CONGRESS
AND
THE PRESIDENCY

Fourth Edition

CONGRESS
AND
THE PRESIDENCY

NELSON W. POLSBY
University of California, Berkeley

PRENTICE-HALL, Englewood Cliffs, New Jersey 07632

Library of Congress Cataloging-in-Publication Data

POLSBY, NELSON W. (date)
    Congress and the Presidency.

    Bibliography: p.
    Includes index.
        1. United States. Congress—Powers and duties.
    2. Executive power—United States.   3. Presidents—
    United States.   I. Title.
    JK1061.P6   1984   320.473   85-19326
    ISBN 0-13-167719-5

Editorial/production supervision: Barbara Alexander
Cover design: Lundgren Graphics, Ltd.
Manufacturing buyer: Barbara Kittle

PRENTICE-HALL FOUNDATIONS OF MODERN POLITICAL SCIENCE SERIES

Robert A. Dahl, Editor

Printed in the United States of America

10   9   8   7   6   5   4   3   2   1

ISBN 0-13-167719-5   01

PRENTICE-HALL INTERNATIONAL (UK) Limited, *London*
PRENTICE-HALL OF AUSTRALIA PTY. LIMITED, *Sydney*
PRENTICE-HALL OF CANDA INC., *Toronto*
PRENTICE-HALL HISPANOAMERICANA, S.A., *Mexico*
PRENTICE-HALL OF INDIA PRIVATE LIMITED, *New Delhi*
PRENTICE-HALL OF JAPAN, INC., *Tokyo*
PRENTICE-HALL OF SOUTHEAST ASIA PTE. Ltd., *Singapore*
EDITORA PRENTICE-HALL DO BRASIL, LTDA., *Rio de Janeiro*
WHITEHALL BOOKS LIMITED, *Wellington, New Zealand*

For Linda, Lisa, Emily, Daniel

CONTENTS

chapter 4

THE HOUSE OF REPRESENTATIVES   114

The Speaker.   Committee and Subcommittee Chairmen.   Committee Assignments. Party Leadership. Party Caucuses. The Distribution of Information. Summary.

chapter 5

NATIONAL POLICY-MAKING I: THE LEGISLATIVE LABYRINTH   138

The Origin of Bills. Reference to Committees. In Committee. Hearings. The Mark-up. The Calendars. The Rules Committee. Floor Action in the House. Floor Action in the Senate. The Conference. The President Acts. Summary and Review: Power in the Process.

chapter 6

NATIONAL POLICY-MAKING II: THE BUDGETARY PROCESS   159

Presidential Planning. Presidential "Ceilings" and Agency Estimates. Presidential Oversight. Congressional Action: Budget Resolutions and Reconciliation. Congressional Action: The Appropriation Process. Summary: The Politics of Budget-Making.

chapter 7

CONFLICT AND COOPERATION   187

Dimensions of Conflict: Differing Electoral Bases. Institutional Sources of Conflict. Instruments of Conflict. The Legitimacy of Conflict. Sources of Cooperation.

PREFACE

To the Fourth Edition

The bicentennial of the American Constitution roughly coincides with the twentieth anniversary of the first appearance of this book. Both anniversaries offer good excuses for thinking about the institutions of American government and how they have evolved over the years. To help readers gain the perspective that time brings, I have in this edition included more in the way of historical information about Congress and the Presidency.

My evaluations of presidents in office now include ten presidents, one quarter of all the political leaders who have held the office. Over time, it has been possible to get a sense of what the modern presidency is all about: conflict and stalemate with Congress, punctuated by brief flurries of legislation; staffs that have grown in size and importance to such an extent as to justify the notion that the Presidency has effectively separated itself from the executive branch, which it now deals with mostly at arm's length and not infrequently in an adversarial way; immersion in foreign affairs; and neglect of party. These patterns appear both for Republicans and Democrats.

In my treatment of Congress, I continue to maintain an explicitly bicameral perspective. Both the House and Senate have undergone considerable changes over the last twenty years, but because they are quite different institutions, they have evolved in different ways. Within our lifetimes, I believe, we have witnessed a transformation of the Senate from an inward-looking, intensely parochial men's club to a publicity-seeking hothouse of policy initiation and senatorial self-promotion. The House of Representatives, for complicated reasons, has both centralized power in the hands of the Speaker and the majority (Democratic) caucus and decentralized it into the hands of subcommittee chairmen.

It continues to be true that national policy is made less by these three institutions—House, Senate, Presidency—separately than in cooperation, and so the plan of the book remains the same as for earlier editions: after an introductory discussion of American democracy, three chapters describing each of the main institutions, and then three chapters describing how they interact.

The central idea of this book has always been, and remains, to give a realistic sketch of the operations of the two more political branches of the American national government: realistic enough so that close and knowledgeable observers would recognize it, sketchy enough so that those less knowledgeable and farther away could take in the main features of these institutions without being inundated by details. The success of three earlier editions suggests that such a sketch fills a need among readers, a need that this edition endeavors also to gratify primarily by adding historical perspective, updating examples, removing archaic language, and correcting mistakes. The first edition of this book was written mostly during the Kennedy administration. Five presidents later, as the American Constitution nears its 200th birthday, there is still plenty for citizens and observers to think about as they consider the problems and prospects of American democracy.

The revisions necessary for this edition were made possible in large part by the energetic assistance of Michael Goldstein, John Gilmour, Steven Stehr, and Peverill Squire, paid for by the Institute of Governmental Studies and the Survey Research Center of the University of California, Berkeley. I thank the directors of both institutions, Eugene C. Lee and Percy Tannenbaum, for their support.

Charles W. Bailey gave me a good critical reading of the chapter on the Presidency. The entire new manuscript was read by Hal Bass, John Zaller, Allen I. Polsby, I. M. Destler, John Hart, Larry Berman, David Kozak, Alan Ehrenhalt, Matthew Pinkus, Eric Davis, Richard Hodder-Williams, and Norman Ornstein. Their comments, which sometimes were very detailed, were of tremendous benefit to the book, and therefore to its readers. Various bits and pieces of new information for this edition were supplied by Dennis Ross, Aaron Wildavsky, and David Cohen. Typing the entire manuscript onto a word processor was accomplished courtesy of Rena Lacey and Beverly Harris. All of the above have my thanks, as do my good friends Linda, Lisa, Emily, and Daniel Polsby. None of the above made any of the mistakes that can be found herein. I made them.

Nelson W. Polsby

Berkeley, California
1986

PREFACE

To the Third Edition

The eminent constitutional lawyer Thomas Reed Powell was once asked, so the story goes, if he would sign an oath to support the Constitution of the United States. "Why not?" he replied. "For all these years the Constitution has been supporting me."

We still have thirteen years to go before the people of the United States can celebrate the bicentennial of the Constitution which contributes so much, among other things, to the shape and contents of this book. For those of us, however, whom the Constitution has been supporting, it seems entirely appropriate that the anniversary of the Declaration of Independence, in 1976, should begin a period when it is in order to reconsider the values and the practices that underlie the conduct of government in contemporary America. It is in this spirit of reconsideration that a new edition of *Congress and the Presidency* is offered.

It is always appropriate for Americans to remind themselves of the extraordinary character of their form of government, a form of government that over a 200 year span has provided basic political freedoms for more people than any in history. No one can observe the fate of democracy in Chile, in India, in Uruguay, or in the Philippines, to take only recent examples, without remarking on the fragility of governments in which repose the great trust that leaders will follow the safeguards of due process, and that ordinary people will choose wisely among real alternatives. Cynics who believe as a blanket proposition that the American political system does not work must confront the dismal evidence of the historical record and ask themselves where they can find better prospects for freedom and human dignity for more and more varied people than in what, sadly, we now may call the world's largest democracy.

In the five years since I last revised this book, two presidents have come and one has departed under most extraordinary circumstances. We have had important changes in congressional organization and brave new beginnings in the budgetary process. I have tried to discuss all these things and at the same time bring up to date the tables, figures, and examples wherever I could.

In this effort I have had the invaluable aid of Byron Shafer, and much assistance also from Shai Feldman, Elaine Kamarck and Matthew Pinkus. The Institute of Governmental Studies of the University of California supplied the services of its typing pool, and in this connection I should particularly like to thank Sidney Dong.

As the years go by, I continue to surprise myself by learning more and more about the subjects of this book. Among my teachers, I should like to mention William Niskanen, who read and commented on the chapter on the budget, Kenneth Shepsle, who gave me timely advice on committee assignments in the House of Representatives, and Elizabeth Drew, Norman Ornstein and Robert Walters, who gave good and useful criticisms—some of which I have taken—of an entire draft of this new edition.

As the pace of change in national politics has accelerated over the last few years it has been harder for observers to keep up with all the new arrangements. I have made a considerable effort to check numerous details, and have had much generous help, but despite our best efforts errors may have crept into a portion of this text, and the double-time march of events may at any moment invalidate other parts. Thus it is with special urgency that I exculpate the kind and knowledgeable people who have devoted their time to making this a better book. If it is a better book, much of the responsibility is theirs; but the opinions, emphases, and mistakes that are distinctive to it are, alas, all mine.

Finally, it gives me the greatest pleasure to rededicate this book to Linda, Lisa, and Emily Polsby, and to add the name of Daniel R. Polsby who, no doubt, even now enjoys Congress and the Presidency as much as his mother and sisters do.

Nelson W. Polsby

Berkeley, California
1975

PREFACE

To the Second Edition

Walter Bagehot published a superb commentary on the English constitution in book form in 1867; in the same year the Reform Act put it out of date. Woodrow Wilson had better luck with *Congressional Government,* as his short preface to the book's fifteenth printing in 1900 indicates. Nevertheless, he said, "inasmuch as [these pages] describe a living system, like all other living things subject to constant subtle modifications, alike of form and of function, their description of The Government of The United States is not as accurate now as I believe it to have been at the time I wrote it." (Woodrow Wilson, *Congressional Government,* 1st ed., 1884, New York: Meridian Books, 1956, p. 19.)

What can happen to Bagehot and Wilson can happen to Polsby. Although for all we know the United States government may be living on borrowed time, it is still a living system, and so it should surprise no reader that in the six years that have elapsed since I wrote *Congress and the Presidency* there have been some changes in these institutions. I have not canvassed them all here, but some things that I could only dimly make out then have become clearer to me with time, events, and the progress of scholarship— a little of my own and a lot by others. And I suppose it is fair to say that a few other matters that I thought were reasonably clear are less so to me now.

Readers may wonder if, in revising the book, I have given consideration to currently fashionable "radical" and "new left" critiques of the American political system. It will not tax anyone's credulity, I am sure, for a Berkeley professor to report that he is aware that such critiques exist. I am not persuaded, however, that this book is the proper place to take full account of them. Radicals, in common with many other American intellectuals, betray little interest in how political institutions actually work. They are more concerned with what they conceive to be outcomes in society than with the complexly interrelated institutions and processes that produce outcomes. The focus here, for better or worse, is on institutions and processes. For the most part, these are real. They exist in time and space, create, spend, and redirect resources, and affect peoples' lives. They should not be ignored. This is true whether or not the reader shares my view that for an increasing number of Americans, though regrettably not for all of them, these institutions have attenuated the chances that their lives would be solitary, poor, nasty, brutish, and short.

Most of what I said in the first edition, consequently, I am content to stand by for this one. I have brought a few allusions in the text up to date and added sections of commentary and amplification where I thought it appropriate or helpful to do so—notably on the Kennedy and Johnson Presidencies, on reapportionment and electoral reform, and on the role of the Senate in the political system.

In spite of the light work I have tried to make for myself, I am, as always, awash in scholarly obligations. I want to thank, in particular, the following friends and colleagues who read and commented on part or all of this second edition, sometimes in great detail: Robert A. Dahl, Elizabeth Brenner Drew, H. Douglas Price, Seyom Brown, Richard F. Fenno, Fred I. Greenstein, Kai T. Erikson, Leslie Gelb, David Cohen, Aaron Wildavsky, Raymond Wolfinger, Andrew McFarland, Paul Sniderman, Robert Jervis, Bill Cavala, William K. Muir, Jr., Robert Axelrod, Byron Shafer, and Jack Citrin. John Palladino, Sam Kernell, Robert vom Eigen, and Joan vom Eigen helped me update the manuscript, and Kathleen Peters typed everything with her usual skill, speed, and imperturbability. The responsibilities, mistakes, and fanciful little touches throughout are, however, all mine.

My work on Congress and the Presidency since the first edition has been facilitated by the Carnegie Corporation through its grant to the American Political Science Association's Study of Congress, the Institute of Governmental Studies and the Institute of International Studies of the University of California, the Social Science Research Council, the Rockefeller Foundation, and the Center for Advanced Study in the Behavioral Sciences.

And I am still greatly indebted to the three ladies to whom this book is dedicated for the fun and amusement they provide when, as sometimes happens, I can get neither from Congress and the Presidency.

Nelson W. Polsby

Berkeley, California
1971

PREFACE

To the First Edition

It is a remarkable fact that American political institutions have survived—indeed flourished—through the strenuous challenges attending the birth of our nation, an explosive expansion westward, civil war, industrialization, urbanization, mass immigration, several depressions, two world wars, and sundry and miscellaneous hostile challenges from abroad. The constitutional order under which these institutions operate has now remained intact for 175 years, longer than virtually any other government in the world. American political institutions are, by any modern standard, impressively venerable. They are also enormously interesting. I hope in this book to suggest why the operations of Congress and the President, in particular, give so much pleasure to the professional student of politics, purely as spectator sport. In addition, to be sure, these two institutions continue to have critical importance in shaping our futures, as they have our collective present and past.

In writing this book, I have relied in part on reading in the scholarly literature and the newspapers, in part on documentary and other primary material, and also on interviews and personal observations. These latter have been made possible over the last few years by generosity from several sources: Ford Foundation grants to the Public Affairs Center of Wesleyan University, which made funds available to me for research assistance; The Social Science Research Council, which has aided me at almost every turn in my pursuit of first-hand knowledge about Congress and the Presidency; and my colleagues in the Government Department at Wesleyan, especially Clement E. Vose, who as chairman made it possible and pleasurable to harmonize teaching and research.

Just as a thief or an embezzler may be kind to his mother, loyal to his friends, and civil to his neighbors, so a short and selective book about Congress and the Presidency may display inadvertent virtues. In this case, any such are probably the result of the strenuous efforts of my friends and colleagues, H. Douglas Price, Theodore Lowi, Fred Greenstein, Joseph Cooper, Micah Naftalin, Robert L. Peabody, John Bibby, Roger Davidson, Edwin Olson, Elizabeth Brenner Drew, Basil Moore, Aaron Wildavsky, Raymond E. Wolfinger, Lewis A. Froman, Jr., and Richard F. Fenno, Jr.; or of my assistants, Peter Morrison, Paul D. O'Brien, Michael Leiserson, John Neff, and Andrew Kleinfeld; or of my typists, Sheila Jones, Martha McCaughtry, and Karen DiStefano; or of my editors, Alfred Goodyear, James J. Murray III, and, especially, Wilbur Mangas, and Robert A. Dahl; or of my wife, Linda. Most of these people read at least parts of the manuscript. All had comments and suggestions that either improved the book or my disposition and sometimes (rarely!) both. But the reader will have no difficulty in assigning responsibility for errors in a book that intends to be only a first approximation, leaves much unsaid, and hence depends so heavily upon an author's own judgment. Indeed, in a book of this kind, the author has no incentive to protest his own inadequacies in a preface because they are so eloquently displayed throughout the volume in question.

Nevertheless, a brief warning. Sometimes I have sacrificed discussion of an institution to a consideration of analytical writing about it. At other points I was moved to do the reverse. Many of the judgments expressed in these pages are by no means widely accepted, and some of them may turn out to be quite wrong. The restrictions of the present format have provided me with an excuse to follow my interests rather than the demands of symmetry or comprehensiveness that a larger text would have imposed. I can only hope that the result will stimulate the reader to work back into the books and articles with which my interpretations agree and disagree, and forward into an enriched understanding of the lively institutions of American democracy.

Nelson W. Polsby

Middletown, Connecticut
1964

chapter 1

ON THE AMERICAN POLITICAL SYSTEM

In 1885, roughly a hundred years ago, a young student of politics named Woodrow Wilson published a book called *Congressional Government*. In it, he said he was going to "point out the most characteristic practical features of the federal system ... with a view to making as plain as possible the actual conditions of federal administration ... striving to catch its present phases and to photograph the delicate organism in all its ... parts exactly as it is today."[1] Nowadays Wilson's book is regarded as a classic commentary for its time on the American system of government.

Despite the obvious immodesty of the aim, the object of the present book is to follow, as best it can, in Wilson's footsteps. For us the task will be somewhat simplified by concentrating on those two great institutions of our national government whose officers are elected by the people and together share responsibility and accountability to the people for all the manifold policies that govern our nation. Congressional and presidential policy-making are important because they embody our theories of democratic government and decisively shape outcomes that affect all of us. And both Congress and the Presidency evolve with the times. Thus, in every generation, the study of Congress and the Presidency is a continuing obligation.

Since *Congressional Government* was written, a great many changes have overtaken our country and expressed themselves through changes in our politics. From a vantage point today, the resiliency and endurance of the American Constitution are much more worthy of note than they seem to have been for Wilson, who wrote when our government was less than a century old and still in the shadow of the post-Civil War Reconstruction. The Presidency was then in eclipse; now, owing to the insatiable coverage of the mass media, the growth of presidential bureaucracies to supervise a

1

vastly enlarged executive branch, and, particularly, the urgent pressure of foreign affairs, the Presidency clearly dominates the Federal system.

Some things, however, have remained the same. The ways of Congress are still labyrinthine and inscrutable. Congress is still more a working legislature than a debating society. However, the distribution of powers between its branches has shifted in interesting ways. The Senate, primarily because of its practices of debate and its greater involvement in policy-making as an advisor and sometime public adversary of the President, has gained a superior toehold in the consciousness of politically aware citizens. The House, on the other hand, is, as it was in Wilson's day, preeminently the home of an old-fashioned legislative politics that values detailed committee work and thrives in an atmosphere of give and take. More often and in more ways, the House is where the domestic plans and programs of Presidents receive their stiffest and most detailed scrutiny and where they most often fail. Through its detailed appropriations procedures, the House maintains a close contact with the machinery of the executive branch; thus it retains substantial power even in a time when the bulk of the news coverage goes to presidential activity of almost any kind and to senatorial speech-making.

HOW MANY BRANCHES OF GOVERNMENT?

The United States Constitution provides for three branches of national government: a legislature, to make the laws; an executive, to "take care that the laws be faithfully executed"; and a Supreme Court, with jurisdiction including the settling of cases and controversies arising under the Constitution. Over the years, as the nation and its government have grown in size and complexity, organizations besides the original three—for example, political parties and interest groups—have assumed a share in government. Government corporations and "independent" regulatory agencies have been established in the interstices of the original three branches. Media of mass communication have sometimes been designated as a "fourth branch of government."

Each of the original three branches has also increased in size and become more specialized. In 1816, the first year for which statistics are available, the entire executive branch numbered 4,479. Today it employs nearly 2.9 million civilians and more than 2 million men and women in uniform.[2] They are organized into a tremendous number of agencies and bureaus, some responsible directly to the President, others responsible to administrative officers selected by the President with the advice and consent of the Senate; a few are supposed to be independent of both Congress and President. Congress, meanwhile, has grown from a Senate of 26 and a House of Representatives of 65 to 100 and 435, respectively. In 1792 each congressman represented an average of 34,436 constituents. Today the average is more than 514,000. Finally, what was originally a six-man Supreme Court has grown to nine justices—eight men and one woman—and has been supplemented by an entire Federal judiciary, consisting of 91 courts of original jurisdiction and 12 appellate courts.[3]

The various branches of government have also changed and modified their functions. The most notable modification came early when, in *Marbury* v. *Madison* (1803), the Supreme Court claimed the right to examine the constitutionality of acts performed by the other two branches.[4] In addition, the judiciary has from time to time engaged in administrative activities, as, for example, in its supervision of local plans for school desegregation.[5] The courts have also, in effect, legislated "interstitially," in areas where Congress was vague, ambiguous, or silent. The executive branch, likewise, engages in judicial proceedings through the actions of administrative tribunals, such as the Immigration and Naturalization Service, which has the power to determine the admissibility of aliens into the United States and to adjudicate their requests for benefits under the law. Agencies of the executive branch legislate by issuing regulations covering classes of events, such as regulations setting standards for the composition, quality, and safety of foods and drugs. Finally, committees of Congress take care that the laws are faithfully executed by undertaking intensive investigations of executive agencies from time to time. These investigations entail reviewing and overseeing the details of decisions reached by the executive departments. Public investigations of private citizens and nongovernmental organizations also provide Congress with a device that in many of its particulars imitates the judicial process.[6]

The point of these observations is to suggest that the bare text of the Constitution is today an incomplete guide to national policy-making. Instead of three branches of government, each with its clearly defined sphere of competence and activity, there may be five branches of government in any particular issue area, or seven, or twenty, or only one. The number of "branches" varies from time to time and from issue to issue. Furthermore, the roles these branches play may vary greatly. An executive agency may "appeal" to a congressional committee, which in turn may instruct another agency to grant relief. The first agency may then ask the President to intervene and "adjudicate" the dispute—and so on, with "legislative," "executive," and "judicial" roles mixed and distributed throughout the national government.

Finally, alliances may spring up across traditional boundary lines at the same time that fierce competition is contained within a constitutional branch. Sometimes the competition between, let us say, the United States Army Corps of Engineers and the Reclamation Bureau of the Department of Interior for jurisdiction over a particular public works project becomes intense; each side brings in allies and defenders from different committees of Congress and from other branches of the Federal bureaucracy, perhaps up to and including the President.[7] In order to understand how a conflict such as this one plays itself out, a reader must suspend belief in what Woodrow Wilson called a literary theory, which views the branches of government as locked in airtight compartments, fixed in number and each operating in its own frictionless universe. Rather, the political activities of Congress and the Presidency that we shall be describing are examples of coalition politics, where there are sometimes only a few "branches" of government to consider, sometimes many.

THE CONTEXT OF POLICY-MAKING

It is quite impossible to classify and count in any way meaningful for our purposes all the complex problems facing the government, but to get a rough idea of what is involved, reflect on the governmental decisions lying behind the following headlines from the front page of a national newspaper on *one* day in 1984.[8]

> U.S. FLOUTS COURTS IN DETERMINATION OF BENEFIT CLAIMS
> VOLCKER SUGGESTS LIMIT ON INTEREST FOR THIRD WORLD
> CAUSE SOUGHT IN BLAZE FATAL TO 8 AT JERSEY PARK'S HAUNTED CASTLE
> DIRECTOR OF FEDERAL DRUG AGENCY CALLS REAGAN PROGRAM 'LIABILITY'
> KOCH ACTS TO CUT ABUSE OF CHILDREN
> UNIONS' ECONOMIC TROUBLES ARE SPURRING MERGER TREND
> MOSLEM STUDENTS IN U.S. REDISCOVERING ISLAM

Clearly, the range of decisions, the number of difficult technical problems, the number of different actors involved in the day-to-day operations of our national government are remarkable. No single President, no matter how shrewd and skillful, no matter how well supplied with staff aid, can hope to give his personal attention to even a substantial fraction of these issues and decisions. Nor can a Congress. In spite of the fact that there are as many as 435 representatives and 100 senators, they make laws only if *coordinated*. A majority of each House (and usually the President's assent) must be secured for each law passed by Congress. There is simply not enough time for either Congress collectively or the President individually to deal effectively with all the problems that come up.

Therefore, both Congress and the President *sample.* Specific techniques they use to handle the decision-making situations they ultimately face will be discussed in detail later. Right now, let us look at a few of the principles on which sampling is based.

There is a tendency, first, for Congress and the President to address those problems, regardless of their intrinsic importance, that are forced on them by the calendar. For example, laws are often written so that they expire after a certain date—indeed, in the case of laws giving money to the armed services, the Constitution requires that they do so.[9] If national policy-makers want to continue such a law in force, they must act promptly to renew it before it expires or they risk the dismantling of valued administrative machinery, the loss of personnel, the misplacement of records, and the interruption of service. Therefore, they do generally attend to the renewal of expiring laws, even when other matters are pressing. Another example: the Constitution gives the President the duty "from time to time [to] give to the Congress Information of the State of the Union, and recommend for their consideration such measures as he shall judge necessary and expedient."[10] In practice, this has meant a major speech at the opening of each congressional session. Since the Constitution prescribes when Congress shall convene (noon, January 3 of every year, unless another day is appointed by law),[11] the President knows he has a deadline to meet. Other, longer-range matters must be pushed aside when that deadline approaches. Thus the first bias in sampling is to do things that the calendar says must be done promptly.

The number of deadlines fixed by the Constitution is not great, but the calendar is inexorable in other ways. Suppose, for example, the President wants Congress to pass a law empowering him to furnish new types of foreign aid. In what way does the calendar constrain him?

There is already a law in effect that deals with the general subject of foreign aid. The President and his advisors must decide whether they want to wait until this law comes up for renewal and tack the new proposals onto it or whether they want to make the program they have in mind a special issue. If they decide to make this a special issue, they must find someone appropriate in each house of Congress to introduce the bill they want. Usually this is a senior member of the committee to which the bill will be assigned. First, however, they must draw the bill up and make sure it says what they want it to say. This takes time, especially if more than one agency wants to look the bill over and signify its approval or disapproval or suggest modifications. Furthermore, the President normally wants a draft of the bill reviewed by experts outside the White House to make sure his proposal is a sound one and to alert the people who are going to have to execute the law to the trend of his thinking.

The executive agencies involved ordinarily supply their congressional supporters with strong and relevant arguments for the bill. They also wish to make up statements of their own to submit when congressional committees hold hearings on it. This means they want to coordinate the submission of the bill with their priority lists for legislation.

The relevant committees of the House and Senate may have other pressing legislation before them, so *their* priorities must be considered. Yet the president's term of office is only four—or, at most, eight—years.[12] It takes time to move the wheels of government, perhaps not enough time to do all he wants to do. So the second bias in national policy-making is toward doing things that can be done quickly.

A third bias, equally understandable, orients decision-makers toward problems that appear to be especially acute rather than chronic. When a crisis occurs, leaders must act. A threatened nationwide railroad strike may demand immediate legislation; other matters must be put aside. Missile bases may be erected in Cuba: the President cannot wait. Gas station owners begin to organize a shutdown for a three-day period unless something is done about their profit margin per gallon: someone must respond. In a sense, then, events govern the priorities established by our national decision-makers. They must keep themselves sufficiently open to the pressure of events to move promptly when necessary. As a result, they are precluded from attending to as many "basic" or chronic demands as they otherwise might tackle.

The pressures of time and events, the multiple competing demands on our national government, mean that, unavoidably, policy-makers are less systematic, less orderly in their decision-making than they would be if they could fully control their environments. Even so, they do make choices. They do pursue policies in part of their own devising. They can regulate many of the demands placed on them. But they must pursue their goals in a complicated world that sets boundaries and constraints on them and that continually forces them into compromises not only in their policy preferences but also in the ways in which they allocate their time and attention.

IS THE SYSTEM DEMOCRATIC?

A fair-minded preliminary characterization would probably concede that, in general, Americans enjoy a "democratic" political system. In recent times, among presumably well-educated people, this view has occasionally been regarded as quaint, irrelevant, or even complacent— quaint because it is more likely to be held by persons over 30, irrelevant because it fails to address pressing social issues, and complacent because the use of the honorific term *democracy* implies a satisfaction with things as they are and an incapacity to recognize or decry injustice. Perhaps what is needed is some other term, without honorific connotations, that concedes the existence of injustice but that nevertheless denotes a system relatively (but not perfectly) open to participation by those possessing requisite skills and interests, relatively (but not perfectly) responsive to the demands of a variety of participants, and run (but not flawlessly) according to a relatively stable and equitable set of rules. Criteria such as these have in the past served to distinguish more and less democratic political systems and have been helpful to observers who wanted to monitor changes in political conditions within one country. Thus, an observer might find it useful to adopt an inductive, empirical approach. One might contrast the legal, political, and social position of black persons in various parts of the United States before Emancipation, during Reconstruction, after the imposition of Jim Crow laws, and today. Or one might compare the condition of our most deprived social groups today with that of Jews in the USSR, Catholics in Northern Ireland, Armenians in Turkey, Chinese in Indonesia, Tamils in Sri Lanka, Ibo in Nigeria, Tonga in Zambia, Asians in Uganda, blacks in South Africa, or Watutsi in Rwanda.[13] Or one might gauge the relative size of privileged and unprivileged groups in different societies. One might ask how widely opportunities to develop the skills requisite to political action are distributed in the population. By such inductive means the relative position of the United States can be established.

To be sure, such an exercise would establish only one context within which the American political system might be viewed, because it leaves open questions of improvement and the extent to which the system approximates or approaches ideal standards. The value of an inductive approach is that it encourages the acquisition of knowledge. Knowledge is helpful not only for accurate observation but also for developing the competence necessary to operate within a complex political system. Thus an inductive approach may facilitate the achievement of ideals more effectively than the mere reiteration of the ideals themselves.

An empirical approach may also contribute to the closer examination of ideal standards. Consider the ideal of majority rule. It would be incorrect to say that our system is one in which majorities always rule, and this fact sometimes confuses observers who believe that the rule of the majority is always a necessary or even a sufficient condition for a political system to be democratic. It is possible, however, to think of several situations in which simple majority rule could operate but in which the system would not be satisfactorily "democratic" from the standpoint of most Americans. For example, suppose duly constituted agents of a majority deprived members of the minority, in a fair vote, of the right to participate in future elections. Or heavy majorities were recorded in elections in which no alternatives were permitted. Or suppose there were occasions when a minority felt intensely about an issue but the majority, which did not care strongly one way or another, still prevailed. In each of these cases, even though majority rule operated, the government would be less open, less responsive, less stable, less equitable, and therefore less democratic than Americans would probably like or accept. Indeed, our national government operates in many instances to thwart the rule of the majority. Here are several brief examples:

1. The electoral college, through which we select our Presidents, pro-

vides that the votes of individual voters be counted state by state. By state law, in every state but Maine, the presidential candidate receiving the most votes within a state is declared the winner of all the state's electoral votes. This means that a presidential candidate who loses the state of New York by one vote but wins Delaware by ten thousand votes receives only three electoral votes while his opponent receives thirty-six electoral votes. The underlying principle of majority rule is, of course, equality in the weight of each individual's vote. Yet the votes of millions of New Yorkers who voted for the loser are in effect not expressed in the final tabulation. Indeed, in this instance, the candidate who received the majority of popular votes in the two states would receive only a bit less than 8 percent (3/39) of the electoral vote.

The electoral college thwarts the majority-rule principle in still another way—by giving small states more electoral votes than they would be entitled to if each popular vote were weighted exactly the same. In 1980, for example, 8,587,063 Californians voted for President. They chose 45 electors, one corresponding to each of California's forty-three members of the House of Representatives, and one for each senator. At the same time, 158,445 Alaskans chose three electors (representing one House member and two senators). If each Californian's vote were weighted equally with each Alaskan's, it would have been necessary in 1980 for California to have had 163 electors, not 45.

2. Malapportionment exists in the Senate, where each state has two votes, regardless of its population. The senators from the nine least populous states, with 2.6 percent of the nation's population, can cancel out the votes of the senators from the nine most populous states, representing a majority (51.2 percent) of the nation's people.[14]

In the House of Representatives, however, the most common cause of malapportionment has been eliminated. Within each state, congressional district lines are drawn by the state legislature. As long as state legislatures were themselves grossly malapportioned, as many were, congressional districts were fairly regularly malapportioned also. Before the Supreme Court began to attack legislative malapportionment, in a series of decisions that began in 1962,[15] great disparities in the populations of congressional districts were not uncommon. Sometimes adjacent districts would have populations varying from a little over 200,000 to over a million.

Today, this sort of extreme disparity is not possible under the law. Within each state the populations of congressional districts must approach equality.[16] Some malapportionment is bound to occur, however, because all states have at least one member of Congress, even though in three cases (Alaska [with 400,481 inhabitants in 1980], Vermont [511,456] and Wyoming [470,816]) their populations are smaller than the nationwide average for congressional districts (one member of Congress for every 514,000 people).[17]

Furthermore, the Supreme Court has not been able to abolish political maneuvering with respect to districting. State legislatures are still political bodies, even though politically they are balanced somewhat differently than they used to be. The one-man, one-vote rule is now more or less followed in House districting, but the system is far from tamperproof. Thus, the legislatures, while accepting the constraint of population equalization the Court has placed on them, have nevertheless still managed on occasion to draw congressional districts with shapes as bizarre as the Massachusetts senatorial district that in 1812 was dubbed "the gerrymander."[18] Thus, a political Pandora's box opens every ten years when the results of the decennial census are tallied. Adjustments then must be made in the allocation of seats among the states, making a wave of reapportionments necessary within each affected state. However, the alternative would be greater numerical malapportionment, so in this respect—and to some degree—the political system has moved toward majority rule since 1964.

3. Many of the practices of the Senate and House thwart majority rule within each body. Often their internal decisions are made by application of the rule of seniority rather than by vote, or by small numbers of members in committees rather than by everybody on the floor. In the House, a great deal of business has been kept off the floor by the actions—or decisions not to act—of the relatively small (13 member) Rules Committee. In the Senate, unlimited debate permits a determined minority to prevent legislative action indefinitely. Filibusters cannot be terminated by a simple majority vote, only by three-fifths of the membership of the Senate (i.e. sixty senators).[19]

4. Even after both houses of Congress act favorably on a bill and it is signed by the President, its constitutionality may be challenged in the courts. If the Supreme Court holds a law to be unconstitutional, the law is voided in spite of the majorities of popularly elected legislators who passed it and the popularly elected president who signed it.

But might not these majority-thwarting institutions also be responsible for the openness, responsiveness, and stability of our system, and hence actually be democratizing influences? It is not at all clear that this is so. What makes our system democratic is more complicated than that; it concerns the fact that each center of special power is for various reasons responsive to somewhat different segments of the population. Furthermore, many power centers share in the making of public policy. This means that public policy is likely to respond to a variety of interest groups. As long as different factions with differing policy preferences control different centers of power, and large numbers of those who are willing and able to learn how to participate have ready access to one or more centers, the system is likely to be reasonably democratic. What, then, makes groups and factions willing to ally with others and admit outsiders? Here we come to four additional, critically important prerequisites of American democracy:

1. Frequent elections of public officials means that it is constitutionally

possible to replace officeholders.

2. The existence of a competitive party system means that sufficient and sufficiently strong alternatives are presented at elections to make the replacement of officeholders not unlikely or at least not politically impossible.

3. The consent of many different politicians must be secured to enact public policy. These politicians may vary in numerous ways: according to their constituencies if elected (safe, not so safe, rural, urban, large, small, one-party, two-party), according to their terms of office if appointed (for life, for a long, set term, at the pleasure of the President), according to their conceptions of their role and their responsibilities, according to their technical knowledge, according to their policy preferences, and so on. These different politicians must deal with one another in order to accomplish their own policy goals.

4. Politicians are generally sufficiently uncertain of the outcomes of elections to be willing, between elections as well as at election time, to accommodate, if they can, the intensely expressed preferences of most groups in the population. Their uncertainty extends to the activities of other politicians. Hence, officials (say, President Reagan) who are relatively inaccessible to a particular group (say, environmentalists) must beware the activities of leaders more accessible to this group (such as liberal House committee chairmen). *Uncertainty* in the face of a well organized electoral politics is the glue that holds together many of the disparate parts of a complex, stable, separation-of-powers democracy.

The operation of the uncertainty principle depends on a further condition, namely, that among groups there be extreme differences in intensity of preferences on issues, with each issue at the focus of concern for one or only a few narrowly specialized groups. In short, if politics is conducted at relatively low temperatures—that is, if friction between contending groups is not intense—it is possible for politicians to seek to accommodate the preferences of most of those who make demands on them. At high temperatures, however, politicians have to choose sides among interest groups. They exchange uncertainty (about what people in an undifferentiated political environment *might* do) for certainty (about what friends and enemies *will* do); they seek less to avoid hypothetical costs than to avert costs that are certain. In these circumstances, the diversity of power centers in American politics and the differences in their accessibility to different interest groups become more important than the uncertainty of politicians in keeping the political system open and responsive.

AMERICAN POLITICS IS COALITION POLITICS

I have mentioned the diversity of power centers in the American political system and the low temperature and pressure that characterize the environment for most policy-making activity. This is true even while some major policies are hotly debated in the public arena. For example, even when thousands of newly concerned citizens focused their attention on military involvement in Southeast Asia, immense leeway for leaders continued to exist in such matters as the regulation of broadcasting, the setting of farm price supports, the acquisition of land for national parks, and scores of other government policies. With respect to these, the vast bulk of all issues at any given time, an observer could note the extent to which political resources are not efficiently or energetically employed to change outcomes and the extent to which policies are unplanned, uncoordinated, piecemeal, and trial-and-error in their conception and execution.

These characteristics of policy-making are not necessarily deplorable. Rather, one would expect policy-making processes of this kind under the following conditions: (1) The constitutional order is highly stable and generally accepted. (2) The society is large, heterogeneous, literate, and mainly prosperous. (3) Political resources and their legitimate use are widely dispersed throughout the population. This would mean in effect that, if most citizens who wanted to could participate in politics and if the demands made on political institutions were moderate and somewhat attainable by those who were willing to seek widespread agreement among politically active segments of the population, then coalitions would—as they often do in American politics—contribute to the legitimacy of governmental decisions by gaining the assent of relevant publics for governmental activity.

American politics is in part the product of quite a lot of good luck, such as the fact that the nation possesses abundant natural resources and territory, enjoyed peace during its period of modernization, never had to overcome the class divisions of a feudal heritage, and had an expanding economy that could absorb and welcome successive waves of immigrants. These and the sheer complexity of the government as set down in the Constitution and the diversity of problems that face it all contributed to the early development of our system of coalition politics. Once in operation, the system has maintained itself not only by continuing to foster its preconditions, but also by indoctrinating, training, and selectively recruiting skilled people for political positions.

As long as political resources are widely (even though unequally) dispersed in a political system, the success of various participants depends on their ability to make alliances, and on their skills at setting policy goals that will distribute rewards to enough interests to make it possible for them to achieve what they want to achieve. This is generally accomplished by consent, not coercion. Therefore, in order to understand contemporary policy-making by Congress and the Presidency, it is necessary to know that they bargain and search for coalitions.

Variations in the institutional resources available to politicians make it easier for some of them to bargain and build coalitions than for others. The President, as we shall see in the next chapter, has greater resources available to him for these purposes than does any other single actor in the political system. This does not mean that he can get his way on any issue he happens to care about. It means, rather, that he is in a better position than anyone else to deal with a wide variety of interests, to propose trade-offs among their competing values, and to develop packages that have sufficiently broad appeal to be formally enacted. Likewise, the great strength of Congress as an institution is that it is sensitive to a wide range of competing needs and must find ways of reconciling and harmonizing them if it is to take action.

The American political system stresses the mutual accountability of many leaders to one another through continuous processes of bargaining, compromise, adjustment, and coalition-building. Circumstances, variations in the kinds of resources available to politicians and in the goals they are seeking, make some coalitions easier to assemble than others. Thus we must sketch in greater detail the resources and goals of presidents, senators, and congressmen in order to see how these politicians adjust to and transform their political environment.

chapter 2

THE PRESIDENCY

THE PRESIDENTIAL COALITION

Perhaps the easiest way to begin a discussion of the American Presidency is to describe the presidential coalition, the combination of interests and political forces that has tended, at least since the New Deal, to form around most candidates for President from both political parties. The presidential coalition has its roots in the political strategies of presidential nomination and election, which in turn are shaped by a few central facts of life.

There is, for example, the fact that presidential elections are contested essentially between two parties, either of which can win.[1] Barring an occasional aberration, winning the Presidency is the supreme goal of both political parties, and they have learned to adapt their strategies to this task. Parties nominate candidates who they believe can win, and they write platforms that attempt to appeal to a broad spectrum of voters and interest groups. But some voters and interest groups are better placed strategically than others. Voters in large, industrialized, two-party states are particularly well situated. The reason for this advantage is the almost universally followed method of counting votes in the electoral college—the so-called unit rule. Enforced by custom and state regulation, the unit rule provides that the presidential candidate who wins a popular majority, no matter how narrow, in a state shall receive the state's entire electoral vote.[2]

The number of electoral votes each state casts is determined by its number of senators (two for each state) and representatives in Congress (which varies according to population). Thus the populous states have large electoral votes and are particularly important. The candidate who wins most or all of them, even by a hair, will probably win the Presidency. Both parties realize this fact and shape their strategies accordingly. They tend to nominate candidates who come from the larger states and who, in the progress of their own careers, have made alliances with urban interest groups, such as labor unions, organizations of black citizens, and other ethnic blocs, and these groups' representatives. In their policy preferences, these groups, by and large, are conventionally described as "liberal"—welfare minded, favoring civil rights activity, and demanding of governmental services.

Although Democrats rather than Republicans are more likely to have firm alliances with groups representing these interests, over the last three decades *both* parties, on the whole, have pursued the strategy of wooing voters in the large, industrialized areas as the first order of business in presidential campaigns. This emphasis has given rise in the Republican party to the charge by conservatives that "me-too" candidacies have weakened Republican electoral effectiveness. However, there is scant reason to believe that in ordinary circumstances more conservative Republican candidates would have won. On the contrary, most politicians, including those most instrumental in selecting Republican candidates, believed that candidates as conservative as, say, Senator Robert A. Taft of Ohio, who was a major power in the party during the 1940's and early 1950's, could not win a presidential election. Public as well as privately sponsored opinion polls have generally borne out this conclusion, and so does the experience of the 1964 campaign, in which the Republican nominee rejected the "me-too" strategy with disastrous consequences.[3] Thus it is not surprising that Republicans (as well as Democrats) have tended to select as their candidates for President politicians from the large states, whose allies are more likely to be industrialists and Wall Street bankers, corporation lawyers, and suburban voters rather than the farmers, small-town professionals, and merchants who contribute so much to the grass-roots leadership of the Republican party. Whatever their personal preferences, successful Republican presidential nominees in recent years have harbored few illusions about the necessity for recognizing the manifold demands that are made on big government.[4]

Thus, in the first instance, the nature of the Presidency is shaped by the process that nominates a President and elects him to office. This process tends to bring to the Presidency candidates whose alliances and promises, if not their personal inclinations as well, spell active government, a government that makes plans and meets demands. There is a passive theory of the Presidency, one that insists on congressional initiative—as if a bicameral body of 535 were designed to be fast on its 1,070 feet. But even modern exponents of a passive Presidency, such as Dwight D. Eisenhower, could not successfully be passive Presidents. If responsiveness to the needs of the presidential coalition were not enough to provoke presidential activity, other factors have made the contemporary Presidency active even when the President was not.

ENERGY FOR THE SYSTEM

Why, in our complex and interdependent political system, does so much depend on the President? "A President has a great chance; his position is almost that of a king and a prime minister rolled into one," said Theodore Roosevelt.[5] That is true. But why is it true? A number of factors, some historical and some institutional, have converged on the President in modern times and radically changed the character of the office as it was conceived of by the authors of the Constitution.

Of the historical factors, none has been more obtrusive, more demanding, or more important than the progressive entanglement of the United States in foreign affairs. The Constitution gives the President an unmistakable, far-reaching, and considerable mandate in this area; the few enumerated duties of the Chief Executive include the power to receive ambassadors from foreign countries, the power to make treaties (with the advice and consent of the Senate), and the rank of Commander-in-Chief of the armed forces. As rapidly advancing technology has shrunk the world, the relevance of these powers to the prosperity, tranquillity and safety of the United States has increased greatly.

A second historical factor in the rise of the Presidency has been the sheer growth of the executive branch, which he heads. As our land area and population have increased and diversified over the last two centuries, the national government has been faced with a variety of new demands— for help, for relief, for services of all kinds. A preferred method for dealing with these demands has been the founding of new agencies within the executive branch. Once they are set in motion, these agencies do not merely respond passively to the accelerating needs of an expanding population; they behave creatively, seeking ways to increase their powers and their size. Here, too, the President's constitutional powers place him at the top of an expanding situation. The Constitution gives him the right, as Chief Executive, to nominate (the Senate consenting) and appoint the policy-making officers of the executive branch and to require their opinions in writing on matters of state. The vague constitutional mandate to see that the laws are faithfully executed means, in effect, that virtually all agencies created by Congress through public laws automatically come under the President's purview.

A third historical reason for the rise of the Presidency can be traced to the relationship between political leaders and followers, in a modern democratic society, as this relationship is filtered through the news media. In the judgment of the purveyors of news, most citizens are not so gripped by political issues that their interest in them can be sustained without the leaven of so-called human interest. In the early days of the Republic, when news was spread by word of mouth and by party-controlled periodical pamphlets, partisan vituperation and personal name-calling provided a rich emotional diet for the consumer of political news. The President was never far from the center of these controversies, since the Presidency, because of its powers to enhance the fortunes of a political party by staffing the government, has always been the most important office of all. Today, in a relatively bland era of "responsible," "objective" news coverage and vastly increased suffrage, the President still remains in the center of the limelight.[6] The news media now ask him to play a more impartial role, as a kind of guardian of national morale, a focus for affectionate emotions, an animate symbol of American sovereignty. It is to be hoped that he will have a sense of humor and a lively family—the media will in any event do their best to endow him with these.

This burden of group emotions and status aspirations that we ask our Presidents to bear has obvious political uses. Most recent Presidents have yielded regularly to the temptation to gain political advantage—either in behalf of their party or in behalf of their policies—by donning the mantle of nonpartisan sanctimony that the contemporary press fashions for them. In any case, whatever an American President does or says is news—automatic, instantaneous news—everywhere in the world. By manipulating the flexible boundaries between public business and private confidences, between firm policy commitments and trial balloons, a clever President can turn his status leadership to enormous political advantage.

Historical changes associated with the growth, industrialization, and modernization of our country have, then, had a great deal to do with the emergence of the President as the principal figure in American national government. Characteristics of the institution apart from these historical changes also enhance the importance of the Presidency.

Consider the scope of the responsibilities allotted to the President. These are virtually as broad as the coverage of the entire body of Federal law. They extend, for example, to the regulation of the economy. Various agencies of the executive branch or appointees of the President have powers to grant subsidies, approve or disapprove corporate mergers, raise and lower tariffs, let contracts (with variations as to their timing, amounts, and geographic locations), condemn land, and regulate credit. This list is not exhaustive.

The President's position at the peak of the executive branch (which, unlike the other two branches of government, is formally organized under a single head) allows him to compel the cooperation of executive agencies in behalf of the policies he wishes to pursue.

A final institutional factor that enhances the position of the President is the discretionary character of the office. He is free to pursue those policies that are of greatest concern to him; he is not required to give equal attention to all problems and all agencies. Hence, it can be expected that most agencies most of the time will conduct their business according to the same pattern no matter who is President; but when a President desires to do so, he can change a particular agency's policies—if he is willing to bear the costs in terms of time, energy, and perhaps also the enmity of bureaucrats and the interest groups who are served by the agency involved.

Within the executive branch, the President must *delegate* powers, but he need not *share* them. The policy preferences he brings to his job, his conception of his role, the demands of the interest groups who are his allies, and the suggestions of his friends, his Cabinet, and his staff—all provide sources for presidential policies. His position at the head of an enormous hierarchy whose concerns reach virtually everywhere, and the wide discretion of his office provide the President with the institutional tools that make it possible for him to move vigorously if he chooses. As we shall see in later chapters, these tools also permit him to move with initiative into areas where he must share powers, such as in the legislative process.

WAYS OF BEING PRESIDENT

There are as many different ways of being President as there are people willing to fill the office. Circumstances permit only one person at a time actually to be President, however, and to face the problems of a particular era. Thus it is difficult to make meaningful comparisons among Presidents and the ways in which they have conducted themselves in office. Nevertheless, the temptation to try is overwhelming. Again and again, commentators attempt to illuminate the problems and possibilities of the presidential office by evaluating the performance of present or recent incumbents. Furthermore, writers on the Presidency have reached something of a consensus in their evaluations—even though these have been heavily influenced by value premises that are only partially articulated in the course of discussions in which they distill out of historical experience personal qualities and administrative practices that seem to be helpful in the conduct of the Presidency. These pages will provide room for a few modern examples of this process of evaluation, covering the most recent ten presidents.

Herbert Hoover (Republican, 1929–1933)

Most contemporary discussion of the Hoover Presidency focuses upon the economic disaster of 1929 to 1933, an event that Mr. Hoover understandably called "the nightmare of my years in the White House."[7] Although the great stock market crash of October 1929 took place only seven months after he assumed office and the ensuing unemployment robbed him a year later of effective majorities in both houses of Congress, the Presidency of Herbert Hoover is considered retrospectively almost exclusively in the light of two questions: Why did he let it happen? Why did he not do something to alleviate its effects?

Stated baldly, the questions seem unfair. Surely no Republican President elected at the end of a fifty-year wave of industrial expansion and business dominance in national politics was in a strong position either to prevent the Depression or to relieve its effects, no matter what his personal style. Nevertheless, attention has been called to what must have been of very marginal importance—Mr. Hoover's administrative fastidiousness, his habit of checking personally into minute details.[8]

> Exposure to detail can be carried too far ... Herbert Hoover is perhaps the classic instance of the man who went too far. For example, Hoover personally read and approved every letter sent by the Budget Bureau to executive agencies "clearing" their individual replies to congressional inquiries on legislation. In suggesting that a President be his own staff director I would not urge that he routinely do the work of the whole staff. One admires Hoover's industry but not his judgment of what to take upon himself and what to leave to others.[9]

Another remark by Neustadt about the Hoover Presidency is even more telling: he refers to Mr. Hoover as "caught in the trap of fighting history."[10] As we shall see, the criterion of judgment that this statement implies plays an important role in the assessment of Presidents. Mr. Hoover's constitutional principles forbade to him many sorts of action that another President might have taken in a crisis.[11] His unwillingness in an acute domestic emergency to use the powers other men have found in the office grievously handicapped his Presidency and deprived it of the esteem of students of the Presidency to this day.

Franklin D. Roosevelt (Democrat, 1933–1945)

All Presidents receive vigorous criticism; for only a fortunate few does praise pour forth in comparable volume and intensity. Franklin Roosevelt is certainly of the elect group. As historian William Leuchtenburg says:

> No one before Roosevelt had so dominated the political culture of his day, if for no better reason than that no one before him had been in the White House for so long, and in the process he created the expectation that the chief executive would be a primary shaper of his times.[12]

The modern era of presidential-congressional relations traditionally opens with Roosevelt's inauguration in March 1933. In the ensuing three months the divisiveness and the normal politics of sectional interest that had dominated Congress over the previous period gave way to a depression-induced cooperation between President and Congress that had not been seen for a generation. The President proposed various measures, and Congress enacted them very speedily indeed, as the accompanying table from the work of one of the foremost Congress watchers of the time, political scientist Pendleton Herring, illustrates.

As Herring says:

The Chief Executive became the chief law-maker.... He displayed remarkable skill in manipulating the attention of Congress and of the public. His messages to Congress were strategically timed and positive and specific in character. Disagreement with his proposals was interpreted by the general public as obstructionism. His swift pace, his boldness in assuming responsibility, and his definite recommendations not only stimulated popular support of his policy, but likewise branded as dissenters and critics congressmen holding to different policies. His radio talks to the nation served the double purpose of reassuring the people and breaking down resistance in Congress. Legislators were made only too well aware of the temper of their constituents.

Congressmen of both parties were willing to follow the President's lead, and he managed his congressional relations with great tact. At the end of the session, he was able to thank both houses for a "spirit of teamwork" between the legislative and executive branches that in most cases "transcended party lines" and made possible "more whole-hearted cooperation" than had been witnessed in "many a long year." Of course the pressure of the emergency and the solid public support behind the President must be understood as modifying normal relations, but even when this is allowed for, a full weight of political sagacity remains to account for the satisfactory contacts with Congress....

Measures were put through this Congress with little difficulty that had been turned down repeatedly in previous sessions.[13]

Historian James T. Patterson describes the mood of the time:

[Roosevelt] did on occasion ask for wide discretionary powers—the economy and banking bills were cases in point. Congress not only granted such requests but usually did so eagerly. By delegating authority, Congress also delegated responsibility, leaving to executive departments the resolution of troublesome policy matters. Congressional delegation of power was so generous that one veteran newsman sighed, "all my adjectives are exhausted in expressing my admiration, awe, wonder, and terror at the vast grants of power which Roosevelt demands, one after the other, from Congress."

Congressional readiness to surrender cherished prerogatives underscored a significant aspect of the 1933 session: in many areas it was considerably less orthodox than Roosevelt. Far from favoring conservative business interests in the manner of the Congresses of the 1920s, it approved an income-tax amendment requiring incomes to be publicized, and it passed the TVA with remarkable ease. Far from ignoring labor, it enacted the labor provisions of the National Industrial Recovery Act, while the Senate passed the Black thirty-hour-work-week bill in spite of Roosevelt's lack of enthusiasm. And far from wedding itself to orthodox monetary theory, Congress passed the Thomas Amendment, pushing Roosevelt in the direction of devaluation or inflation. Congressmen witnessed the end of the gold standard with scarcely a protest....

Above all, congressmen were eager to spend. Under great pressure from constituents to relieve economic distress, they realized that a simple and

TABLE 1 Progress of Selected New Deal Legislation through Congress, 1933

NUMBER OF BILL	TITLE	PROPOSED BY PRESIDENT	PASSED HOUSE	PASSED SENATE	DATE APPROVED	NO. OF LAW OR RESOLUTION	LENGTH OF GENERAL DEBATE IN HOUSE
H.R. 1491	Emergency banking relief	Mar. 9	Mar. 9	Mar. 9	Mar. 9	1	40 min.
H.R. 2820	Maintenance of government's credit (economy bill)	Mar. 10	Mar. 11	Mar. 15	Mar. 20	2	2 hr.
H.R. 3341	Permit and tax beer	Mar. 13	Mar. 14	Mar. 16	Mar. 22	3	3 hr.
H.R. 3835	Emergency agricultural relief; farm mortgage; currency issuance and regulation	Mar. 16	Mar. 22	Apr. 28	May 12	10	5½ hr.
S. 598	Unemployment relief (reforestation)	Mar. 21	Mar. 29	Mar. 28	Mar. 31	5	5 hr.
H.R. 4606	Federal emergency relief	Mar. 21	Apr. 21	May 1	May 12	15	2 hr.
H.R. 5980	Supervision of traffic in securities	Mar. 29	May 5	May 8	May 27	22	5 hr.
H.R. 5081	Muscle Shoals and Tennessee Valley Authority	Apr. 10	Apr. 25	May 3	May 18	17	6 hr.
H.R. 5240	Relief of small home owners	Apr. 13	Apr. 28	June 5	June 13	43	1½ hr.
S. 1580	Railroad reorganization and relief	May 4	June 5	May 27	June 16	68	3 hr.
H.R. 5755	Industrial recovery; public construction and taxation	May 17	May 26	June 9	June 16	67	6 hr.

Source: Pendleton Herring, *Presidential Leadership* (New York: Farrar and Rinehart, 1940), p. 44.

tangible solution was to appropriate, appropriate, appropriate, while leaving taxes alone. Budget balancing, an almost sacred conservative panacea, fell by the wayside. The 1933 session, like those throughout the New Deal, was often a more liberal spender than the administration, particularly when strong pressure groups such as farmers or veterans threatened the hapless congressman with electoral extinction. As one contemporary observer commented, Roosevelt's chief difficulties with Congress in 1933 emanated from such pressure groups. The President, he said, could "do little more than keep order in the bread line that reached into the Treasury."[14]

Roosevelt's Hundred Days, so-called, became a benchmark in presidential-congressional relations. This, according to a pro-New Deal consensus that grew up among observers and analysts, was how presidential-congressional relations ought to work. This view was not grounded in the liberal political preferences of observers alone. It also reflected a taste for the big picture, a preference for assertedly broader, as contrasted with narrower, interests. In addition, it focused upon one leader whose programs and desires could be dramatized and publicized, and gave less emphasis to the unfathomable intricacy of the baroque interiors of the House and Senate. In short, Roosevelt launched American political analysis into a fresh era of what historians sometimes called the "presidential synthesis," in which observers tended to see the system primarily from the president's point of view.[15]

Roosevelt's unqualified success at being his own prime minister did not last far beyond the hundred days, despite the great Democratic victories in the elections of 1934 and 1936.[16] By 1938, stung in particular by the failure of his proposal to pack the Supreme Court, Roosevelt undertook to encourage the defeat in primary elections of anti-New Deal Democrats in Congress.[17] The purge was a flop, and the decentralized character of the American party system prevailed. Soon enough, the New Deal went on the shelf as World War II came closer, and for the rest of Roosevelt's life Congress and presidency alike were preoccupied with wartime concerns.

The elements of Roosevelt's effectiveness as a President are, for many commentators, extensions of his personality. He loved being President, rather than merely working at it. In the view of most contemporary writers, effectiveness as a President entails the enhancement of the powers of the office at the expense of those beneath in the executive branch. Thus they give high marks to Roosevelt's preoccupation with concentrating power in his own hands. One of the most important factors in this quest was Roosevelt's capacity for opening up unconventional sources of information. Although his physical handicap made travel difficult for him, he read widely in the newspapers, saw hundreds of visitors, kept an ear open for politically revealing gossip, and systematically cultivated informal reporting mechanisms.

One source of informal information was the set of complaints generated from subordinates to whom the President had assigned overlapping jurisdictions, as it was his practice to do. By settling the conflicts arising among his appointees, President Roosevelt could retain control over policy-making.[18] Arthur Schlesinger, Jr., says:

> His favorite technique was to keep grants of authority incomplete, jurisdiction uncertain, charters overlapping. The result of this competitive theory of administration was often confusion and exasperation on the operating level; but no other method could so reliably insure that in a large bureaucracy filled with ambitious men eager for power the decisions, and the power to make them, would remain with the President.[19]

Francis Biddle, Roosevelt's Attorney General, shows how this tactic of the President's could cause great difficulty even among members of his Cabinet. Speaking of the Secretary and Undersecretary of State, Biddle writes:

> Hull came to distrust Welles and finally to hate him. The President knew this long before the Secretary came to him with the final ultimatum—one of them must go. Yet before that the President did little to better their relationship, often bypassing Hull by taking up a matter with Welles.... The President cared little for administrative niceties.[20]

Invariably, commentators also mention other personal qualities of Mr. Roosevelt—his buoyant personality, his flair for the dramatic, his superbly modulated radio voice.[21] Because he used these qualities and his love of power in the service of a vigorous Presidency in both the domestic crisis of the Depression and World War II, Mr. Roosevelt's Presidency has had a special claim on the attention of historians.

Harry S Truman (Democrat, 1945-1953)

Harry Truman initially was the victim of the Rooseveltian penchant for making the office of the Presidency coextensive with his own personality, for Roosevelt failed to prepare his successor properly. Louis W. Koenig says:

> Roosevelt was not in Washington a month altogether during the 82 days that Truman was vice-president. The Roosevelt papers disclose that the two met by appointment only twice. Truman himself estimates that he saw Roosevelt only eight times the year before his death, and these meetings contributed little to Truman's preparation for the Presidency.[22]

Mr. Truman never forgot the difference between the man and the office. A major contribution of Mr. Truman's to the history of the Presidency was the progressive institutionalization of the office under his aegis, a systematic rejection, whether conscious or not, of Mr. Roosevelt's preference for an informally run Presidency centering entirely on himself. Under Mr. Truman, the Council of Economic Advisors and the National Security Council came into being and the Bureau of the Budget took on new importance as the center through which presidential control of executive agencies and the President's legislative program could be maintained.[23] "During my administration, [Mr. Truman wrote] there was a continuing audit on the part of the Budget Director in all departments. I had people checking all programs to see how they were shaping up within the framework that had been established."[24]

As Mr. Truman institutionalized the Presidency, he retained many features of centralization that Mr. Roosevelt had encouraged by his own methods. Richard Neustadt says: "Truman saw the Presidency as the place where the buck stopped; he saw the President as the man in charge of government, as maker of a record for his party, and as a voice for the whole body of Americans. The job he had to do, as Truman saw it, was to make decisions and to take initiatives."[25]

Mr. Truman said, "I wanted it to be made clear that as long as I was in the White House I ran the executive branch of the government, and no one was ever allowed to act in the capacity of President of the United States except the man who held that office."[26]

Mr. Truman's way of being President apparently arose from many sources—from a strongly ingrained personal preference for decisiveness and from a sense of history fed by his own wide reading in American history and biography. He had a conscious political theory of the Presidency, a theory of the duties that in a democracy rest upon elected officials to take the responsibility for major public decisions and to render themselves accountable to the people who elected them, and also a theory of presidential representation that harked back to Andrew Jackson. "One thing I always liked about Jackson [Mr. Truman wrote] was that he brought the basic issues into clear focus. People knew what he stood for and what he was against, and ... that he represented the interests of the common people of the United States."[27]

Whereas Mr. Roosevelt's method of keeping control of his administration was to listen to complaints, to collect tidbits of information, to keep his ear to the ground, Mr. Truman's approach was more methodical. He did his homework, carefully went over materials that were prepared for him, and consulted with the people to whom he had delegated specific tasks. As he said: "I believed that the best way to obtain different views, without encouraging rivalries among different members [of the Cabinet] was to have complete airings in the open at full Cabinet meetings ... I would, of course, see Cabinet members individually, but theirs were special problems that affected only their own departments."[28]

Considering the highly partisan fervor that often surrounded his domestic program and his political activities, the small-scale but cumulatively damaging scandals that marred his administration,[29] and the very low ratings that he scored at times in public opinion polls, the judgment of contemporary historians on Mr. Truman is remarkably favorable. No doubt this is largely owing to their evaluation of Mr. Truman's foreign policies.[30] Many of these policies, such as Greek-Turkish aid,[31] the Marshall Plan, and the Point Four Program, sent an unprecedented flood of American resources abroad to restore the economies of European nations that had been shattered by World War II. American entrance into the United Nations and the North Atlantic Treaty Organization also gave the United States close diplomatic ties with other countries—something they had never had in peacetime before. Both sets of policies were pursued on the premises that the world had been shrunk by modern techniques of transportation, communication, and warfare and that America's interests were bound up in the prosperity and safety of her allies. This was a difficult and unfamiliar doctrine to expound to Americans, yet Mr. Truman presided over the change that brought the United States face to face with worldwide responsibilities on a continuing, peacetime basis and through the arduous trial of limited war in Korea. Thus Mr. Truman's stature as a President is tied not to the techniques he used to gather power in his own hands but rather to the purposes to which he put the powers that he had.[32]

Dwight D. Eisenhower (Republican, 1953-1961)

Dwight D. Eisenhower came late in life to partisan politics. Elected by enormous majorities, nevertheless for six of his eight years in office he faced a Congress controlled by the opposite party. Greatly beloved as a leader, he was still generally adjudged by most contemporary scholars to have been a disappointing President.[33] Although recent scholarly opinion has sponsored an upward revision of Eisenhower's reputation,[34] a brief discussion of some of the sources of the earlier disappointment may tell us something about what we expect of our Presidents and something of the trials and frustrations, as well as the opportunities, of the presidential office.

One widely quoted diagnosis of what went wrong with the Eisenhower Presidency—actually a prediction about what would go wrong with it—is attributed by Richard Neustadt to Harry S Truman.

"He'll sit here," Truman would remark (tapping his desk for emphasis), "and he'll say, 'Do this! Do that!' *And nothing will happen.*"[35]

There was much reflection and experience behind his remark. Mr. Truman knew, as few men could know, the difficulties of operating a complicated political organism—one designed to be, at best, only partially responsive to presidential priorities or programs or persuasion. Nevertheless, the conspicuous failures of the Eisenhower administration—the ones that caused the most criticism and attracted the most publicity—were in general not the product of an apparatus—executive or legislative—unresponsive to presidential wishes. Rather, the Eisenhower administration suffered from difficulty in formulating policies to which the government could respond at all or respond without untoward effects. Passivity or ambiguity at critical moments in policy formation seems to have presented a greater problem to the Eisenhower Presidency than lapses of efficiency in policy execution.

It is instructive, for example, to recall President Eisenhower's unwillingness to do anything to strengthen the hand of the executive branch against wild and ill-founded charges of Communist infiltration by Senator Joseph McCarthy, Republican of Wisconsin, despite the President's strong personal antipathy for the Senator. McCarthy's attacks against the State Department and the International Information Administration had already gained wide currency and notoriety by the time Eisenhower assumed office. The problem was alarming, of great magnitude, and unmistakably damaging to the morale and effectiveness of a large and vital part of our government. Observers, hoping that a Republican presidential victory in 1952 would cut McCarthy off from his base of support in the party, could take little comfort from the few clues the new administration gave about how McCarthy would be handled. During the campaign, candidate Eisenhower had excised from a speech in Milwaukee a paragraph praising General George Marshall, the target of one of the Wisconsin Senator's most elaborate attacks. In the early months of the new administration, Scott McLeod, well known on Capitol Hill as a McCarthy ally, was appointed Assistant Secretary of State for Personnel and Security, an extremely sensitive post from the standpoint of frightened employees in the Department.

The new Republican management team in the Information Administration had an especially difficult job, because in the early days of the Eisenhower administration McCarthy was concentrating a heavy barrage of criticism at that agency. The assistant to the agency director describes an attempt to get help at a meeting with a top Eisenhower aide:

> [We told him] morale was terrible and had primarily affected the better personnel, who were dismayed by the seeming impotence of the "new team's" leadership, or absence of it. Would the President give us his backing if we had ... a showdown?
>
> [The man from the White House] blandly answered that he wouldn't dream of approaching the President on the subject. It was Eisenhower's "passion," he said, "not to offend anyone in Congress."[36]

Later, McCarthy went after other agencies in the executive branch. The cumulative effects of his irresponsible behavior finally resulted in a vote of condemnation by the Senate. The election of 1954 deprived him of his committee chairmanship, and he died soon afterward. Throughout the entire two-year period, however, Eisenhower never attacked McCarthy.

> Some of my good friends and most trusted advisors [Eisenhower wrote] would, periodically, become infuriated at his irresponsible actions and urge me to censure him publicly.... It seemed that almost every day I had to point out

that if I were to attack Senator McCarthy, even though every personal instinct so prompted me, I would greatly enhance his publicity value without achieving any constructive purpose.... Lashing back at one man, which is easy enough for a President, was not as important to me as the long term value of restraint.... As the months went by, my advisors gradually became practically unanimous in agreeing with my methods for defeating McCarthyism.[37]

In the case of McCarthy, it is clear that the fact that "nothing happened" in the White House was the result of deliberate choice.[38] Historians may argue over President Eisenhower's conviction that this strategy contributed to McCarthy's eventual decline; our purpose here is only to illustrate the restraint which was such an important feature of Eisenhower's presidential style, even when he reports that his personal instincts strongly urged a less passive response.

President Eisenhower promoted a passive Presidency in other ways. Much authority previously held by Presidents was delegated downward. According to Sherman Adams, Eisenhower's chief of staff for six White House years, this included such matters as control over patronage. With respect to foreign policy, Adams says: "Eisenhower delegated to [Secretary of State John Foster] Dulles the responsibility of developing the specific policy, including the decision where the administration would stand and what course of action would be followed in each international crisis."[39]

Adams makes other illuminating comments about Eisenhower's administrative style:

Because Eisenhower disliked talking business on the phone, [Presidential Assistant Wilton] Persons and I and a few other staff members would speak for him on the telephone on many matters that required his personal attention.[40]

... Eisenhower was not much of a reader. He was impatient with the endless paperwork of the Presidency and always tried to get his staff to digest long documents into one page summaries, which was sometimes next to impossible to do.[41]

As any President must, President Eisenhower fashioned the Presidency to suit many of the needs of his own personal administrative style. Withdrawal from partisan politics, a dislike of rough and tumble, a preference for decision-making at the staff level, leaving him relatively free from detail— all characterized his method of being President. If this method freed him for other things, it also had its costs. Sometimes the President was not thoroughly briefed on matters that he would have been better off knowing about.

An authoritative commentary by Aaron Wildavsky on the administrative snafu known as the Dixon-Yates case discusses one such occasion:

When repeated public questions arose—and the cry about it climbed to a fever pitch, the Administration's disinclination to pursue the matter was so great that the President was put in the position of making untenable statements whose accuracy could have been checked by a phone call.... The President's apparent lack of information concerning Dixon-Yates has led to charges that he was misled by his advisors.... [Nevertheless] it is clear that the Chief Executive either directly or through acceptance of the going procedure, shapes the major channels of information and advice upon which he must base his decisions. While it is important to know how well the President has been served by the men he has chosen to advise him, it is at least as revealing to discover how well the President has permitted himself to be served. This is especially true of a President like Eisenhower who has taken considerable pains to introduce organizational reforms into the White House. There is no evidence to suggest that President Eisenhower was dissatisfied with his own work.[42]

As Wildavsky points out, the weakness in the machinery, if it is a weakness, cannot properly be attributed to a lack of responsiveness to President Eisenhower's own preferences. This was also the case with perhaps the most striking purely administrative dust-up of the Eisenhower years, which took place at the presentation of the budget for the fiscal year 1958.

On the very day that President Eisenhower sent the Federal budget to Congress, he authorized and approved a statement by his Secretary of the Treasury criticizing the budget as too large. Warning of a "depression that will curl your hair," Secretary George Humphrey urged that the Eisenhower budget be cut by the Democratic Congress. Incredulous reporters, seeking repudiation of Humphrey's statement from the President, learned that "that written memorandum—I not only went over every word of it, I edited it, and it expresses my convictions very thoroughly."

Several commentators have said that this contradiction was greatly damaging to the Eisenhower Presidency.[43] It hurt the relations of trust, confidence, and mutual support that Presidents try to build with the executive departments and agencies by reaching agreement on a budget. It exacerbated partisan divisions between the Republican President and the Democratic-controlled Congress and that year jeopardized the mutual security program on which our allies were heavily dependent. Finally, it damaged President Eisenhower's prestige within the professional community of Washington, that large amorphous group in and out of government that consists of members of Congress and their staffs, journalists, lawyers, lobbyists, agency executives, and embassy people—people who as a part of their daily routine keep an eye on political affairs in the nation's capital. To them, that President Eisenhower would allow—indeed, encourage—the repudiation of his own budget on the day it was presented was simply bad political craftsmanship.

But the question is, was this a result of presidential difficulty in persuading some part of the administration to "go along"? Was Eisenhower having trouble persuading people "to do the things they ought to ... do"?[44] Evidently not. Eisenhower's administrative machinery admirably captured his ambivalence toward his own budget.[45] He said "do this," and the budget was sent to Capitol Hill; "do that," and Humphrey's attack was mounted.

What administrative innovations did Eisenhower introduce to further institutionalize the White House? Under Eisenhower, each presidential assistant had fixed responsibilities. Only Sherman Adams, his Chief of Staff, reported directly to the President; everyone else was subordinate to Adams in a highly explicit White House chain of command. Cabinet meetings grew in size to include perhaps twenty or thirty regular participants (UN Ambassador, Budget Director, several White House staff members, Mutual Security Administrator, and so on), and a Cabinet secretariat was established to follow up on decisions reached in Cabinet meetings and to keep the agenda.[46] A congressional liaison operation was set up in the White House under General Wilton Persons, who had previously performed similar functions for the Department of the Army. As in previous administrations, a separate press office was also maintained. Aside from the accretion of activities in the White House and the rather more rigid separation of functions than was usual, however, the main feature of the Eisenhower system of staff organization was the channeling of all lines of communication to the President through Sherman Adams, and later, after Adams resigned, through his successor, General Persons.

Eisenhower protected himself from overexposure; some commentators say that the net result of this and of the zealousness of his assistants to protect him during and after his three episodes of serious illness in office was that he was underexposed to alternatives, to information, and to the opportunities to make decisions. But there is little doubt that insofar as this was true, Eisenhower preferred it that way. His philosophy of government welcomed self-limitation. By virtue of having been elected, he had accomplished his main policy purpose of keeping the Republican party from leading America into a posture of post-World War II isolationism. By doing little else, he maintained the phenomenal popularity with public opinion that was his main resource as a political leader.[47] Other Presidents might suffer, as Harry Truman undoubtedly did, from an inability to get the machinery of government to accomplish the goals they set. President Eisenhower's main burden apparently was a reluctance to jeopardize his popularity by formulating goals, or a distaste for those goals the demands of the system thrust on him.

John F. Kennedy (Democrat, 1961–1963)

John Kennedy, the youngest man to serve as President since Theodore Roosevelt, operated in office quite differently from his predecessor, who, until Ronald Reagan, was the oldest President. Kennedy was a rapid, serious, and voracious reader, had analytical skills of a high order, and hence processed through his own mind a vast quantity of information. It was a part of his style of leadership to emphasize rather than to conceal that he was doing this. Unlike Eisenhower, Kennedy saw virtually nothing of his full Cabinet, preferring to meet with smaller groups and task forces.[48] And the White House staff was far less rigidly compartmentalized than during the previous administration. In some positions, however, there was a fairly clear division of labor, with special assistants for appointments, the press, foreign and security matters, and congressional relations. All of Kennedy's assistants had direct access to the President, and he to them.[49]

Because John Kennedy was a man of great charm, because of the overpowering tragedy of his assassination in November 1963, and because of the brevity of his time in office, it has been difficult for observers to reach balanced judgments about the contribution he made to the Presidency. He came to office as the choice of less than 50 percent of the voters, the winner of the closest presidential election in the twentieth century. His presence at the top of the Democratic ticket was a test of the readiness of American voters to accept the leadership of a Roman Catholic. Analysis of the election suggests that for a sizable number of voters the issue of Kennedy's religion overrode other considerations, and this worked against Kennedy in the popular vote, although not in the electoral college.[50] An important consequence of Kennedy's weakness as a candidate in 1960 was a sharp reduction, in comparison with the off-year election of 1958, in the number of Democrats elected to the House of Representatives.[51]

Thus Kennedy began his Presidency under severe constraint. There could, under the circumstances, be no dramatic "hundred days" such as his well-wishers would have liked.[52] It is not surprising that Kennedy, as a Democrat succeeding a rather conservative Republican, undertook important reorientations of national priorities in a number of areas; however, deprived of his full term of office, he was unable in many cases to see them through.

It is not easy to sort out the main themes of the Kennedy Presidency. With respect to Congress, there was great caution. Presidential-congressional relations were handled gingerly. Kennedy's congressional liaison man Lawrence O'Brien learned his job by listening carefully on the Hill, and in time he enjoyed an extraordinary measure of confidence both in the White House and in Congress.[53] Even before he was inaugurated, Kennedy favored enlargement of the House Rules Committee, but this was not something he could achieve himself or without a coordinated effort based within the House.[54]

Despite the great Rules Committee victory, however, Kennedy feared his margin was too thin in the House to overcome the animosity of conservative committee chairmen. Thus he rationed his New Frontier legislation with great—some liberal critics believed with excessive—care. Sam Rayburn's death in the fall of 1961 brought to the speakership John McCormack, head of a rival clan to the Kennedys in the intensely tribal politics of

Massachusetts, and a strong, though painfully cautious party loyalist. Over McCormack's objections liberal Democrats began using the party caucus to reshape the pattern of assignments to key legislative committees.[55]

Kennedy also gave carefully measured aid and comfort to his allies in Congress who pressed for liberalization of the Ways and Means and Appropriations Committees after the election of 1962. Just at the point when much of this patient gardening could have been expected to begin to bear fruit, John Kennedy was assassinated. His successor, Lyndon Johnson, a devout believer in the efficacy of momentum in legislative affairs, exploited the post-assassination mood and achieved great legislative victories—an unprecedented tax cut, a major civil rights bill.

The legislative record of Kennedy's three years was not distinguished when compared with that of the triumphant Eighty-ninth Congress (1965-67), which, under Johnson, enacted Federal aid to education, the poverty program, and Medicare. There is every reason to believe, however, that the efforts of the Kennedy years in setting priorities, in mobilizing the Federal bureaucracies and the press, and in slowly revamping key committees of the House, made a significant contribution. It can hardly be doubted that Kennedy would have been a much stronger candidate in 1964 than he was in 1960 or that Barry Goldwater would have been a weaker opponent for him than Richard Nixon was in 1960. Thus it is not implausible to speculate that had Kennedy lived to run again, an overwhelmingly liberal Eighty-ninth Congress would have been available to him (as it would have been to virtually any Democratic President in that year) and the final enactment of so many New Deal-Fair Deal measures, which a generation of Democrats had advocated, would have been credited to him.[56]

Because the legislative record is relatively easy to score, Presidents and President watchers use it to evaluate and compare Presidencies. One of the least attractive aspects of the Kennedy-Johnson succession was the passionate squabbling that developed between supporters of both men over who could claim credit with posterity for the enactment in the 1960s of New Deal-Fair Deal-New Frontier-Great Society legislation.[57] Since getting credit for something helps a politician's career, it is understandable that an active politician and his partisans should claim all they plausibly can. When a leader's political career is over, however, and analysts with less at stake begin to weigh in with their judgments, the record can be studied in a new light.

To an analyst committed to neither man, the most significant feature of the Kennedy-Johnson legislative record would surely be its continuity. Both men largely accepted an agenda that had been part and parcel of their national party's basic outlook for a generation. Both came relatively late to an all-out commitment to that agenda, but by the time they reached the Presidency, their commitment to it was firm. Both added and subtracted marginally from the basic Democratic agenda, and both were in major respects constrained by events beyond their control from pursuing it as vigorously as they might have wanted. And, certainly, both brought to its execution highly individual styles of work.

Nowhere were their styles more at odds than in the attitudes that underlay their stance toward the social and political forces that impinged on White House decision-making. Kennedy reached out to visitors with questions about the outside world. He encouraged competition among contending groups in his administration, giving high marks to those who fought for their ideas.[58] He welcomed trial balloons, in which subordinates would suggest a possible line of policy to newspaper reporters, so he could use the reactions from outsiders—interest groups, congressmen—in shaping decisions. Like the skipper of a small boat, Kennedy attended to the winds and tides, running with the wind when he could, tacking when he thought he had to, bailing energetically when, as in the Bay of Pigs episode and on a few other occasions, his administration was momentarily swamped. More than once Kennedy gave voice to a sense of elements "out there" that he could struggle with but not control.[59]

Perhaps the most measured assessment of the achievements of the Kennedy administration by an insider has been that of Richard Neustadt.[60] Of the themes he identifies in the Kennedy Presidency, he gives overwhelming weight to the management of relations with the Soviet Union and the regulation of our defense posture, which was based on avoiding miscalculations and misapprehensions between the superpowers and providing means of responding to conventional military challenges that were not tied to the use of nuclear weapons. This position entailed a sizable expansion of America's military capability, a corresponding expansion of the military budget, and a drastic, important shift in the balance of power within the government—away from military and toward civilian leadership in the setting of priorities with respect to the evaluation of strategic doctrines, in the allocation of missions among the services, and in the choice of weapons systems.

More than any events in foreign affairs, the two early and short-lived crises over Cuba set the tone for Kennedy administration decision-making. The Bay of Pigs episode of April, 1961, three months after Kennedy's inauguration, was an unmitigated disaster, in which President Kennedy and his foreign policy advisors were persuaded by top officials in the CIA to proceed with plans that had been in the making for some time.[61] The utter miscarriage of the plan shook Kennedy's confidence in the military and intelligence bureaucracies he had inherited and gave credence to the maxims of advisors like Richard Neustadt, whose book *Presidential Power* argued that each major decision of the government had to be looked at in the White House from the President's own political perspective, as the only sensible precaution against presidential entrapment by the big bureaucracies of the national government.[62]

When, some eighteen months later, intelligence photographs showed that Russian offensive missiles were being planted on Cuban soil, Kennedy, in utmost secrecy, convened a task force of top foreign policy advisors, dominated by political executives he had appointed, to debate the alternatives. They settled on a strategy of blockade that gave the Soviets an opportunity to withdraw. The Soviets pulled out, producing euphoria in the Kennedy administration. Recalling the decision-making atmosphere years later, when Vietnam was proving so troublesome, a high official was quoted as saying, "There was a confidence—it was never bragged about, it was just there, a residue perhaps of the confrontation over the missiles in Cuba—that when the chips were really down, the other people would fold."[63]

In domestic politics three main themes of the Kennedy administration stand out—reorganization of the Defense Department, modern economics, and civil rights—and all were in one way or another carried forward by Kennedy's successor.

Before President Kennedy installed Robert McNamara as Secretary of Defense, the Defense Department was commonly assumed to be largely ungovernable by civilians.[64] Major decisions were bargained out among military potentates without much participation by the Secretary. This was not an altogether stagnant system, however; incentives to innovate in strategic doctrine were created by the desire of each of the major services to expand at the expense of the others. Nor were civilians totally absent from the decision-making process; at various times, Presidents Truman and Eisenhower both imposed stringent budgetary limits within which interservice rivalry had to take place.

In fact, it was budgetary limits of the Eisenhower years leading to reliance on the doctrine of "massive retaliation" that provided a context for the Kennedy-McNamara reforms. The armed services found it far easier to accept drastic reallocations of missions, consolidation of procurement, and civilian control of the choices among weapons systems while the military budget itself was increasing. In the three years of the Kennedy Presidency, the Defense Department budget increased an average of $7.3 billion per year over the allocation it had received in the last Eisenhower year. "Massive retaliation" gave way to "graduated" or "flexible" response as the central strategic doctrine of the United States. The greater expense was justified on the grounds, first, that building American capability to fight limited wars would decrease the probability that America's enemies would start them, and second, that a more flexible posture of defense opened a greater range of diplomatic options for the Kennedy administration in its maneuvers over the fate of Berlin, the Middle East, Cuba, and Southeast Asia.

As a rising tide of domestic disturbances in the late 1960's turned the focus of public attention from foreign to internal affairs and as the war in Vietnam claimed an increasing share of national resources, some of the justifications for the Kennedy-McNamara strategy were subjected to fierce criticism.[65] There is no doubt that this strategy gave America the capacity to make a sizable commitment in Vietnam, that ultimately this commitment became extremely costly, and that resources were used there that otherwise might have been applied to the amelioration of domestic problems. Moreover, in at least some quarters doubt has been expressed that increased American capability to fight limited wars may have discouraged more vigorous Soviet intervention in the Middle East, kept them from annexing Berlin, forced them to pull missiles out of Cuba, and temporarily thwarted the more ambitious Communist designs on most of Southeast Asia. And since the defense of the Kennedy strategic doctrine (which President Johnson also largely pursued) rests on claims that it prevented dire events that consequently did not happen, the doubts of skeptics can never be definitively resolved.

It is true, however, that in a tense world increasingly populated by nations having the capacity to build and deliver nuclear weapons, none of these weapons has been employed militarily since the American bombing of Nagasaki in 1945. And while our relations with the Soviet Union have not been ideal, since the Cuban missile crisis of 1962 direct confrontations between the two major powers have been avoided.

If the strategic consequences of Kennedy's reorganization of the Defense Department are hard to sort out, the administrative consequences are equally unclear. Secretary McNamara forced program justifications to new levels of detail, precision, and subtlety, and he established civilian control of the Pentagon. He consolidated decentralized intelligence and procurement activities in the Defense Department. Still he was not able to cure the perennial problem of drastic cost underestimates in contracting for major weapons hardware that his new control system was designed to monitor. McNamara's reforms did not vanquish or appreciably rationalize the Byzantine politics of the Eisenhower era's "military-industrial complex," which consisted of shifting and competing coalitions of manufacturers and suppliers of goods and services to the armed services, the various branches of the services, and interested members of Congress. The net effect of these reforms, however, was to deal in the civilian leaders of the government on a more powerful basis.[66]

The great economic achievement of the Kennedy administration was the tax cut of 1964 (actually enacted after Kennedy's death). It was explicitly designed to incur a deficit over the short run in the Federal budget but, by stimulating private consumption, to increase incomes and hence tax receipts over a slightly longer period.[67] Although the theory of economics on which this was based had been widely accepted for thirty years and although the government since Herbert Hoover's day had undertaken smaller-scale applications of this theory, the tax cut of 1964 was the frankest, best-publicized, and most explicitly didactic application of Keynesian economics ever undertaken by the Federal government. Perhaps the greatest success of the tax cut was that it stimulated the economy and won political friends for modern economics in the service of national policy.[68]

The Kennedy administration's record in civil rights is as difficult to disentangle from current events outside the President's control as is its record in foreign affairs. President Eisenhower had hesitated to give moral support to those pressing for civil rights. President Kennedy was very much dependent in Congress on Southern committee chairmen and Southern votes to enact his program. Moreover, he had appointed his brother Attorney General, chief officer of the government in charge of enforcing rulings of the Supreme Court on desegregation in education and public facilities. In so doing, Kennedy accepted an extra measure of political responsibility— and vulnerability—for acts of the Justice Department.[69]

There is general agreement that in the field of civil rights the Kennedy Presidency distinguished itself administratively (as did the Johnson administration), peaceably integrating the University of Alabama (despite the well-publicized defiance of Governor George Wallace), protecting Martin Luther King, Jr., from an irate mob in Birmingham, and desegregating interstate bus terminal lunchrooms by executive order. The Civil Rights Act of 1964, a high priority of both the Kennedy and Johnson administrations, was a historic law that was triumphantly and shrewdly assisted over its most difficult hurdle, the Senate, by Democratic Whip Hubert Humphrey. It provided for initiatives to be taken by the Federal government to enforce the prohibition of racial discrimination in public accommodations and to protect many of the constitutional rights of citizens. These initiatives could take the form of suits by the Justice Department or the cutting off of Federal funds from state and local projects that practiced discrimination.

The Kennedy administration had an unmistakable style, which was exemplified by phrases, such as "beautiful people" and "jet set," that came to be applied to its members.[70] The Kennedy brothers, themselves quite youthful and reared in an atmosphere emphasizing competition, toughness, self-control, and victory, gathered around them persons having mannerisms like their own. It was easy, though not always fair, for the more homespun, middle-aged, and stodgy denizens of the bureaucracies and Capitol Hill to read into the impatience, high spirits, and fashionably smart banter of the ambitious, young Kennedy administration blades-about-town a certain callousness and self-absorption, bred of unfamiliarity with disappointment and nurtured by heady involvement with big doings.[71]

For a time a gap yawned between the White House and the legislative liaison personnel of the executive branch on one hand and Capitol Hill people on the other, growing into what a White House aide once described as a "mutuality of contempt."[72] A friend of the Kennedy administration on Capitol Hill said: "The President's advisors are a part of the trouble. It's not that there is so much friction, it's just that we do not know them and cannot talk their language."[73] Another congressman, a liberal Democrat, agreed:

> These young men come marching up to the Capitol. They wheedle and promise and threaten. When major legislation is being handled on the floor, you will find these men in committee offices just off the floor. They call in members just before the vote and try all kinds of pressures.
>
> One House member was told that, if he did not vote as they wanted him to vote, every military base in his district would be closed.... There have also been threats to take defense contracts out of congressional districts....
>
> They are trying to transfer ward politics to the National Capitol.[74]

Vice President Johnson complained in private to his protégé, Senate Secretary Bobby Baker:

> The trouble with Jack Kennedy's operation is that he's got the minnows in Congress but not the whales. Those kids come up from the White House and start yelling "frog" at everybody and expect 'em to jump.[75]

The *Reporter*'s Meg Greenfield said:

> The most widely shared and loudly voiced grievance that Congress has against administration practices concerns the unremitting attention it receives from those it describes simply and without affection as "the young men." They badger, to hear the members tell it. They hector. They even chase....
>
> Legislators who still cherish the notion that they themselves will decide how to vote appear to have been at various times amused, confused and infuriated by the discombobulation of incoming messages.... "Why are you calling me, son?" an august legislator asked an all but anonymous administration phoner....
>
> To the White House counter-claim that pushing and prodding sometimes help and never hurt, one Congressman replies by citing the case of a young liaison man, the very sight of whom at the cloakroom door, he claims, is enough to cost the administration twenty-five votes. Under questioning he lowered the figure to three, but this time he seemed serious.[76]

Three years of legislative difficulty and the inevitable frustrations of trying to move entrenched bureaucracies had begun to mellow the more flexible and intelligent members of the Kennedy White House by the time of Kennedy's assassination in November of 1963. But for such a group, whose collective impress on the Washington scene owed almost as much to a romantic Camelot mentality, a tacit assumption of their own chosenness and invulnerability, as it did to their idealism and brains, the blow of the assassination fell with devastating force.[77] A few in the Kennedy entourage turned their bitterness on his successor and on those among their number who elected to serve the new President.[78]

Lyndon B. Johnson (Democrat, 1963–1969)

Lyndon Johnson, Kennedy's successor, began to place a distinctive stamp on the office even before all the Kennedy men had left the White House staff. A less cerebral man than Kennedy, Johnson's main strengths were his prodigious energy, an extremely well-developed strategic sense, long political experience, wide political acquaintance, and an overwhelming attentiveness to the operational activities necessary to put across a legislative program.[79] In the early years of his Presidency, Johnson also enjoyed great popularity, which he nurtured by placing heavy stress on the theme of continuity with the priorities of the immediate past.

If John Kennedy's personality and the circumstances of his departure from office have made it difficult to write about his Presidency in a measured way, this is no less true of Lyndon Johnson. Thus accounts of the Johnson Presidency turn again and again to the Johnson personality, as it was and as it seemed to be, when one examines his conduct of the office.

In his years in the Senate, as we will see in the next chapter, Johnson could be observed at his most effective. Johnson as President was much less so, and in part this weakness is traceable to personal limitations. Where policy is bargained over rather than invented or created, by circumstances as well as by public officials, a leader without a detailed grasp of substance can operate successfully, as Lyndon Johnson did in the Senate. But knowing who wants what and how strongly—the most important sorts of knowledge for a legislative broker—is only part of the story for a President. Presidents also have to have a feel for the substance of policy, for understanding how measures will work in a real world that is immensely complex and intractable. Johnson's grasp of these matters in foreign affairs, where he was inexperienced and insensitive to fine distinctions, was unsure. Stewart Alsop has a revealing observation: "When Johnson inherited the Presidency, he at first appalled his foreign policy experts by using Iran and Iraq, and Indonesia and Indochina, interchangeably. Until he became President, those places had not been useful to him in his profession, and there had been no room for them in his mental attic."[80]

The daily pressures and pleasures of the presidential office are such that it is not possible for any President to learn very much totally from scratch. President Johnson's formidable intelligence was for over fifty years harnessed to an equally formidable parochialism. He preferred to apply his energy and ingenuity to the anticipation and solution of concrete problems and to the management of his career rather than to speculation or the gratification of idle curiosity. When the Presidency descended upon Johnson, he fully understood the powers of the office and its potential as a constructive force in American life, but it now appears that in important ways he lacked knowledge of the rest of the world.

Some observers are inclined to attribute this handicap to the circumstances of Johnson's life—to an education at San Marcos State Teachers College rather than at some more cosmopolitan university, to the insatiable demands of Texas politics and Senate cloakrooms during the bulk of his career.[81] Philip Geyelin said:

> He had heard the fashionable concepts, be they containment or disengagement or neutralism or parallelism. But he didn't speak that language because he did not think in it; he thought in analogies to the New Deal or Munich, to "another Korea" or "another Cuba"; the Mekong Delta was to be "another TVA." He was in large measure, then, a self-taught statesman; he couldn't read the music, but he had come a long way on his ability to play by ear....
>
> The trouble with foreigners, the President once said, "is that they're not like the folks you were reared with." Lyndon Johnson was reared with hill-country Texans, and his school was Congress and the New Deal. His interest and expertise were not in policies and still less in ideas.[82]

A number of things Johnson did in office suggest that he was fully aware of this handicap. Most significant was his effort to keep so many Kennedy appointees in his own administration. Three members of the first Kennedy cabinet—Secretaries Dean Rusk (State), Stewart Udall (Interior), and Orville Freeman (Agriculture)—served out Johnson's full term. Virtually all the members of the Johnson administration who fell afoul of the dovish wing of the Democratic party in 1967 and 1968 over the Vietnam war (among them Rusk, Walt Rostow, McGeorge Bundy, Robert McNamara) were originally Kennedy appointees.

Johnson's desire to maintain continuity with Kennedy administration policies apparently led him to an initial acceptance of Vietnam escalation;[83] but it is the persistence of this policy in the face of continued disappointment that needs explaining. One plausible explanation is that President Johnson persisted because in this area he lacked the sure-footedness that is the prerequisite of ingenuity and hospitality to innovation. No doubt pride and the conviction that the policies his administration was pursuing were defensible and ultimately right also led to his persistence in them, but Johnson was not by habit an ideologically inflexible politician or one whose pride was normally invested in particular means so much as in being able to achieve a creditable result.

Although President Johnson was quoted as saying that he believed that his strong and successful pro-civil rights policies coupled with urban riots were the principal cause of his unpopularity toward the end of his term of office,[84] his hope to settle the Vietnam war was the reason he gave for withdrawing in March 1968 as a candidate for reelection. Southern anger over Johnson's civil rights positions could not have harmed him politically to such a degree as to make withdrawal so very attractive. Since 1948, the

38   *The Presidency*

Solid South had not been reliably Democratic in presidential elections; moreover, since then the rest of the national Democratic coalition has more often than not abandoned the South. It was Vietnam that split the national Democratic party, not the race issue. And it was Vietnam that cast a pall over the Johnson Presidency.[85]

Toward the end of the Johnson administration, its policy toward Vietnam began to change sharply. The manner in which this occurred reveals something of the style of the Johnson Presidency.[86] As President, Johnson put great reliance on men whom he could trust personally—with whom, as he said, he "could go to the well." Many of these men had been important figures in their own right in Washington and in Democratic politics since the New Deal. One was Clark Clifford, a Washington lawyer who had been a confidential White House assistant in the Truman administration and whom Johnson picked to succeed Robert McNamara as Secretary of Defense. Virtually the first major problem Clifford faced when he took over the Pentagon in January 1968 was a request from General William Westmoreland, the commander in Vietnam, for a massive new commitment of American troops. Civilian officials in the Defense Department seized on the evaluation of this request as a vehicle through which they could brief the new Secretary in detail about the problems and prospects of the war. Clifford emerged convinced that, within the ground rules imposed by our worldwide commitments, the war could not be won and that ways had to be found to limit and ultimately reduce the American investment there.

This position was contrary to presidential policy; however, by the end of March, after a short period of pulling and hauling within the administration, it had become presidential policy. Clifford had mounted an extraordinary effort to change the President's mind. He encouraged Johnson to convene a council of trusted "wise men" and in effect ask them to evaluate the evidence that had changed his own mind on Vietnam. Some of these men, such as Maxwell Taylor, Walt Rostow, Dean Rusk, and McGeorge Bundy, had been architects of Vietnam escalation. Others— Dean Acheson, Abe Fortas, and Clifford himself—had been sympathetic to the general line of policy. Only a few, such as George Ball, had criticized the policy from within the government. Almost all of them, however, emerged from their deliberations convinced that Clifford was right and that administration policy had to change.

The January 1968 Tet offensive by the Viet Cong forces was militarily devastating to the enemy. It was not read that way in the United States, however, where it greatly embarrassed those in the administration who were optimistic about the course of the war. The polls, demonstrations, and presidential primaries of early 1968, which showed how unpopular the war had become with Americans (especially Democrats), also must have weighed heavily on the minds of policy-makers.[87] But Johnson had long remained intransigent in the face of similar adversity. This persuasion from within his administration—and from men he trusted—cannot be discounted as a force in shifting the policy of the administration. Very soon after the conclusion of the "wise men" was communicated to the President, American policy did begin to change, although this fact was not immediately acknowledged. General Westmoreland in Vietnam was denied his request for a huge new commitment of troops; procedural negotiations began with the enemy in Paris; and the President announced his determination to seek a negotiated settlement in Vietnam unencumbered by the pursuit of another term in office.

In areas where he was more at home—especially in manipulating the press, the bureaucracies, and Congress—Johnson took command of everything to a degree that greatly exceeded the Kennedy style. Members of his staff were much less in the limelight than those in the Kennedy administration, though many of them were of very high caliber. In some respects Johnson tried to give the appearance of running a one-man administration: whenever an agency of the government had good news, there was a standing order to send it to the White House for announcement. The resignations of Cabinet members were timed to allow the President minuscule publicity advantages even though this timing entailed major inconveniences to the men involved.[88]

James E. Anderson, the most thorough student of Johnson as administrator, says:

> There was systematic and extensive monitoring of departments and agencies to provide the president with information on their activities. This information was used for various purposes: to alert the president to potential problems, provide a basis for intervention in agency activities, help protect and promote the president's political interests, and, through the fact it was requested, keep pressure on agencies to carry out presidential purposes.[89]

If Kennedy rode the waves, Johnson, Canutelike, commanded them. He resented all outside attempts, large and small, to commit him in advance to a line of policy, to a presidential appointment, to anything that would reduce his "options." Task forces were mobilized to frame new policy proposals but were required to observe the strictest secrecy.[90] Trial balloons were forbidden. Independent action by allies and subordinates was regarded as a poor substitute for coordinated service in behalf of presidential goals. In the Senate, Johnson had enjoyed six years as Majority Leader without the obligation to pursue a Republican President's priorities. Johnson found that by regulating the pace of Senate business he could maximize his own effectiveness.[91] In applying the lessons of those years to the Presidency, he conceded little to forces that other Presidents had appeased. No serious attempt was made to release the overwhelmingly pro-Johnson Eighty-ninth Congress from its labors in Washington early enough for incumbents of marginal House seats to campaign for reelection. Certainly, by so doing, a few of the fifty-five Democrats who lost House or Senate seats in the 1966 election could have been helped. Relations with local and state party leaders, whose preoccupations centered more on the winning of future elections than on the writing of a glorious legislative record, dwindled. Tremendous effort went into wooing the press, into finding programs with short-run payoffs, and into scoring publicity coups.[92]

Much of this attitude could be justified—and was—on the grounds that the President, as the only one who had to run for election, was the only member of the administration who needed the favorable publicity and, as head of the government, his convenience was paramount. In time, however, this explanation seemed inadequate. Reporters noted the President's unappeasable appetite for adulation, his habit of intruding on and, in little ways, demeaning the people who worked most closely with him. Eric Goldman commented:

> President Johnson's attitude toward his staff was essentially feudal.... When he did not like the length of a Special Assistant's hair, he told him to go to a barbershop; he ordered a secretary to enroll in a charm school. He expected aides to be available at any time for any function. They were as likely to be asked to phone the tailor ("These damn pants hitch up too much") as to confer with an ambassador.... LBJ was full of acts of *noblesse oblige.*[93]

All Presidents in some way or another have been eccentric. It seems unavoidable that anyone who lives so much of his life in the spotlight and under pressure will display casual mannerisms that seem puzzling or unconventional to observers. But for Johnson, who never separated his private person from his public responsibilities, who worked at presidential politics every waking moment, the eccentricities could hardly help but reflect on the conduct of public business.

Sometimes his theatrical instincts paid off:

> In order to discuss the application of Medicare, the American Medical Association requested an appointment with the President, and on July 29th he met with eleven of its leaders at the White House. "I'd never seen anything like it," one of the administration officials who attended the meeting said afterward. "The President made a powerful, moving appeal to the doctors to accept the new law, and reminded them that it had been devised after long and thorough consideration by the people's representatives under our constitutional procedures. He went on in that way for some time, and then he began talking about what wonderful men doctors were, and how when his daddy was sick the doctor would come over and sit up all night with him, and charge a pittance. He was getting terribly corny, but he had them on the edge of their seats. Then, suddenly, he got up and stretched. Of course, when the President of the United States stands up, everybody stands up. They jumped to their feet, and then he sat down, so they sat down, too. He started off again, with another moving statement about this great nation and its obligation to those who had helped make it great and who were now old and sick and helpless through

no fault of their own. Gradually, he moved back to the cornfield, and then he stood up again, and again they jumped to their feet. He did that a couple more times—until they were fully aware of who was President—and then he turned to a memorandum on his desk. He read them the statement in the bill prohibiting any government interference in any kind of medical practice at any time, and also the statement guaranteeing freedom of choice for both doctors and patients, and assured them there would be no government meddling in these matters. Next, he explained that Blue Cross and private insurance carriers, who are the administrative middlemen under the law, would determine the bill's definition of 'reasonable charges' on the basis of what was customary for a given area. Naturally, the doctors went for this, because they have great influence with most of those outfits. Toward the end, he asked for their help in drawing up regulations to implement the law. Then he got up one last time, and said he had to leave. Before he went, he turned to [Secretary of H.E.W. Wilbur] Cohen, who is the A.M.A.'s idea of an archfiend, and shaking a huge forefinger in his face, he said, 'Wilbur, I want you to stay here with these gentlemen, and work things out according to my instructions—no matter how long it takes you.' Afterward, I overheard one A.M.A. man say to another, 'Boy, did you hear how he talked to Cohen?' Of course, Wilbur had written the memorandum.''[94]

As concern over the Vietnam war deepened and dissent became more bitter toward the end of Johnson's term, the press became less tolerant of his foibles. Although comment about them had reached print long before the downturn in his popularity, it became more and more permissible to repeat stories illustrating Mr. Johnson's hunger to domineer in small matters, his lack of cultivation, his manipulativeness and secretiveness.[95] President Johnson's defenders pointed out that many of these complaints were trivial and did not really touch the public business.[96] In other cases, Johnson was merely following the example of Franklin Roosevelt, whose secretiveness and manipulativeness in the service of preserving presidential options were so much admired by writers on the Presidency. But somehow, Johnson seemed to carry the process too far —angrily cancelling major appointments or dropping major policy proposals because news about them had leaked out too soon.[97] "By striking hard at alleged transgressors," Evans and Novak commented, "The President quickly got the message to everyone in his administration that indiscreet officials would not be tolerated. As awareness of this fact seeped deep into the collective subconscious of the federal government, the inevitable reaction was a tendency to clam up. That enhanced the President's personal control over the federal establishment and enlarged the presidential exercise of power."[98]

So it did; but this goal is not desirable to the exclusion of all others. The President cannot run the government without help, and first-rate help is more easily attracted by the expectation of considerate treatment. Evans and Novak continue: "Corporation officials and lawyers had heard about long hours, hard demands, and occasional abuse from above, and some of them were reluctant to join the Great Society."[99]

Nevertheless, Johnson made a number of conspicuously first-rate appointments. The Kennedy administration had been widely congratulated for bringing a fresh and extraordinarily able new group of leaders into public life. Johnson retained many of them and added a few of his own: John Gardner, for example, gave new impetus to the Department of Health, Education, and Welfare; Ramsey Clark distinguished himself as Attorney General by his concern for civil liberties; Erwin Griswold, on his retirement as dean of the Harvard Law School, became Solicitor General; the gifted Clark Clifford replaced McNamara at Defense; and Arthur Goldberg left the Supreme Court to take up the late Adlai Stevenson's UN ambassadorship.

Toward the end, however, the Vietnam war swallowed everything. The popularity demonstrated by Johnson's overwhelming victory in 1964 evaporated in the polls and primaries of 1968; the avalanche of new and liberal legislation that emerged from the Eighty-ninth Congress of 1965-1967 gave way to hostile senatorial hearings that soured Johnson's private relations on Capitol Hill. When the Vietnam war devoured the Health, Education, and Welfare budget, John Gardner resigned. McNamara, increasingly skeptical of Vietnam policy, was eased out. Tension between Johnson and Goldberg, Udall, Clark, and even his old friend Clifford, became open secrets in Washington. Other high officials seem privately to have felt they stayed on too long. In a remarkable article, the usually extremely well-informed James Reston mused: "No doubt some stayed on out of compassion for the President or fear of his wrath and his fascination with the intimidating power of the FBI and the Internal Revenue Service. Others remained out of loyalty or guilt or ambition for position in the future.... Mr. Johnson did not make it easy for his colleagues to differ with him on fundamental issues."[100]

Like all human organizations, our political system relies heavily on the wisdom of the human beings who run it. Because the President alone heads the executive branch, in the end his wisdom counts for more than that of any of the people around him. Thus his weaknesses as well as his strengths, his incapacities as well as his talents, are for his time in office to a greater or lesser degree embodied in and amplified by the machinery of government. Personal eccentricities in private persons normally have small consequences for the neighbors. A President's eccentricities, though publicly on display, may be gratified in small and tolerable ways—by thousands of photographs, by multiple television sets in every room, by desk buttons marked "root beer" and "Fresca."[101] Or they may manifest themselves in larger and less digestible ways. Secretiveness may preserve options but inhibit the rallying of support behind the option finally chosen.[102] The urge to dominate may focus political attention on the leader, but unwillingness to share credit, if carried to an extreme, may deprive the leader of the help he needs. Unwillingness to share power means the President decides what he wants to decide, but it stifles creativity and initiative in those parts of the system close enough for the President to reach but where limitations on his time and energy prevent him from acting. There seem to be no compensating advantages for a President's unwillingness to grant the normal amount of dignity to his closest associates. This trait marks a President as a person of flawed character and leads observers to misinterpret even his most disinterested and public-spirited actions.

It is difficult to tell how history will judge Lyndon Johnson's Presidency. To his contemporaries, his own personal characteristics intrude on a reading of the record—as they did so notably on the writing of it. If his contemporaries are thankful that Johnson had it in him to rise nobly to many occasions—in civil rights, the trauma of the succession, and the grand design of his domestic program— they also regret that often between occasions he fell to petty and vindictive behavior, insensitivity, and maudlin self-justification that in the end may have cost him and his fellow citizens more than he ever could have intended.

Richard M. Nixon (Republican, 1969–1974)

As the twentieth century wears on, it becomes harder and harder for a discussion of particular American Presidents to escape total envelopment in disenchantment and rancor on the one hand or public relations puffery on the other. What of John F. Kennedy remains that has not been transformed into a myth about the martyred prince of Camelot? Now that Lyndon Johnson is in his grave, how long will it be before we are able to see him clearly through the thicket of disappointments that surrounded his last few unhappy years as President?[103]

Then there is the problem of Richard Nixon, the first and only President of the United States in all of our history to resign the office, the first and only President to resign in the face of certain impeachment, the first ever to accept a pardon from his successor, a pardon offered in advance of prosecution for wrongdoing, which he nevertheless accepted without apology to forestall having to take personal responsibility for criminal acts done in his behalf—and almost certainly with his knowledge—some of which caused the indictment, trial, and conviction of several members of his Cabinet, numerous of his closest White House aides, and his personal lawyer.[104]

In all this, surely, there is enough to gratify even Mr. Nixon's well-known taste for the unprecedented. And it poses a problem to the analyst of his Presidency, for a Presidency is made of many things, and not only its most disgraceful moments. Yet in Mr. Nixon's case, what was most disgraceful about his Presidency was most illuminating not only about Richard Nixon and the character he brought to public office, but also about the ways in which the office of the Presidency is embedded in the American constitutional order.

While it is technically correct, it is profoundly misleading to say simply that Mr. Nixon broke the law, was threatened with impeachment, and resigned. Two articles of impeachment rejected by the House Judiciary Committee censured his unilateral order of an attack on Cambodia and his numerous acts of financial self-aggrandizement while in public office—tax chiseling, and spending enormous amounts of government money on his private homes. These deeds outraged many, yet Nixon knew that Presidents before him had acted high-handedly in foreign affairs and gotten away with it. He knew of—and, being an envious man, he undoubtedly envied— Dwight D. Eisenhower's Gettysburg farm stocked with private gifts, and the special tax deal on the proceeds of *Crusade in Europe* that made Ike a wealthy man. He also knew that Lyndon Johnson, who for over thirty years was a full-time public official, had contrived somehow through timely investment in an industry greatly dependent upon government regulation to leave office a millionaire many times over.[105] Yet articles of impeachment were never lodged against them.

One article of impeachment actually voted by the House Committee referred to the abuse of power, the use of the FBI, the CIA, and the Internal Revenue Service to harass Mr. Nixon's political enemies. It is certain that Nixon believed that his predecessors had countenanced, and perhaps initiated, such behavior in the past and had never risked impeachment.[106]

The reason Nixon risked impeachment on all these counts, and on a count of refusing to honor subpoenas pursuant to the House impeachment inquiry itself, boils down to the subject of the first article of impeachment— Watergate. And what was Watergate? Essentially a year-long exercise in the manufacture of lies and evasions in which Nixon and his top staff engaged nearly full-time in order to avoid taking responsibility for an asinine incident, undoubtedly criminal, in which low-level employees of Nixon's reelection campaign committee were apprehended by police while in the act of trespassing upon and trying to bug the offices of the Democratic National Committee, located in the Watergate office building in Washington, D.C.

Soon after two enterprising *Washington Post* reporters established a link between the Watergate burglars and the White House,[107] presidential spokesman Ronald Ziegler, denying everything, proclaimed the Watergate caper "a third-rate burglary." One wonders: Why could Nixon at this point not have cut his losses and taken responsibility for the excessive zeal of his employees? Why did he not dare to risk such a simple, straightforward solution?

One answer no doubt is that he thought he could get away with not doing so. Another is that in the midst of an election campaign, during which the original incident occurred, no politician hands an issue to his opponent, no matter how commanding his lead, no matter how feeble the opponent. Nevertheless, at some point along the road, making a clean breast of it must have seemed far less costly than the convolutions of prevarication and evasion into which the White House staff was forced. A "clean breast," to be sure, would not have involved a comprehensive set of admissions, disclosing the extent to which Mr. Nixon and his agents were engaged in wiretapping, extorting campaign contributions, and other illegal activities, but only a more limited expression of willingness to clean house at the Committee to Reelect the President.

Yet Nixon obviously feared more than anything placing himself at the mercy of the goodwill of the people in charge of the various arenas in which disclosure was demanded: the courts, the press, the special Senate Watergate Investigating Committee, the House Judiciary Committee. He must have felt that in each of these arenas he had no political credit, no goodwill to call on. If this is a correct view of Nixon's judgment, it suggests that Watergate can tell us a great deal about his prior conduct of the office of the Presidency.

It was a strong Presidency, strong in the sense of setting and achieving goals. Yet it achieved its ends to an unusual degree through the device of attacking, crippling, neutralizing, and diminishing the powers of other legitimate power centers in the political system. Underpinning this approach to presidential government were two articles of belief, frequently stated by Mr. Nixon or by one or another of his spokesmen. The first held that the accountability of the President ran solely to his electoral majority. Politics for Mr. Nixon was electoral politics, campaign politics. Election conferred a mandate, an entitlement for him to act in office as his predecessors had acted, in small ways as well as in large ways.[108]

Nixon's second article of belief was a matter of political judgment: that the elite political stratum in this country—not excluding officials of the government itself—was out of step with the dominant mood of conservatism in the country at large. Thus, in his view, his election conferred not only an extraordinary measure of legitimacy upon him, but also a kind of illegitimacy upon many of the very people with whom a President ordinarily does business: the bureaucrats, interest group leaders, journalists, Congressmen, and party leaders of official Washington. These, after all, had for the most part been elected neither in the close election of 1968 nor in his landslide of 1972.[109]

To most of these groups in the course of his Presidency Nixon gave intentional offense, and in each case it was offense of a character that carried with it a clear threat of a very basic kind.[110] It could be said that each of Nixon's predecessors had at one time or another neglected to mend a political fence or two. But Nixon's policies—after a brief period early in his first term when, under the tutelage of his assistant, Daniel Patrick Moynihan, he seemed to be exploring an Americanized version of "Tory radicalism"— consisted of a systematic trampling of his political fences, a direct assertion that the legitimacy of the Presidency entailed the illegitimacy of those other political elites to whom a President normally is accountable.[111]

After beginning with a politically diverse and reasonably visible group of Cabinet appointees, for example, Nixon increasingly moved toward the appointment of relatively faceless officials, people of no independent public standing, no access to constituencies of their own. His first Secretary of Labor, George Shultz, though unknown to begin with, became an early star of the Nixon Cabinet because of his intelligence and quick grasp of problems.[112] The first major reorganization of the Nixon Presidency shuffled Mr. Shultz into the White House. He was replaced at the Department of Labor by an efficient but unprepossessing figure, who in turn gave way to a maverick union official who was not even on speaking terms with the head of the AFL-CIO. This was not the only example, and seemingly by design the access to the President of large and significant interest groups was greatly hampered. Labor, education, the scientific community, conservationists, and others felt not merely that Richard Nixon was a President whose goals differed from their own, but rather that their voices were being choked off, that they were shut out from the White House, and that their case was being rejected before it was heard.

If Nixon's administrative appointments were designed to be increasingly weak in their capacity to carry messages from interest groups to policymakers, they were far stronger in executing orders, in providing a conduit

TABLE 2   Decline in Prior Political Experience of Nixon Cabinet

	PRESIDENT NIXON'S FIRST CABINET	PRESIDENT NIXON'S LAST CABINET
Prior Political experience extensive (includes office-holding)	William Rogers, State Melvin Laird, Defense Walter Hickel, Interior Maurice Stans, Commerce Robert Finch, HEW George Romney, HUD John Volpe, DOT	Rogers C. B. Morton, Interior Earl Butz, Agriculture William Saxbe, Attorney General
Prior political experience moderate (active in state party, etc.)	Winton Blount, Post Office	Frederick Dent, Commerce Peter Brennan, Labor Caspar Weinberger, HEW
Prior political experience slight	David Kennedy, Treasury John Mitchell, Attorney General Clifford Hardin, Agriculture George Shultz, Labor	Henry Kissinger, State William Simon, Treasury James Schlesinger, Defense James Lynn, HUD Claude Brinegar, DOT

from the various arms of the White House executive apparatus—the Domestic Council, the Office of Management and Budget, the National Security Advisor—to the levels of policy execution.[113]

Centralization of policy-making was only half the Nixon administrative program. The other half consisted in systematic attempts to place functionaries who can reasonably be described as political commissars in the bureaus and departments, agents whose job it was to report to the White House on the political fidelity of the executive branch.[114]

A well-known public administrator described the strategy as

> a systematic assault on the integrity of the merit system. Personnel officers were often rendered virtually helpless to withstand this assault as they were either bypassed or given instructions contrary to sound personnel management and often contrary to professional ethics. Top career leaders often were summarily removed with no chance to demonstrate their value and reliability to incoming political leaders. The subversion of the system came not so much from cabinet officers themselves as from White House staff working directly with departmental special assistants or from new assistant secretaries whose work was also orchestrated from the White House staff. "Spies" were placed in some departments to ensure that personnel operations proceeded on a politically sensitive basis.[115]

From time immemorial Presidents and their political appointees have puzzled over the problem of making the enormous apparatus of the executive branch responsive to their will. The legitimacy of this claim is, of course, based upon the results of the last election; a President is presumably elected and makes appointments at least in part in order to carry out his promises with respect to the future conduct of public policy, and the necessary instruments of that conduct reside in the unelected agencies of the executive branch.

Executive agencies, however, are seldom merely passive receptacles awaiting the expression of a President's will. Rather, they embody a number of persistent, ongoing characteristics which from time to time may serve as bases for conflict with presidential directives. Expertise, for example, a body of doctrine about the right way to do things, may well thwart responsiveness to presidential demands. So may alliances between agency executives and the congressional committees that oversee their programs and budgets. So may strong ties between agencies and the client groups whom they serve.

The case of a conservative President facing an executive agency doing what he believes is liberal work is especially poignant. The very existence of a bureaucratic apparatus attests to the mobilization, at some time in the past, of a majority of sufficient strength to pass a law and put an agency to work. So long as the law is on the books, and Congress appropriates funds pursuant to it, the agency presumably has some sort of legitimate standing. Yet it was precisely the existence of all too many of these Federal agencies,

all staffed with people devoted to the execution of programs, that Mr. Nixon
wished to question. In one famous instance, the case of the Office of Economic Opportunity, Nixon attempted illegally to put an agency out of business altogether.[116] In another, that of the President's science advisory machinery, Mr. Nixon succeeded in abolishing an agency after it became clear
that the scientific community, for which the agency was presumably a conduit, opposed administration plans to build an uneconomic supersonic airplane.[117]

In each of Mr. Nixon's attempts to organize and reorganize the executive branch an observer can read efforts to cope with a hostile administrative environment. His adoption of a policy of revenue sharing had the
effect of removing responsibilities altogether from Federal agencies. Nixon
vastly strengthened the White House National Security Office and invented
a domestic counterpart in the Domestic Council,[118] politicized and reincar-
nated the Bureau of the Budget as the Office of Management and Budget,[119]
and drastically increased the number of employees in the Executive Office
of the President.[120] Just as the storm of Watergate broke over his head, he
proposed a reorganization plan that would officially deny Cabinet officers
direct access to the President by shifting supervisory power to four "su-
percabinet" officers who would act as special presidential assistants.[121]

These various devices for limiting the power of government departments, agencies, and bureaus were not necessarily illicit, but they could
scarcely have been calculated to win for Nixon the special esteem of those
thousands of government workers, including many of his own political appointees, whose job it was to make these agencies run effectively.

More serious by far was the lack of comity which the Nixon White
House cultivated toward Congress. The observant journalist Elizabeth Drew
captures the problem nicely:

> There is much in the process of governing, as there is in human relations,
> that cannot be defined or codified; it depends on shared understandings of
> undefined limits. The Nixon Administration, in its dealings with the Congress,
> as in other behavior, did not recognize limits. It placed unprecedented power
> in the hands of White House assistants who were not accountable to the
> Congress. They were not confirmed by the Congress, and were protected by
> the doctrinal shield of "executive privilege" from testifying before the Con-
> gress. Earlier this year, Richard Kleindienst, then Attorney General, told the
> Congress that the President could extend the doctrine of executive privilege
> to all two and a half million members of the executive branch. The Nixon
> Administration's claim was unprecedented. There is no mention of executive
> privilege in the Constitution, and Presidents Truman and Eisenhower were
> the first to make any extensive use of it—against the onslaughts of the late
> Senator Joseph McCarthy. Earlier Presidents had impounded funds appro-
> priated by the legislature, but President Nixon carried this practice, too, to
> new lengths. Other Presidents had gone to war without the approval of the
> Congress, but, at least in the view of some legislators, President Nixon con-
> tinued to wage war in Southeast Asia after Congress had specifically withdrawn

its approval. These legislators believed that the Administration's continued bombing of Cambodia until this past summer was illegal, and so was its secret bombing of Cambodia in 1969 and 1970. The Congress's reaction to the policies of the President on impoundment, executive privilege, and the war was to try to write legislation to codify the limits.[122]

If there was a disrespect for limits in the President's pre-Watergate conduct toward Congress, how can we describe the behavior of the Nixon administration toward those it adopted as its "enemies"—the news media and leaders of the Democratic party? Only as the various Watergate investigations began to publicize such things as a White House "enemies list," consisting mostly of heavy donors to the Democratic party, could the general public get an inkling of what was going on.[123] The targets of White House unfriendliness must have known far earlier, however, that they were experiencing an entirely new level of coordinated hostility from the government. Internal memoranda by presidential assistants Charles Colson and John Dean suggested ways of bringing governmental pressure to bear on political opponents. The bland testimony of John Ehrlichman of a concerted effort to put a reputable and law-abiding citizen named Larry O'Brien— then chairman of the Democratic National Committee— behind bars before the 1972 election did seem to many hardened political observers to carry hostilities to unprecedented lengths.[124]

Managers of the news media must have thought so too. In public they were attacked with unusual venom by Vice President Agnew. A group of Mr. Nixon's friends in Florida got together a challenge before the Federal Communications Commission to the renewal of television licenses of two stations owned by the *Washington Post*. In the White House there was established an Office of Telecommunications Policy, which took on the task (among others) of devising ways of affecting the news coverage of the three networks. And from time to time, presidential aide Charles Colson called or met with the heads of the networks for the purpose of influencing their news policies. According to the later testimony of participants, not all the conversation on these occasions was couched in the language of sweet reason. Frank Stanton, president of CBS, remembers being told just after the 1972 election: "You didn't play ball during the campaign.... We'll bring you to your knees in Wall Street and Madison Avenue."[125]

Ordinarily national politicians and top industrialists live in what the late Representative Clem Miller aptly described as a "cocoon of good feeling"[126] and are not accustomed to hearing believable threats to their livelihood or well-being. It was a rare, and not altogether edifying event in American history when the Attorney General of the United States informed a reporter from a leading newspaper that his boss, the publisher, was about to get a sensitive part of her anatomy "caught in a wringer" if the newspaper persisted in plans to publish a story embarrassing to him.[127]

There were also myriad examples of petty discourtesy and unfriend-liness toward the members of the national press corps, culminating, more or less, in the full FBI investigation of CBS reporter Daniel Schorr, lamely justified afterward by the fiction that he was under consideration for a Nixon administration job.[128]

Before the bulk of the Watergate revelations came to light, even Nixon's fellow Republicans could feel the extent of the alienation of the White House from the rest of the political system. Fund-raising for the 1972 election, for example, including the worst examples of extortion exercised against the leaders of regulated industries, was done not in behalf of the Republican party, but in behalf of the Committee to Re-Elect the President. Gigantic sums were raised—far more than necessary—and from sources normally shared by all Republicans on the ticket.[129]

After his landslide victory, a landslide that benefited virtually no other Republicans, Nixon decided to clean house for his new administration and asked for the resignations of large numbers of his political appointees throughout the government—yet another blow to the party faithful.[130]

Thus, before Watergate became a significant public issue, large numbers of people to whom a President is normally politically accountable in the day-to-day activities of governing had to ask themselves whether the Nixon administration believed in the basic legitimacy of government agencies and their rules, the news media and their right to criticize, Cabinet-level officials and their linkages to interest group constituencies, Congress and its constitutional prerogatives, or even the rest of the Republican party and its political needs. To a degree unprecedented in the history of the modern Presidency, the answer evidently was no.

Yet a President is accountable, and not only to the electorate every four years. He must sustain a governing coalition in order to govern effectively. A political system like ours fragments power and weaves much of the variety of opinion—sectional, ideological, special interest—that exists in the population at large into the fabric of government. That is the design of a constitution that provides for federalism, a separation of powers, frequent elections, overlapping constituencies. No President can escape the consequences of this diversity, and certainly not by attempting to run rough-shod over its legitimate manifestations in official Washington.

A contrast with President Truman is instructive. When Truman fired General MacArthur as commander in the Far East in charge of the Korean War, his popularity with the country at large was low. He also suffered many attacks from Republicans and other supporters of MacArthur. Yet his supporters were even stronger: Secretaries Acheson and Marshall applauded the move. So did Undersecretary of Defense Lovett, a prominent member of the opposite political party. Senators Russell and Kerr staged a long and informative hearing that slowly let the air out of the MacArthur boomlet.[131]

The corresponding moment in Mr. Nixon's career came when he

decided to dismiss his first Special Prosecutor, the entirely too effective Archibald Cox, who had been appointed by his own administration to look into Watergate-related charges. What was popularly called the "Saturday night massacre" followed: Rather than obey the President's order to fire Cox, Attorney General Richardson and his deputy, William Ruckelshaus, resigned. There was what White House assistant Alexander Haig described as a "firestorm" of public criticism.[132] And the Senate Watergate Investigating Committee had some new grist for its mill. By the time Nixon lost public opinion, relatively late in the game, he had already lost nearly everyone in official Washington.

What accounts for all this ill fortune? A small portion of it, as I have suggested, might well have befallen any energetic, strong President who actively pursued conservative principles of government. Like his four appointees to the Supreme Court, Mr. Nixon was not at all a "strict constructionist" of constitutional doctrine in the sense of believing in the restraint of the powerful. Rather, he was an aggressive redresser of what he saw as imbalances in the political system.

Another element no doubt was contributed by Nixon's intensely private style of work, his profound dislike of the cacophony of contending voices, his penchant for orderly, solitary decision-making, for "peace at the center." These traits threw an enormous burden of responsibility onto his immediate White House staff, a group far more accomplished at administrative efficiency than in the exercise of political judgment.[133]

There is also the possibility that Nixon's need for this sort of administrative apparatus carried in its wake the risk that a spirit of alienation would develop between the White House and the rest of the politically active people in Washington, an alienation that would to the men trapped inside the White House come to justify acts of dubious legality.[134]

Finally, the analyst must grapple with the evidence of Richard Nixon's own character and life experience. As one who considered himself an outsider, as one of the excluded ones, he might well have interpreted his electoral victories as mandates for ignoring the political elites who had so often ignored him. Early in his career he had won elections by cutting corners with respect to genteel norms of decency in political debate.[135] He could see that his immediate predecessors "got away" with things that were wrong by copybook standards.[136] Could he be blamed for drawing the conclusion that the copybook was a myth that need not apply to elected Presidents?

Had he not carried matters to extremes, had he not genuinely frightened official Washington, and then, as official Washington shared its knowledge more widely, frightened virtually every politically aware person in the country whose mind was accessible to persuasion on the merits, he might well not have been blamed for such a conclusion.

The most sympathetic chronicle to date of the Nixon Presidency presses the claim that it was as a peacemaker that Mr. Nixon wanted most to be remembered.[137] Evidently, an important goal of Nixon foreign policy was to strive toward a scaling down in the scope of U.S. responsibilities abroad.[138] The chief method that made his goal domestically acceptable was the energetic pursuit, by diplomatic means, of what was called détente with the Soviet Union. Détente could be defined as a condition of ostentatious nonbelligerency in which the two great powers refrained from mutual provocation. There is much controversy over whether this condition went more than skin deep, or whether the prolongation of détente could in time lead to the exploration of a wide range of cooperative activities.

It is notable, in any event, that President Nixon pursued such a course of action in light of his hostile stance toward the Soviet Union throughout most of his public career. Nixon undoubtedly savored the irony that only he, among major American political figures, could have embraced the policy in Southeast Asia of Vietnamization, pressed Strategic Arms Limitations Talks with the Soviet Union, and established diplomatic relations with the People's Republic of China, without having to endure the strident criticisms of partisan opposition spokesman Richard Nixon.[139] To be sure, Nixon heard rumblings of dissatisfaction from the right wing of his own party on foreign policy, but the domestic political risks he ran with his policy were negligible.

Thus an awareness of Mr. Nixon's propensity for partisan excess colors an assessment even of the arena where, his defenders seem certain to argue, he puts his best foot forward. If the initiatives of the Nixon Presidency turn out in a larger perspective to have laid the foundation for a more secure and more just world order, perhaps students in future years will look back upon his stewardship with a kindlier eye than his contemporaries are likely to do.

Gerald R. Ford (Republican, 1974–1977)

At noon on August 9, 1974, President Nixon's resignation took effect, and Vice President Gerald Ford was sworn in as President. His path to the White House was, to say the least, unusual. For twenty-five years Ford had served a Grand Rapids, Michigan, constituency in the House of Representatives, as a loyal, middle-of-the-road Republican and a hard worker for his party on the Appropriations Committee, and then for nearly a decade he was Minority Leader of the House.[140]

When Spiro Agnew resigned the Vice Presidency under a cloud of criminal charges unrelated to President Nixon's difficulties, the 25th Amendment to the Constitution came into play for the first time in history. This provided for a presidential nomination to fill the vacancy, subject to confirmation by both the House and the Senate. Nixon first thought of nominating his sometime Secretary of the Treasury, John Connally of Texas, who had recently switched his party affiliation from Democratic to Republican in anticipation of Nixon's support for the presidential nomination in 1976. But inquiry on Capitol Hill revealed that Connally was not confirmable by the Congress, and so Nixon settled on Gerald Ford, a well-liked and familiar Congressional face.[141]

Before he was confirmed, however, Mr. Ford underwent a minute investigation of his entire personal history by the FBI, under the direction of the House and Senate Judiciary committees, and a searching interrogation by both committees. These Ford passed with flying colors, and upon confirmation he became first in line to succeed President Nixon.

Thus Nixon's was the second involuntary resignation that brought Ford to the Presidency. Mr. Ford was, of course, unelected as President, but he was far from the "obscure" figure some journalists painted him. Obscurity, after all, is in the eye of the beholder; it would have taken only the most rudimentary knowledge of Congress over the last generation for an observer to stumble across Gerald Ford. He had been not merely hand-picked by Richard Nixon but also confirmed in the succession by both House and Senate, bodies whose members are elected by the people as surely as are the electors of the electoral college. And, as a practical matter, Ford was able readily to pick up the reins of presidential power.

In his first month in office he seemingly could do nothing wrong. He was, to begin with, someone other than Richard Nixon, and the waves of relief at this fact from every corner of Washington were almost physically palpable. Moreover, a child of the House of Representatives, he became at once the advocate of the temporarily forgotten legislative virtues of "communication, conciliation, compromise, and cooperation" in dealings between the President and the much-bruised Congress and press corps.[142] The bureaucracies and excluded interest groups had to wait a little longer as he moved slowly to replace Nixon administration political appointees with his own.

Ford's hesitancy in replacing Nixon appointees underscores basic continuities of policy with the Nixon Presidency, despite great contrasts in styles of execution. In this respect, the Nixon-Ford succession resembles the Kennedy-Johnson succession. In both successions there was a great overlap of key personnel, especially in foreign and defense matters and in the management of the economy. Even more than Nixon's, Ford's policy preferences reflected mainstream Republican doctrine.

There were strong incentives for Mr. Ford to clean Nixon appointees out of the White House promptly. The public relations advantages were obvious. Ford rejected the advice of his informal transition team to move quickly, however.[143] He did not wish to stigmatize Nixon staff members who had been innocent of wrong-doing. Moreover, he had no ready phalanx of associates to put into their place. Nixon's holdover chief of staff, Alexander Haig, insisted on his own indispensability and kept sharp elbows out against the newcomers.[144]

An honorific spot was shortly found for Haig as commander of NATO, and Ford installed a group of his own assistants. Most of them were people with whom he had become acquainted in the House of Representatives. Foremost among them was Donald Rumsfeld, once a Congressman from Chicago's north shore suburbs and a younger colleague in whom Ford reposed unusual trust. As it became clear that Ford's easygoing and collegial style of decision-making produced more interaction with the President from staff members than Ford could comfortably assimilate, it fell to Rumsfeld to organize and coordinate the White House. Ford later recalled:

> When I became President—not having anticipated that I would—I initially felt that what I perceived as the Johnson organization was preferable, with seven or eight different people within the White House reporting directly to the President. But I must say, after six months I did find that a President needs one person who at least coordinates people such as the President's assistant for national security affairs, the head of the Domestic Council, the head of the Economic Policy Board, et cetera. Somebody had to organize the day's schedule and the flow of paperwork.
>
> In the last eighteen months, I ended up with an open oval office. Anybody who had a particular problem could come in and see me but had to be channeled through at least one person who had some control over the schedule. Every day, I approved the schedule of people coming in, but somebody in a central office at least gave me options as to whom I wanted to see or the subjects I would discuss during the ten or twelve hours that I was in the oval office each day.[145]

Rivalries for turf continued, as they frequently do in the proximity of the White House. Rumsfeld's ascendancy meant a loss of influence for Ford's appointee as vice president, Nelson Rockefeller, who had originally struck a deal with Ford in which he and his staff would take major initiatives in the coordination of domestic policy.[146] This arrangement never got off the ground, and much energy was dissipated in sorting this relationship out, and in other bureaucratic battling within the White House. Ford did not possess the Rooseveltian temperament that could convert administrative disarray into a presidential asset.[147]

Although Ford was slow to put his own stamp on the White House, he moved with more self-assurance with the Cabinet. His first Cabinet appointments—Edward Levi, President of the University of Chicago, to Justice; William Coleman, a brilliant black Philadelphia lawyer, to Transportation; Washington attorney Carla Hills to HUD; and old Republican war-horse Rogers Morton to Commerce—showed sensitivity to a variety of political demands. When Levi's appointment initially ran into political trouble with key Republican senators, Ford was sufficiently appreciative of the dire need in the Justice Department for a leader of Levi's unimpeachably high quality to persist in the nomination, and a little skillful legislative liaison work performed the remarkable feat of actually changing some senatorial minds.[148]

Amidst these happy auguries, however, Mr. Ford struck one resoundingly sour note just one month after assuming office in his grant of an unrestricted pardon to his predecessor, an act which in a short time reduced his popularity in the Gallup poll by nearly 20 points.[149] In addition to a pardon, the Ford administration granted Nixon wide authority over all documentary materials from the Nixon White House, even material that might figure in future criminal trials. An act of Congress forestalled this foolish and improvident indulgence of Mr. Nixon at the public expense. So, also, did congressional disapproval whittle away at the princely sums Ford requested to aid Nixon in his "transition."[150]

In the two years and four months Gerald Ford served as president, he cast a great many vetoes—on a month-by-month basis, more vetoes than all but four of his predecessors.[151] Congress swarmed with Democrats after the 1974 elections, which were held three months after the departure of Richard Nixon: up from 243 to 289 in the House, from 58 to 62 in the Senate. The House Democratic caucus, burning brightly with post-Watergate indignation, overturned the seniority of three committee chairmen and sliced into the formal powers of the rest.[152] A new congressional budgetary process was begun, in which House and Senate budget committees were established along with an independent congressional agency, the Congressional Budget Office (CBO), staffed by professional budget analysts.[153] In very short order much of official Washington as well as Congress itself came to rely on the work of the staffs of these committees and the CBO in a field where once the Bureau of the Budget had held exclusive sway.

Since Ford could not control Congress, and the next election was for him never far off, his tasks soon narrowed down to the basic conservative business of establishing equilibrium in the government. In this he largely succeeded. As the perceptive reporter for *The New Republic*, John Osborne, said:

> In foreign affairs there was not a single substantive problem area in which [Ford's successors] could do more than follow or at best improve upon the course and policies bequeathed to them by President Ford and [Secretary of State] Henry Kissinger.[154]

The domestic record was less clear: As Osborne observed:

> He inspired hope, instilled confidence. But he did not and evidently could not inspire ideas, action, purpose.[155]

Perhaps so; but it can be argued that after the battering the political system had taken at the hands of his immediate predecessors, hope and confidence were not a small contribution. In part, no doubt, there was wishful thinking in the hope and confidence that people invested in Ford. His attempts to lead the nation by exhortation—as for example in his abortive campaign to "Whip Inflation Now"—were unsuccessful. He was much happier, after all those years on the House Appropriations Committee, dealing with the substance of governing through the budget. He notes in his autobiography that "on the fiscal year 1977 budget ... I ... made at least 150 crucial choices myself."

> Heads of the departments and agencies could appeal to me—and they almost always did. (HUD Secretary Carla Hills was particularly adept at this, and she won three of every four appeals. She marshaled facts and figures to support her positions most effectively.) In November and December, I had spent two or three hours every day just deciding those appeals. The White House logs for those two months, in fact, revealed that the budget had occupied roughly one hundred hours of my time. I was fully prepared to brief reporters myself on the budget's details.[156]

Given the short time he had to serve before election year politics overtook him, and the lack of anything like a Republican majority in Congress, it seems unreasonable to have expected much more. The abbreviated Ford Presidency was an esthetic anomaly; it had a beginning and an end, but no middle. Yet the middle game was clearly the one best suited to Ford's steadfast and stolidly conservative temperament.

Much of what actually takes place in a President's administration goes on within the routines of the institutions of government themselves. So long as the deeply uncharismatic Ford administration escapes the interest of journalists and historians, and invigorates no squadron of memoir writers, it will be hard for outside observers to document the common impression that during the brief Ford Presidency signal improvements of morale took place in myriad agencies of the executive branch, and that professional criteria gained and narrowly political criteria ebbed in departmental decision-making.[157]

The genial face that the President showed to the world was less reassuring after the Nixon pardon, and Mr. Ford's utter lack of fluency as a public speaker fed the impression that he was a bumbler. There was an irony that after a few incidents in which Mr. Ford was seen to stumble in public (getting out of an airplane, taking a header on a ski slope), perhaps the most accomplished athlete ever to serve in the White House[158] should have been portrayed in cartoons and comedy sketches as physically clumsy.[159]

His inability to articulate anything like a grand strategy for his Presidency or a coherent public defense of what he was trying to do, coupled with shaky economic news as well as no hope of a constructive legislative program, rendered Ford a vulnerable target for the right wing of the Republican party. Ford took considerable heat from his fellow Republicans by retaining Henry Kissinger as Secretary of State and by following Kissinger's lead in maintaining the Nixon policy of détente toward the Soviet Union.

A serious contest for the Republican presidential nomination with Ronald Reagan consumed most of Ford's last year in office. Reagan's challenge spooked Ford into reneging on a bargain that his Secretary of Labor, the gifted John Dunlop, had negotiated to define the rights of pickets in the construction industry. This caused Dunlop's resignation.[160] Likewise, fears over his own renomination caused Ford to permit Nelson Rockefeller— who was thought to be too liberal for orthodox Republican tastes—to remove himself from the ticket as a candidate for vice president in 1976.[161]

Thus during his last year in office Ford was severely hemmed in. He ran a close-to-the-vest campaign for the Republican nomination from the White House rose garden, an explicit recognition by his managers that Ford could not begin to match Reagan's Hollywood-honed glibness on the hustings.[162] Incumbency proved to be a resource sufficient to help Ford nose out Reagan for the Republican nomination, but he lost the general election to Jimmy Carter, former governor of Georgia. Carter benefited from the party loyalty of Democrats, much the larger of the two parties, and the old FDR electoral coalition delivered their votes to him.[163] Carter was also a self-proclaimed political outsider, and he could advertise his lack of involvement with all the bad publicity that had been generated in Washington over the previous decade.

Jimmy Carter (Democrat, 1977–1981)

Jimmy Carter, a man much given to exaggeration in his public utterances,[164] did not exaggerate when he described himself as an outsider to Washington and national politics. In the long history of the Presidency, no one ever came to the office less well acquainted on a first-hand basis with the capital and its ways than Mr. Carter. Indeed, besides Mr. Carter only a handful of new Presidents have ever arrived with no experience of Washington at all, the last example being Woodrow Wilson in 1912. And so the Carter Presidency rapidly became a test of the advantages and disadvantages of inexperience in the conduct of public affairs.

It was widely agreed that Mr. Carter possessed many outstanding qualities for the job. His formidable self-discipline, for example, his conscientiousness, and his sheer capacity to apply himself to work sent assurances down the line in his administration that no serious argument on the merits of any issue that came up through channels would be neglected. President Carter's high intelligence meant that no matter how technically arcane or difficult these arguments might be, they would be thoroughly understood. He was loyal to his staff and subordinates and worked well not only with the Georgians who had campaigned with him and went to work for him in the White House, but also, to an unprecedented degree, he made it his business to get on with his vice president, Walter Mondale.[165] He was elected within the context of a sizable overall Democratic majority in Congress, and it was assumed that he could reasonably look forward to a period of harmony between the two branches that his immediate predecessors in the Presidency never enjoyed.

Things did not work out that way. In spite of the fact that middle-of-the-road Democrats in broad ideological agreement with Mr. Carter controlled Congress, legislative-executive relations were strangely distant and occasionally hostile.[166] This turn of events puzzled many Washington observers. The explanation favored by the Carter administration and its friends was that expectations of easy relations were unreasonable given the changes that had taken place in Congress over the previous 20 years.[167] Reforms of congressional organization during the 1970s, according to this argument, had fragmented congressional power. Consequently there was no one place for a President—any President—to go to make deals. In the golden days of yesteryear, so it was said, when Sam Rayburn ran the House and Lyndon Johnson ran the Senate, it was necessary only to get agreement from a handful of powerful committee chairmen, and presidential programs would sail through Congress unimpeded. Nowadays, dozens of subcommittees had gotten into the act, and consequently the problems of managing Congress had multiplied manyfold.[168]

Persuasive as this argument was to many contemporary Washingtonians, for the most part it was historically ignorant. Eisenhower and Nixon faced Congresses dominated by the opposite party, and Harry Truman and John Kennedy had never had substantial majorities of like-minded Democrats to work with in the House of Representatives, as Jimmy Carter did. Only briefly and fleetingly—in Roosevelt's "hundred days," in Johnson's post-assassination Eighty-ninth Congress—had presidential programs enjoyed easy sailing. The Senate had decentralized since Lyndon Johnson's days as Majority Leader,[169] but in the House, while committee chairmen had lost power, they had lost it not only to their own subcommittees but also to the Speaker and to the majority caucus, both instruments of centralized coordination and both in the hands of mainstream Democrats.

It was certainly true, as Carter apologists claimed, that Congress had become an awesomely complex place, and coordination difficult. Sunshine laws and regulations requiring open meetings and roll-calls had vastly increased the number of recorded votes. This situation inspired more grandstanding by individual members. Legislation was more often written on the floor than negotiated out in committee, where an ethic of give and take could prevail and a coordinated legislative strategy could be agreed upon.[170] The capacity of committees to inspire the loyalty of members declined, as did the atmosphere of comity and trust between committees. It was a rare subcommittee chairman who could, in the manner of the powerful committee chairmen of a few years before, protect his subcommittee's legislation from the intrusion of diverse elements, friendly and hostile alike, that lurked on the floor of the entire House. And the Speaker, despite significantly enhanced powers, could deliver the goods only as long as the White House was willing to cooperate with him.

So in the end, the best explanation of the dismal relations between Congress and President during the Carter years boiled down to President Carter's reluctance to adopt the members of his own party in Congress as full partners in the development of legislative alternatives and in the assignment of priorities to them. Two junior members of Mr. Carter's administration write:

> The President sent a flotilla of major proposals to the Congress in the first eighteen months of his administration—cuts in water projects, social security finance, a comprehensive energy program, a tax rebate scheme, hospital cost containment legislation, comprehensive tax reform, welfare reform. Many of these proposals went to the tax-writing committees of the Congress: Senate Finance and House Ways and Means. And because the President had overloaded the Congress and those committees with reforms that would not command ready assent, because he was not able to marshal the administration's resources and develop political support for all the major battles that were required, and because many of his top political lieutenants were untutored in the ways of the Congress (and at the outset didn't seem to care), most of these proposals were either sunk or badly damaged. President Carter's reputation as less than skillful in domestic affairs and with the Congress was thus firmly established.[171]

Tom Wicker of the *New York Times*, a once strong Carter cheerleader, comments:

> Carter simply had too many programs going at once. At one point Speaker O'Neill sent word to the White House that ten or fifteen pending Carter bills were too many—to which three or four did the President give priority? Mr. Mondale and Hamilton Jordan were assigned to pare the list to essentials. They did, but when the President reviewed their work, he restored most of the items they'd eliminated.[172]

Stuart Eizenstat, President Carter's domestic policy advisor, said that Carter

> didn't like to horse-trade. He thought it was a perversion of the process. He felt that people should make decisions on the basis of merit and high ideals. The last way to get his support was to say something would be politically advantageous.[173]

In the beginning, President Carter constructed his office of legislative liaison, against the advice of experienced well-wishers, along the lines of issue specialization rather than according to the sectional and factional structure of Congress.[174] This meant that members of Congress would be dealing with different White House emissaries on different issues, and therefore no orchestration of relationships was possible over a broad front, where a concession on one issue could be compensated for by a reward on another. Moreover, as congressmen soon learned, White House legislative liaison staff were too far down in the White House pecking order to have any power to bargain over the substance of legislation. President Carter's notion was that members of Congress would deal with messengers who could explain what the White House wanted, but he did not give these messengers his full confidence. This limitation hampered their credibility on Capitol Hill.

At the time, much was made of the fact that Mr. Carter's chief of legislative liaison, Frank Moore, was totally inexperienced in Washington. Like most of the other senior White House staff whom President Carter trusted, he was from Georgia, and he had performed similar functions for the President when Carter had been governor. However, inexperience is something that can be cured by gaining experience, as Larry O'Brien, once John Kennedy's new man on the Hill, had found out. Moreover, experienced Hill people were soon hired to beef up the Carter liaison operation as its inadequacies became embarrassing.

The heart of the problem lay not with the perennial sheaf of unanswered telephone calls on Frank Moore's desk, or with an alleged malfunctioning beeper on his belt. It was rather that President Carter had no real intention of collaborating with Congress in policy-making. Policy-making for President Carter was not properly a matter of human interaction, of bargaining, of the harmonization of the priorities of diverse leaders variously situated in the political system. That was "politics," a perhaps necessary part of the process, but not a part of the process to which a conscientious President should concede very much. Policy-making, to Carter, meant identifying problems and applying rational intelligence to the formulation of good solutions. If possible, solutions should strike at the root of problems, should be comprehensive and basic. If they were the right solutions, Carter was convinced, they would commend themselves to Congress, and if not to Congress, then he could appeal over the heads of Congress to the people, as he had done with the Georgia legislature.[175]

By adhering to these beliefs, Carter proved himself to be a man strongly in the grip of a coherent theoretical model of political leadership.[176] It was a model that owed much to Mr. Carter's background as a Navy-trained engineer, and it reminded observers not only of the rigidities of that other engineer-President, Herbert Hoover, but also those of that great constitutional tinkerer and admirer of the Prussian civil service, Woodrow Wilson.[177] Like these predecessors, Jimmy Carter interested himself deeply in reforms of the machinery of government.

His first battle with Congress was over his desire to increase the President's freedom to reorganize the executive branch. Over significant congressional objections, President Carter prevailed. He said:

> an important achievement of my administration when I was governor of Geor-́
> gia had been to reorganize the state government, and I was eager to make
> similar changes in the federal government.[178]

Rather than accept a budgetary process that was built around annual justifications for departures from last year's expenditures, Carter, with much ballyhoo, introduced a requirement that all functions of all agencies be justified annually from the ground up. This "zero-base budgeting," as it was called, was claimed to have inspired miracles of frugality in Georgia state government. At the Federal level it quickly became, in the description of polite observers, a "new way to do incremental budgeting."[179]

The senior civil service was also subjected to a root and branch reform, designed to improve centralized administrative control, which in turn was supposed to reward efficiency and expertise. In short order this reorganization helped to stimulate a significant and unintended flight of senior civil servants into retirement, and morale among the targets of the Carter reform, insofar as observers could tell, went sharply down.[180]

The way in which Mr. Carter constituted his Cabinet provided an early clue to his firm belief in technical rather than in interactive problem-solving.[181] There are at least five communities a President can call upon in making appointments to the top of the government. (1) He can appoint presidential ambassadors, people whose connection with public life or national politics has come about more or less entirely by virtue of their connection with him. (2) He can draw on the large group of his party's Washington careerists. Both major political parties contain talented people who make their careers in Washington, D.C., moving into government at ever higher levels of responsibility as they grow older and more experienced, and, when their party loses a presidential election, moving out again and into Washington law firms, think tanks, and public relations jobs. These public figures are predominantly generalists, who bring to government knowledge of the Washington terrain, and any one of them may be suggested for various Cabinet posts. They are somewhat different from, but partly overlap (3) technical specialists. Specialists make their careers within one issue domain and concentrate on that subject matter whether they are in or out of government. Typically, in their early years they serve at the subcabinet level, then continue their involvement in the subject matter in private professional life before returning to a senior Cabinet position.

(4) Interest group ambassadors consist of political leaders who in the course of their careers have identified themselves with one or more of the

interest group components of the electoral coalition that each major party maintains. Each of the departments of government has bureaucratic staff from whose top ranks technical specialists come. Each also has organized clientele: unions for the Labor department, business for Commerce, banks for the Treasury, law enforcement officials for Justice, and so on. Interest group ambassadors can come from the ranks of leaders of these groups.

(5) Symbolic appointments may overlap with interest group ambassadors, or may not. Presidents have over the years made a considerable effort to include in their Cabinets people who embody certain demographic characteristics that proclaim the broad openness of their administration to social progress. In earlier times, and to a certain degree today, this message was carried by including representatives of different sections of the country or of various ethnic groups. More recently, the appointment of women, Hispanic Americans, and black Americans has been emphasized for these purposes. Such appointees may or may not be drawn from the leadership of organizations active in advocating the interests of the demographic groups in question. In order to satisfy the symbolic interests involved, it is the social identity of the appointee that is most important.

President Carter's first appointments to high positions in his new administration left little room for doubt that he regarded the interest group constituencies of the Democratic party as of negligible importance in constituting his governing coalition. Only his Secretary of Interior and his Secretary of Agriculture had significant ties with Democratic interest groups within the range of their new responsibilities. Mr. Carter's UN ambassador,

TABLE 3   President Carter's Cabinet, 1977

	SPECIALISTS	CLIENT-ORIENTED	PRES. AMBASSAD.	WASHINGTON CAREERIST	SYMBOLIC
State	Vance				
Treasury	Blumenthal				
Defense	Brown				
Justice			Bell		
Interior		Andrus			
Agriculture		Bergland			
Commerce					Kreps
Labor	Marshall				
HEW				Califano	
HUD				Harris	(Harris)
Transportation				Adams	
Energy				Schlesinger	
CIA			Turner		
Natl. Sec. Council	Brzezinski				
OMB			Lance		
Council Econ. Ad.	Schultze				
UN Ambassador			(Young)		Young

Andrew Young, it could be argued, had important experience in grass roots politics and was more than a symbolic black appointment—although he was certainly that as well. However, the rest of Mr. Carter's fifteen or so top appointees were technical specialists or Georgians, with one or two more symbolic appointments thrown in.

This pattern of appointments provided valuable confirmation of what appeared to be the emerging contours of Mr. Carter's theory of the politics of the Presidency. The job of the President and his administration was clearly not to be defined as bargaining policy out in a process of accommodation with interest groups any more than with Congress. The job was to employ the best and most expert talent to find proper answers to the most pressing challenges facing the nation.

President Carter's own descriptions of his preferred method of policy-making in sector after sector illustrate this theory, and its exclusion of Congress, at work. In the field of welfare policy-making, President Carter said:

> My staff, my Cabinet, and I laboriously evolved a complete revision of the welfare system, designed to simplify the program and, through temporary public-service jobs and tax reductions for low-income workers, to move almost two million welfare-dependent people into productive employment.[182]

Likewise for health policy:

> My advisers and I struggled for months to provide a comprehensive health-care system for our country.[183]

The same was true for energy policy, a proposal in connection with which the President declared "the moral equivalent of war":

> Moving with exceeding haste myself, I announced that within ninety days a national energy plan would be made public and sent to Congress for immediate action. This was a major decision— and a controversial one. Because of the short time allowed for completing the project, creating a plan would require maximum coordination among the many agencies involved and would not permit the extensive consultation with congressional leaders that might insure swifter action once our legislation was sent to Capitol Hill.[184]

There is evidence that such coordination as was undertaken under the pressure of President Carter's self-imposed deadline did not embrace a wide network of interested parties, even within the administration itself. Haynes Johnson, the author of the best book on the Carter Presidency, says:

> The trouble was, then and later, Congress was in the dark about what the president was planning.... [Republicans and] Democrats felt equally uninformed—but, then, so did most of Carter's staff and cabinet.

Concern over this secretive approach began to grow as the deadline neared....
[E]ven the president's chief economics advisers hardly knew anything, either
from the president or from Secretary [designate of Energy James] Schlesinger.
[Cabinet Secretary Jack Watson complained:] "What in effect is happening is
that the substance of the energy plan is being put together independent of
economic impact and analysis. And that can be devastating. Some of these
people want to negotiate with Schlesinger before the plans go to the president,
before anything is locked in. There really ought to be some shirt-sleeve sessions."

But try as they did, the top Carter people could not find out from Schlesinger
what specifically was in the works.... Schlesinger did not want to have details
of the plan leak out piecemeal, lest it be destroyed inch by inch by waiting
lobbyists and special-interest groups.

Carter shared this fear, as he confided to the Democratic leaders when he met
them on April 5. [Senate majority leader] Robert Byrd had asked the president
if senators were being included in the discussions on energy policy, adding
that he wasn't aware that they were. A general discussion, critical in nature,
ensued: people who considered themselves experts weren't being consulted.
Others, who had worked with energy-related matters such as air pollution,
had to know, and didn't, how it might affect their legislation.

The President: I understand. Here's the process. Dr. Schlesinger has met with
me regularly one or two times a week. We have brought in forty-five people
from government agencies with legal responsibilities in the energy field. We've
had twenty-one mini-conferences with special-interest groups and ten hearings
across the country. Dr. Schlesinger has given me memos and notes with
alternatives. He is to give me a summary of the comprehensive energy proposal
shortly. I've not seen it but I will, and I will see the draft speech, too. Once
I sign off on it, within the next two or three days, I'll check with Senator Byrd
and Tip [the Speaker of the House] on who in Congress should be brought
in.... I'll have to admit, we've played the evolution of energy policy pretty
close to our vest because if only parts of it were revealed, that would cause
trouble. So neither Fritz, Charlie, nor Bert yet knows what it is.

In other words, less than two weeks before he was to go before the nation
with his most important presidential proposal neither the vice-president, the
chairman of the Council of Economic Advisers, nor his budget director knew
what the plan called for—and neither, fully, did he.[185]

Although Speaker O'Neill constituted a special committee of the House
of Representatives to receive Carter's plan, and that committee approved
the plan in a very short time, interest group politics caught up with the
Carter energy policy in the Senate, and nothing like what he ordered Secretary Schlesinger to put together eventually emerged from Congress. So
all President Carter's secrecy, his demands for speed, his willingness to
delegate but not to share, hastened nothing and encumbered his substantive
plans every bit as much as (perhaps more than) if he had been willing to
collaborate from the beginning with leaders of Congress.[186]

There was a lesson in all this, but President Carter never learned it,
and as time went on, it became apparent that he had no intention whatever

of developing the sort of friendships on Capitol Hill that could help him and the things he stood for during good times and bad. Important members of Congress reported that occasional overtures were made by the President, but these consisted mostly of private audiences at which the President would harangue members on the alleged merits of measures that he favored. Increasingly, President Carter found it difficult to suppress his contempt for Congress as an institution, finding it ridden with "special interests" and less resistant to interest group demands than he believed appropriate.[187]

In time, also, Mr. Carter's natural allies in Congress despaired of cooperating with him, as did leaders of many of the interest groups— especially labor unions— who were natural allies of a Democratic President. All these negative attitudes drifted downward to the general public and sooner or later began to be reflected in low scores for the President in public opinion surveys measuring general confidence in the way he was doing his job.[188]

The collapse of U.S. relations with Iran, shortages of oil and gas, and the drastic upward movement of prices at the gas pump accompanied by long lines, wildcat strikes of truckers, and informal rationing schemes all made it appear that the affairs of the nation were orbiting out of control, and things were getting worse. When in November 1979 the American embassy in Iran was seized and fifty American diplomats were taken hostage by a group of terrorists loosely connected to the new government there, President Carter received the patriotic backing of the American people. This helped him defeat a challenge for the Democratic presidential nomination mounted by Senator Edward Kennedy, but it did not last the full 400-plus days that the hostages were held. Ultimately the seeming ineffectuality of American diplomacy, accentuated by the failure, with loss of life, of a military rescue mission, contributed to a nose dive in President Carter's popularity.[189] So also did the face he showed to the American people. He harangued them as well.

The Carter energy program provided the occasion of what was perhaps the most spectacular episode of his Presidency, in which the President suddenly cancelled a nationally televised address, which was to have been his fifth on energy policy, and ostentatiously retreated to Camp David, the presidential resort in the Maryland mountains.[190] There, for twelve days, while speculation mounted, the President isolated himself from the regular routines of governing while he brought in leaders from various sectors of American life to help him evaluate his Presidency—as always, comprehensively.

At the end of this period of soul-searching, he announced his conclusions in a series of press conferences and speeches: that the American people were suffering from excessive pessimism; that interest groups and their narrow demands were at fault; that he as President had spent too little time out among the people and too much time in the detailed management of public affairs and in Washington.

In short, what the President had learned from his comprehensive assessment was remarkably consonant with the theory of governing that he brought into the Presidency and that was already well established in his behavior. It reaffirmed his belief in the goodness of being an outsider and the corresponding corruption to be found inside Washington. The next step must have seemed perfectly logical to the President's logical mind: he fired everybody at the top of his administration, Cabinet members and White House staff.

Of course he had no intention of accepting all the resignations that landed on his desk. Originally the maneuver was aimed only at two of the thirty or forty-odd top members of his official family.[191] The resulting confusion, entirely predictable by anybody with a shred of common sense— and predicted to the President by, among others, Vice President Mondale[192]—made President Carter a laughingstock among his political opponents and deeply disturbed his political allies, the governments of foreign nations, and international financial markets.[193] Additional members of the Cabinet bowed out, and Democrats on Capitol Hill seethed with rage at the public display of ham-handed incompetence in the management of national affairs to which their Democratic President had subjected the nation. He had, in effect, manufactured a crisis out of whole cloth. Nothing was involved like Vietnam or Watergate, real crises that had entangled two of President Carter's immediate predecessors. The appearance of an emergency was entirely contrived, presumably to symbolize a fresh start. Its chief effect was to compromise even further the feelings of confidence that political leaders in Washington, and through them the American people, felt toward Jimmy Carter.

This suggests that despite the tendency of President Carter to emphasize the contrasts between Washington and grass roots America, there were, and are, intimate connections between members of Congress and interest group leaders who do business in Washington and their constituents out around the country. President Carter not only underestimated these connections, but he overestimated his own capacity to reach out over the heads of the rest of the Washington community and send his own message directly to the American people. He did in fact reach the American people directly, through television, but the message as received would unavoidably be subjected to interpretation, and that is where a President needs friends and allies. There were, to the end of the Carter administration, good and loyal Democrats who were ready to come to the aid of their party, but there was very little they could do to improve the image of a President so determined to do business in a way that defied the logic of a constitutional design that demands cooperation, coordination, and conciliation among the branches of government.

Jimmy Carter's theory of governing ran contrary to this constitutional logic; but for the four years of his Presidency, despite mounting political costs, he was able to indulge his theory. It remains to be explained why, in the face of evidence of its ineffectiveness, Mr. Carter persisted in his view of the right way to do things. There are no final explanations for such phenomena, but it is important to remember that (as in the case of President Nixon) the experience of winning the great prize of the Presidency does administer a healthy dose of self-confidence to newly elected incumbents.

Carter, as he evidently saw it, entered upon the presidential office with few political encumbrances. As he said, he owed the Presidency to no one but himself and to the hard work that he and his campaign staff had put in over a two-year period, laboriously making friends and meeting voters in state after state, tracking the sequence of Democratic delegate-selecting events from Iowa, through New Hampshire, Florida, and so on.[194]

Indeed, the presidential nomination process as it has evolved in the last decade and a half is so long and complex and time-consuming and enervating as to make the mere two-and-a-half month campaign of the general election itself something of an anti-climax. To Jimmy Carter, what the nomination process had established as important was the fact that, against great odds, he had won, and part of the reward of winning was the right to conduct the Presidency in his own way, as his training and habits and ideas and instincts told him to do. If others had theories of governing that were so much superior, let them win the Presidency, as he had done.

Thus, it can be argued that conditions imposed by our system of nominating politics — conditions that emphasize individual effort on the part of candidates and deemphasize cooperative effort under the auspices of party leaders — have an impact upon the conduct of the Presidency. Changes in the nominating process since 1972 have indeed shifted the emphasis in the indicated direction, but of course this new process did not make a President who ignored his party inevitable — only possible. It is likely that a Washington outsider and loner like Carter would have been screened out of a nomination process controlled by state party leaders. Once the nomination process began to depend almost entirely upon the results of primary elections, as it did after 1968, screening of candidates by a process of peer review became impossible, and candidacies like Jimmy Carter's became feasible.[195]

Although Jimmy Carter's theory of governing proved unworkable and unpopular over a broad range of public policies, there were high spots of accomplishment in the Carter Presidency, notably in his personal efforts to improve relations between Israel and its middle-eastern neighbors. The strongest of these neighbors, Egypt, was led by Anwar Sadat, a politician unafraid of bold and dramatic gestures. Carter capitalized on this attribute, and on the depletion of Egyptian resources, to entice the leaders of Israel and Egypt into a marathon negotiating session, personally orchestrated by him at Camp David, that established a framework for peace and the beginnings of cooperative endeavor.[196] This negotiation entailed a remarkable exhibition of patience, stamina, and personal attention to minute details on President Carter's part, and the exercise showed him at his best, where his strongest qualities as a politician could be harnessed to the idealistic ends of peacemaking.

Only in the last months of his Presidency, when the exigencies of a reelection campaign loomed, did President Carter take seriously the need to pay closer attention to the grand coalition of Democrats that had elected him and each of his Democratic predecessors since Franklin Roosevelt.[197] In rapid succession he appointed to his Cabinet politicians with broad grassroots connections in the Democratic party: the mayor of New Orleans, the mayor of Portland, Oregon, and a prominent Jewish business leader. However, the gestures came too late. He had by then established himself as a President who stood apart from his party.

President Carter worked hard and successfully to master the essentials, as well as many of the inessentials, of the programs he advocated, but, in the rueful words of a frustrated congressional ally, he acted as though the politics of being President were a branch of nuclear engineering rather than of human relations. Perhaps the best emblem of his relationship with his own party in Congress came on election day 1980, when it became apparent early on that he would be defeated for reelection. Before the polls closed throughout the West, President Carter conceded publicly to his opponent, despite the pleas of his supporters and staff that an early concession would lower turnout and hurt Democratic candidates farther down on the ticket.[198] It seemed to observers that he was placing a cosmetic need of his own, to appear to be a gracious loser, ahead of the survival needs of congressional colleagues.[199] For an explanation of the sources of the great difficulties of the Carter administration in the preceding four years, it was tempting to look no farther.

Ronald Reagan (Republican, 1981–)

Until the last week of the 1980 presidential election campaign, the result projected by analysts of the public opinion polls was that the election was too close to call. Thus many people were surprised at the outcome: an overwhelming victory for Ronald Reagan in the electoral college (though the election was much closer in the popular vote) and, even more unexpected, the defeat of numerous Democratic senators, giving the Republicans their first Senate majority in twenty-six years.

The result was variously attributed to Reagan's affable demeanor at a last-minute nationally televised debate with President Carter, to Carter's inability successfully to conclude negotiations with Iran bringing the American diplomats held hostage there home, and to what many Reagan supporters concluded was a more deep-seated "turn to the right" among American voters. This latter explanation, in the view of incoming "Reaganauts," as the new President's supporters sometimes styled themselves, nourished the opinion that a mandate had been conferred on them to arrest what they perceived to be a strong tendency for big centralized government to intrude ever more persistently into the lives of ordinary Americans, with subsidies, regulations, petty annoyances, and dictatorial ukases. Mandate or no, relief from big government was what Ronald Reagan had been preaching for the last two decades, and it hardly seemed likely that, elected to the Presidency, he would retreat from his firmly held beliefs.

Careful analysis could not sustain even the more cautious of the claims that a partisan realignment had occurred, but the political climate in Washington does not always respond to careful analysis.[200] Reagan, as much of an outsider to the nation's capital as his predecessor, took pains initially to court rather than to ignore Congress. He installed a professional legislative liaison team with experience from previous Republican administrations in the White House, and he gave them his confidence. And he sharpened his legislative priorities down to a very fine point. These were, at first, all budgetary.

He appointed David Stockman, an able and energetic young congressman, as his director of the Office of Management and Budget and gave him free and immediate rein to cut federal spending. At the same time, the new administration was calculatedly slow in making appointments to the top of the agencies and departments that were going to be cut the hardest.[201] So in effect there were few inconvenient voices in the new administration offering unwelcome substantive objections to plans for budgetary cutbacks. Those sorts of objections would have to be made, if they were to be made at all, in Congress, as the appropriations subcommittees each took up their part of the whole budgetary package.

It was the special good fortune of the Reagan administration that a way was found to short-circuit the congressional process as well. The device was "reconciliation," a recently installed procedure in which the Congress votes an overall budget ceiling and then orders its substantive committees to pare specific entitlement programs and its appropriations subcommittees to cut appropriations down to accommodate to the total. In the Senate, newly controlled by Republicans, it was a foregone conclusion that a vote would be taken, and won, to reconcile Federal spending to the low Reagan ceilings earlier in the budget cycle than was originally provided by law. The great victory on the same issue came in the House, where the conservative coalition of Republican and right-wing Democratic members reemerged in full vigor after some years of hibernation.[202] The triumph of the Reagan legislative team was to bring along virtually every Republican vote in favor of the Reagan package—including the votes of liberal Republicans.

In Congress, both parties span a wide ideological spectrum, and there is usually very little to keep conservative Democrats and liberal Republicans from voting against the mainstreams of their respective parties. Because the key votes on the budget came very early in President Reagan's term of office (all within his first six months),[203] the Reagan legislative team could and did argue that all Republicans, whatever their personal sympathies, owed the President their vote to fulfill the mandate of the people as expressed in the last election. This argument held long enough to get a sizable tax cut through Congress as well. After that, liberal Republicans, with their own fortunes to worry about in the midterm elections, began to pull away from the rest of the Republican party in Congress. Many of them were casualties of the 1982 midterm election, as it became plain that no fundamental realignment of political forces had taken place in the electorate, and the Democratic party regained twenty-six seats in the House.

The bulk of President Reagan's first term of office, after the great initial victories on the budget and taxes, was taken up in legislative stalemate, rhetorical posturing, and public relations gestures. The principal foreign relations initiatives of the administration consisted of a line toward the Soviet Union that varied from distrust to belligerence.[204] This posture slowed, then halted arms control negotiations, placed American missiles in Europe, stimulated considerably higher defense expenditures, and increased U.S. anti-Communist military activity in Central America.[205]

President Reagan's management style contrasted sharply with that of his predecessor. Both Presidents kept high public profiles, but Reagan did not pride himself on his grasp of programmatic details, as Carter did. Members of his administration privately characterized Mr. Reagan as a good listener at meetings, and far more committed to substantive positions than his detractors realized, but the range and depth of his grasp of the wellsprings and ramifications of public policy were for the most part rudimentary.[206] As David Broder wrote:

> Those who work with Reagan quickly come to understand how little his policy views rest on information or facts—how much they rely on his own instincts and long-cherished beliefs.[207]

Reagan's fondness in private as well as in public for homilies of dubious factuality, his carelessness with statistics and with evidence in defense of his views, and his disinclination to immerse himself in the substance of public policy soon established a level of discourse in and around the President that could be characterized as subprofessional.[208]

What President Reagan was fully professional at was public relations. His cheerful demeanor, even when shot by a would-be assassin, his capacity to read a speech and to deliver a prefabricated line in a press conference with an air of spontaneity, suggested that his years as a movie actor were not wasted. The affability that President Reagan projected found a ready response in public opinion, and while there were never majorities in expressed public attitudes for most of the policies he pursued—defense being the major exception—the President himself received considerable popular approval.

The tensions between advocates of right wing ideology versus those of pragmatism were especially acute in the upper reaches of the Reagan Presidency.[209] The President had ample need for both but did not play a strong role in managing the relationships between hard line conservatives, who believed that leading members of the White House staff would not "let Reagan be Reagan," and those staff members who worried about political appearances and advocated a more flexible approach. Both sides could claim some victories, but after a while during the first Reagan term the President's personal advisor and appointment secretary, Michael Deaver, and his Chief of Staff, James Baker, both pragmatists, came to dominate White House decision-making. Baker, a Houston banking millionaire and Princeton graduate, was especially important.[210] He had managed his friend George Bush's presidential campaign in 1980, and joined the Reagan team only after Bush was defeated. Despite his extraordinary competence and the increasing trust reposed in him by the President, friends of the President from earlier days, many of them less willing to give in to what Baker perceived as Washington realities, suspected Baker of ideological softness and of harboring ambitions beyond the Reagan Presidency, if not for himself then for George Bush. Much infighting, which periodically erupted into public, was the result of this cleavage within the administration.

Internal conflicts were said to have worn down Reagan's close friend William Clark, who for a time, despite total inexperience in foreign affairs, was National Security Advisor. Clark eventually was pushed out and became Secretary of Interior.[211] When the President's counselor Edwin Meese was put forward as Attorney General, Baker and his allies were suspected as the source of various charges that delayed Meese's confirmation by the Senate.[212]

It should come as no surprise that, as a major center of power in the American political system, the White House should be the location of a fair amount of jockeying for position. Some Presidents, presumably like Roosevelt, have understood this reality and used the ambitions of others to further their own ends. Other Presidents, like Truman and Ford, with greater or lesser degrees of success, have understood that conflict was inevitable and sought to minimize it. Reagan seems to have thought less and done less about it than most of his predecessors. Rather than running his Presidency with an active hand, he narrowed his role sharply.[213] He required assurance that programs of his Presidency conform to overall goals consonant with his not altogether internally consistent beliefs in reduced central government, lower taxes, and strong defense; and he participated actively in promoting these programs to Congress and to the American people. Debate about the resulting costs of the inconsistencies among these policies—which occurred principally in the form of gigantic government deficits, increasing interest rates, and unfavorable foreign trade balances—shaped much of the political agenda during the first Reagan administration.[214]

PROBLEMS IN EVALUATING PRESIDENTS

Some Presidents, fortunate in their instincts, their advisors, and their opportunities, have been great goal setters. Harry Truman and John Kennedy shared the distinction of bringing forth exciting policies and plans. Other Presidents have had superb executive talents. Lyndon Johnson seems sure eventually to be regarded as one of these, as were Coolidge and Hoover—two quite different men—in their time. And, of course, Franklin Roosevelt's performance on both counts is universally accounted as exceptional. In any event, the President's job must partake of both. There are two fundamental problems involved: deciding what to do, and seeing that it is done. A President, or an administration, may be good at one and not the other. Furthermore, a failure at one task may sometimes, as I think was the case with President Eisenhower, help to explain failure at the other.

It may be that in inspecting the criteria by which Presidents are judged we shall learn more about judges of Presidents than about Presidents themselves. However, the risk is worth taking. The Presidency is, after all, a role. Like other roles, it develops in response to identifications, demands, and expectations that impinge on it from outside, and some of these expectations are recorded in the form of evaluations of presidential performance.

Two Theories of the Presidency

The first and most significant problem in evaluating a President is to decide how to weigh his own theory of his proper place in the American political system. Some Presidents did less than they might have because they believed that this was their proper role in the constitutional order. One President who has written eloquently in defense of this point of view is William Howard Taft:

> The true view of the Executive function is, as I conceive it, that the President can exercise no power which cannot be fairly and reasonably traced to some specific grant of power or justly implied and included within such express grant as proper and necessary to its exercise. Such specific grant must be either in the Federal Constitution or in an act of Congress passed in pursuance thereof. There is no undefined residuum of power which he can exercise because it seems to him to be in the public interest.[215]

An alternative view was held by Theodore Roosevelt:

> I declined to adopt the view that what was imperatively necessary for the Nation could not be done by the President unless he could find some specific authorization to do it. My belief was that it was not only his right but his duty

TABLE 4   Popularity of President in Foreign Crisis

BEFORE CRISIS		AFTER CRISIS
June 1950 37 pro/45 anti	United States enters Korean War (Truman)	July 1950 46 pro/37 anti
August 1956 67 pro/20 anti	British, Israeli, French attack Suez; U.S. refuses to aid them (Eisenhower)	December 1956 75 pro/15 anti
July 1958 52 pro/32 anti	U.S. sends Marines to Leba- non (Eisenhower)	August 1958 58 pro/27 anti
May 1960 62 pro/22 anti	U-2 incident, summit meetings collapse (Eisenhower)	Early June 1960 68 pro/21 anti
March 1961 73 pro/7 anti	Bay of Pigs, Cuba (Kennedy)	April 1961 83 pro/5 anti
October 1961 61 pro/24 anti	Missile Crisis, Cuba (Kennedy)	December 1961 74 pro/15 anti
Late July 1964 59 pro/	Gulf of Tonkin incident (Johnson)	Early August 1964 65 pro/
Early May 1975 40 pro/43 anti	Mayaguez incident (Ford)	Early June 1975 51 pro/33 anti
Early Nov. 1979 32 pro/55 anti	Iran Embassy takeover (Carter)	Early Dec. 1979 61 pro/30 anti
Late Oct. 1983 49 pro/41 anti	Grenada invasion; (Reagan) Beirut bombing	Late Nov. 1983 53 pro/37 anti

Sources: Hazel Gaudet Erskine (ed.), "A Revival: Reports from the Polls," *Public Opinion Quarterly*, vol. 25 (Spring 1961), pp. 135-37; and Gallup releases for indicated periods.

to do anything that the needs of the Nation demanded unless such action was forbidden by the Constitution or by the laws. Under this interpretation of executive power I did and caused to be done many things not previously done by the President and the heads of the departments. I did not usurp power, but I did greatly broaden the use of executive power. In other words, I acted for the public welfare, I acted for the common well-being of all our people, whenever and in whatever manner was necessary, unless prevented by direct constitutional or legislative prohibition.[216]

The beginnings of this conflict in constitutional interpretation and practice have been traced back to the founding of the Republic. Leonard White found that in those early years:

The Federalists emphasized the necessity for power in government and for energy in the executive branch. The Republicans emphasized the liberties of the citizen and the primacy of representative assemblies. The latter accused their opponents of sympathy to monarchy and hostility to republican institutions.... Hamilton ... insisted on the necessity for executive leadership of an otherwise drifting legislature; Jefferson thought the people's representatives would readily find their way if left alone to educate each other by free discussion and compromise.... By 1792 Jefferson thought the executive power had swallowed up the legislative branch; in 1798 Hamilton thought the legislative branch had so curtailed executive power that an able man could find no useful place in the government.[217]

Contemporary evaluations, even after the chastening experience of the Nixon Presidency, are likely to favor an activist view of the Presidency. "Mediocre" presidents, according to Arthur M. Schlesinger, Sr., "believed in negative government, in self-subordination to the legislative power."[218] Presidents such as Hoover and Eisenhower, who believed they should not seize power at the expense of Congress, have been downgraded for their performance in office.

Occasionally, evaluations of Presidents based on their theories of the Presidency mask disagreement over substantive policy. Passive Presidents serve the demands of the presidential coalition less well than active Presidents. Thus, constitutional theories may influence specific policies and the chances that the needs and desires of masses of citizens will be met. Unavoidably, therefore, preferences with respect to public policy enter into evaluations of presidential behavior by the back door of constitutional disputation.

Three Arenas of Performance

There are additional criteria in evaluating presidential performance apart from the observer's view of the appropriateness of the role a particular President chooses to play and its impact on public policy. It is quite common to speak of performance in foreign affairs, in administering the business of the executive branch, and in getting a program through Congress. Each of these arenas presents great difficulties to the evaluator.

The extent to which a President succeeds with Congress, for example, may hinge on simple good fortune in the makeup of the House and Senate, or even of certain key committees of Congress. Or it may depend on the sorts of things he asks them to do and the aid he receives from outside events in convincing them of the need for action. Still, congressional box scores are kept, showing how well the President's program is doing. Comparisons between programs that are relatively modest and those that are relatively ambitious, between presidential successes in times of crisis and in times of relaxation are almost meaningless but are made.

It is hard to imagine a great President during an era of good feeling in foreign affairs. International crises and winning battles have historically provided the ideal setting for presidential leadership. Invariably, the short-run popular response to a President during an international crisis is favorable, regardless of the wisdom of the policies he pursues.[219] Table 4 illustrates the point. Even fiascoes from the standpoint of American policy produce quite remarkable short-run transformations of public sentiment. So also with the longer view of historians. Presidents who have mobilized the energies of the nation against specific external threats have been rated high.[220]

Perhaps the arena in which it is hardest to gather data is the purely administrative. Both Grant and Harding are treated severely in the history books because of the large-scale scandals that marked their administrations. Nowadays, internal and legal controls on the bureaucracy have been greatly strengthened, but even so the sheer size of the executive branch precludes presidential supervision of petty graft or corruption far down the line. Closer to the top of the executive branch, the main problem is normally not overt stealing but favoritism stemming from a conflict of interest. This sort of thing is extremely difficult to identify. Administrative discretion is wide, compelling substantive arguments may exist for a decision, and in some cases movement in any direction may be susceptible to interpretation as favoritism. Even so, scandals of a sort have occasionally developed in recent administrations. Several of President Truman's advisors were accused of influence peddling and one was convicted of income tax evasion. President Eisenhower's top White House aide was forced to resign over charges of improper use of his office. In President Nixon's case there was apparently systematic extortion from businessmen doing business with the government; however, "fund-raisers" were on the whole not officials of the government but rather connected to Nixon's campaign organization. Vice President Agnew, very much in a class by himself, was forced out of office while charged with receiving kickbacks on Maryland road contracts, paid to him while he was vice president, but actually referring to activity when he was governor of Maryland.[221]

Bert Lance, President Carter's budget director, was required to resign from public office to fight charges, of which he was subsequently cleared, of improper banking practices before he joined the government, and a special prosecutor was appointed to investigate charges that the President's top assistant, Hamilton Jordan, had used illegal drugs. Another Carter White House aide, a physician, resigned over an irregular drug prescription.[222]

Incidents of sharp practice—such as insider stock trading—in the private financial lives of several high-level appointees in the Reagan administration were given ample publicity, and a top presidential assistant was revealed to have received loans and favorable financial treatment from people who subsequently were appointed to various federal jobs.[223]

For the most part, since Watergate, such scandals as have reached public print have been tame stuff. Most of the financial wheeling and dealing that has involved big money took place in the lives of political appointees before they became government officials. There has also been a little cronyism, and some instances of bad judgment about the use of federally subsidized transportation, and one Reagan high-level appointee evidently illegally recorded some telephone calls.[224] None of this would have caused much notice a few years ago, but regulations governing the conduct of Federal officials, and the disclosure of the private affairs of new appointees to public office, have recently become more elaborate. The more rules there are, the easier it is to find transgressions of them.

Absence of widespread or widely publicized scandal is one mark of a successful administration. Another, equally tenuous, is a reputation for being on top of the job. Presidents are watched closely by their subordinates, by congressmen and senators, by lobbyists, journalists, the embassies of foreign governments, and so on. Sooner or later, these diverse President-watchers begin to develop a shared, composite picture of each President and the way he operates. A President's reputation with this community suffers if he does not do his homework (e.g., read a substantial sample of the reports that are sent across his desk), if he fails to grasp the substance of issues as they are presented to him, if he unduly restricts the range of his acquaintance and his exposure to information. In these circumstances, a President is regarded as unreachable, as rigid, and as administratively weak.

Luck

Finally, however, we cannot rule out the tremendous role that luck plays in establishing a presidential reputation. So many circumstances that impinge mightily on the fate of nations are beyond the realm of presidential discretion. If things turn out well, we praise the President; if badly, we blame him. But we can only guess at the difference he and his policies have made.

Thus when we evaluate a President, we may be making a variety of judgments. We may be expressing agreement or disagreement with his theory of the proper role of the Presidency in the political system. We may be judging his performance in the realm of foreign policy, or as an administrative leader, or as a lobbyist with Congress. Or we may be responding favorably or unfavorably to the circumstances in which he found himself, regardless of his best efforts.

MACHINERY OF PRESIDENTIAL POWER

The Presidency has always been a big job. It could be argued that at one point in history it was a big job for a single leader. Today, a huge executive branch "takes care that the laws are executed," and at the head of this establishment sits not a single man, but a superbureaucracy, the Executive Office of the President. In turn, at the apex of this conglomeration of agencies, is the President himself.

The many jobs or roles or "hats" of the President have often been enumerated: Chief of State, Chief Executive, Supreme Commander of the Armed Forces, Chief Diplomat, Chief Legislator, Chief of Party, Voice of the People, Protector of the Peace, Manager of Prosperity, World Leader. An impressive list.[225] But the main point about it is, as Richard Neustadt says, that the President must wear all the hats at once.[226] Perforce, some hats sit more precariously on that single head than others. The President is only one man, and he is subject to severe constraints on that account. He can be at only one place at a time. There are only twenty-four hours in his day. He has only two arms, two legs, two ears, two eyes. He is subject to illness, to fatigue, to deadlines, to conflicting demands, and to a glut of information. The job of the agencies in the Executive Office is to give the President the extra arms, hands, brains, and time that he needs to make decisions, to keep his hats from falling off, to make policy, and to see that it is carried out. As these agencies have taken shape, they have developed characteristics and problems of their own. These have to be understood if we are to understand the contemporary Presidency.

The White House Office

Closest to the President is, of course, the group of aides and assistants he gathers around him in the White House. This group has grown greatly in size and importance over the years. In the administration of Franklin Roosevelt, as Joseph Alsop remembers:

> There literally was no White House staff of the modern type, with policy-making functions. Two extremely pleasant, unassuming, and efficient men, Steve Early and Marvin McIntyre, handled the President's day-to-day schedule and routine, the donkey-work of his press relations, and such like. There was a secretarial camarilla of highly competent and dedicated ladies who were led by "Missy" LeHand.... There were also lesser figures to handle travel arrangements, the enormous flow of correspondence, and the like. But that was that; and national policy was strictly a problem for the President, his advisers of the moment (who had constant access to the President's office but no offices of their own in the White House), and his chosen chiefs of departments and agencies.[227]

World War II changed presidential staffing greatly, as the Federal government's needs for the procurement of equipment to fight the war led inexorably to needs to stabilize and guide the domestic economy. The President's attention was taken up with managing the war, and in the emergency a special agency was created, the Office of War Mobilization (later the Office of War Mobilization and Reconversion), that in effect became a domestic Presidency.[228] When the war was over, presidential staff never shrank back to its prewar size. Under Eisenhower the functions of White House aides were differentiated and regularized, including the customary appointments secretary, a press officer, and, most significantly, an office of legislative liaison.[229]

The Office of the Press Secretary is an example of a unit within the White House in which a constant need is filled in slightly different ways from one administration to the next.[230] One important source of variation is the degree of closeness that the press secretary enjoys with the President. One long-term White House correspondent rated the Eisenhower-Hagerty and Carter-Powell combinations particularly high, for example, because the press secretary's intimacy with the President made journalists feel that their point of access to the White House would be particularly useful to them.[231] On the other hand, Ron Ziegler, who was press secretary for Nixon, began as an outsider and thus was not highly regarded by the press. He was much more useful from the administration's viewpoint, however, because his low status meant that he knew very little about what was going on and thus could not reveal much embarrassing information. At the depths of the Watergate crisis Ziegler became a personal confidante of Nixon's and had to be relieved of some of his duties as a spokesman.[232]

In the Nixon administration the press office was split into two sections, with Ron Ziegler in charge of dealing directly as spokesman with Washington correspondents accredited to the White House, and Herbert Klein as "director of communications" with longer-range public relations tasks targeted on the out-of-town media. This division of labor was more or less continued in the Carter and Reagan administrations, and there is now both a press secretary and an Assistant to the President for Communications.[233] Together, these offices have a professional staff of 40.[234]

No matter how the structure of the press offices have varied, the tasks remain largely the same. The press secretary holds daily briefings for the hundred or more credentialed White House correspondents who inhabit the large room in the basement of the west wing, during which he informs them of the movements and activities of the President.

The press secretary is the official "voice" of the administration and speaks on the record in response to queries of the press regarding administration policy. His task is to present the administration's story in the most favorable way possible. The job of the journalists in attendance sometimes finds them at odds with the press secretary, since they must try to get "good stories" that do not necessarily adhere to the official line. This frequently leads the press and the secretary into an elaborate game of cat and mouse in which the journalists attempt to induce or trap the secretary into giving them a good quote while the secretary measures out every word, hoping to avoid saying the wrong thing.[235]

In addition to officials already mentioned, the White House sometimes houses a number of people who undertake specific tasks as they arise, such as looking into an explosive Latin-American situation or mounting a campaign for a reciprocal trade bill. More often in recent years these functions have been performed by subunits of the Domestic Council or the National Security Council. Other officials spend their time writing speeches for the President. The organization of this office is entirely up to the President; it exists entirely to serve his interests as he defines them.

The Office of Management and Budget

The largest permanent presidential agency, with just under 600 employees, is the Office of Management and Budget (incorporating the activities of the former Bureau of the Budget), which has a variety of tasks defined by law. This is the agency that has routine charge of the "program of the President." As we shall see in a later chapter, bills introduced in Congress are routinely referred to agencies in the executive branch for opinions. These opinions are cleared through the Office of Management and Budget, which makes sure that they are in accord with policies laid down by the President. The Office also allocates funds to the executive branch in three-month installments and, in a complicated process described in Chapter 6, has major responsibility for the preparation and clearance of all requests for money made to Congress by all Federal agencies. The Office also undertakes administrative surveys of various kinds in the executive agencies at the President's request.

Special Expertise Agencies

The Council of Economic Advisors is designed to offer the President continuing advice and counsel on the state of the economy. This agency was formed just after World War II, reflecting the concerns of those years that the return to a postwar economy would cause great economic dislocation and unemployment.[236] Actions by the government can do much to change the economic picture; the President must have a flow of information and advice always at hand to help anticipate these changes as well as changes caused by outside events that may have an impact on government policy. Increasingly, the Council also provides information and policy advice designed to assist Presidents in their use of governmental power to affect economic growth, prices, wages, levels of employment throughout the domestic economy, and the balance of payments abroad.

From 1962 until it was abolished by President Nixon in 1973, the Office of Science and Technology served a similar function for the President. Presidents vary greatly in their interest in scientific advice. President Johnson was far less interested in the opinions of scientific advisors than President Eisenhower, who set up the office; indeed, as criticism of the Vietnam war from academic precincts increased, Johnson saw less and less of his science advisor. After an early attempt to rejuvenate the office, President Nixon and his senior White House staff became quite disenchanted with scientific opposition to Nixon administration projects like the antiballistic missile system and the supersonic airplane. Early in his second term Nixon reorganized the OST out of existence and assigned its functions to the head of the National Science Foundation.[237]

The need at the presidential level proved to be durable, however, and under President Ford a presidential-level Office of Science and Technology Policy was reintroduced, with somewhat reduced authority. The rationale for this office is that scientific advice to the President is, like economic advice, nowadays a critical necessity. In 1939, before this was regularly provided for, Albert Einstein wrote a cautious letter to President Roosevelt, calling to his attention "recent work" that "would ... lead to the construction of bombs, and it is conceivable—though much less certain—that extremely powerful bombs, of a new type may thus be constructed."[238] Since that time, the findings of pure science have intruded on national policy-making at an ever-increasing rate. Now government is the principal support of and customer for science of all sorts—pure and applied, physical, biological, and even social. Not only must Presidents react promptly to scientific news, they must also make choices—increasing Federal support here and cutting it back there—that help determine what the scientific news is going to be. As the physicist I. I. Rabi pointed out in 1957 to President Eisenhower:

> There was no one around the president ... who could help him make decisions involving technology and to be aware of any scientific component that might exist in policy matters coming before him. He should have a full-time scientific adviser—a person he could live with easily.[239]

The Office of Science and Technology Policy, staffed by a small number of scientists and scientific administrators who are in touch with the various scientific communities, is designed to help with this task.

The U.S. Trade Representative, originally called the Special Representative for Trade Negotiations, was established in 1963. This office is charged with conducting international trade agreements and monitoring U.S. international trade relations more generally. Chronic American trade deficits, owing to relatively high U.S. labor costs, obsolete capital equipment, governmental deficits, and interest rates, have brought new prominence to the position. William Brock, the trade representative in the first Reagan administration, played an important part in discussions over restrictions on Japanese auto imports, and in textile negotiations. The Trade Representative does not have sole authority over his appointed domain. The State Department and the Commerce Department are both competitors for this increasingly visible piece of turf.[240]

   The presidential agency now known as the Policy Development Office has had several different names and a slightly uncertain existence since it was created by President Nixon in 1970 as a domestic counterpart to the National Security Council. Under Nixon it was known as the Domestic Council and was headed by John Ehrlichman, with a mandate to coordinate domestic policy initiatives of the Nixon administration.[241] This office also served as a cover for many of the Nixon administration functionaries who engaged in activities subsequently exposed in the unraveling of the Watergate scandals.

   President Carter abolished the Domestic Council and created in its place a Domestic Policy Staff, which was headed by his industrious and fair-minded assistant, Stuart Eizenstat. Here was where virtually all Carter administration domestic policy was given staff consideration for submission to the President, including those programs initiated in Cabinet departments. The Reagan administration renamed the organization the Policy Development Office and substantially reduced its size, from a staff of 80 to 40.

The Cabinet

   Tradition decrees that the presidential Cabinet shall consist of the operating heads of the main departments of government.[242] Presidents have had great leeway in deciding how this group of top-level administrators is chosen and the extent to which it is used as a collective entity, either to thrash out interdepartmental problems or to advise the President. President Eisenhower's practice was, as I have mentioned, to use an expanded and augmented Cabinet quite extensively as a sounding board and policy-making group.[243] Most of Eisenhower's successors, on the other hand, have preferred to deal directly with those Cabinet members involved in a particular problem and have avoided large-scale formal meetings. In some presidencies, with the growth of policy-making activity in the White House itself and the increased influence of such bodies as the National Security Council and the Office of Policy Development, the Cabinet has few collective functions. In others, the Cabinet is the starting point for more focused policy-making organization. Presidents Ford and Reagan, for example, formed councils staffed by White House officials which brought Cabinet-level agencies together for the purpose of coordinating plans.[244]

The National Security Council

   The National Security Council is a Cabinet-like group, by statute consisting of the President, the Vice President, and the Secretaries of State and Defense. The chairman of the Joint Chiefs of Staff and the director of the Central Intelligence Agency are statutory advisors to the Council. This group meets to make formal determinations of policy in areas affecting foreign and defense affairs. Considering its importance, the politics of its inner workings have not been much explored, although, once again, there are indications that Presidents Eisenhower and Kennedy treated the Council in much the same ways that they treated their Cabinets—Eisenhower tending to open up meetings to a large number of formal participants, Kennedy tending to create working task forces to deal with specific problems.[245] Under President Nixon, the staff of the NSC was greatly expanded and became the core of "the central machinery in the process of policymaking for national security...."[246] A report by President Nixon says:

> The National Security Council itself met 37 times in 1969, and considered over a score of different major problems of national security. Each Council meeting was the culmination of an interagency process of systematic and comprehensive review. This is how the process works: I assign an issue to an Interdepartmental Group—chaired by an Assistant Secretary of State—for intensive study, asking it to formulate the policy choices and to analyze the pros and cons of the different courses of action. This group's report is examined by an interagency Review Group of senior officials—chaired by the Assistant to the President for National Security Affairs—to insure that the issues, options, and views are presented fully and fairly. The paper is then presented to me and the full National Security Council.[247]

This system, which operated under presidential aide Henry Kissinger, was the earliest organizational innovation of the Nixon White House and was used by Nixon as his chosen instrument to ensure presidential control of foreign policy.

As time has gone on, the NSC staff has become more and more important, a natural outgrowth of the desire of Presidents to manage the foreign affairs of the United States themselves.[248] Under President Carter, the NSC even had its own press officer, and the advisor, Zbigniew Brzezinski, became a major spokesman for governmental policy. This had happened once before, under Richard Nixon, who used his NSC advisor Henry Kissinger rather than the Department of State to conduct American diplomacy.[249]

Tensions between the NSC and the State Department are thus built into the structure of government and exist more or less because Presidents desire them to exist, as a means of facilitating their own personal involvement in foreign policy making. There is also a straightforward substantive rationale for an organization like the NSC, as Peter Szanton argues:

> The decision to establish the National Security Council (NSC) and staff after World War II was based on the widespread perception that matters previously treated as either military or diplomatic could no longer be separated. Each was part of the larger problem of national security. Since no single cabinet agency comprehended the full range of security issues, two conclusions followed. The departments responsible, mainly State and Defense, had to work more closely together; and at some level above those departments, their dif-

ferences had to be resolved and their perspectives integrated into a broader view of national security.

Similar considerations apply today, but far more broadly. The distinction between foreign and domestic matters, eroding for 50 years, has now virtually disappeared. Are grain sales to the Soviets a foreign or domestic issue? Under which heading do military registration, energy policy, and trade agreements fall? Each is significant both at home and abroad, and each involves not just State or Defense, but much of the cabinet, all of the Congress, and a bewildering array of domestic economic and political interests.

Yet below the presidency, the executive branch is still organized in functional departments designed to deal only with particular aspects of major issues. And they see those issues, presidents soon come to believe, in quite parochial terms. Presidents must therefore do far more than merely preside over the resolution of differences among departments. They must fill the gaps between their perspectives, force exploration of alternatives they do not raise, and establish a framework within which each must work.[250]

The Central Intelligence Agency, the main agency in charge of gathering foreign intelligence for the U.S. government,[251] is, according to the organization chart, a presidential agency, and the Director reports directly to the President and not through some other Cabinet officer. Because of the CIA's great size, it is not housed in proximity to the White House, and its director, although he typically has frequent and regular access to the President, in other respects operates in a manner analogous to that of the other chiefs of large governmental bodies.

Ephemeral Agencies

Some agencies have floated in and out of the purview of the Executive Office, gathering the prestige of close proximity to the Presidency before they were lodged somewhere else in the executive branch. This was true, for example, of the Arms Control and Disarmament Agency, once a special project of White House aide Harold Stassen in the Eisenhower administration and now a special agency housed in the State Department. The Office of Civil Defense, now in the Pentagon, had a similar history.

Other presidential agencies expand and contract with the demands of the times. During World War II the director of the Office of War Mobilization and Reconversion, in the White House, was virtually President in domestic affairs.[252] After the war, however, the agency was cut back. Vestiges of the agency now remain in the White House as the Federal Emergency Management Agency. Under President Johnson the director of this office (which was then called the Office of Emergency Planning) was used primarily as a liaison with governors and as a clearinghouse to help solve administrative problems between Federal and state executive agencies.[253]

Presumably, all these and other presidential aides can perform a variety of functions. They can protect their chief from burdensome irrelevancies.

They can tell him what is going on both in the government and in the world. They can ascertain whether people in the executive agencies and in Congress are doing what the President wants them to do. And they can help the President to decide what he wants to do in the future and to anticipate difficulties and opportunities. How well or how badly they do these jobs depends on many things: on the difficulty of the circumstances that confront them, on the willingness or the ability of the Chief Executive to use their services, and on their own skill and diligence.

ARE PRESIDENTIAL POWERS GREAT OR SMALL?

Let us conclude this preliminary, general treatment of the Presidency by asking if presidential powers are great or small. We know they are many. As we shall see, the President is the initiator of much legislation, and his veto can be overridden only by a two-thirds majority in each house of Congress. He can provide a coherent legislative program, party leadership, a budget coordinated with tax revenues. His appointees staff the top levels of the executive branch and, as vacancies occur, the judiciary. He may decide which programs to emphasize, which to supervise perfunctorily, which to change, which to ignore.

On the other hand, there are many practical limitations to the President's powers. Deadlines must be met. Routine business hems him in. Although very little legislation can pass over his veto, well-placed and determined groups in Congress can thwart his desires as surely as he can thwart theirs.

In addition, many of the problems he faces are intractable, if not insuperable. The President must make decisions even when there is no way of knowing what decisions ought to be made. He must deal with allies who are sometimes petulant and enemies who are sometimes hostile and often devious.

Measured against the opportunities, the responsibilities, and the resources of others in our political system and in other nations, the powers of the Presidency are enormous. It is only when we measure these same powers against the problems of our age that they seem puny and inadequate.

chapter 3

THE SENATE

Although vast powers are vested in the presidential office, the Chief Executive is much like other executives. He shares dilemmas of leadership common to many others in and out of government. Congress, on the other hand, is a unique institution. The analogies to parliaments which predominate in intelligent conversation about Congress do not do justice to the powers of our national legislature. For unlike parliaments the world around, the American Congress dissolves neither itself nor the government when it has a serious disagreement with its Executive. Moreover, Congress does not meet briefly and hurriedly, as some of our state legislatures do. Rather, it continues to function and to wield substantial power in season and out, quite independently of the preferences of the other branches of government.[1]

To examine Congress closely, it is necessary to look at each house separately. The Senate and the House of Representatives share many characteristics, but they also differ significantly.[2] The Senate, with only 100 members, is smaller. Its members also have more prestige and attract a lot more publicity;[3] members of the House regularly resign voluntarily to run for the Senate, but no one in modern times has voluntarily done the reverse. Until 1913 each state legislature elected two senators for six-year terms.[4] Since then, under the provisions of the Seventeenth Amendment, senators have been popularly elected; but they still are chosen from statewide constituencies, and each state, regardless of population, has two senators. The Senate is a continuing body in the sense that at each biennial congressional election, only one-third of its members runs for reelection, and the six-year term gives senators greater job security than congressmen, who must run for office every two years.[5]

THE SENATE IN THE POLITICAL SYSTEM

Whereas the House of Representatives is a highly specialized machine for processing bills and overseeing the executive branch, the modern Senate is, increasingly, a great forum, an echo chamber, a theater, where dramas—comedies and tragedies, soap operas and horse operas—are staged to enhance the careers of its members and to influence public policy by means of debate and public investigation.[6] In both the House and the Senate a fundamental commandment to new members is "specialize."[7] This means vastly different things in each house, however. "Specialize" to a representative means "attend to your knitting"—work hard on the committee to which you are assigned, pursue the interests of your state and region. In the Senate everyone has several committee assignments. Boundaries between committees are less strictly observed than in the House. Access to the floor is much less regulated. Therefore, the institution itself gives few clues and no compulsions to new senators wondering what they should specialize in. For senators, specialization seems increasingly to mean finding a subject and cultivating a nationwide constituency that has not been preempted by some more senior senator.[8]

It is a cliche of academic political science that in legislative matters it is the President who initiates policy and Congress that responds, amplifying and modifying and rearranging elements that are essentially originated in the executive branch. But where do innovations in policy come from *before* the President "initiates" them? Old Washington hands know the answer. There is very little new under the sun. A great many newly enacted policies have been "in the air" for quite a while. In the heat of a presidential campaign or when a newly inaugurated President wants a "new" program, desk drawers fly open all over Washington. Pet schemes are fished out, dusted off, and tried out on the new political leaders. There is often a hiatus of years—sometimes decades—between the first proposal of a policy innovation and its appearance as a presidential "initiative," much less a law. Commentators have only recently recognized the role of the Senate in gestating these ideas, by providing a forum for speeches, hearings, and the introduction of bills going nowhere for the moment. This process of gestation accomplishes a number of things. It maintains a sense of community among far-flung interest groups that favor the innovation by giving them occasional opportunities to come in and testify. It provides an incentive for persons favoring the innovation to keep information up to date on its prospective benefits and technical feasibility. And it accustoms the uncommitted to a new idea. Thus the Senate is in some respects at a crucial nerve-end of the polity. It articulates, formulates, shapes, and publicizes demands and can serve as a hothouse for significant policy innovation, especially in opposition to the President.

How long has this been going on? Certainly since World War II, there has been a general movement of political resources and public attention toward Washington and away from local and regional arenas.[9] This trend has been reinforced by the growth of national news media, especially television. The impact on the Presidency of this nationalization of public awareness has been frequently noted. To a lesser extent, the same effect can be noted for all national political institutions. Of these, the Senate has gotten the most mileage out of its increased visibility. The Supreme Court has remained aloof. Until recently, successive Speakers refused to allow televised coverage of any official House function.[10] The bureaucracies have been expected to leave the public formulation and defense of their programs to their political executives, especially the President. From the beginnings of national television in the early 1950's, only the Senate had no constraint placed on its availability for national publicity, except for the ban on photographing or televising activity on the Senate floor itself.

As senatorial names—Kefauver,[11] McCarthy, Kennedy, Goldwater, McGovern, Sam Ervin—became household words over the last three decades, most governors slipped into relative obscurity. Where once a governor's control of a political "base," by virtue of his leadership of a state party organization, was the single overwhelming resource in deciding at a national party convention who was presidential timber, television and the nationalization of resources have eroded gubernatorial power.[12] Federal programs, financed by the lucrative Federal income tax, are being distributed among the states in part as senatorial patronage. Governors are by no means always ignored in this process, but their influence is on the whole much reduced. Meanwhile, at the state level, services have not kept pace with demands, and taxes are often inequitable and unproductive. Responsible governors of both parties have often tried to do something about this problem, but such activity has led to donnybrooks with state legislatures, great unpopularity, and, on some occasions, electoral defeat.[13]

The decline of the influence of governors and of state party leaders in the presidential nominating process and the shift of public attention to national politics and national politicians are still not enough to explain how the modern Senate became an incubator of policies and presidential hopefuls. Historical accidents have also played a part. The first was Lyndon Johnson. Ambitious for the Presidency and immensely skilled, as we shall presently see, Johnson sedulously perpetuated the myth of a Senatorial inner club while destroying its substance.[14] Joseph Clark, newly elected to the Senate in 1957, described a lunch Majority Leader Johnson gave for freshman Democrats. "As we sat down ... we found at our places copies of [William S. White's book on the U.S. Senate] *Citadel* ... autographed 'with all good wishes' not only by its author ... but by the majority leader as well. During the course of the lunch ... Senator Johnson encouraged us to consider

Mr. White's book as a sort of McGuffey's *Reader* from which we could learn much about the 'greatest deliberative body in the world' and how to mold ourselves into its way of life."[15]

Yet if the essence of the description of the Senate in *Citadel* was collegiality among the fellowship of the elect, the essence of Johnson's Senate operation was the progressive centralization of power in the hands of the Majority Leader. By the time Johnson left the Senate, in 1961, after six years as Democratic Leader, the "inner club" of White's description could command little of its old power. It had too long been merely a facade for Johnson's own activity, a polite explanation for the exercise of his own discretion in committee appointments, legislative priorities, and tactics. Under the loose rein of Mike Mansfield, Johnson's successor, the Senate became a genuinely collegial body whose corporate work was pretty much determined by presidential programs and priorities. It never recaptured the sense of cohesion, community, and separateness that obtained "in the old days," before Johnson. Younger people came in, and liberal majorities on legislation became by no means uncommon.

When Mansfield retired in 1977 to become Jimmy Carter's ambassador to Japan, the Democrats, still the majority party, chose as his successor Robert Byrd of West Virginia, an assiduous traffic manager who avoided leadership on substantive issues.[16] After the election of 1980, the Republicans captured a slim Senatorial majority, and the new majority leader, Howard Baker of Tennessee, discovered that traffic management, not policy coordination, had become the main responsibility of the leader of the Senate. And so it has remained for Baker's successor, Bob Dole.[17]

In recent years the Senate has become a thoroughly individualistic, not a collegial, place. In the words of a close observer, "the Senate has become a collection of casual acquaintances whose focus is on the world outside the chamber."[18] Senators' staffs have grown to such a size that managing them has become an important senatorial chore—and dependence on them an unavoidable necessity.[19]

In 1891 exactly 39 people worked as staff for the entire U.S. Senate (at the time there were 88 senators) and committee staff totaled 41. In 1981 the number had grown to 3,638 personal staff and 1,022 committee staff. This adds up to approximately 36 people directly responsible to each senator in Washington, plus whatever number of jobs senators control on committees and subcommittees. These committee staff aid senators in their legislative activity. Personal staff—in Washington or in offices located in senators' home states—are focused predominantly on giving assistance to constituents in their dealings with the government—"casework," as it is called.[20] Former Senator Dick Clark (D-Iowa), who was himself once a congressional staff member, characterized the staff-senator relationship as one of "dependence." "Domination, no. Dependency, definitely. In all legislation, they're the ones that lay out the options." For example, on a proposed code of ethics: "the staff spent ten hours drawing up a proposed outline.... Then we spent two hours studying it. We worked hard on it—but they drew up the options."[21]

To an increasing extent, Senate staff also look for ways in which the members with which they are associated can become active. Examples of this policy entrepreneurship by staff members have, in particular, entered the literature through the writing of a number of former employees of Warren Magnuson (D-Wash.). One of them describes an experience working as an intern in Magnuson's office when an idea for a minor bill was suggested to him by a Seattle physician; he and other members of the staff sold Magnuson on the idea and then proceeded to write the bill and shepherd it through the Senate. Magnuson's personal involvement in the process was almost purely perfunctory.[22]

Staff people in the Senate have enabled a style of senatorial service that in its search for national constituencies has little in common with that of the older, more insular Senate preoccupations. Nevertheless, the newer sort of senator is not regarded as a maverick. Rather, such senators are national politicians, something that the mass media have made it increasingly possible for senators to be.[23] They are following a style of service hit on by several postwar senators, notably pioneered by Arthur Vandenberg of Michigan and, in the 1950s and 1960s, brought to full flower by Hubert Humphrey.

Much earlier than most members of his generation, Humphrey sensed the possibilities in the Senate for long-range political education. He spent the Eisenhower era incubating ideas that in a better climate could hatch into programs. In the late 1940s and early 1950s a flood of Humphrey bills (many of them co-sponsored by other liberal senators) on all aspects of civil rights, medicare, housing, aid to farm workers, food stamps, job corps, area redevelopment, disarmament, and so on died in the Senate. A little over a decade later most of them were law, and Humphrey had in the meantime become a political leader of national consequence.[24] The force of his example was not lost on younger senators.

In recent years it has proven to be possible for senators to reconcile their ambitions for large public accomplishments with accommodation to Senate norms. The Senate is now a less insular body than it was in former times, and the fortunes of senators are correspondingly less tied to the smiles and frowns of their elders within the institution.

THE DISTRIBUTION OF POWER: THE DEMISE OF THE INNER CLUB

This description of the contemporary Senate—as an individualistic, staff-saturated, publicity-hungry, and public-regarding institution serving the ambitions of many of its members to achieve star billing in connection with national issues—is drastically at odds with the picture provided by observers of the place as late as the mid-1950s. In the first edition of this book, published in 1964, objections were raised to this earlier portrait which seemed to me already out of date, a portrait of an institution in which close-knit collegial relationships dominated the Senate's status structure, and an "inner club" repelled and punished outsiders and determined significant outcomes. The question was whether the formal structure of the Senate was less revealing of the actual distribution of power within the institution than was usually the case with political organizations. Writers attempted to capture and codify "folkways"—informal prescriptions of behavior—an understanding of which was supposed to help one disentangle the mysteries of senatorial power and influence.

In order to see how far the contemporary Senate has come in a brief two decades, and to provide historical perspective, it is instructive to recreate that portrait just at the point— roughly 1960, give or take a few years— at which serious students of the institution could see it begin to fade.[25]

The Senate, it was argued, was really run by a clique of interacting senators, an "inner club," small in number and not necessarily the most senior in rank, who were emotionally in tune with one another, who followed the folkways, and who were widely recognized as "Senate types." It was said that senators, if they aspired to this inner club, were required to adapt their behavior to fit Ralph Huitt's famous composite description:

> [He is] a prudent man, who serves a long apprenticeship before trying to assert himself, and talks infrequently even then. He is courteous to a fault in his relations with his colleagues, not allowing political disagreements to affect his personal feelings. He is always ready to help another Senator when he can, and he expects to be repaid in kind. More than anything else, he is a Senate man, proud of the institution and ready to defend its traditions and perquisites against all outsiders. He is a legislative workhorse who specializes in one or two policy areas.... He has a deep respect for the rights of others ... making his institution the last citadel of individualism.... He is a man of accommodation who knows that "you have to go along to get along"; he is a conservative, institutional man, slow to change what he has mastered at the expense of so much time and patience.[26]

I have noted that the picture of senatorial life that this description gives has some historical validity. However, even twenty years ago, as Huitt went on to show in the classic article from which this summary is drawn, it had become extremely misleading. In order to see why, it is helpful to examine the following questions:

First, what are the folkways, as described in the books, magazines, and journals, on which real senatorial leadership was supposed to be based?

Second, who were the members of the inner club?

Third, in what sense did powerful senators actually follow the folkways?

Finally, what does this suggest about the distribution of power in the Senate even then, and about the roles available to senators who wished a significant share in the power of the institution?

The Senate's folkways were described most succinctly by Donald Matthews in an article that achieved wide currency and acceptance.[27] They consisted of:

1. Practices of the Senate that granted individual senators few or no opportunities for deviation. Examples include the operations of the seniority system and the rules of comity governing floor debate.

2. Prescriptions of "good" behavior that applied to freshman senators only. During the period of apprenticeship, which lasted until the next class arrived two years later, the freshman senator was expected to perform many thankless tasks cheerfully, such as presiding over floor debate. He was expected to seek advice from senior senators, make no speeches or remarks on the floor unless specifically invited, and take the initiative in getting acquainted with other senators.[28]

3. Prescriptions of "good" behavior that applied to all senators in their relations with one another. Examples included the following commandments: make speeches only on subjects on which you are expert or that concern your committee or your state; do not seek publicity at the expense of less glamorous legislative work; do favors for other senators; address your colleagues in a friendly manner; speak well of the Senate as an institution; keep your word when you make an agreement.

In truth, these folkways could provide little help to senators who sought to unravel the secrets of the inner club. Freshmen were apparently not the only senators excluded, and nonfreshmen who conformed as freshmen were not necessarily "in."

Who was in? Who, specifically, were the Senate men who in the "Citadel" era were supposed to have dominated this institution? "They [are] men of the type and character," said Dean Acheson, "who, in a quiet way, are apt to dominate any male organization. The main ingredients of such men are force, likeableness and trustworthiness. Alben Barkley, Walter George and Arthur Vandenberg were, perhaps, the *beaux ideals*."[29]

Perhaps not. William S. White, while granting Barkley and George entrance to the inner club, said, "The late Senator Arthur Vandenberg ... for all his influence upon foreign relations ... was never in his career a true Senate type, no matter how formidable he was as a public man."[30] For White, Senate types displayed "tolerance toward [their] fellows, intolerance toward any who would in any real way change the Senate," and commitment to the Senate as "a career in itself, a life in itself and an end in itself."[31] Yet certified Senate types, White acknowledged, such as Senators Robert Taft of Ohio or Richard Russell of Georgia (and he might have added Bob Kerr, Hubert Humphrey, and Lyndon Johnson) did run for President.

White's argument was that they did this, not because the Presidency was a higher or more preferable office, but because it was "another" ambition of theirs.[32] Even in the late 1950s, this argument was unconvincing.

Other Senate insiders could be observed tampering with the decor of the institution in a variety of ways. The reformist agitations of insider Hubert Humphrey (later Majority Whip) abated only slightly after the celebrated speech early in his Senate career suggesting the abolition of insider Senator Harry Byrd's Committee on Reduction of Nonessential Expenditures in the Executive Department.[33] Perhaps more significant was Majority Leader Lyndon Johnson's successful reform of the committee assignment process on the Democratic side of the aisle in 1953. This change of real and undeniable significance, which took power away from senior senators and vested it in more junior ones, was effected by a man widely recognized as the most inside of insiders. As Huitt says, "One of [Johnson's] most successful political acts was his decision in 1953 to put all Democratic senators, even new ones, on at least one important committee."[34] Johnson also participated in a human drama of some poignance a few years later, when the elderly Senator Theodore Francis Green of Rhode Island, "a member of the very hierarchy of the Club,"[35] was persuaded to relinquish the chairmanship of the blue-ribbon Foreign Relations Committee to the next-ranking J. William Fulbright of Arkansas, who was, White said, "not ... quite a Senate type."[36]

On the matter of tolerance, it is hard to judge senators from a distance. If, however, as White suggests, the practice of tolerance separated members of the inner club from those outside, we must assume that he is implying that Senator Walter George of Georgia, for example, was a more tolerant man than, say, Senator Herbert Lehman of New York, whom White places outside the inner sanctum.[37] But that is not the way all of their contemporaries remembered them.[38] Indeed, it is instructive to recall the anecdote with which Mr. White introduces Senator George and the Senate type.

> No skin in all the world is more easily abraded than senatorial skin. Once, for an illustration, the Attorney General of the United States, Herbert Brownell, Jr., was condemned to the pit of Senatorial displeasure for daring to permit his department to prepare a memorandum raising certain questions about a ... proposed Amendment to the Constitution.... The incident struck the then Dean of the Senate, Mr. George of Georgia as [Mr. White's choice of words is enlightening] intolerable. It was his conclusion, expressed in the tragically wounded tones of which his majestic voice was capable, that Brownell was "a very *odd* Attorney General," and worse still, that his offensive paper had undoubtedly been written by "some cloik" [clerk] in the Justice Department.[39]

Tolerance, lack of presidential ambition, undeviating acceptance of the institutional status quo—all on closer inspection fail to differentiate members of the inner club from those who languished outside. What about the more diffuse folkways that seem to reward the agreeable sorts of people who manage their interactions with their fellows smoothly? Was there, perhaps, an identifiable personality type that foreordained membership in the inner club?

It is difficult, without an exhaustive set of identifications from those in the know, to say who was and who was not in the inner club at any given time,[40] but I think we can reasonably assume that those senators who were elevated by their colleagues to high party posts within the Senate could be regarded as Senate types. This leaves aside the great number of self-selected leaders whose interest in particular policies made them important in the Senate and that group who were "in" by virtue of seniority. Both groups, because of the method of their selection, would be less subject to peer review and less likely to display personal characteristics compatible with the folkways than senators formally selected to leadership by fellow senators.

Even in this latter group, however, the variation in personal characteristics was quite striking. From the forties onward, observers noted the gregariousness of Hubert Humphrey and the diffidence of Mike Mansfield; the geniality of Alben Barkley and the brusqueness of Robert A. Taft; the adroitness of Everett Dirksen and the hamhandedness of Kenneth Wherry; the humorlessness of William Knowland and the wit of Eugene Millikin; the secretiveness of Styles Bridges and the openness of Arthur Vandenberg; the self-effacement of Ernest McFarland and the flamboyance of Lyndon Johnson; the steadiness of Thomas Kuchel and the unpredictability of Russell Long; the urbanity of Hugh Scott and the folksiness of Robert Byrd.[41] The contrasts could undoubtedly be expanded indefinitely, but the point would remain the same: no clear standards of eligibility for membership in the inner club, if there was one, seem likely to emerge from an examination of personality characteristics of senators.

We must pause to ask: Was there an inner club at all? Or was power distributed in the Senate more widely? It is worthwhile to remember that there are only 100 U.S. Senators. Each one enjoys high social status, great visibility, a large staff, and substantial powers in his[42] own right. Each one has the right, by the rules of the Senate, to speak on the floor of the Senate on any subject for as long as he desires to do so. Where a tremendous amount of business must be transacted by unanimous consent, any single senator can, if he chooses, effectively stall and harass the machinery of government. But these are ultimate sanctions, rarely employed by an individual senator though more frequently by groups of senators. In any event, settled Senate practice is to take account of the wishes of every interested senator with respect to the convenient scheduling and disposition of most Senate business. Senator Richard Russell described this practice in debate on the floor:

> I have heard questions asked [the Senate majority and minority leaders] for 30 years—Senators come up to them and say, "What time are we going to

vote? What time are we going to vote?" Of course neither the majority leader nor the minority leader knows any more about the time the Senate is going to vote than does the Senator asking the question, but he is supposed to have some pleasant and reasonable answer. Another day a Senator will say, "Well, I cannot be here Thursday, so you cannot vote on such and such a bill on Thursday." Likely as not, the majority leader or the minority leader had agreed with the author of the bill to have it acted on on Thursday. That is only one instance of perhaps 10,000 different commitments that they make.[43]

This is still the way it works, as long-time Senate staff member William Hildenbrand told Alan Ehrenhalt:

Everybody who wants to be accommodated is accommodated.... If somebody doesn't want a vote on a Monday, there's no vote on Monday. The leadership just coordinates the individual requests.... [Senate majority leader Howard] Baker has 53 constituents, and he has to serve them.

Ehrenhalt continues:

The constituent problem must have flashed through [minority leader Robert] Byrd's mind late one summer night in 1980, his last year as majority leader, as he stood on the floor trying desperately to find a time the following Monday when the Senate could vote on the 1981 budget resolution. One senator after another announced that a particular time would be inconvenient. Byrd was reduced to writing all the preferences on a long yellow legal pad, a process that made him look more like a man sending out for sandwiches than the leader of a deliberative body.[44]

Ralph Huitt describes a striking example of the way an individual senator can have a decisive impact on legislative outcomes. His subject was William Proxmire, then a freshman senator from Wisconsin.

The provocation was a bill to allow the Metropolitan Sanitary District of Chicago to increase the amount of water it may withdraw from Lake Michigan by a thousand cubic feet per second for a three year test period. Similar bills had been passed by both houses twice before (by the Senate in the closing hours of a session with scant debate) only to be vetoed by the President because of objections raised by Canada. Once more it appeared that the bill would come up in the flood of last minute legislation, and with committee and leadership support, it seemed sure to slide through the tired Senate. Moreover, because the Canadian position was now ambiguous, the President might sign the bill. But the pressure for adjournment which was the greatest factor in favor of the bill's passage could also be its doom—if its opponents had sufficient nerve. Their hope was to stall consideration as long as possible, then make it clear that the cost of passage was extended debate. It was a simple, time-proven strategy, but not one designed to make friends. Proxmire was by no means the only man fighting the bill—there was a militant bipartisan coalition on each side—but he was probably the most determined and certainly the most conspicuous. It was he who blocked unanimous consent to allow any deviation from the rules in handling the bill.[45] Thus he objected to a meeting of the Public Works Committee while the Senate sat, and to the bill's being reported to the Senate after the expiration of the morning hour—tactics which brought sharp rebukes from two senior members but delayed the bill a day. And it was he who held the floor from nine till midnight the last night of the session, until the water diversion bill was put aside for other business; and he who sat through the early morning hours, armed with a score of amendments and great piles of materials, ready to resume the debate. When the session ended at 4:11 in the morning the unfinished business of the Senate was a Proxmire amendment to the water diversion bill.[46]

Even foreign policy, by tradition a special preserve of the President, is not immune from the ministrations of enterprising senators. Consider the following:

> When, at last, the Senate had voted on final passage of the battered foreign aid bill, Majority Leader Mansfield wore his habitual expression of martyred resignation. Chairman Fulbright of the Foreign Relations Committee appeared grateful to be alive.
>
> Only Senator Morse, Democrat of Oregon, was triumphant. The bill passed, but with $500 million less than its backers had hoped. It was largely due to Senator Morse's exertions and the exhaustion of the other Senators. Nobody wanted to take him on.
>
> The foreign aid bill did nothing for anybody else in Washington. The Senate leadership was flouted. Secretary of State Rusk protested in vain. The President pleaded too late. The President's men in the Senate ... were too tired to fight— at least with Wayne Morse.
>
> Senator Morse alone came out of the tedious battle with something like prestige.
>
> His domination of the debate does not make him a leader. His forces were a motley group of defecting liberals and soured Southerners who may never march under the same banner again.
>
> Besides he is a lone wolf . . . Senator Morse combines qualities of exceptional ability, supreme egotism, self-righteousness and vindictiveness that do not make a man a favorite with his fellows. . . .
>
> But if he is disliked, he can no longer be discounted as a power in the Senate. He is getting mail from all over the country, hailing his attacks on foreign aid.
>
> Presidential blandishments were of no avail. Invited to the White House, the Senator sat down with the Chief Executive for 45 minutes and went over the program.
>
> "Then I came back up here," he told his friends with a wolfish grin, "and put in a couple of more amendments.". . .
>
> He threatened the Whip with a country-by-country review of the whole foreign aid program. Senator Humphrey hastily withdrew his amendment. . .
>
> Senator Morse was satisfied . . .
>
> He went on to threaten "further debate of great length" if the Senate conferees on the foreign aid bill came back with a conference report that undid any of his work . . .

It was one time when the Senate was content to have the Senator disposing of all problems, great and small, in what the President this week called "an untidy world." The leadership was out trying to cope with Senator Mundt's sticky and inopportune amendment on the wheat sale to Russia.

So Senator Morse had a perfect day. Even the passage of the bill, against which he voted, of course, could not mar his self-satisfaction. He had left his mark on foreign aid for all the world to see.[47]

Morse, one of two senators to vote against the Gulf of Tonkin resolution under which President Johnson prosecuted the Vietnam war, was a true lone wolf. Nevertheless, on occasion he got his way.

A more recent instance featured Senator Henry Jackson, Democrat of Washington:

Last year he was chiefly responsible for passage of an amendment requiring the U.S. to maintain parity with Russia on all weapons in the SALT agreement. More recently, he introduced the Jackson Amendment to the trade bill; it denies most-favored-nation status to any country that does not permit free emigration—a measure aimed at the Soviet Union's refusal to let Jews leave for Israel.

Jackson is not only determined, he is also effective—a fact that is recognized by allies and opponents alike. He does his homework; he is earnest and honest. He is nothing if not himself; plain-spoken, no shaggy locks, rimless glasses or any other concession to youth or fashion. He operates from an almost impregnable position in the Senate, where he is chairman of the Interior and Insular Affairs Committee and a member of the Armed Services Committee, the Joint Committee on Atomic Energy, and the Government Operations Committee.

Most important, he is chairman of the Permanent Investigations Subcommittee of Government Operations, a post he has used to mount assaults on Administration foreign policy. Says a Senate dove who disagrees with Jackson: "Senators like John Tower, Barry Goldwater and Strom Thurmond, who hold a view of the world that is similar to Scoop's, have been at a loss to know how to cope with a self-styled Republican conservative in the White House who has undertaken to establish normal relations with the Soviet Union. Jackson has found the Achilles' heel in Nixon's foreign policy. He has opened fissures that have dealt very strong blows to that policy."

For all this tough talk, Jackson is as skilled at compromising an issue as at dramatizing it. Partisan of big defense that he is, he has worked behind the scenes to scale down Pentagon budget requests so that they would be acceptable to the Senate. Though he is adamant about maintaining U.S. forces in Europe, he joined Senator Sam Nunn in introducing an amendment to the Defense Appropriation Bill that would require European nations to share the cost of the troop commitment; the amendment was passed. He and his staff are huddling with both the White House and Soviet diplomats to try to work out a compromise on the trade bill . . . His own political conduct is punctilious; he does not indulge in inflammatory rhetoric or *ad hominem* attacks. "I hate emotion in anything," says Jackson, "even in religion. If you master the facts, then you can posture yourself in such a way that you can persuade people of your point of view." . . . Obviously, U.S. foreign policy depends at least to an extent on where Jackson stands.[48]

It is clear that individual senators can, according to the rules and customs of the Senate, play a powerful hand in the disposition of legislation reaching the floor, even without the immensely useful fortifications of seniority, membership on a relevant substantive committee, a committee chairmanship, or a position of formal leadership. Nevertheless, let us inquire into the distribution of these prizes, for much that happens off the floor, where so many legislative outcomes are actually settled, depends on the strategic locations of friends or foes of bills and their diligence and skill in shaping results to suit their preferences. There are a number of strategic locations, as a sampling of commentary on the recent history of the Senate will rapidly reveal:

> [Senator Robert S.] Kerr [Democrat, of Oklahoma] was correctly rated the most powerful member of the Senate, though not one of its nominal leaders, in the . . . (eighty-seventh) Congress . . . The base of Kerr's power was never his major committees. Rather, it was his chairmanship of the Rivers and Harbors Subcommittee of the Public Works Committee, an obscure post that makes few national headlines, but much political hay. Kerr not only used it to consolidate his position in Oklahoma by festooning the state with public works but placed practically all Senators under obligation to him by promoting their pet home projects. He never hesitated to collect on these obligations later, when the votes were needed.[49]

* * *

> The [Senator Warren G.] Magnuson [Democrat, of Washington] muscle stems from several sources. In the Senate, where seniority almost automatically confers clout, 29-year veteran Magnuson is Number Five. That, however, hardly tells the whole story. His Commerce Committee literally holds life-or-death power over the nation's railroads, airlines, truckers and maritime industry; considers all legislation concerning the communications and power industries; has jurisdiction over today's two hottest issues, consumer protection and the environment; and supervises virtually all of the federal regulatory agencies. "When the Nixon Administration took office," says New Hampshire Senator Norris Cotton, the Commerce Committee's ranking Republican, "I warned the White House not to clear the agency appointees just with me. I advised them to clear them with Maggie first. And they do."

> There is still another source of Magnuson power: the chairmanship of Appropriations Committee's Subcommittee on Health, Education and Welfare. This seemingly innocuous position gives Magnuson virtual control over the $27-billion appropriations for HEW, the second biggest item in the federal budget. Explains Cotton, a good friend of Magnuson's who also happens to serve as ranking Republican on the HEW Subcommittee, "The other subcommittee members have too many obligations to get involved in all the details of the HEW appropriations. So Maggie and I sit there day after day for months

going over each item. The rest of the subcommittee will generally go along with our decisions."

For a man who has walked the corridors of political power for a generation, there is a basic unpretentiousness, even a simplicity, about Warren Magnuson. In his rumpled blue suit with its out-of-style narrow lapels, wandering out of his office to exchange small talk or try out his latest story on his staff, he looks more the kindly small-town lawyer than one of the most powerful men in Washington.

Beyond that easygoing geniality, however, lies the keen mind of a man determined to leave his mark on history. Scornful of the liberals who grandstand in the Senate chamber, Magnuson prides himself on his "kitchen work," the behind-the-scenes Committee drudgery that produces the avalanche of legislation of which he is so proud. A man with a fantastic memory, he remembers the details of virtually every bill he has dealt with in his 35 years in the Congressional kitchen. Recalls Washington lawyer William Kohler, who served on Magnuson's staff for many years: "Many times I would go in to brief him on an upcoming bill. He would read it quickly and remark that it contained the same provisions as a bill that had failed to pass ten or twelve years before. I would go back and look it up, and he was invariably right."[50]

* * *

In the past seven months, soft-spoken Alabama Democrat James B. Allen has administered two terrific legislative beatings to ... Senate liberals, and has emerged as a master practitioner of the "new style" Senate filibuster.

In December, Allen led a filibuster to block [liberals] from attaching a public campaign financing bill to a routine measure extending the federal debt limit. Last week, using the same techniques, he choked off a . . . move to use another debt-ceiling extension bill as a vehicle for tax reform and tax cuts.

To be sure, Allen had warm support from the White House and from Senate conservatives. But he exhibited an amazing knowledge of the Senate rules, an admirable tactical sense, and the patience and endurance needed to stay on the floor all day long for nearly two weeks and make certain his opponents didn't grab a procedural advantage.

Here since 1969, Allen, 61, is a deep-dyed conservative, a staunch foe of school busing who has gradually taken over leadership of the anti-busing forces in the Senate, and a political ally of Gov. George C. Wallace, under whom he served as lieutenant governor. He is quiet, slow-talking, courteous, sometimes witty in a sly country way.

Allen knows very well how to use the filibuster, even though the technique has radically altered in recent years.

In the old days, before Mike Mansfield (D-Mont.) became Senate Majority Leader when Lyndon B. Johnson moved to the vice presidency, there was a giant Southern conservative bloc united against civil rights legislation. A filibuster meant getting the floor and holding it and being prepared to speak all night if your opponents attempted to wear you down by forcing round-the-clock sessions.

One of the last such marathons was in August 1957, when Strom Thurmond held the floor for 24 hours and 18 minutes against a civil rights measure.

Thurmond's feat, made possible by the fact that the South Carolina senator (he was then a Democrat, but has since switched to the Republicans) is a physical fitness enthusiast, is unlikely to be matched again.

Mansfield has changed the whole technique by refusing to schedule round-the-clock sessions. He thinks they are ridiculous, endanger the health of older senators, and actually help the filibusterers rather than those who want to shut them off.

"What you wear down is not the filibusterers but the moderates. And too many people were coming in here to all-night sessions in bedroom slippers," Mansfield said.

He explained that to keep holding the floor, the filibuster team needed only shifts of three or four members on the floor for several hours at a time.

The anti-filibusterers, in contrast, [needed] many more people constantly ready to ward off a surprise attempt to kill or further entangle the legislation the filibusterers didn't want.

So now, instead of the picturesque but fruitless all-night sessions, the Senate uses a much more polite and less exhausting procedure. Things are done by signals, and if the filibusterer happens to be off the floor, he is sometimes notified to come back if he wishes to object to an opponent's attempt to move the business forward.

"Yes, I always make it my business to inform the opposition leader. In the long run it pays off," Mansfield said. Eventually it comes down to whether the proponents have the ... votes needed to break the filibuster. "We get the job done," said Mansfield, "sooner or later we get a cloture vote."

Under the new style filibuster, a senator doesn't actually have to talk and hold the floor for 20 or more hours. He and one or two of his allies simply have to be on hand to signal that they will seek to talk and will object if anyone tries to get a vote on the proposition they are opposing.

For this reason, a debate-limiting cloture petition is sometimes filed before an hour's debate. A senator makes known that he is going to filibuster, but without actually dragging "Gone with the Wind," a Bible and sack of nourishing candy-bars out to the floor.

His opponents then give him credit for having done what he has only signaled he intends to do, and they file cloture immediately. This happened in last week's debate, when a tax-reform amendment was introduced by Sen. Hubert H. Humphrey (D-Minn.) and a cloture petition on it was filed at once by Mansfield, without a single word of debate or even an explanation of the amendment.

Mansfield, Kennedy and Humphrey knew opponents would block a vote, so they moved immediately to short-cut the verbal barrage and get a test of cloture. (Two days later the cloture move failed by 18 votes, ending the tax fight and giving Allen his big victory.)[51]

* * *

Senator Eastland was the politician's politician. You could make deals with him. Publicly, he might rant and rave, as when James Meredith racially integrated the University of Mississippi in 1961, but behind the scenes he worked closely with President Kennedy and Attorney General Robert Kennedy to defang Mississippi's governor, Ross Barnett, who did not have a very bad dose of the smarts, and who the Washington Establishment feared might make a terrible situation even worse. Senator Eastland got along equally well with Lyndon Johnson; he reached his zenith during the Nixon years when the so-called Southern strategy was in vogue. Yet, he took Senator Edward Kennedy under his wing when the youngest of the Kennedy brothers arrived in the Senate and told him, "Boy, your brothers never made it here because they used the Senate to run for president. You may want to run for president someday yourself, but you'll be happier here and make more friends if you'll do your homework. Don't try to avoid the ditch-digging. It's part of the job." Senator Eastland also gets along with his colleagues by allowing his committee members—as chairman of the Judiciary Committee and ranking Democrat on Agriculture—many patronage plums and large staffs; though few know it, he always has been one of the top fund raisers for the Democratic Senatorial Campaign Committee through tapping his affluent oil and agri-biz contacts.[52]

* * *

Though still indisputably the boss, Majority Leader Mike Mansfield (D-Mont.) has turned over much of the responsibility for the day-to-day conduct of Senate business to his assistant leader, Majority Whip Robert C. Byrd (D-W.Va.).

Byrd, in turn, has devoted himself conscientiously and tirelessly to the job.

He is winning high marks for fairness and ability even from some Northern Democrats who completely disagree with his views on the war, civil rights and welfare.

This has greatly strengthened Byrd's position to bid for the top job should Mansfield step down at the end of this Congress, as some expect. However, in the secret caucus at which Senate officers are elected, many of these same Northerners would oppose a promotion for Byrd, solely because they believe he would make a poor national spokesman for their party . . .

The growing strength and assurance of Byrd as a leader has been evident for some time. Absolutely tireless, he stays on the floor long hours each day engineering legislative agreements and moving the Senate business forward . . .

When he astonished Washington in early 1971 by beating the glamorous Edward M. Kennedy (D-Mass.) for the whip post, 31 to 24, several Northern Democratic senators . . . feared he would stifle "the liberals" and use his leadership to advance conservative causes.

Now, some of these same Northerners will say privately— virtually no one will speak "on the record" in delicate matters of inner Senate power, where a misstatement might invite retaliation—that Byrd has done an excellent job. . .

To a substantial extent, Mansfield in recent months has delegated to Byrd the crucial power of scheduling legislation, arranging unanimous consent agreements on times to vote, and working out delicate maneuvers to keep business moving.

Though little understood by the public, these powers have great influence over the outcome of legislation. The capacity to win concessions by delaying legislation, to force a vote when "your" side is best prepared while the other is in disarray or has many absentees, to forestall such maneuvers by the other party—these can make or break legislation.

Byrd has proved to be a superlative maneuverer, and has been extremely careful to "protect the interests" of all Democratic senators—for example, in arranging speaking time, and in notifying individual members when legislation in which they are interested comes to the floor.

He worked with Northern Democrats to obtain a vote on the poverty bill when a GOP stall was threatened, and he has moderated his position on a few votes recently—supporting the D.C. home rule bill, voting against the nomination of Richard G. Kleindienst as Attorney General, and endorsing stronger powers for the Equal Employment Opportunity Commission.

It was these same qualities, when Byrd was only a minor figure in Democratic leadership as secretary of the caucus, that enabled him to beat Kennedy. His steady accretion of respect from some Northerners who dislike his political views will make him a formidable contender at such time as Mansfield steps down.[53]

* * *

As the Republican minority leader of the Senate in the 1960s, Everett Dirksen, Mr. Baker's father-in-law, had been famous for his oracular, highhanded approach to the job—threatening, for example, to withhold coveted committee assignments or hold back floor action on particular legislation as a means of forcing recalcitrant Senators to vote the party line. It was a familiar technique in an era when Senators spent a lifetime in the chamber, amassing political I.O.U.s and nursing grudges. Today, 54 Senators are in their first term.[54] They have little sense of institutional devotion and no disposition to be bullied.

Howard Baker's approach to the job reflected the changing makeup of the Senate—he enlarged attendance at leadership meetings, for example, inviting freshmen and those with a special interest in the particular piece of legislation under discussion. His approach also reflected a very different personality: Mr. Baker is a patient builder of coalitions, generous with his time and slow to anger. He is also one of the great listeners of all time and a man of considerable personal charm and humor. Last year, for example, [1981] when Senator Slade Gorton, Republican of Washington, wondered why the majority leader was sitting out a debate, Mr. Baker offered one of his down-home epigrams: "Ain't got no dog in this fight."[55]

* * *

The office of Democratic Leader, it is true, combines all the most important elective positions—Chairman of the Conference, of the Steering Committee, of the Policy Committee (the Republicans fill these positions with four different

men). Each position adds something to his influence and to the professional
staff he controls. The Steering Committee handles committee transfers and
assignment of new members . . . As Chairman of the Policy Committee he
has substantial control over legislative scheduling (in close collaboration with
the Minority Leader) which gives him not only the power to help and hinder
but an unequalled knowledge of legislation on the calendar and who [wants]
what and why. A tactical power of importance [is] . . . the right of the Majority
Leader to be recognized first when he wants the floor [which can be exploited
to] initiate a legislative fight when and on the terms he [wants].[56]

It is probably not possible to identify *all* the institutional nooks and
crannies that can provide a base of power for a United States senator. In
any event the same base is often used differently by different men. For
example, whereas Lyndon Johnson as Majority Leader pretty much ran his
own show, his successor, Mike Mansfield, was more comfortable sharing
substantial power with his assistants as well as with his party's Policy and
Steering Committees.[57] It may be useful, just the same, to see how the more
obvious strategic positions were distributed among senators in the Ninety-
eighth Congress (1983-1984). Among these positions, one might include
elective leadership posts, memberships on party policy (agenda) and steering
(committee-assignment) committees, committee chairmanships (or, in the
case of the minority, position as ranking member), chairmanships of subcommittees, memberships on more than two regular legislative committees,
and memberships on the Appropriations Committee.

Although there are considerable inequalities in the distribution of these
prizes, virtually no senator in the Ninety-eighth Congress was without some
institutional base that guaranteed him a disproportionate say, either in some
substantive area of public policy or in the behind-the-scenes management
of Senate business. Of fifty-four Republicans (the majority party), fifty-two
were chairmen of committees or subcommittees and one—Howard Baker—
was the Majority Leader; forty-three out of forty-four Democrats were ranking members of committees or subcommittees. Only two senators, therefore,
for the time being had no institutional base that was particularly helpful to
them: Frank Lautenberg (D-N.J.) and Pete Wilson (R-Calif.), both newly
elected. These figures mean that very junior senators are now sharing far
more of the action than ever before. A little earlier, when chairmanships
were slightly less spread about, a Capitol Hill veteran told a reporter: "If
you're walking down the hall and you pass a member [of Congress], always
say 'Good morning, Mr. Chairman.' If it isn't so, you won't offend him, but
chances are it will be true."[58]

Obviously, some senators have more institutional positions to operate
from than others, but this misses the point that in a legislative body not
even the best-placed senator can hope to accomplish his legislative ends
without the help of other senators, who may be less favorably situated. As
Alan Ehrenhalt says:

With its loose rules and collegial leadership style, [the Senate] has allowed its tradition of individual rights to turn into tolerance for virtually unlimited individual obstruction. A senator whose constituency does not like a piece of legislation can not only block its passage for weeks; he can sometimes keep it off the floor for good.[59]

Consider the techniques for cooperative endeavor, both over the short run and the long run, that can be observed in an anecdote such as the following:

Magnuson rarely makes a speech on the Senate floor. Hardly shy, he just thinks it is a waste of time. Floor speeches, as every Senator knows, are delivered for the media and the voters back home. The real decisions are made before a bill gets on the floor by the men who run the Senate. There is no more familiar sight in the Senate aisles than Magnuson, unlit cigar clenched between his teeth, holding quiet conversations with his colleagues. "If you've got the votes," he says, "you don't need a speech. If you need the speech, you don't have the votes."

A demonstration of the behind-the-scenes Magnuson clout occurred in the closing days of Congress last December. With the SST down the drain, Magnuson's home town of Seattle (home of Boeing, the prime contractor) was beleagured by an unemployment rate of 12%-13%. To help alleviate the problem, Magnuson wanted to pass a bill extending unemployment compensation an additional 26 weeks in areas with extremely high unemployment. Since the Administration opposed the measure, Magnuson tried that oldest of Senatorial ploys: an amendment to a bill that the Administration desperately wanted. In this case, it was the bill stepping up tax cuts and restoring the investment credit.

That should have been the end of it. But Magnuson was far from through. He then began to press the Congressional power levers he knows so well. Within a few hours of the committee vote, he sidled up to his old friend, Russell Long, Chairman of the Finance Committee, bemoaning the fate of the unemployed in Seattle. Left unmentioned were all the favors that Magnuson had done for Long over the years, like giving Long, whose state boasts the bustling port of New Orleans, the chairmanship of the Commerce Committee's Subcommittee on the Merchant Marine. Long remembered an obscure bill dealing with unemployment, already passed by the House, that had been languishing in his committee. If Magnuson wanted to attach his amendment to this bill, Long offered to try and push it out of committee in the few weeks remaining before adjournment.

That night Magnuson called his friends on the Finance Committee urging them to attend a meeting Long had called for the following morning. The Committee voted out the bill the next day, and Magnuson had the vehicle to which his amendment could be added on the Senate floor. Then he made a rare pilgrimage to the House side of the Capitol to call on Wilbur Mills. The canny Ways and Means Chairman, fully aware of Magnuson's power to return the favor, agreed to let the amendment through his committee. Magnuson, ever the pragmatist, told Mills that if Ways and Means became balky, he could go along with a compromise of thirteen weeks' additional unemployment compensation instead of 26.

Then came another hurdle: No legislation was being considered because the Senate was tied up in extended debate over President Nixon's Supreme Court nominations. So Magnuson went to Majority Leader Mansfield, who agreed to interrupt the Supreme Court debate if Magnuson could get his amendment through in thirty minutes without debate or a roll call. That afternoon, co-ordinating signals with Mansfield and Long, Magnuson offered his amendment.

But there was still a final roadblock: Senator Carl Curtis, a conservative Ne-braska Republican, objected. Magnuson went over, placed his arm on Curtis' shoulder and spoke quietly to him for a few minutes. Nobody knows what was said, but Curtis shrugged and withdrew his objections. The bill and the Mag-nuson amendment sailed through.[60]

One conclusion that we can draw from such a narrative is that the need for cooperative effort and uncertainty about the precise composition of any particular winning coalition make senatorial bargaining necessary, dilute the power of the most entrenched, and enhance tremendously the powers of all senators, however low on the totem pole.

Senators, moreover, do not agree unanimously about the relative de-sirability of different institutional positions. Although at the extremes it is possible to rank committees according to their apparent desirability, there are considerable gray areas. This can be illustrated by comparing two at-tempts to rank Senate committees in order of their attractiveness to senators (Table 5). In the first column, which was calculated by Donald Matthews, committees are ranked according to the average seniority of the senators newly appointed to each committee from the Eightieth through the Eighty-fourth Congresses.[61] The reasoning here is that the committees attracting the senior members would be more desirable, first, because seniors would be likeliest to know which committees were most important and, second, because their seniority would make it possible for them to win appointment, even though competition were keen for vacant seats. In the second column, showing George Goodwin's findings, committees are ranked by their net gain or loss of members due to transfers of senators from the Eighty-first through the Eighty-fifth Congresses, corrected for the overall size of com-mittees.[62] The reasoning behind this tabulation is quite similar to that for the first—presumably senators migrate toward desirable committees and away from undesirable ones. Column III corresponds to the first column, and column IV to the second, using data comparing the ninety-seventh and ninety-eighth Congresses (1981-1982, 1983-1984). It is clear that, if any-thing, choices have become more dispersed in recent years.[63]

Part of the dissimilarities among the lists can be explained away by the narrowness of differences in the raw data on which the rankings are based. However, it is interesting to reflect that committees low on both

TABLE 5   Senate Committees Ranked According to Two Criteria of Desirability[a]

I	II
1. Foreign Relations	1. Foreign Relations
2. Appropriations	2. Finance
3. Finance	3. Commerce
4. Agriculture	4. Judiciary
5. Armed Services	5. Appropriations
6. Judiciary	6. Armed Services
7. Commerce	7. Agriculture
8. Banking	8. Interior
9. Rules	9. Banking
10. Interior	10. Labor and Public Welfare
11. Post Office	11. Public Works
12. Public Works	12. Government Operations
13. Government Operations	13. Rules
14. District of Columbia	14. Post Office
15. Labor and Public Welfare	15. District of Columbia

III	IV
1. Appropriations	1. Labor and Human Resources
2. Rules and Administration	2. Rules and Administration
3. Armed Services	3. Banking, Housing, and Urban Affairs
4. Environment and Public Works	4. Foreign Relations
5. Veterans' Affairs	5. Agriculture, Nutrition, and Forestry
6. Finance	6. Armed Services
7. Energy and Natural Resources	7. Finance
8. Agriculture, Nutrition, and Forestry	8. Appropriations
9. Governmental Affairs	9. Budget
10. Labor and Human Resources	10. Commerce, Science, and Transportation
11. Foreign Relations	11. Environment and Public Works
12. Banking, Housing, and Urban Affairs	12. Governmental Affairs
13. Budget	13. Judiciary
14. Commerce, Science, and Transportation	14. Veterans' Affairs
15. Judiciary	15. Energy and Natural Resources

[a] Space Committee, created 1958, omitted.

earlier lists—Government Operations, Labor and Public Welfare, and Public Works—provided major sources of power in the past for senators as disparate as Robert Kerr and Patrick McNamara, Joseph McCarthy and John McClellan, John Kennedy and Lister Hill. There are, in other words, several ways in which a post can come to be desirable.

When a senator brings unusual skill, resourcefulness, or luck to seemingly minor posts in the institution, sometimes he is remarkably and disproportionately rewarded. Senators Joseph McCarthy and Estes Kefauver, on strikingly different missions, catapulted themselves to national prominence, which they preferred to popularity within the Senate, by imaginative use of minor subcommittees to which they fell heir rather early in their senatorial careers. Brian McMahon, Thomas Hennings, and Henry Jackson carved out unlikely empires, small but significant, by making themselves specialists in atomic energy, constitutional rights, and national security policy machinery respectively.[64]

The division of labor in the Senate has a curiously ad hoc quality: roles within the Senate are as much adopted by senators when it suits their interests as they are doled out by institutional forces beyond the control of individuals. There are two senses in which the term *role* may be used. In one sense, roles are job descriptions; the Senate has members who primarily investigate the executive branch, members who speak to the society at large, members who specialize in a wide variety of substantive policy areas, members who seek primarily to deliver Federal funds to their home state, members who engage mostly in backstage politicking and legislative coalition-building, and so on. Role also refers to the stable expectations that develop around the ways people fit into the informal society of group life; the Senate has its sages, its clowns, its mavericks, its fools. The number of senators who are distinctively placed in job roles is almost certainly quite high; the number who are distinctively located in the informal social life of the Senate is almost certainly quite low. All groups of any substantial size have their deviant members, but the existence of mavericks does not necessarily demonstrate the existence of an inner club.

MAVERICKS

Because mavericks[65] frequently have vivid personalities and do unusual things, reporters pay attention to them. Besides, watching the deviant members of any group can bring the characteristics of normal behavior into sharper focus and this helps outside observers to understand the group and its norms. In a place like the Senate, one is tempted to assume that unconventional members are without much influence over others. But this is not necessarily true of Senate mavericks. Indeed, because they are willing to go to great lengths to get what they want, mavericks may sometimes wind up having more real power than they at first seem to have.

What are mavericks like? Is there such a thing as a typical maverick? Probably not; senatorial mavericks at one time or another have exhibited a variety of behavior patterns and these have proceeded from a variety of causes. Some behavior that is regarded as deviant in the U.S. Senate would undoubtedly be regarded as deviant anywhere; excessive drinking is one obvious example. In general, however, senators regard themselves as part of a working body rather than a social club. For this reason, they may take notice of behavior that impairs the functioning of the legislative process but ignore behavior that might be regarded as extremely deviant in the society at large or in a purely social organization. One example is the Senate's treatment of the notorious Senator Joseph McCarthy of Wisconsin. William S. White says:

> The whole history of the Institution shows this general view of Senatorial conduct: First a strong disinclination to proceed at all against *any* Senator . . . It was this tradition that lay at the bottom of the Senate's long hesitation before it dealt with Senator Joseph R. McCarthy of Wisconsin . . . When . . . he was at length condemned . . . it was for purely *Senatorial* offenses.[66]

Repeatedly attacking the leadership of one's own party in the Senate, failing to keep one's bargains, extreme intractability or stubbornness or uncooperativeness, unwillingness to "listen to reason," conducting interminable one-man campaigns in behalf of hobbyhorse projects—these may be regarded as deviant behavior patterns by senators within the context of the network of informal clearances, courtesies, obligations, and loyalties that facilitate the work of the institution.[67] Senators who frequently exhibit one or more of them may come to be regarded as mavericks. They may be mavericks because of their psychological needs and predispositions, their political principles, the expectations of meaningful segments of their constituencies, or for any combination of reasons. The result is that they engage in behavior thought to be inappropriate for the conduct of business or disruptive of relationships regarded by most members as necessary, stable, and enduring.

A keen understanding of the accommodative nature of legislative activity, where, after all, a majority of senators must be marshaled in order to pass legislation, is widespread in the Senate. Senators also understand the general run of pressures—of time, of obligation, and so on—that is their common lot. Inattention to these facts of political life is quite understandably regarded as deviant. An example of such deviance is illustrated in a case study:

> The hearings became what it would be fair to call tedious. A contribution to tedium was Senator Malone (R-Nevada); nearly three-fifths of the record— that is, 1,200 pages of testimony—resulted from his questions and statements. [Witnesses were largely] confined to saying in answer to these statements, "That is right," and Malone through his remarks made the bulk of the record. Frequently the chairman urged Malone to speed up, but to no avail. Evening sessions were conducted, at which it appears that frequently Senator Malone alone was present to interrogate witnesses and hear testimony . . . Even his colleagues became irritated with him; his most acrimonious run-ins were with two [likely allies].
>
> [On the final vote, the side he favored] was the victim of Malone's own intransigence. He was against reciprocal trade for "Three years, two years, one year or three minutes." The ethos of a parliamentary body was lost on

him. Like most laymen outside the Capitol, he saw the issue as a bipolar one
. . . Malone was the sort of man— laudable in the public arena but indigestible
in a negotiatory decision-making body—whose decision rule on voting was
simple. He voted for what he believed in and against what he opposed [but
in this case causing his own side to lose].[68]

In the main, and as this example illustrates, most of the harm that
comes to mavericks in the Senate—if, indeed, any harm comes to them—
is self-inflicted. Ralph Huitt has demonstrated that the Senate is an extremely hospitable place, which perforce tolerates a wide range of personal
styles rather comfortably and which permits senators to respond in whatever
way they think best to the multiplicity of demands their variegated constituencies place upon them.[69] In the modern Senate it is only when an unusual
senator meets an unusual political situation that trouble develops. Thus
Senator Wayne Morse of Oregon ran afoul of a hairline party split when in
1953, in a most unusual act, he left the Republican party and became an
Independent. He was not reappointed to his old committees. "The Republican leadership denied any wish to discipline Morse. What they wanted was
to control the Senate. As [Senate Majority Leader Robert] Taft pointed out,
the Republican margin was paper-thin; with Morse an Independent the
Senate division stood at 48-47-1."[70] Morse was dropped from his committees
by the Republicans because otherwise they could not have controlled majorities on those committees under the terms of the Legislative Reorganization Act, which apportions committee assignments according to the overall
party ratio in the Senate. So Morse was left places on what were regarded
that year as the two least important committees, Public Works and District
of Columbia. These assignments did Morse no permanent harm, however:
"Wayne Morse received better committee assignments from the Democrats
[two years later] in 1955, just before he joined their party, than he had lost
two years earlier."[71]

PARTY LEADERSHIP: LYNDON JOHNSON'S SECRETS OF SUCCESS

The wide and generous distribution of power in the Senate and the relative
geniality with which deviants are tolerated suggest that devices for coordinating the work of the institution are weak indeed. In some respects they
are weak, but they exist, and in dedicated and capable hands they can be
made to yield impressive results.

Many devices for coordinating the Senate are the product of tacit
bargains, mutual adjustments, individual clearances, and other piecemeal
accommodations among senators. These are necessary because the division
of labor parcels out power over such a variety of substantive problems in

so many different directions. A second source of coordination for senatorial behavior arises out of the party loyalties and partisan (and sometimes ideological) identifications that most senators, as intensely political people, bring to the institution. If unanimous or nearly unanimous sentiment fails to coordinate voting, party loyalty of a voluntary kind has a major impact.

Beyond these tacit and institutional factors and in spite of the wide diffusion of senatorial power, one office, that of Majority Leader, is or can be preeminent. The Majority Leader is in charge of getting a legislative program—usually the President's—through the Senate. The powers to stall, amend, modify, and block legislation—in short, *negative* powers—are widely distributed in the Senate. The power and the responsibility to get things done, especially big things, is predominantly in the hands of party leaders. Other senators recognize that their leaders, who are elected by their respective senatorial party caucuses, have this responsibility; yet the specific tools they place in the Majority Leader's hands to help him do this job are not overly impressive. A variety of tasks that must be routinely performed in the Senate, such as placing senators on committees or making up an agenda for floor action, provide the main strategic opportunities for the party leadership. This is particularly true when these routine functions are used to put together legislative proposals that are satisfactory to a majority coalition or when they are used to round up hard-to-find but necessary votes.

The Republican and Democratic parties in the Senate handle their routine functions somewhat differently. This difference has consequences for the powers of the party floor leaders. The Republicans traditionally spread their formal powers more thinly about: one senator acts as floor leader; another acts as his assistant; a third chairs the Policy Committee, which acts as a reasonably coherent party voice on the legislative agenda; a fourth senator heads the Republican Committee on Committees; a fifth has the honor of chairing the caucus of all Republican senators; and a sixth acts as chairman of the Republican Senatorial Campaign Committee. On the Democratic side, the floor leader chairs the caucus, the Policy Committee (on agenda), and the Steering Committee (on committee assignments). He has an assistant, also known as the Whip, and there is a secretary to the caucus, also nominally a leadership position. The Campaign Committee is also run somewhat independently.[72]

By common consent, the most effective Majority Leader to serve in recent times was Lyndon Johnson, Democrat of Texas, who led his party in the Senate from 1953 to 1960.[73] An examination of his success in this job will be helpful in understanding the Senate, the legislative process, and, more generally, the process of government in the United States.

It is possible to explain at least part of Johnson's formidable reputation historically. He was Majority Leader under quite unusual and, on the whole, quite favorable circumstances. President Eisenhower, whose term of office coincided with Johnson's period as Democratic leader, wanted very little in the way of new legislation from the Senate, and, being of the opposing party, Eisenhower was entitled to only a modicum of cooperation from the Democratic majorities of 1954 to 1960. This situation left Johnson free to set his own priorities and pursue goals comfortably within reach. There was no necessity to do what a Majority Leader of a President's own party must do—extend his energies and spend his influence in behalf of a schedule of priorities and demands that are not his own and that could be strategically more difficult to accomplish. The Speaker of the House was Johnson's old friend, mentor, and fellow Texan, Sam Rayburn. Sometimes legislative proposals that would have created difficulties for the Senate Majority Leader could be effectively bottled up in the House. Finally, just by chance, William S. White, another fellow Texan, good friend, and strong partisan of Johnson's, was during Johnson's stewardship covering the Senate for the *New York Times.* This gave the Majority Leader handsome and timely recognition, something rarely accorded legislative leaders in the predominantly President-oriented news media of America. Thus moderate external demands and an exceptional array of coincidental extrasenatorial resources helped Johnson achieve preeminence as a senatorial leader.

It would be incorrect to suggest, however, that on this account Johnson's reputation was unmerited. A variety of political skills and abilities made it possible for him to use his advantages and his resources with great success. Among these resources were his phenomenal energy, which he used, quite consciously, to maintain daily communication with almost every Democratic senator. Many social psychologists and some political scientists define leadership as centrality in a communications network.[74] Johnson, in effect, made himself the leader by putting himself at the center of an enormous number of bargains in the Senate, especially bargains concerning the allocation of time in the chamber and the division of labor. These bargains, in turn, ramified in several directions. Notably, they gave Johnson a tremendous head start at being at the center of bargains over policy. He was in a position to know more about the relative intensities of senators' preferences on a variety of issues; in this way, he could create coalitions of senators who would never have thought to get together on their own but who, under Johnson's guidance, could be brought together to help one another on projects important to them. In return, they would give Johnson support on items that for them mattered less.

Any leader who performs this brokerage function for a while is bound to become reasonably skilled at it, and Johnson profited enormously from his on-the-job training in legislative maneuvering. At the same time, he built up a deposit of goodwill for favors done in the past. This, in turn, could be invested to produce bigger and better results for senators who then would feel obligated to help with the "tough ones," and so it went. Johnson himself was not unaware of the process. He once described how he worked to Arthur Schlesinger, Jr.:

> The Treatment began immediately: a brilliant, capsule characterization of every Democratic Senator, his strengths and failings, where he fit into the political spectrum; how far he could be pushed, how far pulled; his hates, his loves. And who (he asked Schlesinger) must oversee all these prima donnas, put them to work, knit them together, know when to tickle this one's vanity, inquire of that one's health, remember this one's five o'clock nip of Scotch, that one's nagging wife? Who must find the hidden legislative path between the South and the North, the public power men and the private power men, the farmers' men and the unions' men, the bomber-boys and the peace-lovers, the eggheads and the fatheads?[75]

Another quality of Johnson's that seems to have contributed to his success as Majority Leader was a relative indifference to most policy outcomes coupled with an interest in finding constructive legislative solutions even in the face of considerable disagreement among his colleagues on the substance of policy. To Senator Johnson, public policy evidently was an inexhaustibly bargainable product. Few issues incited him to intransigence, and thus he could arrange for solutions and compromises that would have been unimaginable to an equally constructive but a more substantively committed man. Having few strong policy preferences, Johnson could also expedite the inevitable without regret. Doing this gave him a reputation for being on the winning side, which was another resource at his command, because he could sometimes use this reputation as a bluff and get away with it.

Party leaders in the Senate are not without inducements—a coveted committee assignment, perhaps, or an appointment to an honorific commission whose meetings will be held in Paris or Bermuda, or a pet bill rescued from oblivion, or an accommodation in the schedule. The Senate is, after all, an ongoing institution that meets continuously. There are many routine ways in which senators can make one another's lives pleasant or inconvenient if they choose to do so, and these opportunities generally come more often to the party leaders, who are the custodians of Senate routine.[76] On the whole, however, these inducements are small change in the busy lives of senators.

It should be added that Johnson's successors have not chosen to operate a centralized leadership in Johnson's whirlwind fashion. They have not exercised much of the power to manipulate the routines of Senate debate. Frequently they have refrained from indicating a preference whenever a fight has developed, as it has on several occasions, for lesser positions in the Democratic leadership. They have encouraged extensive and open deliberation in the party conference and have relinquished much of the power Johnson had assembled to influence committee assignments. These are now determined in part by a semiautomatic matching up by the staff of senators' preferences with vacancies, and in part by political maneuvering within the Democratic Steering Committee of ideologically like-minded blocs of senators.[77]

SUMMARY: COORDINATION AND DECENTRALIZATION

We can summarize our discussion of power and leadership in the Senate by noting resemblances between the Senate and any sizable group of human beings who meet and do business together fairly often. We can think of the Senate not as an institution controlled by a small group of powerful senators surrounded by everyone else, but as a group that divides labor and power— unequally to be sure, but still significantly—among almost all its members. Some of its members are regarded as deviants and mavericks, and some of these enjoy less personal prestige, but even they are not necessarily powerless. The ties of party, regional interest, and policy preference are the ones that bind senators to one another in coalitions. Personal tastes and habits play a part, of course, as they do in shaping the ways senators do their jobs and approach their constituencies and the executive branch.

Despite a number of devices that party leaders have at their disposal to concentrate power in the Senate in their own hands, the forces making for decentralization of power in the Senate are even more striking. When partisan or factional lines are drawn closely, each senator's support on legislation becomes more valuable and can be quite difficult to obtain, if senators choose to make the lives of their leaders miserable.

Decentralization of power is also reflected in the committee system, which parcels out substantive legislation entirely to bipartisan committees, run almost exclusively according to seniority. Within their domains, the committees are quite beyond any but the most perfunctory control of the parent body. Senators are expected to specialize in this aspect of their work, surely the only rational possibility in a time when issues are complex and require technical mastery as well as wisdom. These people are extremely busy and so they not only specialize themselves in one or two subjects but also rely on fellow specialists in matters in which they are not competent. Reciprocity on substantive questions of public policy as well as in matters of housekeeping is regarded in the Senate as a necessary condition of life.

Coordination is accomplished mainly through party loyalty and party leadership. Party leaders depend especially on the cooperation of committee chairmen and the President. When they are in agreement, party leaders can exercise great power. They have control over the agenda and over the machinery for rounding up votes within the Senate. Rank-and-file senators recognize that party leaders may legitimately use this machinery in behalf of the program of the party and especially in behalf of measures high on the priority list of the President. Senate party leaders also exercise influence in the allocation of committee assignments, and they often have access to extrasenatorial sources of influence, such as those found in the executive agencies. Finally, changes in the Senate's position in the political system have made for decentralization. Staff play a much more significant hand in the structuring of decisions than heretofore, as well as in fortifying senators for the multiple public roles that they increasingly play. Senators now seek to cultivate national constituencies on their own, receive great amounts of publicity, and are more likely than heretofore to find independent advocacy more satisfying than coordinated legislative activity.

chapter 4

THE HOUSE
OF REPRESENTATIVES

On April 3, 1964, Everett G. Burkhalter, a Democratic Representative in Congress from California, announced that he would not be a candidate for election to a second term. In an illuminating statement to the press, the California congressman explained why: "I could see I wasn't going to get any place. Nobody listens to what you have to say until you've been here 10 or 12 years. These old men have got everything so tied down you can't do anything. There are only about 40 out of the 435 members who call the shots. They're the committee chairmen and the ranking members and they're all around 70 or 80."[1]

A little over ten years later, after a landslide election, seventy-five newly elected Democratic members appeared in the House of Representatives. By then, a series of reforms had begun to change the congressional landscape. At the party caucus that met to organize the Ninety-fourth Congress, Democrats voted by secret ballot to depose three committee chairmen. A fourth voluntarily stepped aside after publicly embarrassing himself in a series of incidents attributed to alcoholism. A leader of the newcomers said: "The winds of change have arrived at the House."[2] A congressional freshman added: "The reforms of two and four years ago set the stage.... There were enough votes now that the changes came fairly rapidly."[3]

It was not altogether clear, however, even a decade afterward, what lasting impact these changes would have. Clearly, the House has been evolving new patterns of power over the last twenty years, and these new patterns have great significance for the way the House functions in the national government. Nevertheless, it must be said that the individual representative remains far less visible than even the beginning senator. A newly elected senator enters immediately into the big whirl of Washington social and political life. He and his brethren[4] sit four notches up the table from their House colleagues according to the strict protocol of Capitol society.[5] His comings and goings are likely to be chronicled by the society pages. The press releases prepared by his sizable staff often find their way into print. He frequently joins in the well-publicized debates on public policy that the Senate stages from time to time. He is a member of several committees and is consulted when the business of the Senate touches concerns of his own, as, for example, when a presidential appointment from his party and his state is scheduled for confirmation. If he wants to take the trouble to present a fairly convincing case, he can block the appointment by saying that the prospective appointee is personally unacceptable to him. This action invokes "senatorial courtesy." His colleagues can be counted on to protect his position in the party politics of his home state by voting against the nominee.

The visibility and eminence of senators makes the Senate a less than cosy place to do business. Each senator is to a certain degree the product of his staff and what they do for him. He is exposed to public inspection both at home and in Washington, is quite often active in the politics of his home state, and, in short, is a public personage with numerous, diverse, pressing public obligations and connections. In such circumstances, the norms of the Senate, powerful as it is as a social institution, cannot reach senators and shape their behavior in the same sense that the norms of the House can shape the behavior of the relatively anonymous individuals who labor there.

Compared with the Senate the House is a big institution, consisting of 435 members, allocated among the states according to their populations. Each member runs for election every two years, in a single-member district whose boundaries are established by the legislatures of the various states. Collectively, the House is quite as powerful as the Senate. Both houses share fully the power to legislate; bills must pass each house in order to become laws. The Senate alone has the power of confirmation, giving it the right to advise and consent to major presidential appointments. And the Senate alone ratifies treaties. The House has other advantages, however. Under the Constitution, it originates all bills raising revenue, which means all tax bills, tariff bills, and bills pertaining to the social security system (because of the revenue-raising aspect of the latter types of legislation). By an extension of this constitutional privilege, bills appropriating money to run the Federal government also start in the House. The mere privilege of initiating bills does not mean they cannot be changed in the Senate, but the power of initiation does set the terms of legislation, often suggesting limits beyond which the Senate cannot go if it wishes bills on a given subject to pass at all. The House enjoys another advantage. Because of its size, it can apportion work among more hands than can the Senate. One result is that the House has developed over the years a corps of members who are devoted subject-matter experts to a degree quite unusual in the Senate.

Busy senators, due at three meetings at once, must rely to a much greater extent on their staff.[6] House members can dig into subject matter themselves. The mastery of subject matter on the House side of the Capitol is conspicuously displayed in the appropriations process (to be discussed in Chapter 6), but it also crops up in other matters. For example, Robert Kastenmeier, chairman of the relevant subcommittee of the House Judiciary Committee, is the reigning expert in the field of copyright law. Les Aspin's hard work has made him the House's contemporary virtuoso performer on disarmament policy. These and others like them are the contemporary successors of a long line of House subject-matter specialists whose unpublicized but enormously influential work is recorded in the laws of the land: other examples from recent history are Wilbur Mills and Barber Conable on taxes, Francis E. Walter on immigration, Albert Rains on housing, Charles A. Mosher and Emilio Daddario on science, John Fogarty and Paul Rogers on health, and Carl Elliott on education.

On the whole, individual rank-and-file representatives must be regarded as somewhat less powerful than individual senators. Internally, power in the House is today held by a larger group than Representative Burkhalter said—perhaps as many as half of the total membership.[7] So large a bipartisan group is seldom united, and except for the party leaders its members generally concern themselves only with sharply limited areas of public policy. On such a matter as making up the schedule of activity on the floor, Senate Majority and Minority Leaders customarily touch bases with all senators who ask to be consulted on a given question. In the House, on the other hand, only those members who, because of their committee assignments, are legitimately concerned with a piece of legislation are normally consulted when the schedule for debate is arranged. We also may contrast the unlimited debate of the Senate with the strictly controlled debate in the House. In the House, the most senior committee members act as the managers of bills flowing from their committee to the floor. They allocate among themselves and other members limited segments of time, as suits their preferences and strategies as well as the demands of members, usually according to a formula dividing time equally between the parties, with driblets of time going mostly to majority and minority members of the relevant committee. As far as the preferences of individual members are concerned, floor action resembles a car pool in the Senate, a bus line in the House. The Senate runs by unanimous consent; the House, by a codified set of rules.

THE SPEAKER

It would be foolish to conclude that the Senate is the more powerful body because the average senator is likely to have more powers than the average representative. Buses are, after all, capable of moving passengers as far and as fast as car pools. Hence it is necessary to inquire into the identity of the driver. We look first to the Speaker of the House as a center of power. The Speaker, by tradition and practice the active leader of the majority party in the house, the "elect of the elect," second in succession to the Presidency, occupies an office of great prestige and importance in the Federal government. An examination of power in the House would naturally begin with him.

Woodrow Wilson wrote in 1884 about the impressive powers residing in the office of Speaker.

> The Speaker is expected to constitute the Committees in accordance with his own political views ... [and he] generally uses his powers as freely and imperatively as he is expected to use them. He unhesitatingly acts as the legislative chief of his party, organizing the Committees in the interest of this or that policy, not covertly or on the sly, as one who does something of which he is ashamed, but openly and confidently, as one who does his duty.[8]

At that time, the Speaker also sat as chairman of the then five-man Rules Committee, which controls the flow of legislation to the floor of the House. In 1885, however, once legislation reached the floor, the Speaker's control was severely diminished, largely because of the "disappearing quorum," a time-honored device that members used to delay or defeat legislation. Because a quorum consists of an absolute majority of the whole House of Representatives, any large minority could halt the business of the House indefinitely by suggesting the absence of a quorum: even though they were present in the chamber, they would simply not answer to their names when the roll was called. Normally, doing this was enough to stall business.

In 1890 Speaker Thomas Reed abolished the disappearing quorum. He called off to the tally clerk the names of those members he saw in the chamber who had not answered to a roll call. This tactic caused a huge uproar, but after four days of battle Reed was sustained by a vote that, in effect, went along party lines. Soon afterward, a new set of rules, composed by Reed, was adopted. It changed the quorum required for the Committee of the Whole from a majority of the House to 100 members, thus making it much easier to do business on the floor. In addition, all members present could be counted by the Speaker, and the Speaker was given powers to declare motions as dilatory and hence out of order. Later, the constitutionality of these rules was upheld in the Supreme Court, and when the Democrats next controlled the House, in the following Congress, they themselves used the Republican Reed's rules.[9]

From the Fifty-first to the Sixty-first Congresses (1890-1910) the Speaker was clearly supreme in the House. Reed had added the effective control of floor action to the formidable arsenal of weapons off the floor that had previously been at the Speaker's disposal. But a Republican successor, Joseph Cannon (Speaker, 1905-1910), fell victim to the splits within the majority party which eventually led to the formation of the Bull Moose and Progressive parties. In 1910 the House of Representatives' experiment with strict majoritarianism and party discipline was terminated with a revolt against Speaker Cannon by a coalition of Democrats and Progressive Republicans led by George Norris of Nebraska.[10] A former parliamentarian of the House and congressman comments:

> The power of the Speakership in the halcyon days of Reed and [Joseph] Cannon lay principally in three rules: the appointment of the Committees of the House, chairmanship and control of the Committee on Rules, and the arbitrary powers of recognition....
>
> The revision [of the rules] of 1911 was the most drastic since the promulgation of Jefferson's Manual. The power to appoint committees was taken from the Speaker; he was made ineligible for membership on the Committee on Rules and the power of recognition was circumscribed by the Calendar Wednesday Rule, the Consent Calendar, the Discharge Calendar and restoration to the minority of the right to move to recommit.[11]

Curiously, the Reed rules were not a casualty of this episode; to this day the Speaker has substantial powers to monitor floor debate. Most of the weapons Reed gained have remained securely within the control of the Speaker, but the weapons Reed already *had* passed from the Speaker's grasp.

Today, the Speaker has regained considerable power. This is a phenomenon of the 1970s, a result of electoral shifts that reduced the number of conservative Southerners in the Democratic caucus and augmented the number of Northern liberals. For the first time since the early New Deal, mainstream Democratic sentiment such as could be found in the presidential wing of the party dominated the Democratic caucus. The caucus, in a series of structural reforms, took power away from committee chairmen and gave power to subcommittees and to the Speaker.

Among the Speaker's new prerogatives were (1) sole discretion to appoint members to the House Committee on Rules, the committee that regulates the flow of business to the floor of the House; (2) discretion to refer bills to more than one committee, concurrently or serially; (3) the chairmanship of the Democratic Committee on Committees. An old prerogative that took on new meaning was his leadership of the caucus itself.

The first Speaker to enjoy these new powers was Thomas P. (Tip) O'Neill of Massachusetts, a genial veteran of the Rules Committee who had come up the ladder as Democratic Whip and Majority Leader behind Hale Boggs of Louisiana. Over the last half century, Northern urban Democrats have for the most part alternated with Southern populists in the leadership of the Democratic party. The Speaker is elected by the majority caucus, as is his next in command (and, as it has turned out, next in succession as well), the Majority Leader. Until January 1985, when the position became an elected one, these two leaders in turn appointed the Whip, who in the normal course of events has found himself well situated to run for Majority Leader once that position is vacated. Thus O'Neill was appointed by Boggs as Whip and became Majority Leader when Boggs was lost in an airplane crash. When the Speaker, Carl Albert of Oklahoma, retired in 1977, O'Neill moved up the next notch to become Speaker. Albert's career showed the same pattern; he had originally been appointed Whip by one of the great figures of congressional history, the formidable Sam Rayburn of Texas, who was Speaker for 16 years, during which time the Speakership was relatively weak in comparison with today.

Rayburn, the "indestructible, imperishable and indomitable,"[12] was not, however, a weak man. He possessed enormous legislative skill, great rectitude, and earthy charm. He sat in the House for nearly fifty years, accumulating knowledge, friendships, and political debtors. Rayburn had no wife or family, only a career in the House, which he pursued with fierce concentration. He could gain legislative results not only because he was Speaker, but because he was Rayburn. None of his successors, not even O'Neill with the augmented powers of the Speaker at his disposal, would have the chance to build the personal following that through luck, time, and his own peculiar genius made Rayburn within the limits of his era an effective Speaker.

The Speaker today has many weapons, small and not so small, that he can use to influence the course of legislation. As chief executive of the House for its internal business, he can help his friends by allocating to them extra office space or recommending them favorably to the committee of his party that distributes minor patronage appointments on the Capitol grounds. He can provide members with access to executive agencies in behalf of their projects "back home," an edge that might make a difference in a difficult election campaign. He can help members of his party improve their committee assignments by exerting his influence in his party's committee on committees, and in the case of the Rules Committee, whose members he appoints, he can exercise even more direct influence. He can speed a member's pet bill through the unanimous consent process or through suspension of the rules. He can enhance a member's prestige in the House by asking him to preside over the Committee of the Whole, and he can increase a member's political opportunities and contacts by appointing him to one or more of the various public boards, commissions, and delegations on which members of Congress serve—the annual delegation to the International Parliamentary Union, the board of the Woodrow Wilson Centennial Commission, and so on. These perquisites are not without their importance in a world where political careers and fortunes rise and fall as the result of unknown combinations of minor accidents and contingencies.

COMMITTEE AND SUBCOMMITTEE CHAIRMEN

The chairmen of the 22 standing committees have not escaped the reforms of the mid-1970s; indeed, they have been the big losers as their autonomy has been circumscribed in a number of important ways: (1) They must form subcommittees, a minimum of four for any committee having more than 20 members; (2) they must refer all incoming bills promptly to a subcommittee; (3) they may not chair more than one subcommittee themselves and even this occurs only if their party colleagues on the committee elect them in a secret ballot; (4) they may not monopolize control over committee staff, which, since the reforms, are largely hired and fired at the subcommittee level.[13]

The combined effects of these reforms have been to push power downward in the system, toward subcommittees and their chairmen, and upward toward the Speaker. In the last big reform before the 1970s, which took place in 1946, the committee chairmen had been the big winners. In January 1947, under the Legislative Reorganization Act of 1946, the number of committees was drastically reduced from about 47 to 21, and their legislative tasks were clarified. This act served to reduce materially the discretion of the Speaker in assigning bills to committees, because it did away with most of the shadow areas where two or more committees shared jurisdictions. Previously, the Speaker could kill bills by routing them to unfavorable committees and could save bills by sending them to favorable committees, when more than one option existed.[14] The reorganization made this much more difficult, and at the same time it strengthened the hand of committee chairmen.

Most congressional committees have divided into many subcommittees since the reorganization of 1946, and these look less to the Speaker than to the chairmen of the full committees for leadership. As the chairmen lost significant influence in the 1970s, subcommittees have gained autonomy with respect to staffing and subject-matter jurisdictions; thus it is increasingly with the subcommittee chairmen, newly secure in their jurisdictions, now more frequently abetted by competent staff and highly specialized in their focus upon public policy, that power can be found in the House.[15]

The chairmen of committees in the House are formally elected by the whole House at the beginning of each Congress by nomination of the Majority Leader. Since 1919 they have virtually always been those persons of the majority party who are most senior in consecutive service on each committee.[16] Committee rank is counted by party and by committee service, not by service in the whole House. The chairmen are now only nominally the executive officers of the committees. More or less devolved to subcommittee chairmen are powers to hire and fire staff members, allocate the time and supervise the efforts of the staff, and substantially determine the business of the committee, as to both amount and content, subject to informal consultation with and persuasion from party leaders in the House, high officials of the executive branch, and, to an increasing extent, their own committee colleagues. After the Democratic caucus deposed several chairmen at the opening of the Ninety-fourth Congress, there appeared to be far less inclination among chairmen to risk the consequences of behaving in arbitrary or unresponsive ways toward significant numbers of their colleagues. Moreover changes in the rules governing the committees had materially reduced their power to do so.[17]

A few of the prerogatives left to the chairmen of committees, however, have proven useful in giving chairmen leverage over the work product of their committees. Chairmen are still exofficio members of all subcommittees. They have a major influence over subcommittee budgets, including the administrative budget that funds travel for all subcommittees. Subcommittee decisions to hire and fire staff, though mostly initiated by subcommittees, must be cleared through chairmen of the full committee in a process of consultation. Full committee chairmen may exercise editorial control over reports and press releases flowing from subcommittees. Also full committee chairmen may or may not move subcommittee business, such as bills emerg-

TABLE 6 Committees of the House of Representatives, 97th Congress, 1981–1982

COMMITTEE	NUMBER OF SUBCOMMITTEES	NUMBER OF MEMBERS
Agriculture	8	43
Appropriations	13	55
Armed Services	7	45
Banking, Finance, and Urban Affairs	8	45
Budget	0	30
District of Columbia	3	12
Education and Labor	8	34
Energy and Commerce	6	42
Foreign Affairs	8	37
Government Operations	7	40
House Administration	6	19
Interior and Insular Affairs	7	43
Judiciary	7	28
Merchant Marine and Fisheries	5	36
Post Office and Civil Service	7	27
Public Works and Transportation	6	46
Rules	2	16
Science and Technology	7	40
Small Business	5	40
Standards of Official Conduct	0	12
Veterans' Affairs	5	32
Ways and Means	6	35

(There are also several select committees, e.g., on Aging and on Intelligence; and joint committees, e.g., Economics, Library, Printing, and Taxation.)

TABLE 7   Committees of the House of Representatives, 97th Congress, 1981–1982

COMMITTEE	JURISDICTION
Agriculture	Agriculture generally, protection of birds and animals in forest reserves, crop insurance and soil conservation, dairy industry, farm credit, general forestry, human nutrition and home economics (food stamps), rural electrification, commodities exchanges.
Appropriations	Appropriation of the revenue for the support of the government.
Armed Services	Common defense generally, military pay, selective service, military application of nuclear energy, strategic and critical materials necessary for common defense, scientific R&D in support of the armed services.
Banking, Finance, and Urban Affairs	Banking and currency generally, deposit insurance, Federal Reserve System, gold and silver coinage, public and private housing, valuation of the dollar.
Budget	Concurrent resolutions on the budget, review of the operations of the Congressional Budget Office.
District of Columbia	All measures relating to the municipal affairs of D.C., other than appropriations.
Education and Labor	Education and labor generally, Child labor, labor standards and statistics, child nutrition, vocational rehabilitation, wages and hours of labor, work incentive programs.
Energy and Commerce	Interstate and foreign commerce generally, national energy policy generally, Department of Energy and Federal Energy Regulatory Commission, inland waterways, railroads, interstate and foreign communications, securities and exchanges, consumer affairs, travel and tourism, public health and quarantine, biomedical R&D.
Foreign Affairs	Relations of the U.S. with foreign nations generally, embassies, foreign loans, UN organizations, international economic policy, export controls.
Government Operations	Budget and accounting measures other than appropriations, reorganization in the executive branch, Federal procurement, general revenue sharing, review and examination of GAO recommendations, general oversight authority over all government programs.
House Administration	Employment of persons by the House, Library of Congress, Congressional Record printing, measures relating to accounts of the House generally, Federal elections generally.

TABLE 7 Committees of the House of Representatives, 97th Congress, 1981–1982 *(Continued)*

COMMITTEE	JURISDICTION
Interior and Insular Affairs	Forest reserves and national parks created from the public domain, Geological Survey, irrigation and reclamation, Indian affairs, military parks and battlefields, mineral land laws, mining interests generally, public lands generally, domestic nuclear energy industry regulation generally.
Judiciary	Civil and criminal judicial proceedings, bankruptcy, civil liberties, constitutional amendments, federal courts and judges, immigration, claims against U.S., patent and copyright, antitrust, national penitentiaries.
Merchant Marine and Fisheries	Merchant marine generally, oceanography and coastal zone management, Coast Guard, fisheries and wildlife, Panama Canal, international fishing agreements.
Post Office and Civil Service	Census and collection of statistics generally, all Federal Civil Service, Postal Service generally, Hatch Act, holidays and celebrations, population and demography.
Public Works and Transportation	Flood control and improvement of rivers and harbors, construction and maintenance of roads, pollution of navigable waters, public works (including dams and bridges), water power, transportation (except railroads), regulatory agencies (except ICC, Amtrack, and Federal Railroad Administration as they relate to railroads).
Rules	The rules and joint rules and order of business of the House.
Science and Technology	NASA, National Science Foundation, scientific R&D, National Weather Service, Bureau of Standards, environmental R&D, all energy R&D.
Small Business	Assistance to and protection of small business.
Standards of Official Conduct	Measures relating to the Code of Official Conduct.
Veterans' Affairs	Veterans' measures generally, veterans' cemeteries, VA hospitals, readjustment of servicemen to civilian life, compensation, education and vocational rehabilitation of veterans.
Ways and Means	Reciprocal trade agreements, revenue measures generally, the bonded debt of the U.S., deposit of public monies, tax-exempt foundations and charitable trusts, Social Security.

ing from subcommittees, with speed through the full committee stage of deliberation.[18]

Of the twenty-two committees of the House, three outrank all others in importance: the Rules Committee, whose agenda-making function is treated in the next chapter; the Committee on Appropriations, discussed in Chapter 6; and the Committee on Ways and Means.[19] The Ways and Means Committee originates all laws raising revenue, including tax laws, laws regulating foreign trade (because of their tariff aspect), and laws pertaining to the social security system (including medicare).[20] Because of the complexity of the bills this committee writes, and because of the temptation that exists for congressmen to add special exemptions and provisions to tax bills, legislation originating in the Ways and Means Committee normally comes before the House under rules of debate that limit amendments.

Tables 6 and 7 list the names of the standing committees and their jurisdictions. House committees under the Reorganization Act of 1946 were consolidated to provide unified supervision of particular executive departments and agencies.[21] This is not an ironclad arrangement, but it holds in general. The prestige of House committees to a certain extent is tied to the size of the agencies they supervise, the size being measured in terms of employees or, more often, in terms of the share of the Federal budget they spend. The importance of committees thus changes over time. When the Committee on Science and Astronautics was started in 1958, it was anticipated that the committee would not be important.[22] Its members originally were a few senior men who elected to leave high-ranked but subordinate places on other committees plus a large group of freshman members. In only five years the budget authorized by the Science Committee grew from $48 million to over $3.5 billion, essentially all of which was actually appropriated. Subsequently, the original chairman, a congressman not highly regarded by the leaders of his party, died; his replacement was more willing to share power with young and vigorous subcommittee chairmen. As the prestige and importance of the committee grew, nonfreshman members of both parties (including the Majority Leader) asked to be transferred to the committee. Then, as the space program slowed down in the 1970s, the Science and Astronautics Committee's prestige waned. By the 1980s, with a new name and enlarged jurisdiction including energy research and development, the Science and Technology Committee was on the rise again.

The effects of the Legislative Reorganization Act of 1970 and subsequent actions of the Democratic caucus have tended to reduce the powers of committee chairmen. "Each chairman," says one well-informed commentator, "is now theoretically regularly accountable to the full Democratic caucus. Control over subcommittee jurisdictions, chairmen, activities and powers now rests with subcommittee chairmen (who can be checked by the committee Democratic caucus) instead of committee chairmen, as previously.

Informal powers of persuasion are limited by the increasing openness of committee meetings.''[23]

Now all but two House committees, as Table 6 indicates, are divided into subcommittees.[24] Power on these subcommittees is determined in part by the personalities of the subcommittee chairmen and the ranking minority members, and how harmoniously they work together, and in part by the extent to which subcommittee business is at the focus of national political attention and activates the programmatic or ideological commitments of members and interested outsiders.

Until quite recently, chairmen had control over committee staffs: how many employees they hired, who they were, and what they did. The chairmen were well aware that numerous, competent, and active staff members led to a product quite different from the output of a corporal's guard of somnolent incompetents. A second source of a chairman's influence came through manipulating the division of labor among committee members. Chairmen, by custom, decided if there were to be subcommittees, whether subcommittees should have explicit jurisdictions, the extent to which subcommittees had adequate or competent staff aid, and who chaired and sat on subcommittees. These powers were not unlimited; custom also decreed that senior committee members should be consulted in the process and that minority assignments should be made by the "shadow" chairman, the ranking minority member.

It sometimes happened that members became chairmen of committees in areas where they were actually opposed to the enactment of legislation. In such a case, the powers of the chairman were used to obstruct, often with considerable success.[25] In other cases, a chairman was somewhat circumscribed because a majority of his committee (including both Democrats and Republicans) were out of sympathy with his views. In such an instance, the chairman had to proceed with care, because it was only custom that permitted him to run his committee without hindrance; more formally, the chairman was subject to majority rule within the committee. From time to time, chairmen saw their committees "taken away from them" on one or another issue. At least one chairman, Graham Barden of the Education and Labor Committee, resigned from Congress after his committee was packed with new members who supported liberal legislation for education and labor, as he did not.[26] By the beginning of the Ninety-fourth Congress a formidable arsenal of additional sanctions could be brought into play against chairmen by committee majorities. Chairman Harley Staggers of the House Committee on Interstate and Foreign Commerce, for example, was removed by his fellow Democrats on the committee from his chairmanship of the Investigations subcommittee. Each subcommittee was in addition given the power to set its own budget and agenda and hire its own staff.

COMMITTEE ASSIGNMENTS

The assignment of members to committees is one of the most significant activities not only for members, who after all must live with the results, but also for legislative outcomes and public policy. The process of committee assignments differs between the parties and is quite complicated for each.[27]

The Republicans have a Committee on Committees, consisting of one representative from each state that sends a Republican to Congress. Each representative votes with the strength of his state delegation—one vote apiece for Alaska or Vermont in the Ninety-eighth Congress, eleven votes for Ohio, fourteen for New York. The real business of this committee is conducted by a subcommittee, consisting mostly of representatives of the large state delegations plus one representative from the small states, all meeting with the party leader (the Minority Leader in recent Congresses). This subcommittee fills committee vacancies with freshmen and with members who are requesting transfer; they report back to the full committee, where their decisions are customarily ratified—because, after all, the subcommittee members have enough votes to win in the full committee. This process worked to the disadvantage of Republicans from small state delegations until a mini-rebellion took place in the 1970s. As a Republican freshman described it:

> Before, the senior guy from each of the big states—like Bob Wilson—would sit on the committee and cast seventeen votes because there are seventeen Republicans from California, whereas the members from states with only one Republican had only one member, Don Young.
>
> Young, from Alaska, would sit there, and he might represent fifteen single-state members, but he had only one vote, instead of fifteen, and that is the way it had been for sixty-five years. And there were all those one- and two- and three-member state delegations—the people that represent all those states were always appointed by the leader.
>
> But in a conference here a couple of weeks ago, we changed all that, so now it is one man, one vote. The guy from the one-member state will cast fifteen votes if that is how many members he represents, and the minority leader no longer has the power to appoint those people. We will caucus and choose them ourselves.
>
> So, instead of the big states—the top five or six, Ohio, California, and so forth—dominating all the key assignments henceforth, it will be one man, one vote, on the executive committee of the Committee on Committees.[28]

The qualifications of members are not irrelevant to the process. The Committee on Committees takes into account the career backgrounds of applicants, their district's interests, their seniority, and their reputation for "soundness," which means, in some cases, willingness to do business equably and, in others, adherence to conservative policy positions. It is not at all unheard of for senior members on key committees to check into the public records and private views of members who aspire to their committees.[29]

On the Republican side, then, each state delegation is formally represented in the committee assignment process. On the Democratic side, state delegations and their spokesmen are also important but are less formally engaged in decision-making. The Steering and Policy Committee of the caucus sits as the Democratic Committee on Committees. Its chairman is the Speaker (or, when the Democrats are in the minority, the Minority Leader). Other exofficio members are the Majority Leader, chairman of the campaign committee, the chairman and secretary of the caucus, and the chairmen of the Rules, Appropriations, Ways and Means, and Budget committees. In addition, there are nine members appointed by the Speaker: the Whip and four deputy whips, one representative from the freshman class of newly elected Democratic representatives, one representative from second- and third-term members, one from the Black Caucus (recently consisting of 21 Democratic members), one from among women Democratic members. The remaining 12 members are elected from geographic zones. All members of the committee are entitled to nominate representatives for vacancies on committees and to vote on nominations. In practice, however, the geographic zone representatives take the lead, especially in placing new members from their own parts of the country, of whom the rest of the committee members may have heard only slightly. Deans of state party delegations normally help their members in making a favorable case before the Committee on Committees.

State delegations are sometimes regarded as having title to certain committee posts by custom—Virginia, for example, long claimed two seats on the Agriculture Committee. When a valued seat on a committee falls vacant because of the death, defeat, or resignation of a member, all eyes automatically focus on the delegation of the departed member in the expectation that it will provide a suitable successor. Beside strict delegation succession, other criteria of suitability, including acceptability to party leaders—and to the rank and file, since assignments are ratified in the caucus—appropriate experience or training, and so on, are of course applied. Republican members' initial committee assignments are pretty much negotiated by the leadership, the heads of their delegations, ranking members of key committees, and the subcommittee of the Committee on Committees. Democratic members will confer with the party leadership, their state delegations, their geographic representative on the Committee on Committees, and all other members of the Committee on Committees as well. In both parties it is usually necessary for members to "run" for committee posts. Only members of large state delegations that are "entitled" to specific vacant seats can afford not to; other members must make a case to receive the assignment they desire, except when there is no competition for an assignment.

The importance of state delegations cannot be overemphasized. Some of the larger state delegations systematically distribute their members among important committees. For example, under Speaker Rayburn, the large Texas delegation (twenty-one Democrats in the Eighty-seventh Congress) did especially well. In the Eighty-eighth Congress, their first without the Speaker, they had a member on Rules; one on Ways and Means; two very senior men on appropriations; the chairmen of Veterans' Affairs, Banking and Currency, and House Administration; and other members strategically located. One small delegation, Arkansas, by virtue of good luck, long tenure (an advantage mostly accruing to one-party states), and, in several cases, the friendship of Mr. Rayburn, did nearly as well. Their four representatives in the Eighty-eighth Congress were the chairman of Ways and Means, the chairman of Commerce, a member of Rules, and the fourth-ranking member on Agriculture.

Another way of seeking advantage in committee assignments is represented by the Illinois Democratic delegation—an unusually cohesive bloc of fourteen votes in the Eighty-seventh Congress (1961-1963), consisting mostly of representatives sent to Congress from the territory of the Cook County (Chicago) Democratic machine. This delegation was fortunate in having as its representative in charge of committee assignments Representative Tom O'Brien, former sheriff of Cook County, who was an old friend of Speaker Rayburn. Mr. O'Brien was reputed to have provided the Speaker in 1937 with the margin by which he won election as Majority Leader.[30] One of Mr. O'Brien's major legislative goals was placing members from his zone in the first place in any group newly assigned to a committee, thus making an Illinois member senior within the committee to members of equal seniority in the Congress. This device could be expected to pay dividends for the state of Illinois many years after Mr. O'Brien had passed from the scene.[31]

With respect to committee seniority, the rules of the House say only that members are to be seated in the order in which they are presented to be voted on in an early session of each Congress in the resolution prepared by the party committees on committees. In the Eighty-sixth and Eighty-seventh Congresses (1959-1961 and 1961-1963), however, Illinois freshman always came first on the list of newly assigned members regardless of alphabetical order, seniority on the Committee on Committees, or date of entry of members' states into the Union—all of which are given in *The Precedents* as methods for allocating committee seniority among members of equal seniority in the House.[32]

PARTY LEADERSHIP

Voting in the House, as in the Senate, is predominantly along party lines.[33] This is not simply because there are such sharp ideological divergencies between all the members of each of the two parties. Rather, the act of voting is regarded as a public act, with ramifications that run beyond the confines of the House community. In roll-call votes, the parties in the House "make a record," and congressmen draw the overly simple lines that they carry back into their home districts to campaign with. Generally, the people back home have few ways of assessing a congressman's performance on the job other than taking note of his attendance at roll calls and keeping track of how he votes. As we will see in the next chapter, roll-call votes can be quite misleading because of the enormous number of less public opportunities open to a congressman to express himself on a bill. Nevertheless, roll calls are the public face that Congress wears, and they do determine the fate of legislation.

At voting time, party leaders are most in evidence. Each party in the House has a whip system, which operates not so much as a device to coerce or even persuade members as it does simply to inform the leadership of the dispositions of members toward legislation. Each party leader has a small staff that prepares summaries of the forthcoming week's legislative business for party members. In addition, approximately fifteen members of each party, drawn from geographic zones, act as assistant whips. They assist the deputy whips and the Whip of each party in counting noses and estimating the probable outcomes of important votes. They are no longer important in bringing members to the floor, however. Now that a high proportion of all votes taken in the House are recorded, this activity has been largely automated. When members are called to vote, lights and bells go off throughout the Capitol and House office buildings, recorded messages are available on the House telephone system, members carry beepers and have in their offices television monitors which broadcast House floor proceedings over a closed circuit.

A member described the job of the Whip in these terms:

The whip is more the eyes and ears of the leadership than anything. On controversial matters, they like to know what the chances of success are. So the deputy whips count noses and the whip's job is to evaluate the count—especially to assess the doubtfuls.... A lot of these eastern guys have a Tuesday through Thursday club [which means that they spend the rest of the week in their home districts]. The whip takes the duty of telling them if the signals change so they can get back here if they're needed.[34]

Since the advent of electronic voting and televised floor coverage, the Whip's job has changed. The day to day task of bringing members to the floor has largely been automated, and the Whip is much more valuable as a confidant and consultant to the Speaker on longer-range strategy, and as a conduit of communications from rank-and-file members to the "leadership" by means of the network of deputies and assistants that each party maintains.

The third member of the majority party leadership team, along with the Speaker and the Whip, is the Majority Leader. His job in the House is to lead his party on the floor: he is the custodian of the weekly schedule; he makes *pro forma* motions from the floor, and, if he desires, he leads his party in debate on substantive issues. Off the floor he divides the duties and functions of leadership, negotiating with committee chairmen and the White House, informally persuading reluctant members to "go along" with the Speaker. Who does what and who consults whom are matters the incumbents of the offices work out for themselves.[35]

For a short time after the revolt against Cannonism and the rules changes weakening the Speaker, the majority party was run "from the floor" by a strong Majority Leader who operated through the caucus.[36] However, Rayburn's long incumbency blurred somewhat the distinctive role of the Majority Leader. On the Republican side, there is a policy committee that through its pronouncements gives some guidance to members. A similar function on the Democratic side has been served by the incumbency of a Democratic President and his administration. Under a Republican administration, Democratic policy leadership is divided among several leaders, of course including the Speaker and the formal House leadership, and the Democratic Steering and Policy Committee, which is constituted identically to the Committee on Committees. The Democratic Study Group, an informal caucus of liberal Democrats, has been another major source of policy leadership within the House Democratic party but certainly not the only one. There are caucuses of smaller numbers of members on a wide variety of issues.[37] Also state delegations in some instances provide policy guidance to members. As we shall observe in later chapters, the program of the President and his executive departments constitutes a rallying point for members of the President's party, though it does not bind them.

PARTY CAUCUSES

The fundamental fact of political life in the House is party: the two parties are communities that elect their own leaders, have established policy positions, and determine committee assignments. Informal social groupings of congressmen seldom cross party lines. The parties have separate cloakrooms, sit separately on the floor, and maintain separate clubs and meeting places outside the Capitol building. Increasingly in recent years changes in the general composition of each congressional party have had considerable influence on policy outcomes and to a degree have changed the responsibilities of party leaders.

Although there are some floating and some overlapping Democrats who defy precise pigeonholing, for most purposes we can think of the Democratic party in the House as being composed of three loosely coordinated factions of almost equal size. First, there are the traditional Southern Democrats, who vary from the most liberal to the most reactionary on social welfare issues. Some of these members are still constrained by the implacable sentiments of those who vote in their constituencies to oppose civil rights measures, now usually expressed as a distaste for governmental intervention of all sorts. Others have become responsive to the growing numbers of black voters in their constituencies, and to the inward flow of Northern migrants. This group is declining in importance as more Southern Republicans are elected to Congress; in recent years there have been about seventy Southern Democrats, including a substantial number of committee chairmen, in the House. About one-third of these are "mainstream" Democrats, who vote with their party majority twice as often as not.

The second faction is made up of Northern urban Democrats, many of whom who owe their nominations and elections to strong political parties at the local level. Many of these congressmen come to the House late in life and do not work overly hard at legislative tasks. Consequently, only a few urban Democrats have made a significant mark on the House as individuals, although collectively they account for a large number of votes for the programs of Democratic Presidents. In the past, urban Democrats have been unfailingly liberal on welfare and civil rights matters, but increasingly they have reflected the concerns over racial issues of the working-class neighborhoods they represent.

For most of the last thirty years the vast preponderance of Democratic committee chairmen and party leaders in the House have been drawn from these two groups, both of which serve predominantly one-party electorates giving them extremely safe seats. These leaders shouldered the major responsibilities for dealing with House Republicans, Senate conference committees, interest groups, the White House, and, not infrequently, their own misgivings on legislative matters. Nowadays, they must reckon as well with a third group, far larger and better organized than before. This group consists of programmatic liberal Democrats, who come from all sections of the country including the cities and the South, as the effects of successive Voting Rights Acts have begun to change the character of Southern electorates so as more nearly to reflect the sentiments of a wider range of the population. These Democrats have as their main interests the pursuit of programs reflecting traditional Democratic concerns with social welfare, civil liberties, and racial equality. They took the lead in the late 1950s in establishing the Democratic Study Group, which in recent years has pooled their information and concerted their tactics on a wide range of issues. The Study Group has pressed for reform of House rules, and in this as in other areas, has had many notable victories. It has formed the nucleus in the House for an informal whip system to coordinate the maneuvers of House liberals on civil rights. In earlier years tightly organized Southern Democrats ran rings around the somewhat more numerous but much less experienced House liberals on all manner of issues. The Study Group brought those days to a close. At one point in the 1960s they upset a committee-assignment arrangement favorable to conservatives; at another, they vastly strengthened the hand of the Speaker—against his own wishes—in controlling the legislative process. By such means they have achieved recognition as a significant force in House Democratic politics. Their views are now directly reflected in the activation of the caucus and in the committee assignment process.

At the beginning of each Congress, all the members of each party in the House meet in caucus to select their leaders and ratify committee assignments. By organizing the largest bloc of Democrats in the Caucus, the Democratic Study Group has gone far in stiffening the resolve of House Democratic leaders to represent the programmatic traditions of the national party even when the President is Republican.[38]

The Republican conference, as its caucus is called, is by no means as ideologically diverse as the Democratic. The handful of Republican liberals from the Northeast and a few other urban-suburban constituencies are not sufficiently numerous to make a dent in the course of Republican party policy in the House. The main concerns that in recent years have divided most House Republicans have had to do with the flexibility, constructiveness, and efficiency with which the Republican minority position has been pursued. Twice in recent memory, in 1959 and 1965, the Republican conference has deposed its party leader, each time moving toward a younger, more vigorous man.[39] These moves reflect the main cleavage in the Republican party in the House—not between liberals and conservatives but between junior and senior congressmen. It is quite usual for congressmen without much seniority to complain about the management of the House, as Representative Burkhalter did. Junior Republicans have been in a position to do something about it, because of their numerical strength within their caucus. As Table 8 shows, Republicans with six years of service or less in the House have over the last two decades made up almost half the strength of the party caucus; Democrats similarly situated have recently approximated the Republican percentage, but this was not the case until after the Watergate landslide election of 1974. In 1965 these young Republicans voted overwhelmingly to replace the aging Minority Leader, Charles Halleck, with Gerald Ford, 14 years his junior; they also supported moves to broaden the base of leadership in the Republican congressional party. However, because junior Republicans are on the average as conservative as senior Republicans, these changes did not have much impact on the course of public policy. Younger Republican members through the years have, if anything, been more aggressive in their partisanship than senior Republicans. In recent years some of the more vocal of them have been supporters of supply-side economics and what they call a conservative opportunity society. When President Reagan needed them in 1981 to pass his budget and tax measures,

TABLE 8   Members of Congress Serving Three Terms or Less

CONGRESS	ELECTED	REPUBLICANS	DEMOCRATS
87th	1960	37% (74/172)	31% (81/260)
88th	1962	47% (84/177)	36% (92/258)
89th	1964	47% (66/140)	43% (126/292)
90th	1966	51% (97/187)	34% (84/247)
91st	1968	46% (87/189)	30% (72/242)
92nd	1970	45% (80/177)	28% (72/255)
93rd	1972	44% (84/192)	30% (71/240)
94th	1974	47% (66/144)	41% (120/291)
95th	1976	48% (69/143)	48% (141/292)
96th	1978	44% (69/158)	52% (145/277)
97th	1980	57% (109/192)	40% (98/243)
98th	1982	57% (95/167)	45% (121/268)

Source: *Congressional Directory* (Washington, D.C.: Government Printing Office, annually).

virtually every Republican in the House, including the small number of liberals, voted with the President.

It is not far wrong to say that from the waning of the New Deal in the

TABLE 9   Percentage of all Contested House Roll Calls on Which the Conservative Coalition Appeared and Won, 1962–1981

YEAR	COALITION APPEARANCES	COALITION VICTORIES IN HOUSE
1962	14%	44%
1963	17	67
1964	15	67
1965	24	25
1966	25	32
1967	20	73
1968	24	63
1969	27	71
1970	22	70
1971	30	79
1972	27	79
1973	23	67
1974	24	67
1975	28	52
1976	24	59
1977	26	60
1978	21	57
1979	20	73
1980	18	67
1981	21	88

Source: *Congressional Quarterly* (January 9, 1982), p. 51.

mid-1930s until the mid-1960s the House, both in voting and in its organization, was in many respects dominated by a coalition of Republicans and
Southern Democrats.[40] This "conservative coalition," when it did not actually command a majority of votes, as it frequently did, simply outmaneu-
vered the majority of the majority party. Table 9 documents the appearance
and considerable success of this coalition over the years.

Reapportionment, the rise of the Republican party in the South, and
the determination of the Democratic caucus to assert itself, under the prod-
ding of the Democratic study group and alert tacticians such as Representative Richard Bolling,[41] have strengthened opposition to the conservative
coalition. Majority rule within the Democratic caucus weakens the conservative coalition only as long as liberal Democrats are elected to Congress in
large numbers, but few doubt, at least in the short run, that liberal Democrats
will continue to form the largest bloc in the House.

THE DISTRIBUTION OF INFORMATION

Life in any legislative body is bound to be difficult for its members. There
is an enormous amount of routine business that has to be transacted but
that involves only a few members. For everyone else this business constitutes
a distraction, yet it must be done. On the other hand, sometimes extremely
controversial and important measures demand the close attention of all
members for indeterminate periods of time—two days, three days, or even
a week. Then they must put aside everything else in order to be available
for voting on amendments and on final passage of a bill. Legislative life is
often a matter of "hurry up and wait," with the schedules of congressmen
for long periods of time being controlled by the strategic maneuverings of
their party's leaders and the opposition.

Time pressures are expressed in other ways too, such as by the two-
year term. This means that many members are campaigning for office all
the time. Attentiveness to the constituency is reflected in the frequent trips
many members make back home; indeed, a few congressmen spend most
of their time in their home districts even when Congress is in session. Most
congressmen also devote the major portion of their staff (usually consisting
of 17 or 18 people) and much of their own time to what they call casework,
complying with requests for help from constituents.[42] This often involves
helping constituents—individuals, firms, and local communities—make rep-
resentations before agencies of the executive branch, for a favorable administrative ruling or for such things as a Small Business Administration
loan or an Economic Development Administration grant. The casework may
involve submitting a private bill to admit an immigrant, and clearing the
bill through the watchdog procedure that both parties in the House, and
to a lesser extent in the Senate, have set up to guard against unjustifiable

exceptions to public laws. The number and variety of casework activities is great; they do not, in general, have very much directly to do with the congressman's strictly legislative work, but they help the congressman maintain a link with his constituents, and they also help him learn about the inner workings of the various executive agencies that are administering the laws he makes.[43]

Obviously, it is not possible for most congressmen to learn a great deal about the provisions and consequences of most of the bills they vote on. Time is short; the bills are many and sometimes technically complex. Congressmen are busy, and their staffs are overloaded with work. As a result of these inexorable pressures, congressmen have worked out shortcuts to inform themselves on legislation. Fortunately, many of the decisions they have to make are on issues that have been around a while. Members economize on their information costs, and on their risks, by voting the way they did the last time. Like their constituents at election time, many of them also use party loyalty to help decide how they will vote. Others are particularly alert to the preferences of their state delegations. Voting with the party or with one's state delegation is at the least a sound defensive maneuver; when a congressman votes against one or both, he is "sticking his neck out," laying himself open to criticism from people whose support he needs, either back home to be reelected or in the House to speed his private bills through or to obtain a coveted committee assignment.

A congressman may, of course, vote on the merits of bills if he can inform himself about their merits. This is a complicated process, however. Most politicians realize that in practice bills often do not do what they are intended to do, that grants of wide discretion and latitude are commonly made to administrative agencies, that there are always numerous competing demands for Federal funds. Hence, in order really to understand the import of a bill, it is necessary to read the bill, the committee report that explains it, and perhaps the published testimony of hearings; and it may also be necessary to seek out committee staff members who can explain the distribution of forces in society that have mobilized for and against the bill. Even then, the correct decision does not automatically present itself. Sometimes a bill a congressman favors is watered down in the legislative process, and he must decide whether he would rather take half a loaf now or hope for demands to build up behind the bill so that he can try for a full loaf later. There are times when a legislator would rather have the bill, other times when he would prefer to have the issue. Another dilemma is created when his party leaders in the Congress are urging him in one direction and local party leaders are urging him in another. He needs to inform himself not only about what the legislation is designed to do and about who is for it and who against it, but also what the consequences are for himself of choosing one course of action or another. He arrives at conclusions and votes even when there seem to be costs and benefits, advantages and disadvantages, on both sides of a question. As Representative Jerry Voorhis wrote: "It would be a great deal easier if only one could answer, 'Fifty-five percent aye,' or 'seventy percent no,' or 'I vote aye but with the reservation that I do not like Section 3 of the bill,' or 'I vote no but God have mercy on my soul if I am wrong, as I may very well be.'"[44]

Normally, no congressman has the time to satisfy his uttermost curiosity on a large number of bills and even larger number of amendments that are offered for roll-call votes. He may ask a friend on the relevant committee: "Do you really think this will solve your problem?" or "How strong are the interest groups behind this bill?" or "What objections did the executive agency that will administer this raise?" From brief, cryptic, informal exchanges such as these, often made over the telephone, or as congressmen mill about on the floor to answer routinely to quorum calls, a representative's opinion on the merits of a bill may crystallize. In general, congressmen read very little material unconnected with their committee work. If they do, it is more likely to be newspapers and magazines than books. They rely on their colleagues, the news media, constituents, and lobbyists to tell them about pending legislation. They rely on the mail and visits back home to keep them abreast of constituent problems.[45]

In their area of specialization, determined almost entirely by their committee assignment, congressmen are much better able to get an intellectual grasp of the merits of legislation. Lobbyists may seek them out; executive agency people try to inform them; official committee trips and hearings fill in concrete details on public policies, the way they are executed, and the attitudes of interest groups toward them. And congressmen may find themselves consulted by others, just as they ask their colleagues to inform them in areas outside their competence. Few congressmen serve on more than one major committee. This rule enforces specialization and encourages technical expertise in a small range of issues and reliance on shortcuts in most other areas. This is one key respect in which the House operates according to a division of labor whereby individual members fan out across the spectrum of issues on which the group must make a collective judgment, and each member has an opportunity to contribute disproportionately in his area of specialization. Some members gain greatly in their personal reputations within the House for performing this set of tasks especially well.[46] Senators who serve on two or more committees spread themselves more thinly.

SUMMARY

Whereas the Senate is exposed on every side to public acclaim and attention, the House, because of its size and intricacy, confuses casual observers; hence its members are relatively enclosed and insulated. Senatorial debate is long and voluminous; it attracts and holds the attention of the press and of public-opinion makers. House debate is comparatively short, pointed, and often technical. Senators are famous people whose doings are noticed and whose sayings are celebrated; some of them use their office as a springboard for their presidential ambitions. House members other than the Speaker are anonymous, whether they want to be or not. There are too many of them. To busy Capitol Hill journalists, they seem to come and go too fast. Thus they are deprived of the limelight, even those House leaders whose decisions matter more than the deeds of any ten senators.[47] Finally, the sheer number of members in the House has forced the growth of customary ways of doing things—incomprehensible rituals to outsiders but absolutely indispensable for the efficient conduct of business. The intricate rules governing debate or the customs concerning the allocation of committee seats are examples. The House is, much more than the Senate, a world all its own.

chapter 5

NATIONAL POLICY-MAKING I:
The Legislative Labyrinth

The task of the student of Congress and the Presidency would be greatly simplified if there were a typical process by which a bill becomes a law, that is to say, a process typical in some sense other than the narrowly formalistic. But most bills do not become laws; they are introduced, referred to committees, and there languish and die.[1] So even to speak of a bill's actually becoming a law is to speak of an atypical event. The figures for the Ninety-seventh Congress (1981-1982) are shown in Table 10.

Furthermore, bills have all shapes and sizes. Some propose to authorize the expenditure of billions of dollars; others tinker with existing laws, expanding or contracting the powers of executive agencies; still others provide for the relief of individual citizens. Bills may be short and straightforward or long and technical. They may deal with a handful of Federal employees, as does a bill to equalize the salaries of judges of the Court of Military Appeals with those of other judges of comparable jurisdiction. Or they may deal with many people, including vast numbers of private citizens, as does a bill setting rates at which Federal income taxes are levied. A bill may excite great concern—or none at all—among interest groups, journalists, executive agencies, and electorates. All the different kinds of bills are exposed to different political contingencies, different parliamentary pitfalls, different strategies and tactics. No single case study can do these various contingencies justice. On the other hand, neither can a summary statement, such as will be attempted here.

THE ORIGIN OF BILLS

Bills begin their formal existence by being dropped into a hopper, a mahogany box that sits on a clerk's desk, by a representative in the House and

TABLE 10 **Disposition of Bills, 97th Congress**

	HOUSE	SENATE
Bills introduced and referred to committee	7,458	3,124 (total, 10,582)
Bills reported by committee	576	607
Bills enacted into law	251	172

Source: *Congressional Record*, Daily Digest, 97th Congress, 1st Session (January 6, 1982) and 2nd Session (December 23, 1982).

by being sent to the clerk's desk by a senator in the Senate. The process is separate for the House of Representatives and the Senate, but since no bill can become law without being passed in identical form by both houses, some coordination is necessary. This can take place in a variety of ways. Perhaps the most usual is for identical bills to be introduced at about the same time in each house of Congress, for their provisions to be remolded in somewhat divergent ways in the separate houses, and then for their differences to be reconciled for joint action at the last stage, in the conference committee.[2]

Where do bills come from? The President's preeminence as legislative leader is most obvious in this first stage of the process. The Constitution requires that the President "from time to time give to the Congress information of the State of the Union."[3] In recent years this message has been delivered at the opening of each session of Congress and has been used by Presidents as an opportunity to announce their legislative programs. Specific messages embodying the President's legislative recommendations follow on the heels of the State of the Union message. Friendly senior congressmen and senators from the various committees, usually the chairmen, are consulted and asked to introduce in their respective houses bills prepared by the executive agencies. These bills are referred in a semiautomatic process to the appropriate committees for study.

Not all bills introduced in Congress are inspired by the executive departments or included in the presidential program. Some embody a congressman's or a senator's own ideas, and some are offered at the request of an interest group or a constituent.

REFERENCE TO COMMITTEES

There is an art to drafting bills. In part, bills are written so as to be sent to committees that will act on them favorably. This is not always as easy as it sounds, however. Here is a sample dilemma: In the House of Representatives it has often been easy to get bills in support of labor or education passed out favorably by the Committee on Education and Labor, but not with the bipartisan support of the committee. This lack of full support, in turn, jeopardizes the chances for the bill to clear the Rules Committee and reach the floor, and it also means that a coalition of Republicans and conservative Southern Democrats might defeat the bill even though a majority of Democrats (presently the majority party in the House) supported it. But let us suppose that the bill is on a subject that permits its proponents some room to maneuver, that it provides, say, for medical education. Instead of placing the program in the hands of the U.S. Office of Education, which is mistrusted by conservative congressmen, and routing it through the Committee on Education and Labor, the bill can be written so that the program comes under the aegis of the Surgeon General of the United States, who is the head of the Public Health Service. In that case the bill would be referred to the Commerce Committee, whose jurisdiction includes public health legislation. If this committee deals with the bill, its chances of survival are greater, but the chances that it would be as strong or as liberal a bill as one from the Education and Labor Committee are slim; indeed, the more conservative Commerce Committee would be less likely to approve any bill at all. Or consider civil rights. Suppose that supporters of civil rights wanted to write a bill pertaining to racial discrimination in commercial practices and that the two committees to which the bill might be sent, depending on how it was titled and written, were the Commerce Committee and the Judiciary Committee. Suppose also that the committees were chaired as shown in Table 11. In order to avoid having the civil rights bill bottled up in committee, it must be written a bit differently for each chamber and referred to the Judiciary Committee in the House and the Commerce Committee in the Senate.

This is in fact how the 1963 Civil Rights Bill was handled. Walter Oleszek gives a couple of more recent examples:

> [In 1977] Sen. Pete V. Domenici, R-N.M., sought legislation imposing fees on barge operators who ship freight on the nation's canals and rivers. These operators had never paid any waterway charges for using the national network of federally built and maintained locks, dams, and channels. Traditionally, proposals similar to Domenici's had been designated as "tax" measures and were referred to the Senate Finance Committee, which has jurisdiction over revenue-raising legislation. In that committee, such measures encountered strong opposition and had never won approval. In an effort to bypass the Finance Committee, Domenici designated his proposal an "inland waterways

TABLE 11   Chairmen, Selected Congressional Committees, 1963

	HOUSE	SENATE
Commerce	Oren Harris, Ark.	Warren Magnuson, Wash.
Judiciary	Emanuel Celler, N.Y.	James O. Eastland, Miss.

charge"; as a result, the bill was referred jointly to the Senate Public Works and Commerce committees. Domenici, a member of the Public Works subcommittee that had jurisdiction of the waterways measure (the Commerce Committee deferred to the Public Works panel), won Senate passage of the measure in June 1977.

Another drafting technique by members is to introduce legislation that amends statutes over which their committees have jurisdiction. Noted Rep. Bob Eckhardt, D-Texas (1967-81):

You can phrase your new bill as an amendment to some Act that the Committee has previously dealt with, and then the bill will go to that Committee. For instance, I had the Open Beaches Bill. I had a strong interest in it. By phrasing it as an amendment to certain legislation involving estuarine matters, I could get my bill referred to Merchant Marine and Fisheries, because that Committee had previously processed the statute my bill amended. Had I amended certain bills dealing with land use, I could have got it referred to the Interior Committee.[4]

Thus strategic maneuvering designed to keep a bill alive begins while it is being written and certainly before it is introduced. Sometimes it is possible to word bills ambiguously and hope for a favorable referral.[5] But the committees guard their jurisdictions; the parliamentarians (who do the actual referring of bills under the direction of the Speaker in the House and the Majority Leader in the Senate) know the precedents, and only a case of genuine ambiguity gives the Speaker or the Majority Leader any real option in referral.

Still, occasions do arise. In 1962 an interstate water compact for New England rivers was reported out of the House Public Works Committee, which deals with water-resource management. A closely similar bill for the Delaware River Valley came out of the Judiciary Committee, which deals with Federal-state compacts. When quizzed on the apparent discrepancy in the handling of the two bills, the chairman of the public works subcommittee pointed out, in somewhat resigned tones, that the ranking Democrat on the Judiciary Committee, Francis E. Walter, was from the Delaware Valley and was "mighty interested" in the bill and that it therefore had "just gravitated" to the Judiciary Committee.

IN COMMITTEE

Once bills are in committee, automatic processes carry them no farther. From this point onward they must be carefully and assiduously nurtured or they die. Needless to say, those bills in which the committee chairman is personally interested are given the most prompt attention,[6] but even for a chairman it is futile to promote legislation that cannot command widespread support, at least from the leadership of his own party or from a vast majority of his colleagues on the floor.

In every session of Congress each committee has a great many bills referred to it, more bills than it can possibly attend to. The committee chairmen play a strategic role in selecting the bills that committees will take up, but in this decision the preferences of the White House and the chairman's own legislative party leaders weigh heavily. Chairmen pride themselves on their success in obtaining passage of legislation reported favorably out of their committees. The chances of success are enormously enhanced if the full weight of the party leadership is behind a measure. If party leaders are indifferent, the entire burden of assembling a majority on the floor falls on the chairman; if party leaders are opposed, it will probably be very difficult to build this majority.

Chairmen who oppose White House measures may delay taking up the offending bill or may seek to water it down or substitute legislation on the same subject more satisfactory to themselves. A firm and intense majority on the committee may successfully oppose a chairman who wishes to do this, and some committees now conscientiously enforce rules that require chairmen to refer bills to an appropriate subcommittee by a specified time. Such majorities are rare, however, for several reasons. Avoidance of conflict within committees is so much easier for all concerned. Committee chairmen may take an active hand in assigning new members to their committee and in shaping the size and jurisdiction of future subcommittees. Chairmen can reward their friends by giving them the sponsorship of bills or taking up legislation they may want or need. Finally, the chairman who opposes his party leadership and the President may in fact have a reasonably accurate sense of which provisions in a bill will actually attract a legislative majority.

In the House there is a provision, the discharge petition, by which the signatures of a majority of members of the whole House (218) can force any bill out of committee after it has been held there for thirty days, even if the committee has voted it down. In the Senate, committees can be bypassed by amending legislation on the floor with the provisions of bills bottled up in committee. This was the method, permitted under loose senatorial rules of germaneness, by which medicare was brought to a vote in 1962. However, neither of these devices is much used. Senators and representatives are loath to play fast and loose with their own procedures. Many fear the wrath of powerful committee chairmen thus affronted. Many feel a responsibility to work according to the regular order, even at the sacrifice of policies they favor. One liberal congressman commented: "members are reluctant to sign a discharge petition. It could be construed as a vote of no confidence—as an attack upon the committee system or on the integrity of the members of the committee.... As long as we have the committee system we need to try to make it work, but what about the public interest? It is heart-rending to see how slow...."[7]

Each major committee seldom aims at producing more than one bill of substantial scope in a session of Congress, and this bill is usually on a subject selected by the President in consultation with the relevant executive departments. Minor bills, favored by executive agencies, interest groups, and/or individual congressmen, may flow through the committees at a brisk or slow pace, depending on the habits and inclinations of the chairman and on his instructions to the staff.

On all bills that the chairman decides to take up, it is usual for him to begin by instructing the staff to solicit comments from the executive agency that will be charged with administering the bill's provisions if it becomes law. This is routinely cleared through the Office of Management and Budget, which takes care that the agency's comments are not inconsistent with the presidential program.[8] A negative response from the agency usually dooms a bill unless its congressional sponsor is especially vehement, resourceful, and influential. A favorable executive response may move a minor bill swiftly toward the floor; if the bill authorizes an expenditure of less than a million dollars and appears to be noncontroversial, it can be sent rapidly out of committee. In the House it is placed on the consent calendar and will probably be passed *pro forma* when this calendar is called, as it is on the average of twice a month. In the Senate, similarly, the Majority Leader asks periodically for unanimous consent to pass noncontroversial bills.

On major legislation or controversial legislation, the committee deliberates more slowly. If the chairman favors the bill in question, he will undoubtedly choose to become its sponsor and will schedule the bill for early consideration by the committee. Or he may send the bill to a subcommittee.

Some committees have over the years built up traditions of decentralization and subject-matter specialization that have led them to spin off major responsibilities to subcommittees. It is quite common for the relations between subcommittees and the full committee to be in flux. For example, observers noted a tendency for Chairman Carl Vinson of the House Armed Services Committee in the latter years of his long chairmanship to allow greater autonomy to his subcommittees and their chairmen. Likewise, subcommittees seemed to be growing in importance as the House Science and Astronautics Committee gained in stature and responsibility. When a strongly liberal majority of Democrats entered the House in the Ninety-fourth Congress, one of their first acts was to press the Democratic caucus to force the powerful tax-writing Ways and Means Committee to form subcommittees, rather than work in the full committee as had been the practice under the chairmanship of Wilbur Mills. The House Appropriations Committee, as we shall see, depends heavily on subcommittees. The membership, size, and jurisdictions of these have in the past been controlled closely by the chairman of the full committee, but now Appropriations

Subcommittee chairmen are voted upon in secret ballot by the Democratic caucus, and the membership of the committee is strongly influenced by the party leadership.

Although the peculiarities of subcommittee-committee relations can also affect the outcome of legislation, for the sake of simplicity let us examine the process when, as sometimes happens, the committee chairman refers a bill to a subcommittee of which he is also chairman. The staff solicits and receives material backing the bill from the appropriate executive agency, and the chairman instructs the staff to arrange for hearings.

HEARINGS

Hearings serve a variety of functions. Ideally, they are an effective research device, a way of focusing the attention of congressmen on the substantive merits of a proposed bill and its possible pitfalls. In an ideal world, of course, issues are raised *de novo*, and legislators' minds are clean slates. In the real world, however, the subjects of major legislative proposals are familiar to committee members long before they reach the stage of hearings. Sometimes these proposals have been the subject of protracted partisan debate, and interest groups often exist on all sides of the issue. Therefore it is not uncommon for hearings to become rather perfunctory, with spokesmen for the various points of view coming before the committee and delivering speeches that the members have heard many times before. As one congressman said, "I get so bored with those repetitious hearings. We've been listening to the same witnesses saying the same things the same way for ten years."[9] Still, all this is necessary—to make a record, to demonstrate good faith to leaders and members of the House and Senate, to provide a background of demonstrated need for the bill, to show how experts anticipate that the bill's provisions will operate, to allay fears, and to gather support from the wavering. Not only does it tell congressmen what the technical arguments for and against a bill are, but, even more important, it tells them *who*, which interests and which groups, are for and against bills and how strongly they feel about them.

The committee staff at the direction of the chairman can manipulate the roster of witnesses before the committee and can ask witnesses unfriendly to the bill to file statements rather than appear in person. Here is one account of the strategic use of hearings:

> Senator McClellan is known as the most adroit committee chairman on the Hill when it comes to generating publicity for something that he is concerned about, or that he wants to appear to be concerned about. A former rural prosecutor of the jury-rail-thumping variety, he has always made great use of simplicity in conducting Senate hearings. Characteristically, he has stuck to the main point and one side of that point—his. In this case his point was the

same one that he had been making all along—that decisions of the Supreme Court endangered the nation's stability. But he also said "I want to get the other side of it and see what can be presented in opposition to these bills." To accomplish this, he invited fifty-odd witnesses to testify, only half a dozen of whom opposed his viewpoint, and he inserted in the record scores of letters, editorials, and statements favorable to his position, with only a handful opposed.[10]

Committee chairmen do often play scrupulously fair with all interested parties and allow everyone to speak his piece. The timing and length of hearings are of course strategically important. Sometimes it is desirable from the chairman's point of view to drag hearings out perhaps until the other body can act. Often, leaders on the House side of the Capitol who desire to pass a bill find that pressure for it builds up if the Senate can be allowed to act first. Therefore, a chairman may drag House hearings on until the Senate acts favorably. On the other hand, House leaders may wish to move quickly, because if the Senate passes an unacceptable bill before the House acts, then opponents of the bill in the House will be galvanized at once into opposition. House opponents of a measure realize that when a House bill that differs greatly from a Senate bill on the same subject is sent into conference, the combined result may be too close to the Senate version for them. Conference committees have great leeway, and the House conferees may be drawn from senior members of the substantive committee reporting the bill, who are proponents of the bill.[11] Even if formally instructed to the contrary by a vote of the House or Senate, conferees can agree to delete provisions of the bill that passed their chamber, but of course if they do so, the chances that their report will be accepted in the chamber decline. When the conference report returns to the House and Senate floors for a vote, no amendments are in order, and opponents of some of a bill's provisions can only vote yes or no on the whole package. On issues where there is an overwhelming consensus that *some* legislation is necessary, opponents of a conference report are at a great disadvantage. And so House committee chairmen sometimes try to keep one step ahead of possible opposition by hastening bills through hearings.

The format for the hearing varies with the committee and the circumstances. At each hearing the ground rules may change ever so slightly, but in general it works as follows: Witnesses from the executive agencies, first of all, are invited to appear in order to describe how they anticipate the bill will operate and in order to record their support for the bill. After the government witnesses and interested congressmen and senators appear, it is customary for witnesses from interest groups to testify for and against the bill. Usually each witness makes a prepared statement and then is questioned by members of the committee in order of seniority, starting with the chairman, then the ranking minority member, and so on, alternating back and forth between the parties. Ordinarily, time is limited and so it is quite unusual for all members of the committee on either side to get a chance to question witnesses on the record in any great detail.

Committees vary in the opportunity they give to their more junior members. One of the ways in which congressmen tell whether a committee is being run democratically is the extent to which opportunities are provided for newer members to interact with witnesses at hearings. Those committees that place a time limit, usually five minutes, on questions from any one member are the committees that are most solicitous of junior members. Nowadays, this custom is the norm.

Frequently, hearings are badly attended, and only members most interested in the bill are on hand, with committee staff members providing most of the audience. This is not true, of course, when for one reason or another the hearings are being covered by television cameras, or on special occasions, such as when the Secretary of Defense presents his annual statement on America's defense posture to the Armed Services Committee, or when the Joint Economic Committee receives the annual report of the Council of Economic Advisors.

Not all hearings are organized to consider specific legislation. Sometimes committee chairmen will ask that hearings be organized simply to furnish general information to the members or in order to investigate the execution of laws by an executive department. Committees differ in the extent to which they hold investigatory hearings without a specific legislative purpose. The infamous, and now defunct, House Committee on Unamerican Activities was the committee that was most active in holding hearings that did not especially pertain to any specific legislation before it.[12] Even when there is no particular bill before a committee, however, the general legislative purpose of inquiring whether present laws within the committee's jurisdiction are adequate is legally sufficient to justify holding hearings.

Some committees, less famous by far than HUAC or the subcommittee on investigations of the Senate Government Operations Committee, have used hearings quite consciously as a device for the general education of members. The Jackson subcommittee on national policy machinery of Government Operations in the Senate, for example, conducted what amounted to a high-level seminar for senators, and the Senate Watergate hearings under the aegis of Sam Ervin most certainly had a significant impact on legislators as well as the public at large.

THE MARK-UP

At the conclusion of hearings, the subcommittee may meet and consider the bill. The bill will be read line by line, and the various members will voice their approval or objections to its provisions. It is at this point, the mark-up, where the bill is amended and rewritten so as to gather the necessary support in the committee to make it possible for the bill to survive its subsequent trip through the Congress. If the bill can be written here so as to receive substantial support, its chances of survival later are immensely improved. If, on the other hand, the provisions of the bill are such as to divide the committee, the chances of the bill's survival are much less. Representative Clem Miller has described the mark-up process:

> The committee staff has a proprietary interest in our bill. The bill we went to hearing with was probably its creature to begin with. Its details were worked out in conferences with the executive department "downtown." The staff knows every byway in the bill, has hedged against every technical problem...
>
> What we are seeking is maximum majority support at mark-up. The hostility of the [subcommittee] chairman is almost fatal and division between the Majority members almost equally so...
>
> After hearings, to be sure of some unity, the subcommittee chairman calls a meeting of Majority members to look over some possible changes in the bill. The Chairman insists on informality. It is a "discussion." Nothing is to be "final." Your "ideas" are sought. One member wants a much tougher section in one part of the bill. There is a chance of agreement. The staff had anticipated this with some appropriate language. Another member, not primed by a staff man, throws out an innocent suggestion which it turns out the Chairman is most opposed to. The "suggestion" is permanently shelved.
>
> Quickly the friction points are reviewed, and assent is secured for our Majority position. We are now ready for the executive session[13] of the full subcommittee, the marking-up with a united front...
>
> The Minority function at the subcommittee mark-up is to test every major segment of the bill, looking for weakness. One member leads off with a challenge to the whole bill. He has a substitute which is disposed of in a second. Then the bill is read, line by line. At the appropriate places, the Majority amendments are offered. There is some discussion. Staff members hover behind members, counseling in whispers. A vote is taken and the clerk reads on.
>
> At step after step the Minority amendments are offered. The attitude is offhand and perfunctory. If a glimmer of interest or a shade of response is elicited from the Majority side, the proposal is pressed. One amendment does seem reasonable. A word or two is said in its behalf. The chairman stirs about unhappily, seeing an opening wedge in Majority unity. It is disposed of, but the restlessness is noted for future exploitation by the Minority in full committee and on the Floor. Finally, the bill has been read. The disagreements— first among Democrats, then between Democrats and Republicans—have resulted in much new language, changing the shape of the bill, accommodating to our needs.[14]

Perhaps the most important factor in determining whether or not a bill emerges at all is the extent to which there is a widespread belief, at least among the majority, that there should be some legislation or other on the subject being considered. If even a medium-sized minority feels that there is really no use or necessity for the contemplated legislation, the number and variety of objections they can raise are quite staggering. If, on the other hand, everyone believes that some legislation is desirable or inevitable, the chances that a bill will emerge are much greater. Under these circumstances, both majority and minority are willing to compromise at least sufficiently to provide for some kind of legislation.

After a suitable amount of bargaining, the subcommittee may take a vote on the bill and report to the full committee. In some cases, the full committee provides only a perfunctory review of subcommittee action. In other cases, however, amendments that failed to be adopted in the sub-committee may be in order in the full committee, if their proponents wish to bring them forward. On some committees, doing this is regarded as bad form, but on an increasing number it is regarded as perfectly acceptable to sustain subcommittee conflict within the full committee.

Customarily, by this time the chairman has instructed the staff to prepare a report. The report is an explanation of the bill from both a substantive and a political standpoint. The purpose of the report is to explain the bill and its contemplated effects to members of Congress and also, on occasion, to the courts, who later, in the course of litigation, may look at reports to ascertain legislative intent. The report may include minority views. It is a point of pride with committee chairmen to bring their minority along with them as much as possible. In committee, at any rate, the process is very similar to that in the subcommittee. Once the bill is marked up and the report written, it may be voted out of committee. It then goes on the calendars of the respective houses.

THE CALENDARS

In the Senate there are only two legislative calendars; from them the Majority Leader, in consultation with the Minority Leader, the legislative liaison from the President, committee chairmen, and interested senators, selects bills for floor action. The method and timing of introduction may be manipulated at the discretion of the Majority Leader to his strategic advantage.

In the House there are five calendars. One, the consent calendar, has already been mentioned.[15] A second calendar is for bills introduced for the relief or benefit of named individuals or groups. A third, rarely used, is the calendar for bills discharged by petition from committees. The other two calendars are for public bills of some importance; bills are listed on them on a first-come (from any committee), first-served basis. This method of setting priorities has been found to be unacceptable, and so these calendars are never called. Rather, substitute methods for placing bills on the agenda are used. Some committees are granted privileged use of the floor, most notably the Appropriations Committee, which can bring its bills to the floor whenever it is ready to report them and suitable arrangements for their consideration can be made with the Speaker and Majority Leader.[16] The Rules Committee is also privileged to bring to the floor special orders making it possible for the House to consider specific bills. These special orders are voted by the Rules Committee and brought to the floor at the request of leaders of the various committees of the House. Thus, normally when a bill is voted out of a House committee and is entered on a calendar, the next step is for the chairman to ask the Rules Committee for a special order taking the bill from the calendar and placing it before the House. The Rules Committee chairman may be quick or slow in responding to this request. Normally, however, he will respond with reasonable promptness and schedule a hearing at which the managers of the bill from the substantive committee and its opponents can appear before the Rules Committee and state the case for and against the granting of a special order.

THE RULES COMMITTEE

By the time a bill gets to the Rules Committee, political lines on it are drawn fairly clearly. Up to a few years ago the Rules Committee was not a perfunctory procedural hurdle; its members considered bills on their merits and on the basis of party strategies. Over the last two decades, however, the Rules Committee has been changed more than any other committee of the House. These changes occurred because the committee was such a formidable roadblock and was especially effective in thwarting the plans of Democratic Presidents. In the 1960s the committee was packed with mainstream Democrats; in the 1970s, as the influence of mainstream Democrats in the Democratic caucus crested, Democratic appointments to the Committee were taken out of the hands of the Committee on Committees and given to the sole discretion of the Speaker.

Before these changes took place, however, there were three major factions within the committee, as there are within the House generally. First, Republicans regularly voted against reporting to the floor legislation, both foreign and domestic, on which there was any substantial partisan division in the substantive committee or on which Democratic Presidents placed high priority. They formed an alliance with the second faction, conservative Southern Democrats, who also opposed Democratic presidential programs for expanding the welfare activities of the government, increasing the size of governmental bureaucracies, intervening in the economy, or sending aid abroad. The third faction consisted of Northern Democrats, who were allied with a few Southern liberals and moderates. They normally united to back programs sponsored by the House Democratic leadership and Democratic Presidents.

On some issues, especially when the Presidency was in Republican hands, these patterns of alliance broke down. Civil rights is a conspicuous example. The usual strategy was for Democrats in the Judiciary Committee (from which civil rights legislation normally comes in the House) to accede to some Republican suggestions during the mark-up. The idea was to gain the support of a body of Republicans sizable enough to make possible a coalition between Northern Democrats and Republicans on the Rules Committee. Meanwhile, normally liberal Democrats from the South allied with their conservative Southern brethren. However, the Southerners did not have enough votes to defeat Northern Democrats and Republicans on the granting of a rule.

The main weapon of the South in the Rules Committee over most of the last four decades was the shrewdness of its senior members, such as Eugene Cox of Georgia and Judge Howard Worth Smith of Virginia, who from the Eighty-fourth to the Eighty-ninth Congress was chairman of the committee. A colleague of Judge Smith's described his political skill (and, in a sense, the political skill of all legislative craftsmen inside the House) in the following terms:

> One of the interesting things is to watch the way he plays all these different things the way a great conductor conducts an orchestra. It's really fascinating. If he sees he's going to be overrun here, unless it be in the civil rights field ... but on an economic issue, or a welfare issue ... let's say there are five or six of them, he'll play them as carefully as he can and very skillfully to kill as many as possible, but if he has to knuckle under in order to get "X" by going along with "A" he will. It's really magnificent skill.[17]

The devices Judge Smith used to discourage legislation he opposed were many and various. The committee had no regular meeting time but rather convened at the call of the chairman.[18] When legislation obnoxious to the Judge was pending, it was not unknown for him to delay convening his committee, sometimes for long periods of time.

> In August 1957, he vanished from Washington, leaving his committee without the power to call itself to order, while the civil rights bill gathered dust in its files. Word seeped back from Virginia that Judge Smith had gone to inspect a barn that had burned on his near-by dairy farm.
> "I knew Howard Smith would do most anything to block a civil rights bill, but I never suspected he would resort to arson." Speaker Rayburn quipped, somewhat wryly.[19]

Or he could stall by piling up other bills ahead of the one he wanted to bury. When at last the bill he disliked was reached, it was possible to hear a long parade of witnesses against it and have lengthy and searching questions waiting for its proponents. Both these tactics would consume days, perhaps until the Rules Committee members who were key proponents of the bill had to be out of town; then he could abruptly call for a vote.

Alternatively, gentlemanly fair play required further delay while the Judge's colleagues met their other obligations.

Thus hamstrung, the managers of a bill often tried to strike a bargain with the Judge and his conservative allies, amending one section or removing another in return for prompt action, in fear that there would be no action at all. It was this bargaining process that the Judge referred to when he once spoke on the floor about the powers of his committee.

> You know, it so happens that the Rules Committee has a little something to do about when these bills come to the floor. I want to assure you that if there is any ... deal going on or has gone on, I am going to use what little finagling and delaying, and so forth, that I can bring to pass on this situation to see that does not happen.... You know, we southern boys are pretty good old horse traders. I was raised to be a pretty good horse trader myself.[20]

Much of this is now in the past. Neither Judge Smith nor his successor, the equally conservative William Colmer of Mississippi, could control Democratic committee assignments to the committee, and the composition of the committee was changed over the years to approximate the will of the majority of the majority party. Now, by a rule of the Democratic caucus, the power to appoint members of the Rules Committee has been taken out of the hands of the party committee on committees and vested solely in the Speaker. Before 1959 the committee was composed of twelve members divided in a two-to-one ratio between the parties, reflecting the House tradition that the majority party should have control over and responsibility for the agenda. However, the defection of two conservative Democrats (Smith and Colmer) could and did tie the committee up and prevent legislation favored by the majority party to reach the floor. One liberal Democrat ticked off the score in the Eighty-seventh Congress:

> For example, the area redevelopment bill passed the Senate in 1959, but the [Rules] Committee refused to report the House version. Through the almost forgotten procedures of Calendar Wednesday, the bill finally reached the floor in May, 1960, and passed after many procedural roll calls. In June, 1960, a discharge petition was used to circumvent the Committee and bring the Federal pay-raise bill to the floor for approval.... The threat of a discharge petition finally forced committee action on the 1960 civil rights bill. The threat of Calendar Wednesday prodded the Committee into clearing the school construction bill, although the Republican-Southern Democratic alliance within the Committee ultimately blocked the bill by refusing to report a resolution sending it to conference.[21]

A Rules Committee deadlocked on most matters of domestic policy was tolerable to liberal Democrats in Congresses gripped by problems of World War II or in Congresses whose major accomplishments were in foreign affairs, as they were under President Truman, or even, as from 1953 to 1961, when a Republican was in the White House. However, with the advent in 1961 of a Democratic President, who would need the assistance of his party in bringing his program to the House floor, it became clear to Democrats in the House that something drastic had to be done about the Rules Committee. Something was; after a very intense and protracted struggle between mainstream Democrats and liberals on one side and conservative Democrats, mostly Southern, and the vast majority of House Republicans on the other, the size of the committee was expanded by three—two Democrats and one Republican. Sam Rayburn saw to it that the Democrats who were appointed were party loyalists, and since that time no other sort of Democrat has been appointed to the committee. With the growth in recent elections of the liberal wing of the House Democratic party, the party caucus has taken on new significance and has on occasion given instructions to the Rules Committee about the disposition of legislation. In consequence, the Rules Committee, which at one time captured nationwide attention by its capacity—and willingness—to say "no" to the best-laid plans of Presidents, Speakers of the House, and committee chairmen, now has all the fascination of an open valve, and it is no longer an interesting committee to members. There has, in recent years, been little demand to serve on the Rules Committee, and the number of members has dropped back to 13. Its chairman is expected to consult with the House leadership and to run the committee's business so as to be accommodating to leadership strategies. The business of the committee itself is to determine the structure of debate on all major issues, the order in which amendments are to be offered, and the time allocated to each subject. This ability is highly significant in organizing the legislative process in the House, but the Rules Committee does not operate as autonomously in this sphere as it once did. The power of the Speaker to appoint committee members is more than adequate to keep the Rules Committee cooperative over the long run.

At the conclusion of hearings before this committee, the committee votes whether or not to grant a special rule making in order floor debate on the bill that has just come before them. If the vote is affirmative, the chairman and the ranking minority member each appoints a member of the committee from his side of the table to take the rule to the floor.

FLOOR ACTION IN THE HOUSE

When a special order is granted by the Rules Committee, this fact is rapidly communicated to the House leadership, the Speaker and the Majority Leader, who schedule the bill for debate. They have some flexibility in this process and may wait for strategic reasons or reasons of convenience. On the scheduled day two members of the Rules Committee, one each from the majority and the minority, appear on the floor of the House and ask that the committee resolution setting the terms of debate on the bill be given immediate consideration. This resolution is itself debatable, and sometimes debate on the resolution provides a hint of the controversy that will ensue when the bill is debated directly. Only in rare instances is the resolution from the Rules Committee not adopted; when it is, the House resolves itself into the Committee of the Whole.

The membership of the Committee of the Whole House is identical to that of the House of Representatives itself, but parliamentary rules in the committee are somewhat relaxed. Proponents and opponents of the bill from the substantive committee—customarily senior members from the majority and minority sides—move up to long tables on either side of the center aisle in the house.[22] They will manage the time for debate, make split-second decisions whether to support or oppose amendments, and keep a weather eye on the attendance of friends, waverers, and foes.

In 1970 House rules were changed to permit the recording of names on teller votes in the Committee of the Whole, and the installation of electronic voting apparatus has greatly speeded up voting to a fifteen-minute period per recorded vote. The quorum is 100, not a majority of the House as in regular proceedings. This smaller quorum makes it more difficult to halt proceedings to bring supporters to the floor. And as the bill is read, amendments may come up unexpectedly. An observer says:

> In the Committee of the Whole a premium is placed on effective organization and on the sense of commitment that will hold members on the floor hour after hour. Thus, early in 1961, administration supporters were caught off guard on a controversial minimum wage vote, which was lost 186 to 185 (with a dozen or more "supporters" skulking in the cloakrooms, or House barbershop).[23]

At the conclusion of debate in the Committee of the Whole, the committee rises and reports the bill back to the whole House with such amendments as may have been agreed to. At that point the Speaker asks if a separate vote is demanded on any amendment reported favorably. Any member may demand such a vote. After all such votes the title is read a third time. A motion to recommit may be offered, and then a vote is taken on final passage. If the bill is passed, it is sent to the Speaker for his signature. It is then sent to the Senate.

FLOOR ACTION IN THE SENATE

The Senate may or may not have been waiting for the House bill. It is not uncommon for Senate committees to undertake hearings on their own bill on a subject. Senate committees hear bills and mark them up in a process very similar to that in the House. However, these committees are much smaller than House committees; thus individual senators have greater opportunities to question witnesses and participate in the mark-up. On the other hand, senators have many more committee assignments than representatives, so unless the bill is within a senator's area of special interest or attracts his attention for some reason, he is likely to depend heavily on staff members. Senate committees may permit television to cover their proceedings; House committees were forbidden this option by Speaker Rayburn, and this rule only recently has been reversed. In any event, ordinary committee hearings of the Senate rarely attract the interest of the television networks. The networks usually ask to cover only investigative hearings, which are more likely to provoke a sensation. When a bill is reported out of a Senate committee, it goes on a single calendar, from which it may be taken at any time by the Majority Leader and presented as the order of business before the Senate.

Senate debate is less restricted than debate in the House as to both time and substance. In the House there is a strict rule of germaneness, but in the Senate germaneness is required only for short periods of time. Senate debate is normally more attractive to the news media than is House debate; it is certainly more voluminous, as can easily be seen by comparing the number of hours the House and the Senate are in session. Whereas the House in the Ninety-seventh Congress managed to get its business done in 1,420 hours and 7 minutes, the Senate took 2,157 hours and 47 minutes (fifty more legislative days) in which to accomplish virtually the same tasks.

A famous feature of senatorial debate is the filibuster. This refers to the occasions when senators, by prolonging their talk, tie up the Senate for days (sometimes weeks) at a time and thus stall the legislative machinery so as to win concessions on the substance of the legislation being debated. A filibuster, which can be halted only by a vote of three-fifths of the membership of the Senate, may be undertaken for a variety of purposes. Proponents claim that this is a valid way of bringing sharply to the attention of the country the imminent passage of laws that they feel are unjust or unwise. Opponents regard filibusters as inimical to the rule of the majority.

The conditions under which a successful filibuster may be launched are fairly well understood. First, it should take place as far toward the end of the legislative session as possible, because its main effect is to stall legislative machinery. If the wheels of progress can be stalled long enough, some bills strongly preferred by nonfilibustering senators will be lost in the end-of-session shuffle. When enough bills are jeopardized, their proponents presumably will become willing to withdraw their support of the measure being filibustered and will agree to scuttle the issue for that session of Congress. Thus the closer to the end of the session the filibuster takes place, the greater its chances of success.

A second condition for successful filibusters is that numerous senators participate. At least one-fifth of the Senate seems to be necessary to carry on a full-scale filibuster. Historically, one of the major techniques of the leadership when attempting to defeat a filibuster was to call for round-the-clock sessions. This tactic was employed in order to exhaust marathon speakers. The speakers, in turn, could retaliate by suggesting the absence of a quorum throughout the night hours, thus necessitating the physical presence in the chamber of all senators, not merely those filibustering. If a quorum could not be mustered, Senate business was stalled without the expenditure of extra energy by filibusterers. When tactics such as these were employed, the Senate took on the appearance of a besieged fortress. Cots were set up in hallways. Senators wandered bleary-eyed around the Capitol, awaiting a call to the floor. As few as twenty senators could provoke this kind of situation for some time before they were exhausted, but a smaller number could not sustain this sort of filibuster, because it was so much easier to muster the three-fifths majority against them that was necessary to close off debate. Nowadays, even after general debate is concluded, a determined filibusterer (as we saw in the case of Senator James Allen in the Senate chapter) can offer amendments—lots of amendments—and prolong disposition of a measure for long periods of time.

Perhaps the most important characteristic of filibusters is that they are exceedingly rare. Generally, senators do not undertake to waste their time and that of their colleagues in such a fashion unless they are prompted by strong external stimulus. In the case of Southern senators, for example, such stimulus would historically have been the extreme position of their constituencies with respect to civil rights legislation, which almost made it mandatory for them to make a fuss that was easily audible back home.

If a bill evades the severe controversy implied by the filibuster, it can be debated and voted on promptly in the Senate. Normally, however, the Senate and the House pass bills that are not identical in every particular. Therefore either house may ask for a conference in which their differences are resolved.

THE CONFERENCE

Conference committees are appointed, for the House by the Speaker, and for the Senate by the vice president, on the recommendation of the chairmen of the substantive committees handling the legislation. The conference committees normally consist of senior members from the substantive committees or subcommittees that had the most to do with managing the bill, with the majority usually outnumbering the minority in a ratio that reflects the party ratios on the full committee. The entire delegation from each house votes as a unit in conference committees. Occasionally it is possible to pack a

delegation by varying its size, but this normally requires cooperation between the committee chairman and the presiding officer of his house.[24]
These *ad hoc* committees meet and attempt to reconcile the differences
between the House and the Senate bills. They are generally given great
latitude in reporting a consolidated bill back to their respective houses.
Sophisticated members take advantage of ideological differences between
the two houses, when they occur. For example, when the Senate was reliably
liberal and the House considerably less so, liberal members of the House
frequently made no attempt to insert liberal provisions into House measures
initially but arranged for them to be put into the Senate version of the bill.
In this way they could avoid the possibility that the House of Representatives
would explicitly reject provisions they were interested in. Once there is such
an explicit rejection in the House, it is very difficult to pass any conference
report that includes the offending language, because conservative House
members will make much of the fact that the House has already rejected
the provisions of the bill. Thus the technique is to see that the liberal
provisions are introduced on the Senate side and then make every effort to
ensure that the combined bill that comes out of the conference has predominantly Senate provisions in it. Conferees may also put new matter into
the bill by a broad interpretation of their powers. Reports of conference
committees are privileged business in both houses. Furthermore, no amendments may be made to these reports in either house. The reports may,
however, be voted down or returned to conference, with instructions in the
House or without instructions in the Senate. Thus Senate conferees have
somewhat greater leeway; House members may fear being bound by instructions if they stray too far from the provisions of the bill passed by the
House.

Close observers have often noted differences between House and Senate members of conference committees. Conference committee behavior
often reflects greater degrees of technical specialization by House members
and preoccupation with matters other than the business at hand by senators,
a situation that leads senators to rely more heavily upon their committee
staffs. This is strikingly illustrated in one case by the conference committee
that met on the Securities Act of 1933.

> The rules of a Conference Committee are apparently not unlike those rules
> that govern collective bargaining negotiations.... Senator Fletcher was the
> chairman of the Senate group and Sam Rayburn [then chairman of the House
> Commerce Committee] headed the House delegation.... On the Senate side,
> there were such distinguished names as Carter Glass of Virginia, James Couz-
> ens of Michigan and Hiram Johnson of California. Senator Robert Wagner of
> New York was also a member of this Conference Committee. Although he
> signed its final report I cannot recall his appearance at any of the sessions....
> The House, on the other hand, had no such distinguished personalities except
> for Sam Rayburn, although each of its members was far better acquainted
> with the subject matter at hand than the representatives of the Senate.

Jockeying occurred in the beginning as to the procedures that should be adopted. In its midst, Senator Glass, who had been rapidly scanning the House bill, broke out into a tirade to the effect that he was the proponent of legislation dealing with banks and their relationships to the sale of securities and that he wanted no interference with his handling of these issues. We pointed out to him that the House bill had carefully excluded from its operations all securities issued by banks.... He growled, thumbed the bill for any further references to banks, found none, and shortly thereafter left the committee never to reappear.

Senator Fletcher, with the courteousness that always characterized him, suggested to Rayburn that he should accept the chairmanship of the committee at least for the first meeting. Rayburn agreed and shortly thereafter suggested that the first business was to come to a determination of which bill should become the basic working draft of the Committee. Rayburn quietly asked Senator Fletcher if he did not desire to make a motion on this matter. The Senator replied by moving that the Senate bill should be made the working draft. Rayburn took a vote on this motion and, finding that all the Senators voted for the motion and all the members of the House voted against the motion, applied the unit rule and declared that since the vote was a tie the motion failed of adoption and consequently the House bill would become the basic draft. That was the last we heard of the unit rule and the last of Title I of the Senate bill....

Work moved reasonably smoothly thereafter and Title I was completed by Friday. Senator Fletcher never requested to alternate the chairmanship, and, absent any request from him, Rayburn continued to guide the proceedings. The Committee met daily. Its sessions carried on throughout the mornings.... The representatives of the House were assiduous in their attendance, the Senate Members less so.[25]

In the era that has arrived since the passage of the Securities Act of 1933, the House typically does its most important legislating in bills that are broader in scope and more complex in their provisions. They tend to cut across more interests in the society and engage more committees of the House, and they require that the Speaker build broader coalitions than committee chairmen and floor managers of bills once needed to do.

THE PRESIDENT ACTS

Once a consolidated bill is agreed on in conference and passed in identical form by both houses, it goes to the President for his signature. If the President fails to sign the bill within ten days of the time he receives it (Sundays excepted), the bill becomes law unless Congress has adjourned. If Congress has adjourned, the President's failure to act constitutes a pocket veto and the bill fails of enactment. The pocket veto seems like a technicality of minor significance, but it is not, because the final days of a congressional session are hectic, and a great deal of legislation is passed under the pressure of adjournment. Congress, too, is constrained by the calendar: every two years it must adjourn long enough for House members and at least one-third of the Senate to go home and campaign for reelection. Understandably also, in years when there is no election, members of Congress are under some pressure to adjourn at least long enough to snatch a Christmas vacation with their families.

More formidable than the pocket veto is, of course, the veto. Under the Constitution, the President may return a bill to the house that originated it with his objections. The bill then may be reconsidered but must pass both houses of Congress in identical form by two-thirds majorities in order to become law. This means, in effect, that one-third of the votes plus one vote in either house constitutes a presidential majority, at least for the purpose of preventing the passage of legislation. The President may employ the threat of veto to discourage the consideration of legislative alternatives earlier in the process. This threat must normally be taken seriously, because it is a rare issue on which a President cannot find sufficient allies in the House or Senate to prevent passage over his veto.[26]

SUMMARY AND REVIEW: POWER IN THE PROCESS

The mere chronicle of the complicated and tortuous passage of bills through the legislative process should give some concrete meaning to the notion that there are many points in the American political system where it is possible for interested groups and interested parties to advance their cause. The considerable powers of committee chairmen and committee staffs, of the House Rules Committee, of the Speaker, of the Senate Majority Leader, and of the President and the executive agencies in the legislative process are nowhere more apparent than in the massive artistic production that is involved in producing a legislative product of any substantial significance. Even so, most of the dispersed powers in the process are essentially negative: legislation can be stalled or defeated in so many different ways, by so many different people. The powers to create formulas acceptable to successive majorities in committees and on the floors of both houses of Congress, formulas that are technically workable and politically feasible—are more concentrated. They rest most heavily with the President and his congressional agents, with the majority leadership in House and Senate, and with the members of Congress who manage the bills in House and Senate committees and on the floor.

chapter 6

NATIONAL POLICY-MAKING II:
The Budgetary Process

In the American political system, both Congress and the President shape national policy-making. It is, as one observer correctly noted, "a system of separated institutions *sharing* powers."[1] Probably the most significant set of national policies over which both Congress and the President share powers is the Federal budget.

The budget, according to David E. Bell, President Kennedy's first Director of the Bureau of the Budget, is

> ...a major means for unifying and setting forth an overall executive program....
> [It] reflects [the President's] judgment of the relative priority of different
> Federal activities. Thus, the President's budget necessarily reflects his policy
> judgments and the Congress in acting on the President's budget necessarily
> reviews these policy judgments as to the relative importance of alternative
> uses of national resources...
>
> The essential idea of the budget process is to permit a systematic consideration
> of our Government's program requirements in the light of available resources;
> to identify marginal choices and the judgment factors that bear on them; to
> balance competing requirements against each other; and, finally, to enable the
> President to decide upon priorities and present them to the Congress in the
> form of a coherent work program and financial plan.[2]

One of the Eisenhower administration's major financial officials agreed: "The American system of government provides no good alternative to reliance on the budget process as a means of coordinating and reviewing the activities of the departments and raising periodically for Presidential decision and review their effectiveness in actual performance."[3]

The budget is an enormous document, formulated annually. Until 1967 it reflected only the administrative expenditures of the government, but it now includes the rather sizable payments made by trust funds held by various governmental agencies, such as Old Age and Survivors Insurance and the Federal Unemployment Trust Fund.[4] The budget must be enacted into law, pursuant to the provision of the Constitution that "no money shall be drawn from the Treasury, but in consequence of Appropriations made by law."[5] This means that appropriations bills must be enacted annually before the wheels of government can turn and that these bills must come from Congress.[6]

But the budget, as a document, is in the first instance the President's. It is the President who must decide whether to retrench, expand, or hold the line in program planning, whether to risk a deficit, accumulate a surplus, or balance the budget. He must decide where and how to cut back existing programs and where and by how much other programs are to be encouraged to grow. Early each year it is the President who submits the detailed document to Congress. In February 1984 the budget called for the expenditure of $925.4 billion for fiscal year 1985.

Formulating and enacting the Federal budget is not merely a matter of bookkeeping; it is an intensely political procedure. The budgetary process determines to a great extent in any given year what activities the Federal government will undertake and to what extent it will undertake them. And so it is not surprising that the process by which a budget is born should call forth responses from the various parts of our political and governmental system and reflect in microcosm some of the major forces in national policy-making.

The fiscal year of the Federal government begins on October 1. For convenience, we can divide the budgetary process into five stages, beginning in March of the calendar year before the money is to be spent, that is, 18 months before the start of the fiscal year. (See Figure 1.)

PRESIDENTIAL PLANNING

Negotiations on the shape of the budget begin at a theoretical level. Economists in the Executive Office of the President, working for the Council of Economic Advisors (CEA) and the Office of Management and Budget (OMB), meet with economists from the Treasury Department and attempt to arrive at a mutually satisfactory forecast of levels of Federal revenue and expenditure for the year beginning two Octobers hence.[7] Some attempt is made to keep the budget in a known relationship with the expected income of the Federal government. Some Presidents have expressed strong desires for "balanced" budgets, in which expenditures never exceed income. However, it is very difficult to bring a Federal budget into precise balance,

FIGURE 1 Major Steps in the Budget Process

MAJOR STEPS IN THE BUDGET PROCESS

PERIOD BEFORE THE FISCAL YEAR	FISCAL YEAR	BEYOND FISCAL YEAR
MARCH JAN.	OCT. SEPT. 30	

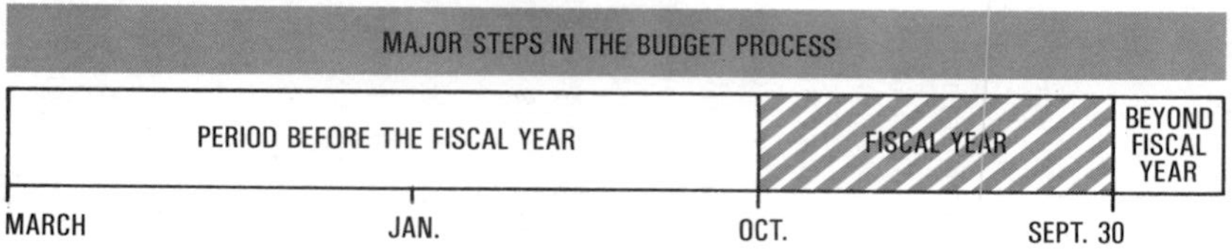

FORMULATION of President's Budget

Spring Budget overview and guidelines developed.

Summer Agencies prepare budget requests.

<u>Fall</u> President and OMB review requests.

January President submits budget to Congress.

EXECUTION of Enacted Budget

OMB apportions funds and agencies make allotments.

Agencies reprogram and transfer funds and request supplemental appropriations.

President proposes impoundments.

Beyond the fiscal year, post-auditing occurs and final budget data are made available.

CONGRESSIONAL BUDGET PROCESS

March–May Committees submit "views and estimates"; Congress adopts first budget resolution.

May–September Congress considers spending, revenue, and debt legislation and then adopts binding second budget resolution.

During Fiscal Year

Congress considers supplemental and continuing appropriations and adopts revised budget resolution.

From: Allen Schick and Robert Keith, Manual on the Federal Budget Process (Washington, D.C.: Library of Congress, Congressional Research Service, 1982), p. 4.

primarily because Federal revenues depend in large measure on the state of the economy as a whole. When domestic production and consumption are high and unemployment low, the government takes in more money. The income of the government is largely pegged to income taxes, which are dependent on domestic prosperity plus the level of inflation.[8] When businesses and private individuals make more, they pay more in taxes, swelling the government's coffers and permitting a higher level of Federal expenditure within a balanced budget.

If a recession occurs, production falls and unemployment increases, so individual and business incomes decline and the government takes in fewer tax dollars. This means that the government can finance fewer of its activities from current income. If the President is determined to balance the budget under these circumstances, he must cut back on Federal expenditures. It is more likely, however, that he will seek ways to stimulate the economy, which, his economic advisors devoutly hope, will eventually increase the flow of governmental income, although in the short run it is likely to further unbalance the budget.[9]

In an economic recession, the so-called automatic stabilizers of the economy, Federal payments that alleviate recessions, come into operation as required by law. One such stabilizer is the payments by the unemployment insurance program, which in the short run increase as the number of unemployed increases. The graduated Federal income tax is another major automatic stabilizer, because tax payments to the Federal government decrease as income decreases (although in recent years this has been offset by the effects of inflation, which have reduced the purchasing power of the dollar but kept many thousands of taxpayers in relatively high tax brackets).[10] In addition, the Federal government may, at the discretion of the President, accelerate the pace at which expenditures that are going to be made anyway are disbursed, as when the timetable on new defense contracts or public works is advanced so that work can commence more rapidly.

These and many other activities of the Federal government affect corporate and private decisions to invest and consume. The cumulative impact of all these decisions determines the level of the economy, and so it is no mean trick to forecast Federal income from six to eighteen months ahead.[11]

In order to forecast Federal expenditures for this period, it is necessary to get some idea of the demands Federal agencies will be making for funds. The OMB has in hand estimates that the agencies have already made of their needs for the fiscal year they are considering, but the larger agencies are asked to review these estimates and to project their probable needs for as long as five years ahead. As these estimates are reported to the OMB, they are examined and discussed with the agencies.

Meanwhile, the President discusses the preliminary forecasts with Cabinet members. At this point, discussions are being shaped toward two key decisions, both of which are made by the President and his top-level economic advisors.[12] The first decision relates to the fiscal policy the government will follow for the year. The President must decide whether to try to balance the budget, accumulate a surplus, or agree to deficit spending, which is spending at a higher rate than current income permits. This involves selling government bonds either to banks or to the public and increasing the so-called national debt, which is the amount in dollars of all outstanding marketable obligations of the government. This first decision sets a policy that will ultimately govern how much money all the various agencies of the government will be able to plan on spending in the year ahead.

The second major decision, actually a large cluster of decisions, is what the government will try to buy with the money available. The President and the OMB director go over the main items of the budget, and the President sets policy guidelines in which the extent and direction of new programs are decided in the light of expected demands and expected resources. Expected resources are estimated by the revenue forecasts and fiscal decisions already described.

Forecasts of expected demands are equally difficult to determine. In the case of expected revenues, the most useful information for forecasting the state of the economy the next year is the state of the economy now. So also for demands: the basic fact of overriding importance in determining next year's expenditure level in this year's budget is last year's budget.[13] Naturally, there will be changes, but looked at in the large, the changes are marginal. This fact can be seen by examination of Table 12, which gives the annual percentage of increase or decrease in appropriations for thirty-seven agencies (all concerned with domestic policy) over a twelve-year period centering on the 1950s.[14] Although the Reagan administration made a major effort to change things in the 1980s, Mr. Reagan's Budget Director David Stockman could still say:

> . . .[T]he budget isn't something you reconstruct each year. The budget is a sort of rolling history of decisions. All kinds of decisions, made five, ten, fifteen years ago, are coming back to bite us.[15]

TABLE 12   Range of Variation in Annual Appropriations for Thirty-seven Agencies over a Twelve-Year Period

Percentage change from previous year	0–5	6–10	11–20	21–30	31–40	41–50	51–100	101+
Cases (one agency per year = 1 case)	149	84	93	51	21	15	24	7
Total Cases: 444								

Source: Aaron B. Wildavsky, *The Politics of the Budgetary Process* (Boston: Little Brown, 1964), p. 14. Data from Richard F. Fenno, *The Power of the Purse* (Boston: Little, Brown, 1966).

TABLE 13   Percentage of GNP and of National Budget Spent on Defense, 1966–1984

	DEFENSE BUDGET AS A PERCENTAGE OF TOTAL BUDGET	DEFENSE BUDGET AS A PERCENTAGE OF GNP
1966	43.1	8.0
1967	45.3	9.2
1968	46.0	9.9
1969	44.9	9.1
1970	41.7	8.4
1971	37.5	7.6
1972	34.3	7.0
1973	31.2	6.1
1974	29.6	5.7
1975	26.7	5.8
1976	24.6	5.5
1977	24.2	5.2
1978	23.3	5.0
1979	23.7	5.0
1980	23.2	5.2
1981	24.0	5.5
1982	25.4	6.1
1983	26.4	6.5
1984	27.8	6.7 (est.)

Source: U.S. Bureau of the Budget, *The Budget in Brief, Fiscal Year 1985* (Washington, D.C.: Government Printing Office, 1984), pp. 69, 82.

In general, barring mobilization crises, there is a similar picture even for defense spending. Consider Table 13, which gives the percentage of the gross national product (GNP) and the percentage of the national budget spent on defense from 1966 to 1984. Table 14, which compares the Federal budget with the gross national product, reveals essentially the same thing: that changes in the budget are marginal from year to year.

The budget document is the President's, and he is expected to exercise leadership in budget politics. But because so much of the budget is directly tied to the performance of the economy, there are limits to the extent of the President's ability to use budgets for his own purposes. For example, a deteriorating economy not only reduces government revenues, but also increases the amount of money the government must pay out in the form of unemployment insurance, welfare payments, and food stamps. When inflation increases, government expenditures on Social Security, which are tied to the inflation rate, also rise. Allen Schick, a leading authority on contemporary budgeting, watched Jimmy Carter change his budget three times for the 1981 fiscal year as the result of "deteriorating economic conditions and spiraling program costs":

During the year [1980], automatic increases in uncontrollable accounts had done more to change the budget than had all the discretionary actions of the White House. The budget had become the destroyer of presidential dreams, compelling the chief executive to concede to forces beyond his control.[16]

PRESIDENTIAL "CEILINGS" AND AGENCY ESTIMATES

When the President has made basic decisions on the size of the budget, its role in the economy, and its general allocation pattern, the OMB director notifies the heads of the bureaus and departments about these preliminary decisions. He does this by means of a letter to the bureau heads asking for firm estimates of their agency's needs for the coming year and informing them of presidential budget policy—"ceilings" for each agency and guidelines about the proposal of new programs. It is difficult to describe precisely what presidential "ceilings" consist of and what they are used for. Maurice Stans, director of the Bureau of the Budget[17] under President Eisenhower, was once asked whether there was an overall "ceiling" for the 1961 budget. He replied:

I have not fixed a ceiling this year and did not fix one last year.

I do think that it is important, in considering a budget of this size, to take a look at it at various levels. By that I mean I think the Department of Defense should determine what kind of defense it can provide for $40 billion.

If this is done and everything is given its proper ranking in priority, then it can be determined whether or not it provides an adequate program, which items are next in rank of priority that should be considered, and which items are marginal or least essential. This does not mean I think that the defense of the country can unquestionably be satisfied for $40 billion. It means that as a matter of method I think the Department should start with a figure of that general magnitude and see what kind of a budget it can prepare at that level, and what, if anything, is then left out that is still sufficiently important that it has to be added.

That, in my opinion, is not a ceiling at all and it is not a target either. It is a method of procedure that I think is a desirable one to follow.[18]

David Bell described ceilings in these words:

There are cases ... in which ... the President would give some kind of preliminary planning dollar figure to an agency.... In such cases, however, we would not regard this, nor would the President regard this as a ceiling in the literal sense. We would regard it as a preliminary planning figure. The agency head would be expected to submit to the President a budget which would show what could be done for that figure, but he would also be expected to submit to the President any additions, any changes in that figure, which he regarded as necessary to carry out the agency's mission.

TABLE 14   Federal Budget and GNP Compared

	FEDERAL BUDGET AS A PERCENTAGE OF GNP
1966	18.6
1967	20.3
1968	21.4
1969	20.2
1970	20.2
1971	20.4
1972	20.4
1973	19.6
1974	19.4
1975	21.9
1976	22.2
1977	21.5
1978	21.4
1979	20.8
1980	22.4
1981	22.8
1982	23.8
1983	24.7
1984	24.0 (est.)

Source: *Budget of the United States, Fiscal Year 1985,*
pp. 9–60.

The President would not expect to end up with the figure that he started with. He would expect that after considering the detailed figures, the detailed budget, and the agency heads' opinion of the changes that would be desirable, the President would make a different and final judgment in the fall of the year.[19]

There is, in other words, a process going on in which successive approximations of a final figure are being made. The presidential ceiling is one such approximation, but, depending on how flexible Presidents decide they wish to be, it is open to negotiation and to appeal from agencies and is subject to modification.

At this point, the major focus of activity shifts to the agencies and bureaus within the executive branch, at a subdepartmental level. Figure 2 gives a simplified view of the organization for one department; it will help in visualizing the types of organizations in which budgetary activity at this stage is taking place. Bureau chiefs, receiving the letter from the OMB setting out presidential guidelines for their estimates, proceed to call for budget estimates from their offices and divisions. This call gives policies and priorities to be observed within the bureau.

These estimates and the justifications that accompany them will serve

FIGURE 2 The Department of the Interior

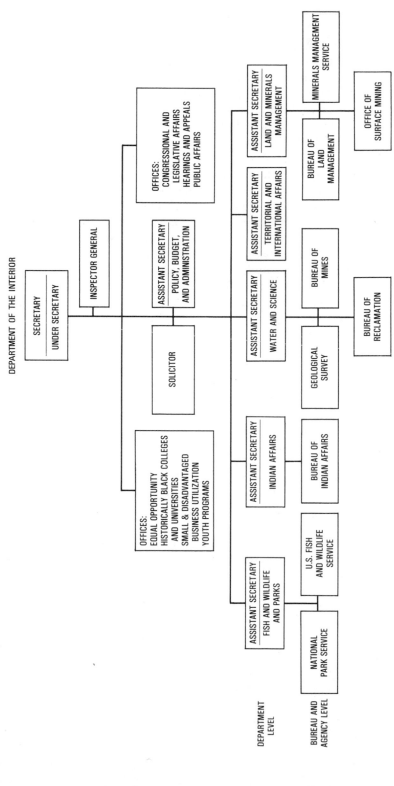

DEPARTMENT OF THE INTERIOR

SECRETARY
UNDER SECRETARY

INSPECTOR GENERAL

OFFICES:
CONGRESSIONAL AND
LEGISLATIVE AFFAIRS
HEARINGS AND APPEALS
PUBLIC AFFAIRS

ASSISTANT SECRETARY
POLICY, BUDGET,
AND ADMINISTRATION

SOLICITOR

OFFICES:
EQUAL OPPORTUNITY
HISTORICALLY BLACK COLLEGES
AND UNIVERSITIES
SMALL & DISADVANTAGED
BUSINESS UTILIZATION
YOUTH PROGRAMS

ASSISTANT SECRETARY
FISH AND WILDLIFE
AND PARKS

ASSISTANT SECRETARY
INDIAN AFFAIRS

ASSISTANT SECRETARY
WATER AND SCIENCE

ASSISTANT SECRETARY
TERRITORIAL AND
INTERNATIONAL AFFAIRS

ASSISTANT SECRETARY
LAND AND MINERALS
MANAGEMENT

NATIONAL
PARK SERVICE

U.S. FISH
AND WILDLIFE
SERVICE

BUREAU OF
INDIAN AFFAIRS

GEOLOGICAL
SURVEY

BUREAU OF
MINES

BUREAU OF
RECLAMATION

BUREAU OF LAND
MANAGEMENT

MINERALS MANAGEMENT
SERVICE

OFFICE OF
SURFACE MINING

DEPARTMENT
LEVEL

BUREAU AND
AGENCY LEVEL

Source: U.S. Government Organization Manual 1984/85 (Washington, D.C.: Government Printing Office, 1984), p. 833.

many purposes. Within the executive branch they will be the basis on which claims for a larger allocation are made, either in support of or as an appeal from presidential guidelines. It is here that agency executives show that it is necessary to expand the scope of their activities in order to do their job under the law or that it is necessary to spend more in order to maintain their current level of service. The same sorts of justifications will have to be presented first at the departmental level, where agencies within a department may have to compete for funds, then at the presidential level, at hearings conducted by examiners of the OMB, and still again before the appropriations subcommittees of Congress.

Under President Johnson a concerted attempt was made to reorganize the traditional methods for justifying budgetary demands so that expenditures could be more directly related to the missions and programs of agencies and to the results these programs were supposed to achieve. The Planning, Programming, Budgeting System (PPBS) was modeled on Secretary McNamara's efforts in the Defense Department to assert control over defense planning and procurement.[20] Although McNamara brought an important measure of civilian control to the gigantic Defense Department, the missions and expected benefits attributable to the activities of other departments did not prove easy to codify, and PPBS was abandoned in 1971.[21] President Carter revived a similar management scheme, which he called "zero based budgeting." It also failed.[22]

Estimates from the offices and divisions are put together in detail at the bureau level and submitted to scrutiny at the department level, usually by a departmental budget committee, which may include budget officers from the principal subdivisions within the department, the departmental budget officer, and the assistant secretary for administration of the department. The task of this group is to bring budget requests from the department's subdivisions into line with departmental policy, as laid down by the Secretary of the department, with presidential policy, as expressed through the OMB, and with congressional sentiment, as expressed in years past at appropriations subcommittee hearings and through informal contacts between departmental and bureau congressional liaison and budget officers, on the one hand, and congressmen, senators, and Appropriations Committee staff, on the other hand.

The requests from the subdivisions, and the manner in which the Secretary handles the process, will also reflect bureaucratic judgments about the success of various programs, and the demands of the groups that make up the clientele constituencies of the departments. An agency like the Department of Housing and Urban Development, for example, maintains programs of direct interest to home builders, tenants' rights organizations, the Urban League, the National League of Cities, the Governors' Conference, mortgage bankers, and so on. Most of these interests are organized in the sense that they have professional staff looking after their interests in Washington, carefully observing the course of policy-making, and intervening in behalf of programs they favor.

Thus the process of harmonizing a departmental budget with the various demands and policies of these different groups is not mechanical, but political. Departmental policy-makers must calculate whether the time is right to forge ahead with a particular program, and if so, how far ahead. They must count the costs of cutting back another program in terms of the interest groups affected and their access to key congressmen. The major decisions, and especially cases of disagreement, are settled by the departmental Secretary.

PRESIDENTIAL OVERSIGHT

Before the Budget and Accounting Act of 1921, the process on the executive side had less presidential participation and ended at this point, with the departmental estimate. Budgetary requests from individual departments were assembled at the Treasury Department and transmitted in a single document without alteration; the rest was up to Congress. In 1921 the Bureau of the Budget was created in the Treasury Department as an agency through which departmental requests could be filtered. When the Bureau was moved to the Executive Office of the President in 1939, the budget became a major device for presidential control of the executive bureaucracies.[23]

At this stage of the process, departmental budget requests are submitted to the OMB, which goes over them with some care. OMB agency specialists discuss requests informally with departmental representatives and hold hearings at which agency budget and operating officials make formal presentations in defense of their requests. Here, once again, major attention is devoted to deviations from expectations, to changes in requests from last year, to justifications for new programs, to performance statistics such as those reporting workloads of employees, and to deviations from presidential guidelines.

As the OMB grew in strength during the Nixon administration, these hearings took on a heightened importance for the rest of the bureaus and agencies of government. Only the Defense Department maintained a degree of autonomy since its budgetary guidelines came from the National Security Council rather than from the OMB, and since the department's budget, traditionally the last one received in the OMB, never was given more than a *pro forma* review by the OMB director. It is regarded in the government as symbolically significant that whereas the hearings of all other departments are held in the OMB offices, OMB hearing examiners travel to the Pentagon to examine the defense budget, and these are customarily far more perfunctory and more subject to the influence of the Cabinet officer involved than is true of any other set of departmental hearings.

When these hearings are completed, the OMB puts together a recommendation to the President, who has a final opportunity to go over the results and to propose last-minute adjustments. As soon as his decisions are made, letters are prepared and sent to the agencies informing them of the budgetary requests the President intends to send to Congress in their behalf. There is then a short period in which emergency appeals from top executives of bureaus and departments may be entertained, but by this time the calendar is crowding in on all participants in the process. The budget must be printed, proofread, bound, and transmitted to Congress in January.

The budget has been described as a vast network of bargains. The President has his ceiling to protect and certain programmatic interests. Agencies want to give service to their clientele and often want to expand their programs. Interest groups served by agencies maintain a keen interest in the capacity of agencies to serve them. Through the continuous participation of the OMB in the process of budget-making, the President bargains with the executive agencies. When he sends his final letter to departments and bureaus, the President seals the bargain and adopts as his program the various programs of the agencies for which money has been requested. It is still incumbent on each department and bureau to make its case before Congress, but now the President is at least formally on their side of the bargaining table, not across the table as heretofore.[24]

Some agencies may still feel slighted or shortchanged by the outcome of this process since the mixture of activities they now must advocate reflects OMB choices rather than their own. Their part of the bargain nevertheless entails defending their section of the President's budget before Congress. Bureau chiefs may not openly volunteer their disagreements with the final figures, but they may, and occasionally do, respond to direct questions in congressional appropriations hearings with "personal opinions" at variance with official budget requests. Appropriations subcommittee hearings contain examples of this:

> *OFFICIAL:* If I go into those questions my personal opinions might conflict with the Budget Report.... But I want to make it clear to the committee that I have acquiesced in the limiting figure of the budget.
>
> *CONGRESSMAN:* You want this committee not to increase the amount of this budget?
>
> *OFFICIAL:* Oh, no; I recognize in Congress the power to do what it wants with this budget.
>
> *CONGRESSMAN:* Do you feel that it [service] is adequate?...
>
> *OFFIICAL:* It is all I am permitted to come here and ask you for.
>
> *CONGRESSMAN:* How much would you like to ask for?
>
> *OFFICIAL:* Oh, 50 percent more.
>
> *CONGRESSMAN:* What did you ask the Department for?
>
> *OFFICIAL:* $885,314,000.
>
> *CONGRESSMAN:* What did you get from the Bureau of the Budget?

OFFICIAL: $780,000,000.

CONGRESSMAN: Between the two, they only cut $100 million. Did you ask for too much?

OFFICIAL: No, sir.

CONGRESSMAN: Do you think you could use that $100 million if Congress voted it?

OFFICIAL: I think we could use the bulk of it yes, sir.[25]

OFFICIAL: We requested direct loans of REA, for example, we requested direct loans of ---

CONGRESSMAN: How much did you request for REA?

OFFICIAL: $438 million for electric loans.

CONGRESSMAN: $438 million. Can you tell the committee when this new policy as set forth in this budget was arrived at? Was that after it had reached the OMB?

OFFICIAL: Yes.

CONGRESSMAN: After it reached OMB?

OFFICIAL: Yes.

CONGRESSMAN: Now that is not new money, is it, Mr. Miles? When you speak of REA, are you talking about authorization or are you talking about money?

OFFICIAL: New authorization.

CONGRESSMAN: New authorization. What other items do you have scattered throughout this budget where there is a substantial reduction in the request of the Department by OMB. Give one or two others, for instance.

OFFICIAL: For the Agricultural Research Service, we requested $196 million.

CONGRESSMAN: The amount included in the proposal as submitted to the committee is how much, Mr. Miles?

OFFICIAL: $180 million.

CONGRESSMAN: Go ahead and give us one or two more.

OFFICIAL: We requested $94.6 million for the Cooperative State Research Service, and the budget includes $73.7 million for that Service.

CONGRESSMAN: What about Extension Service?

OFFICIAL: We requested $232.8 million for the Extension Service. The allowance was $196.8 million.

CONGRESSMAN: Since you had your figures pretty well justified as you submitted them, Mr. Miles ---

OFFICIAL: We did. But we can only look at programs from the point of view of the Department of Agriculture and others have a responsibility to look beyond that for the total Government. We are not in a position to evaluate our request against requests of other departments and agencies.[26]

If agencies are not always completely loyal to the budget as it is sent to Capitol Hill, it is because this document, when it arrives for congressional action, is a presidential document, reflecting presidential priorities and containing the most minute and comprehensive summary of what the President wants his administration to undertake in the fiscal year ahead.

Presidents are occasionally disloyal to their own budgets, claiming that Congress must take the responsibility—and incur the political costs—of cutting them somehow. This position understandably enrages the President's opponents in Congress, since it means the President is publicly challenging them to do precisely what he has refused to do himself. Because this process is so complex, only Washington insiders are likely to understand how anomalous the spectacle is of a President unwilling to cut his own budget who nevertheless insists that Congress must do it. Correspondingly, on the congressional side, members may

> vote for reductions in appropriations bills, thereby taking credit for being responsible economizers. At the same time, they have voted for huge increases in entitlement programs by relaxing eligibility requirements and raising benefit levels that later resulted in higher spending in the uncontrollable accounts.[27]

Just before the President sends the budget to Congress, he may take special pains to acquaint key congressmen with its major provisions and with the economic and political premises on which these provisions are based. While the budget is being put in final shape, the Economic Report of the President and his State of the Union Message are receiving their finishing touches. Each of these three documents is written and designed to be read in the light of the other two. All three are delivered to Congress by the President in the opening days of each session, in late January.

CONGRESSIONAL ACTION: BUDGET RESOLUTIONS AND RECONCILIATION

Under the provisions of the Congressional Budget and Impoundment Control Act of 1974, the President's budget is received by two sets of committees. One set consists of the budget committees of the House and Senate.[28] These committees are charged with the responsibility of holding hearings on the budget document as a whole, and of submitting to their respective houses a concurrent resolution (which does not require the President's signature) establishing overall totals for the major categories of expenditure, and reconciling these guidelines with estimates of expected revenue. By May 15 the House and Senate must agree upon these guidelines and must, in effect, endorse an overall level of expenditure for the government in light of expected revenues. Once the appropriations committees of the House and Senate are well underway in their work, and more is known about revenues and expected deficits or surpluses, the budget committees are expected to meet again and by September 15 produce a concurrent resolution setting a limit to overall expenditures. If the various appropriations subcommittees bring in appropriations bills that total more than the September guidelines allow, it will be necessary for the appropriations subcommittees to reduce the expenditure totals called for in their bills; otherwise, the House and Senate must agree to an amended—that is, increased—set of guidelines.

In practice, the September resolution, which is supposed to be binding, comes too late to influence a budget due to be completed in a couple of weeks. Consequently, the earlier resolution has become steadily more important, and as its importance has increased since 1980, its date of adoption has been delayed.

Date of Adoption of First Budget Resolution

FISCAL YEAR	DATE OF ADOPTION
1977	May 13, 1976
1978	May 17, 1977
1979	May 15, 1978
1980	May 23, 1979
1981	June 11, 1980
1982	May 21, 1981
1983	June 23, 1982

Source: Testimony of Les Aspin in "Congressional Budget Process," *Hearings Before the Task Force on the Budget Process of the Committee on Rules*, House of Representatives, 97th Congress, Second Session, September 15-29, 1982, p. 34.

In some cases, it is impossible to set budget ceilings without making changes in existing laws. In order to cut spending on food stamps, for example, it may be necessary to tighten the rules governing eligibility for the program, an action that in turn requires changes in the law that set up the program. When changes of this kind are necessary to enforce budget ceilings, the budget committee attaches "reconciliation instructions" to its resolutions in which it asks the relevant substantive committees of Congress to make the requisite changes. In 1981 this produced a substantial cutback in expenditures on entitlement programs, but it is not expected that such drastic measures will be employed frequently. By attaching "reconciliation instructions" to the resolution, the first budget resolution is made binding—rather than advisory, as originally envisioned—on other congressional committees, which are required to fit their programs to the spending limits set in the resolution.

Upon passage of the budget resolution containing reconciliation instructions, action reverts to the various substantive committees of the House of Representatives to adjust authorizing levels. At the same time, the Appropriations Committee begins to mark up appropriations bills flowing in from its subcommittees, if it has not already begun, and the substantive committees whose entitlement programs have been targeted for reconciliation savings must begin their work.

First budget resolutions containing reconciliation instructions have also stipulated to the committees a date by which they are to report their reconciled legislation, usually about a month after the passage of the resolution. This committee legislation does not go directly to the floor or to the Rules Committee, but to the Budget Committee, which performs a stapling function: it transforms the committee bills into one large cluster of bills, and then sends it onward to the Rules Committee.

The House and Senate Budget Committees, which are charged with the primary function of producing these budget resolutions, have gone about their business in rather different ways. The Senate committee was created as a separate entity of the Senate, a new committee with a new set of tasks. Under its first chairman, Edmund Muskie (1975-1980), a bipartisan alliance was forged with ranking minority member Henry Bellmon, and the committee customarily wrote its resolution in interminable mark-up sessions, in which they would go through each set of governmental functions laboriously, striving to set a budget figure for each that would gain majority support. After that they would add it all up, usually deciding that the total was too high. Back they would go over the functions again and try to whittle them down so that the budget total would be acceptable, too. Committee action was open and bipartisan. Transcripts of committee mark-up sessions on display in the publications office of the Senate Budget Committee show, from the sheer tonnage of the volumes, that under Muskie's chairmanship long hours in committee were spent trying to hammer out bipartisan accords that would stand up on the Senate floor. Since 1981 the Senate Budget Committee has been highly partisan, and the length of the transcript has diminished greatly as the committee is more often used to ratify decisions made elsewhere, such as (during the period of Republican control of the Senate) in the committee's Republican caucus, the Reagan White House, or the Office of Management and Budget.

The decision style in the House Budget Committee has been markedly different: partisan from the start and focused on the chairman and his staff. The House committee, because of the limited tenure of its members, all of whom retain permanent committee assignments elsewhere, has had a more difficult time establishing itself as the sort of entity to which members might give their loyalty. In the House, passing budget resolutions has become a major test for the committee's leadership, and sometimes it does not succeed. The second committee chairman,[29] Brock Adams of Washington, established a pattern of strong, independent committee leadership, a pattern that persisted in the cautious, conciliatory, and successful chairmanship of Robert Giaimo of Connecticut (1977-1980). Jim Jones of Oklahoma, the fourth chairman, took seriously the emerging responsibility of the chairman to shape budget resolutions, which after wide consultation he wrote in private with his staff. This system caused some animosity among those committee members who preferred a more open style. Before convening the committee mark-ups on the resolution, Jones was a very busy man, for he talked to nearly all—if not all—Democrats in the House to see what it would take to get them to vote for the resolution. He defined his task as assembling a majority in the House as a whole, and he operated so as to put himself in the center of these negotiations. Negotiations within the committee have consequently had much less importance in the House than in the Senate.

Budget resolutions, though they take no notice of any appropriation under $100 million, nevertheless are based on fairly detailed program assumptions. As originally designed, the first budget resolution was supposed to contain *targets*, and the second budget resolution was supposed to be binding. This is why the 1974 Congressional Budget Act originally called for reconciliation, the enforcement tool, to be used in conjunction with the second resolution. However, because there are only two weeks or less between the passage of the second resolution and the start of the fiscal year, there was no time actually to reconcile appropriations to the second resolution. Thus in 1980 the House and Senate both voted to put reconciliation language into the first resolution, thus making the first resolution more consequential. In a few short years the second resolution has withered in importance, and it may not survive much longer.

In order to meet the substantial intellectual burdens imposed by the creation of this new set of demands for overall guidelines, Congress provided that each of the budget committees should have its own staff, and in addition established a Congressional Budget Office, a professional organization whose job it is to provide economic estimates and forecasts as well as alternative projections of expenditures for the use of the budget and the appropriations committees.[30]

Liberal beliefs in the efficacy of overall planning, plus a desire to curb the Nixon administration's profligate impoundment policies combined with conservative anxieties about growing Federal expenditures and budget deficits to create a coalition in both House and Senate favoring the establishment of these committees and the enormous increase in staff that they involved. No doubt liberals expected more rational and just expenditures of funds, and conservatives expected smaller Federal budgets as a result of this innovation in public policy.[31] Although neither set of expectations seems fully to have been realized, the big winner so far has been the Reagan administration, which used a reconciliation resolution in 1981 to force reductions in program spending along a very broad front.

Under normal procedures as they existed before 1981, legislation to cut a total of $40 billion from over a hundred programs would have to have been written separately for each program and sent to the various substantive committees and subcommittees having jurisdiction over them. There, almost certainly, nothing more would have happened. The President's influence would have been dissipated, for although he is powerful, he could not hope to prevail on each and every one of the hundreds of votes that he would have had to win to push a $40 billion budget cut through Congress. By writing his entire spending program into the first budget resolution of 1981, however, and adding reconciliation provisions at that point, Reagan had only to win two big votes: on the amendment attaching reconciliation to the resolution, and on the budget resolution itself, which directed the committees to make legislative changes saving specified amounts of money. These changes were adopted into law as a single bill, one of the largest bills ever passed on a single vote.[32]

The decentralization of congressional power and responsibility among authorizing, appropriating and budget committees, party leaders and the Congressional Budget Office and the multiple votes that ordinarily need to be taken along the legislative path for any given measure tend to insulate members of Congress from casual observation. By aggregating a large number of budgeting decisions into a single omnibus measure, reconciliation tends to focus a fair amount of attention on this vote, and, as President Reagan showed in 1981, allows the president greater budgetary influence in Congress. This may prove to be a factor in determining whether this process is modified or discontinued in the future.[33]

CONGRESSIONAL ACTION: THE APPROPRIATION PROCESS

The submission of the budget to congressional budget committees for overall guidelines is the newer of the two tracks the budget follows in Congress. There is also a second, concurrent track, the appropriations process, which I shall now describe.

The Constitution provides that "All bills for raising Revenue shall originate in the House of Representatives."[34] This rule has, over the years, been given a broad interpretation. By a tradition based on this language, all "money" bills, both for taxing and for spending, now begin in the House, and so while the budget goes to both houses simultaneously, by custom the House of Representatives acts first on it. The budget is referred to the Committee on Appropriations—with 55 members, the largest committee in the House. There it is split into thirteen parts of various sizes and sent to subcommittees, each of which processes a bill dealing with a specified group of agencies and governmental functions.

The membership, size, and jurisdiction of these thirteen subcommittees are partly the handiwork of custom, which helps in determining what sorts of subcommittees there will be. Partly, they are shaped by the committee assignment process, through which energetic Majority and Minority

Leaders can, over the years, pack the committee with members of their choosing. Partly also, so long as the House is controlled by the Democratic party, they are shaped by the Democratic caucus, which in 1975 asserted the power to vote separately and secretly on the chairmen of all appropriations subcommittees.[35]

Formerly the chairman of the committee could use his power to constitute subcommittees and appoint members to them. This gave him considerable control over the extent to which subcommittees favored the programs coming under their jurisdiction.

> Since the early 1970s, however, members have been allowed to pick their subcommittees in accord with a seniority-based procedure. Inevitably, this self-selection has led to a predominance of program advocates on subcommittees.[36]

The Appropriations Committee has traditionally been regarded as something of a law unto itself, even within the House. It guards all its prerogatives jealously. It resists attempts by the Senate to originate appropriations bills. It attacks all legislation that provides for the financing of government programs through Treasury loans or revolving funds, thus escaping the toils of the budgetary process. Nevertheless, increasingly in recent years it has lost ground in protecting its jurisdiction. In fiscal year 1983 entitlement spending such as social security payments and interest payments on the national debt together accounted for 62 percent of all outlays. Although interest payments do receive appropriations, the committee can exercise no discretion as to their amounts and must appropriate as much as is needed, lest the government default on its debts. Nondefense discretionary spending accounts for only 17 percent of all spending.[37] And the Appropriations Committee has lost power in the squeeze between the budget committee, whose guidelines impose an overall ceiling on appropriations, and substantive House committees, which have established entitlement programs funded by means other than appropriations.[38]

The committee is universally regarded as hard-working, even by the most craftsmanlike House standards. Subcommittee hearings are famous for their detailed, lengthy, sometimes harsh scrutiny of budget items.

> Hearings on a routine major bill may run for six weeks of nearly daily sessions. Swelled on the one hand by matter prepared in advance (like the justifications) and by information worked up later at the request of committee members during the hearings (usually inserted at the point where the question appears), the printed hearings have become monumental.[39]

The traditional view of the committee is that, with the possible exceptions of generous subcommittees in charge of defense and health budgets, each of the subcommittees is united in a common task:

... to guard the Federal Treasury. Committee members state their goals in the essentially negative terms of guardianship—screening requests for money, checking against ill-advised expenditures, and protecting the taxpayer's dollar. In the language of the committee's official history, the job of each member is "constantly and courageously to protect the Federal Treasury against thousands of appeals and imperative demands for unnecessary, unwise and excessive expenditure."[40]

More recently, this norm has been diluted. Allen Schick quotes a committee staff member:

The Appropriations Committees have been living off a claim to past glory. It might have been true in the past that the committees really cut the request of the President, but it certainly hasn't been true in recent times. Most of the cuts are picked up in supplemental appropriations or in the next budget. Nowadays, true cuts are so seldom that it would be newsworthy to have a big one.[41]

Distinguishing among "Housekeeping Functions" ("for the continuing operation of Federal agencies"), "Defense and International Programs," and "Client-Oriented Programs," Schick shows that the committee made very small cuts—about 2 or 3 percent— in the Housekeeping area between 1970 and 1975. In this same time period the Defense and International Programs experienced deep cuts, while the Client-Oriented Programs (such as Agriculture, Public Works, Veterans Administration, Education) were given substantial increases.[42]

Agency heads from the executive departments appear on Capitol Hill at subcommittee hearings and, just as they have done "downtown," before the OMB, they defend their budgetary requests. The arduousness of this experience can be suggested by a few excerpts from the transcripts of hearings:

OFFICIAL: We have already closed two regional offices, one the Los Angeles office, moving to somewhat smaller quarters.

CONGRESSMAN: Did you say the Los Angeles office?

OFFICIAL: Yes, Mr. Chairman.

CONGRESSMAN: Will you repeat that statement again, because I want to be sure it is on the record. You have done what, now?

OFFICIAL: We are moving to smaller quarters, sir.

CONGRESSMAN: In Los Angeles you are moving to smaller quarters?

OFFICIAL: I am afraid so. On the other hand, they are more centrally located.

CONGRESSMAN: Well, that is a consolation.

OFFICIAL: We are moving to a Federal building, which although smaller, it will place us near a large segment—

CONGRESSMAN: You are now moving to the Valley?

OFFICIAL: No, we are moving to Westwood.

CONGRESSMAN: Westwood?
OFFICIAL: That is where I went to school.
CONGRESSMAN: So did I, but that does not mean that that is the center of the population.
OFFICIAL: Well, sir, there is the Federal building at 11000 Wilshire.
CONGRESSMAN: It was a mistake to build that building to begin with. But we are not going to go into that at this moment. To go back to the answer you started to give us with regard to closing some of these offices, I am glad you are not closing the Los Angeles office.
OFFICIAL: We are making it more efficient.
CONGRESSMAN: More efficient. I was going to say more inefficient. But more efficient.[43]

* * *

CONGRESSMAN: [Last year] I think we appropriated about $100 million.
OFFICIAL: $97.1 million.
CONGRESSMAN: For 1974 you are down to $25 million. Are you going to carry out the intent of Congress with that large a reduction?... Now, is this another one of those heartless cuts down at OMB? Is this cutting off of the kids' milk the same as the cutoff of the veterans' benefits?... Are the kids next?
OFFICIAL: No. This would provide sufficient funds to insure that a child has either a full lunch available to him ... or ... has at least milk available to him.
CONGRESSMAN: Has a sufficient amount of research gone into this, so that you are not going to deprive those youngsters?
OFFICIAL: In my judgment there has....
CONGRESSMAN: Please send me the justification for this. I want to see whether you have researched this enough so that you are not going to cut out those kids.[44]

The appropriations subcommittees exercise to the full their prerogative of examining the justifications for Federal programs. This may mean making requests for specific services to constituents and looking into work loads, both of which are checks into the ongoing performance of executive bureaucrats. But there are severe limits on the time of subcommittee members and staff. They cannot hope to inquire into every aspect of executive performance. They cut corners by asking about items they may know something about or by trying to find things that look "fishy" or by concentrating on deviations in requests or performance from prior years.[45]

The powers of the subcommittees extend further. As the "saucers that cool the legislative tea," in the colorful phrase of a subcommittee chairman,[46] these subcommittees may effectively nullify the will of Congress expressed through ordinary legislation by refusing to appropriate money authorized by law. On the other hand, they are not permitted to appropriate where there is no authorization; to do so would be legislating in an appropriations measure, an act that can be blocked on the House floor by a simple point of order. On such occasions the offending section is removed. When the committee wants blanket protection against points of order, they must go to the Rules Committee for a special order or rule waiving points of order against it.

Hearings are followed by mark-up sessions, as in the case of authorization bills. Here, however, the thirteen subcommittees do the real work. Each of these subcommittees, once it is put together with the blessing of the chairman, is quite independent. "One subcommitteeman chairman exclaimed: 'Why, you'd be branded an imposter if you went into one of those other subcommittee meetings.... Each one does its work apart from all others.'"[47] The subcommittees also do their work relatively free from partisan discord. "Since they deal immediately with dollars and cents, it is easy for the members to hold to the idea that they are not dealing with programmatic questions, that theirs is a 'business' rather than a 'policy' committee."[48]

When all the bargains are finally struck in the subcommittee, the bill is presented to the full committee for ratification, not for change. "It's a matter of 'you respect my work and I'll respect yours.' 'It's frowned upon if you offer an amendment in the full Committee if you aren't on the subcommittee.' 'It's considered presumptuous to pose as an expert if you aren't on the subcommittee....' Members agree that subcommittee recommendations are 'very rarely changed.'"[49] Two observers of the Eighty-eighth Congress have given an excellent picture of how full committee compliance is encouraged:

> Most sessions of the ... Committee are as ritualistic and meaningless as a gathering of the Supreme Soviet in Moscow. A subcommittee's report on a bill isn't even seen by the full Committee until members file into the meeting room. Before they have a chance to glance at the report [the chairman] gavels the bill through. The entire process takes about five minutes.
> This system makes it impossible for a Committee member to influence the contents of a spending bill unless he happens to be a member of the subcommittee involved—with one little exception. The exception is [the committee chairman] himself, who wanders in and out of all subcommittee meetings, making a suggestion here and influencing a decision there. He and only he is familiar with the full scope of the Committee's work.[50]

A junior member of the committee said, "When the main committee meets, the subcommittee report is on your desk. You've never seen it before. You know how thick it is? This thick! [about two inches.] Well, you thumb through it, and meanwhile [the chairman] asks if there are any questions. You can't even ask an intelligent question."[51]

Nowadays the norms of comity are weakening and subcommittees are more often challenged in full committee. Likewise the full Appropriations Committee is more often challenged on the floor. When an appropriations bill is ready to be reported, the chairman arranges for time on the floor directly with the Speaker and Majority Leader. His committee has privileged access to the floor without recourse to the Rules Committee.[52] Before 1974 the Appropriations Committee rarely released its reports before the day on which debate was to be held. This practice was very unpopular; as a result, during a flurry of rules changes in 1974 a three-day layover between the reception of reports and debate was instituted. This has made a sizable difference in outcomes. Before 1974, when the committee was united, as it usually was, it almost always got its way. A tabulation of the appropriations histories of thirty-six bureaus dealing with domestic policies for sixteen years (1947-1962) showed that the House deviated from committee recommendations only 10.1 percent of the time. The rest of the time, Appropriations Committee recommendations prevailed to the last dollar.[53] In the 1970s, committee unity on the floor diminished, and with it, the committee's capacity to withstand floor amendments. From 1974 to 1980 an average of 75 amendments were adopted to appropriation bills; in the prior seven years the average was only 22.[54]

Schick reports that there were 200 financial amendments to appropriations bills (as opposed to nongermane riders) in the Ninety-first and Ninety-second Congresses (1969-1970 and 1971-1972) in the House. That means an average of 50 per year and three or four per bill.

> Proposed increases outnumbered amendments calling for reductions. Also as might be expected, demands for higher spending were more successful than proposed decreases. Less than 10 percent of the reductions were passed, but 40 percent of the increases received majority support. Overall the House committee had a success rate of almost 75 percent, slightly better than the long-term average computed by Fenno for the period from 1947 to 1972.[55]

While the *proportion* of successful amendments remained about constant, the absolute *number* of amendments both offered and passed increased. This increase is consistent, as Schick points out, with the long-term increase in floor amendments in the House.[56]

Inroads have been made on the procedural advantages once enjoyed by the committee. Committee mark-ups, once closed, are now open. The appointments in each Congress of the committee chairman and subcommittee chairmen are all subjected to approval of the Democratic caucus, by secret ballot. This means that there are incentives for chairmen to be more responsive to spending pressures from within their party. Votes in the Committee of the Whole, in which floor consideration of appropriations bills takes place, are now publicly recorded.[57]

Moreover, the disposition of the Appropriations Committee to cut back on programs has declined, at least in part, because the party composition of the committee has been shifted to provide a 3-2 Democratic majority and the subcommittees have been slightly enlarged. The influence of conservatives in the Democratic caucus has declined over the years. All of these changes have reduced the effectiveness on the committee of the conservative coalition which once could regularly outvote the more liberal Democrats.[58]

Changing the composition of the Committee has had additional effects. As Schick explains:

> The addition of liberal Democrats not only changed the political complexion of the committee; it also undermined socialization and cooptation of new members. With many newcomers joining the committee in each Congress, it was not possible for the slow "learning" process to successfully educate the recruits in the traditional committee norms. Moreover, a number of the new Democrats joined the committee to subvert its traditionally conservative approach on spending issues.[59]

When appropriations bills reach the Senate, they have been thoroughly worked over. Senatorial scrutiny is much less detailed and generally much more sympathetic to the agencies. In appropriations, the Senate is traditionally regarded as an appeals body. Agencies are expected to complain in hearings about those aspects of the House bill that seem likely to do them the most damage. The Senate often restores these cuts.[60]

In part, the Senate Appropriations Committee is more liberal than its counterpart in the House because of its position as legislatively second in line and because of the way the House Appropriations Committee defines its role. There are other reasons as well. In the House, Appropriations is an exclusive committee, occupying all of a legislator's time and absorbing all his committee loyalties. Not so in the Senate: Appropriations Committee members all serve elsewhere. Subcommittees are manned predominantly by senators who are members of the substantive Senate committees that passed the bills enacting the programs whose appropriations are before them. Thus, in the House, money bills have traditionally been seen primarily in the context of assaults on the treasury; in the Senate, as financial extensions of programs, as expressions of legitimate social and political demands.[61]

The mechanics of the conference process are the same for appropriations bills as for other bills. When House and Senate bills are not identical, representatives of both sides meet and hammer out a compromise. The result then goes directly to each house for a final vote, without amendment.[62] Because appropriations are necessary for the very running of the government, the likelihood that such bills will be rejected by the House or Senate at the last stage or vetoed by the President is remote. This situation places an extra measure of responsibility and power on members of appropriations conferences.

Occasionally—and regularly of late—this process is not completed by the beginning of the fiscal year, as the following table shows:

	1977	1978	1979	1980	1981	1982
Bills enacted by start of fiscal year	13	10	5	3	2	1
Number finally enacted	13	12	12	11	9	10

Source: Aspin testimony, *op cit.*, p.35.

When a bill is not ready, even though the fiscal year for which it makes appropriations has begun, the Appropriations Committees report continuing resolutions, which provide for financing of government activities month by month on the same basis as in the preceding year.

There is also a procedure by which agencies can request appropriations to supplement the amounts in their annual appropriation. This process is essentially the same as I have already outlined, only it usually proceeds at a somewhat faster pace and as the result of a special request not included in the budget. Presidents can submit balanced budgets to Congress and then unbalance them by making heavy use of supplemental requests. Having what looks like a balanced budget at the start of the fiscal year is a useful propaganda device. The government frequently spends more than the budget asks for, however. There are, as well, some reallocations among programs as the result of the budgetary process. Moreover, often receipts are less than predicted. Table 15 in this chapter gives the figures for a recent thirty-year period.

Finally, in addition to regular appropriations, continuing resolutions, and supplementals, there is a fourth appropriations device: rescission bills. Rescissions, which are repeals of appropriations, are sometimes contained under the program headings in the first three classes of bills, but they sometimes are provided for in individual bills. They are used where the underlying authorization to spend is repealed or lapses, where the intent of Congress can be achieved by spending less money, or where for policy reasons an administration desires not to spend money as enacted. Unless Congress enacts a rescission bill within 45 days after the Office of Management and Budget impounds an appropriation,[63] the OMB is obliged to commit the funds. These procedures were spelled out in the 1974 Congressional Budget and Impoundment Control Act, which was enacted to curb President Nixon's profligate use of impoundments as a means of executing policies he could not persuade Congress to support. Since the enactment of this legislation, impoundments are no longer a significant arena of conflict between Congress and the President.

TABLE 15 The Extent to Which Federal Budgets Predict Actual Federal Expenditures, 1953-1983 (in Billions of Dollars)

YEAR	FEDERAL BUDGET	PREDICTED SURPLUS (DEFICIT)	ACTUALLY SPENT	ACTUAL SURPLUS (DEFICIT)	OVER (UNDER) SPENDING	OVER (UNDER) ESTIMATE OF RECEIPTS
1953	84.6	(14.4)	74.1	(9.4)	(10.5)	5.4
1954	77.6	(9.9)	67.5	(3.1)	(10.1)	3.4
1955	65.4	(2.9)	64.4	(4.2)	(1.0)	2.2
1956	62.1	(2.4)	66.2	1.6	4.1	(8.1)
1957	64.6	0.4	69.0	1.6	4.4	(5.6)
1958	71.2	1.8	71.4	(2.8)	0.2	(4.4)
1959	73.6	0.5	80.3	(12.4)	6.7	(6.2)
1960	76.3	0.1	76.5	1.2	—	1.3
1961	79.1	4.2	81.5	(3.9)	2.4	(5.7)
1962	80.9	1.5	87.8	(6.4)	6.9	(1.0)
1963	92.5	0.5	92.6	(6.2)	0.1	(6.6)
1964	98.8	(11.9)	97.7	(8.3)	(1.1)	(2.5)
1965	97.9	(4.9)	96.5	(3.4)	(1.4)	(0.1)
1966	99.7	(5.3)	130.9[a]	(3.8)[a]	34.9[a]	(36.3)[a]
1967	153.6	(3.8)	158.4	(8.8)	4.8	(0.2)
1968	169.2	(2.1)	178.9	(25.2)	9.7	(13.4)
1969	183.7	2.4	184.6	3.1	0.9	(1.6)
1970	192.9	5.8	196.6	(2.8)	3.7	5.0
1971	212.8	(18.6)	211.4	(23.0)	(1.4)	5.8
1972	236.6	(38.8)	231.9	(23.2)	(4.7)	(10.9)
1973	246.3	(25.5)	246.5	(14.3)	0.2	(11.4)
1974	268.7	(12.7)	267.9	(4.7)	(0.8)	(7.3)
1975	304.4	(9.4)	324.2	(45.2)	19.8	15.9
1976	349.4	(51.9)	364.5	(66.4)	15.1	(0.6)
1977	395.8	(44.6)	400.5	(44.9)	4.7	(4.3)
1978[b]	459.4	57.7	448.4	(48.8)	(11.0)	2.0
1979	500.2	(60.6)	491.0	(27.7)	(9.2)	(23.7)
1980	531.6	(29.0)	576.7	(59.6)	45.1	(14.5)
1981[c]	611.5	16.5	657.2	(57.9)	45.7	28.7
1982[d]	695.3	(45.0)	728.4	(110.7)	33.1	32.5
1983	757.6	(91.5)	796.0	(195.4)	38.4	65.5

[a] In 1967 the BOB abandoned the "administrative budget," which portrays a smaller portion of Federal spending, and began calculating on the basis of a "unified budget," which includes transactions in the large Federal trust funds.
[b] Carter revision of Ford's budget.
[c] Carter revision of Carter.
[d] These figures are Reagan's revision of Carter's budget.

Sources: *Congressional Quarterly* (January 17, 1964), p. 109; *Congressional Quarterly Almanac* (annually since 1964); and *Budget of the United States, Fiscal Year 1985*, pp. 9–60. The figures for "sources of error" are arrived at in the following way. Over (under) spending is the difference between the Federal budget and the actually spent columns. Over (under) estimate of receipts is the budget plus the predicted surplus (or minus the predicted deficit) minus the sum of the actually spent and actual surplus (deficit) columns.

SUMMARY: THE POLITICS OF BUDGET-MAKING

The budgetary process comes close to being the ideal illustration of the maxim that power in the American political system is dispersed and shared among a large number of participants with widely varying obligations, constituencies, and policy preferences. It also shows how political leaders sample selectively among numerous opportunities to make decisions.

Budget-making is often admired on the presidential side because of what is regarded as excellent presidential coordination of budget policy; at the same time, the alleged fragmentation of the congressional appropriations process is often roundly criticized, though less often since the advent of budget committees and the CBO. In fact, the contrasts between the ways in which Congress and the President handle budgetary policy are today not as compelling as the similarities between the two branches. In spite of appearances to the contrary, neither Congress nor the President considers all programs in relation to all other programs. Both, in practice, take account of expected revenues in deciding how much to spend. Disagreements between congressional appropriations and presidential requests do not reflect "more adequate" presidential information, but rather differing responses to the demands of various groups in society for Federal programs, differing evaluations of the same sorts of information, and differing preferences about what sorts of public policy are desirable.

If there are real differences in the policies preferred by congressmen and Presidents, there are also real similarities in the processes by which they arrive at their decisions. Both executive and legislative policy-makers accept the major outlines of the budget from year to year. In making their contributions to the marginal adjustments of budget allocations, both Congress and the President take account of: (1) What agencies received last year. Deviations from former allocations draw attention. It is, practically speaking, rarely possible to ask an agency to justify *all* its activities in detail, but they can be asked to explain why they want more or less than what they have previously succeeded in justifying and receiving. (2) World developments. When Sputnik went up, so did the budget for the National Aeronautics and Space Administration. When war broke out in Korea, this fact was rapidly reflected in the Defense Department's budget. (3) Agency reputations for accurate estimating, hard work, and "integrity." Just as some agencies are "glamorous" and reap the rewards of headline attention and others are dull and prosaic in the image they project, so also on a more professional level some agencies make better reputations than others and gain and suffer accordingly. Some draw more partisan flak than others. Agencies may develop different relationships with their OMB examiners and their appropriations subcommittees, but in both arenas the criterion of professional integrity comes into play in decision-making. (4) Prior programmatic commitments. It is rare that a well-established program will be crippled in the appropriations process. (5) Interest group demands. Some interest groups have better access to Republicans, some to Democrats, some to Congress, some to the President, some direct to agencies; therefore their demands are likely to be met selectively in the different arenas. (6) Economic ideologies and general economic conditions. Liberals and conservatives in Congress and the executive battle over whether gains in economic prosperity should be spent in the public or the private sector, and likewise they have different opinions about the effects of government spending when the economy is in recession. They have differing views on the harm that deficits do to economic activity generally, and on where and how to reduce deficit spending, whether to raise taxes or cut welfare or defense. Many of these disagreements are reflected in budgetary decision-making and in the justifications that politicians use in defending their decisions.

chapter 7

CONFLICT AND COOPERATION

Conflict and cooperation between Congress and the President are not merely the result of whim or willfulness at one end or the other of Pennsylvania Avenue. There are institutional reasons that make it difficult for Congress and the President to see eye to eye, and there are characteristic practices and tactics that help on some occasions to overcome these differences. It is difficult to deal with the question of conflict between these two institutions dispassionately, for an enormous volume of rhetoric favoring one side or the other has accumulated in both the popular press and the writings of political scientists. Much of this rhetoric revolves around the legitimacy of disagreement between Congress and the President; there is not much question over the fact of disagreement. It may be useful nonetheless for us to begin with that fact. From there I propose to discuss possible sources of disagreement, or reasons for disagreement, between Congress and the President. Then, briefly, I will take up the methods and instruments by which disagreement is expressed and move to a discussion of the legitimacy of conflict between the two branches of government. The chapter ends with a discussion of cooperation between Congress and the President.

DIMENSIONS OF CONFLICT: DIFFERING ELECTORAL BASES

Disagreement between Congress and the President is generally measured in two ways. The platform of the party winning the Presidency normally contains a great number of policy proposals. If, as usually happens, the same party wins a majority in Congress, the gap between presidential platforms and legislative output is often held to reflect the extent of disagreement between the President and Congress. This gap is normally very wide. As a matter of fact, it is not unusual for the presidential platforms of *both* political parties to be in substantial agreement on a wide range of issues, yet the policies they recommend are not enacted by Congress. How can this be so?

A presidential platform is an unusual document. It is written at the national party convention, and its avowed purpose is to appeal to voters and groups of voters who will be electing a President. Platforms must be appealing but they need not be terribly practical. They need not promise only those policies that are likely to be enacted. They need not mention any of the costs of what they propose, only the benefits. They need not reflect the actual relative strength of demands made on the political system once the election is over. They need not even reflect the priorities of the political leader who is elected President. And they are certainly not intended to reflect the goals or priorities of all the varied people who are elected to Congress. Given all these peculiarities of party platforms, it is easy to see why they do not anticipate legislation more closely. They are written by the presidential wing of the party as an appeal—not to Congress or even to the congressional wing of the President's party, but to voters.

A more sophisticated measure of disagreement between Congress and the President can be achieved by turning to those appeals that the President makes directly to Congress and seeing which proposals, or how many of them, are enacted. The newspapers and magazines keep a running box score while Congress is in session, and much of the comment that flows from Washington revolves around the state of this box score. Presidential "triumphs" occur when a bill is enacted. Congressional "obstruction" occurs when a policy that the President has asked for is held up at one point or another in the legislative process. When a bill is "watered down," as members of Congress seek a formula that can command the successive majorities that must be mobilized in Congress, it is not clear who wins in the box score.

These box scores are, to be sure, somewhat arbitrary in that they reflect somebody's judgment on which measures are to be included and which excluded. On the whole, box scores appearing in the popular press are somewhat unrealistic in that they are usually weighted heavily toward presidential priorities and newly proposed legislation. Renewals of old programs, although they may occupy much congressional time and effort, rarely appear in the accounts, nor does noncontroversial legislation. Box scores are, in other words, designed less to monitor congressional output than to keep tabs on presidential success in moving a program through Congress. In general, better than two-thirds of measures on which Presidents have taken a clear-cut position are enacted in some recognizable form by Congress, as Table 16 shows.[1]

TABLE 16   Disagreement Between President and Congress

YEAR	PRESIDENT	SUCCESS RATE
1954	Eisenhower (R)	82.8%
1955		75.0
1956		70.0
1957		68.0
1958		76.0
1959		52.0
1960		65.0
1961	Kennedy (D)	81.0
1962		85.4
1963	Kennedy/Johnson (D)	87.1
1964	Johnson	88.0
1965		93.0
1966		79.0
1967		79.0
1968		75.0
1969	Nixon (R)	74.0
1970		77.0
1971		75.0
1972		66.0
1973		50.6
1974		59.6
1974	Ford (R)	58.2
1975		61.0
1976		53.8
1977	Carter (D)	75.4
1978		78.3
1979		76.8
1980		75.1
1981	Reagan (R)	82.4
1982		72.4
1983		67.1

Sources: *Congressional Quarterly* (January 24, 1964), p. 181, and (January 12, 1968), p. 43; *Congressional Quarterly Almanac* (1965) and annually thereafter.

From the 1930s to the 1970s many of the controversial items that repeatedly failed of enactment cast the President in a conventionally "liberal" and Congress in a "conservative" role. The President wished to expand the role of the Federal government in protecting the civil rights of black citizens; congressional objections referred to states' rights and property rights. The President asked for medical care for the aged under Social Security; congressional objections called forth the specter of socialized medicine. The President sought expanded Federal aid to education; Congress worried about the question of states' rights in the face of the possible imposition of Federal requirements, desegregation of school systems, and aid to parochial schools. The President attempted to mount a "War on Poverty"; congressmen claimed beneficiaries of the program had police records.

These conflicts had reality not merely because principled and dedicated politicians stood on both sides of each issue. They also reflected differences between Congress and the Presidency as institutions. These issues, and many others like them—foreign aid, reciprocal trade, and tax reform are three other examples—customarily divided Presidents and significant segments of Congress along liberal and conservative lines. This has been easiest to see when the President is Democratic and especially sensitive to his most probable winning presidential coalition, which is predominantly liberal, activist, and urban in its orientation. This coalition may be contrasted with typical winning coalitions in Congress, which have depended so heavily for their formation on seniority and expertise. There have been clear advantages in this system for congressmen and senators from one-party states with small electorates.[2] The attention of these members has not so constantly been diverted from legislative business; their ties back home have been easier to maintain, and their chances of falling by the wayside in massive party turnovers have, of course, been much less than those of their brethren from competitive two-party areas. And so over the years, they rose to positions of power in the all-important committee systems of Congress.

In sparsely populated and one-party areas, the interests that dominated—for example, tobacco, textiles, and segregation in the South—were quite different from those that dominated in urban, two-party areas, which consisted of such groups as laborers employed in manufacturing and racial and ethnic minorities. Thus the germ of conflict over policy was contained in the very rules by which congressmen, senators, and Presidents were elected and sustained in office.

Over the last half-century, Congress has almost always been controlled by Democrats, but the President has been Republican for over half of the last thirty years (see Figure 3). These electoral results are constantly reshaping the terrain over which presidential-congressional relations are battled out. To come to fruition, presidential initiatives demand tractable congressional coalitions. These coalitions are formed out of the raw materials supplied by voters in the several states and in the 435 congressional districts. It is voters who decide how many Democrats and how many Republicans sit in Congress, and it is voters who decide from what party the President shall be chosen.

From 1930 to 1980 Democrats held the Presidency for thirty-two years and Republicans eighteen. For a good part of the time, however, Democratic programs were stalled and frustrated because congressional sentiment was more evenly divided, regardless of the party labels of incumbents. In the

FIGURE 3 Party Control of Congress and the Presidency

Year	HOUSE DEM.	HOUSE REP.	SENATE DEM.	SENATE REP.	PRESIDENCY
1929-30	163	267	39	56	Hoover (R) 1929-33
1931-32	216	218	47	48	
1933-34	313	117	59	36	Roosevelt (D) 1933-45
1935-36	322	103	69	25	
1937-38	333	89	75	17	
1939-40	262	169	69	23	
1941-42	267	162	66	28	
1943-44	222	209	57	38	
1945-46	243	190	57	38	Truman (D) 1945-53
1947-48	188	246	45	51	
1949-50	263	171	54	42	
1951-52	234	199	48	47	
1953-54	213	221	46	48	Eisenhower (R) 1953-61
1955-56	232	203	48	47	
1957-58	234	201	49	47	
1959-60	283	153	64	34	
1961-62	262	175	64	36	Kennedy (D) 1961-63
1963-64	258	176	67	33	Johnson (D) 1963-69
1965-66	295	140	68	32	
1967-68	248	187	64	36	
1969-70	243	192	58	42	Nixon (R) 1969-74
1971-72	255	180	54	44	
1973-74	242	192	56	42	Ford (R) 1974-77
1975-76	291	144	61	37	Carter (D) 1977-81
1977-78	292	143	61	38	
1979-80	277	158	58	41	Reagan (R) 1981-
1981-82	243	192	46	53	

American system of separated branches of government, electoral results must be turned by acts of institutional leadership into legislative coalitions, a set of transactions separate and apart from the voting that puts Presidents and members of Congress in office. In general, two great coalitions have dominated congressional business.[3] One has consisted mostly of Democrats subdivided into their various species: liberal Democrats, mainstream Democrats, urban Democrats, Northern Democrats, Western Democrats, and more than a handful of mainstream Southern liberal Democrats. These, plus a few maverick progressive, silk-stocking, or suburban Republicans, make up the more liberal coalition. The "conservative coalition" has generally consisted of almost all the Republicans plus conservative Democrats, mostly Southern (recently called "boll weevils"), with a few Westerners.[4] Most commentators on presidential-congressional relations over the last fifty years have spent a lot of time and energy calculating the ways in which ebbs and flows in the electoral results have added to and subtracted from these coalitions.

These sorts of calculations led to the observation that over a twenty-year period there has been a significant shift among the congressional delegations of the South from Democratic to Republican. In 1960 there were 106 congressional seats in the eleven states of the old Confederacy. Seven of those seats were held by Republicans. After the 1980 election, 30 Republican House members came from the 108 seats allocated to the South.

This does not mean, however, that Southern conservatism has become more influential in Congress. On the whole, Southern Republicans filtered into open seats instead of knocking off incumbents, and these seats had predominantly been held by conservative Democrats.[5] There has always been a modest number of mainstream or liberal Democrats from the South, from rural areas where the New Deal brought electricity and farm price supports, for example, or from big cities like Houston and New Orleans, with large working-class and black populations, and from areas, like Miami or San Antonio, heavily populated by Spanish-Americans. In 1960 twenty-five Southerners voted with the rest of the Democratic party on House roll calls more than twice as often as they voted against; that number was still twenty-five in 1981, a fact suggesting that the net gain of Southern Republicans in Congress has *all* been at the expense of conservative Southern Democrats.[6]

Consequently, for those significant decisions taken in the House Democratic caucus, as in the 1970s many were, the voice of conservative Southerners was greatly diminished. This helps to explain how, in the late 1960s and 1970s the caucus became an instrument of the Democratic party's mainstream.

Behind micropolitical movements of this kind we can see lurking larger forces such as were once identified by E. E. Schattschneider as "the nationalization of American politics," the reduction in the distinctiveness of regional political trends, owing in part to migration, in part to the advance of technological innovations like air conditioning and television.[7] Almost certainly in particular the influence of television has been very great in accelerating the tendency for political information and political sentiment in the United States to be uniform across the country.

When the President is Republican and one or both houses of Congress are controlled by Democrats, it is much harder to generalize about their respective policy positions. The basic winning coalition in national politics is still, on the whole, liberal, but a Republican President, even one elected with only a minority of the vote, might nevertheless feel tempted by a "Southern strategy." He could hedge, let us say, as President Nixon did, on the enforcement of school desegregation while, on the other hand, sponsoring a liberal program of payments to replace an unsuccessful welfare system. Likewise, members of Congress, especially senators, could find themselves very pleasantly in the limelight as they mounted attacks on mediocre (and conservative) Supreme Court appointments, pressed for the end of an unpopular war, or fought for more aid to education.

In the mid-1970s older electoral bases for congressional-presidential conflict began to erode. Several factors contributed to this erosion. First, party realignment in the South caused a large number of safe Democratic House seats to fall to Republicans. This shift moved the control of the Democratic party in Congress decisively north and into the hands of the increasing number of senior congressmen and senators from Northern, safe, urban seats. Second, the net effects of reapportionment and stable voting habits in the North ensured that there would be a substantial number of Northern safe seats and that these would be held by liberal congressmen.[8] This made it possible, third, for Congress to evolve from 1958 into the 1970s into an institution less dependent upon seniority and more responsive to majority rule of the majority party, especially through the revitalized use of the Democratic caucus of the House of Representatives. Finally, on the presidential side, the rules by which party nominations were made underwent revision tending to strengthen the hand of splinter groups within and outside the two-party system and to increase the necessity for ideological appeals by presidential candidates.[9] A difficulty of this newly emerging system was that it weakened the deliberative machinery within parties, and hence the capacity of party organizations to arrive at a presidential candidate by negotiation among leaders. This weakening depressed the chances for nomination of widely acceptable candidates and correspondingly increased the presidential chances of candidates who made relatively uncompromising or narrowly factional appeals. The net effect of this change in the presidential nomination system, though difficult to foresee in detail, seemed to increase the probability that presidential nominees would be more doctrinaire, that is, either more liberal (if Democratic) or more conservative (if Republican) than they would have been under the old system. The probability that the fortunes of the electoral process would produce a President ideologically out of phase with any given Congress thus remained fairly high.

INSTITUTIONAL SOURCES OF CONFLICT

Even in those times when electoral results do not divide Congress and the President, *institutional* factors facilitate conflict between the two branches. These factors may drive a wedge even between a President and those people in Congress who were elected as supporters of presidential programs from constituencies like the President's own.

Perhaps the most fundamental of these institutional sources of conflict can be described as a difference in the time perspectives of members of the two branches. Consider the "efficient minority" of congressmen, both liberals and conservatives, who regard Congress as their vocation and who have risen in the hierarchies of the House or Senate sufficiently to have a noticeable impact on legislative outcomes. The unit of time to which a member of this group is most attentive in gauging the consequences of his behavior is the career. Normally, he will think of his career as open-ended and having no fixed terminal point. The questions he must continually pose to himself are: How will my behavior today affect my standing in this house tomorrow, the next day, and in years to come? How may I act so as to enhance my esteem in the eyes of my colleagues? How may I lay up the treasures of obligation and friendship against my day of need? Or, if he is oriented to public policy, how may I enhance the future chances of policies *I* favor?

In contrast, the President and his agents must focus on the presidential term of office as the unit of time most relevant to them. Eight years is the very most they have in which to do what they want to do. Subtract one year at the end as a lame-duck period. Discount the period of time just before elections, especially the critical period just prior to the decision whether there is to be an attempt at a second term or not. Subtract also the time that will have to be devoted to crises, especially international ones. Finally, subtract whatever time has elapsed already. How much time remains? Not very much, and yet there are so many programs that they may want to advocate, so many policies they desire to put into practice.

The conflict that arises from the difference in time perspectives even between responsible, loyal, and decent members of the two branches is this: The President is intent on the problem of the moment, which is to pass high-priority items in his program. He asks his congressional allies to spend power in behalf of this goal. The congressman, who has to worry about the possibility of a future transfer to a desirable committee or a private bill that he thinks may mean political life or death at some future time, is naturally inclined to hoard power or to invest it so as to increase his future stock of resources. Meanwhile, the President's opponents in Congress are not so constrained. If they are of the opposition party, they may content themselves with simple party regularity. If they are of the President's party, they need only refrain from bestirring themselves. Or if they fight, they can fight in behalf of their own preferences or those of their district, but not necessarily those of the President.

A second institutional dilemma that strains presidential-congressional relations is the age-old strategic question: "Help thy friends or woo thine enemies?" No matter which horn of the dilemma the President chooses to confront, the other is bound to cause him grief. Dean Acheson gives a famous example:

> Dealing with the two senior foreign relations Senators took a good deal of time.... The simple thing would have been to talk with them together; but

simplicity would have been, if not disastrous, at least hazardous. Connally loved to heckle Vandenberg. Vandenberg when aroused could respond in a way calculated to move Connally another notch toward disagreement for its own sake. So the procedure was first to see them separately, to get each so far committed that only the sheerest wilfulness could undo it. But which to see first? Here was a tricky decision. Both were fairly good about not leaking the content of our talk to the press. But each found it hard to resist leaking the fact of a private talk. Once this was done, the second to be seen knew that he was the second. With Connally, this was instant cause for offense. We were members of the same party; he was loyal and proved; yet I turned to his rival first—if, indeed, I had done so. It was to him a poor explanation that Vandenberg was the Chairman of the committee, in the years in which he was.[10]

Here is an instance from the Kennedy administration:

Some of the Executive's relations with Congress have not helped the aid program. For example, its chief ball carrier in Passman's House Appropriations subcommittee, the major fortress of aid opponents, is Representative Silvio O. Conte, a three-term liberal Republican from Massachusetts. Yet Conte is rarely consulted on strategy and on occasion has been snubbed by thoughtless underlings in AID. When the University of Massachusetts, located in Conte's district, received a $178,000 AID contract for a farm training project in Nyasaland last February, Conte read about it in his home-town newspaper in the form of a joint "announcement" by the state's Senior Senator, Republican Leverett Saltonstall, and the newly arrived Senator Edward M. Kennedy. Five days later Conte's office received a routine press release containing the same information.[11]

Immediately upon taking office in 1969, President Nixon was faced with similar problems. As Nixon was the standard-bearer of the minority party in this country, elected with only 43.4 percent of the popular vote, it was clearly desirable for him to broaden the base of his support as he put together his administration. The complaints were not long in coming.

To hear some Republicans tell it, Democrats were the only guys getting jobs in this Republican administration. Senator Robert Dole of Kansas, only half jokingly, has been urging fellow GOP lawmakers to include this line in their letters of recommendation: "Even though Zilch is a Republican, he's highly qualified for the job."

According to Mr. Flemming [of the White House] the complaint isn't grounded in fact, since Democrats have received only about 8 percent of the jobs. Yet the Democrats still control Congress, so Mr. Nixon must give them some patronage in hope of winning support for his legislative program. "You can't just go around with a meat ax when you have to work with them," Senator Bellmon remarks . . .

Not everyone is happy. Senator Dole laments his inability to place a single Kansan in the Administration so far. "There must be a spot for one between now and 1976," he says. "A janitor maybe?"[12]

And from the Carter years:

> Tired of reading about President Carter's improving relations with Congress?
> Read this. Moderate Republicans who've backed Carter on voter registration,
> water projects, and other tough issues gripe that they get no help or thanks
> from the White House. "I've been with him on two or three close ones, and
> I've never heard a word from Frank Moore," says a GOP congressman. Moore
> is Carter's chief congressional backpatter.
>
> Case in point: in the House Appropriations Committee, Republicans agreed
> to side with Carter and approve military aid to Nicaragua. But the White
> House had failed to line up the committee's Democrats, who voted solidly
> against the aid. Committee Republicans lost the vote—and also lost whatever
> faith they had in Moore's lobbying operation.[13]

Presumably the ideal way to handle the problem is for the President
to keep both his friends and his enemies happy. But then the question is
bound to arise whether the President's friends are being sufficiently differentiated from his enemies. What profit accrues to a congressman who regularly sticks his neck out for the administration if congressmen who do not
are amply rewarded just as he is? In practice, limits on the time and other
resources available to the President and his aides set boundaries on the
extent to which *either* activity is pursued. Mistakes are bound to occur.

A third institutional factor encumbering presidential-congressional relations concerns the gains and costs of uncertainty to both. Congressmen
and senators often find it useful to refrain from committing themselves on
legislation in order to bargain with interest groups and within the House
or Senate or perhaps simply in order to avoid potentially dangerous controversy. The President, on the other hand, has a stake in knowing the lay
of the land as early as possible so he can see what he needs to do to win.
Therefore the conflict between secrecy and disclosure can be added to the
ones already mentioned.

Relations between White House functionaries and members of Con-
gress have seldom been easy. One recalls widespread congressional re-
sentment, in former administrations, of Harry Hopkins, Dean Acheson, and
Sherman Adams. This did not noticeably abate for Nixon's team of H. R.
Haldeman and John D. Ehrlichman or for Carter's top assistant, Hamilton
Jordan.[14]

One way for people in the White House to avoid problems with congressmen is to ask far less of them in a way of performance, and clearly
some Presidents have taken this tack. However, this course of action—or
rather inaction—hazards the displeasure of the President's natural allies
among interest groups. If carried to an extreme, it may even jeopardize the
President's control of his own administration and his own or his party's
chances of retaining the Presidency itself.

INSTRUMENTS OF CONFLICT

The means that Congress and the President have available with which they can express disagreement and induce cooperation—in short, their weapons in the intramural political struggles of Washington politics—are probably well enough known to demand only a brief recapitulation.

The President can veto legislation desired by congressmen. He can no longer prevent the spending of funds appropriated by Congress for purposes he does not approve, but there are still possibilities for foot-dragging,[15] since he has an enormous range of discretion over the activities of the executive branch. This includes his power of appointment, a power that reaches into every state, embracing United States attorneys, Federal judges, and collectors of ports. Other appointments made mostly at presidential discretion include those to the Supreme Court, to independent regulatory commissions, to top managerial posts in the various departments and agencies of the government, to ambassadorships, and to honorific boards and commissions—some of them *ad hoc*, such as the Presidential Commission on Intergovernmental Relations, and some more permanent, such as the Fine Arts Commission, which advises on the design of public buildings in Washington, D.C.

A President can create goodwill and forge alliances by prudent use of his appointment powers. In order to protect his own political position, he has the obligation to find appointees who are competent and also politically acceptable. Normally, these matters proceed on a state-by-state basis; some attempt is made to strengthen the hand of the party and distribute rewards in states where the party leaders are allies of the President.

Sometimes "clearance" with state party leaders is quite formal and elaborate, sometimes not. Minor appointments have been delegated to the congressman from the district involved, if he is of the President's party. This congressional patronage helps to build a bridge between the President and his party's members in Congress. In like manner, senators of the President's party clear the Federal judgeships and most of the other important Federal appointments made to citizens of their respective states.

When senatorial confirmation is required by law, as it is in the case of the more important appointments, senators employ a cooperative device to ensure clearance. This is senatorial "courtesy," so called. When a senator from the President's own party announces that a nominee to high office from his state is personally obnoxious or embarrassing to him, the Senate customarily refuses to confirm. This is a powerful weapon but is used sparingly; senators prefer to encourage consultation by less visible means, by arranging for delays in the confirmation process while appropriate apologies or even more concrete tokens of contrition are proffered them by minions of the executive branch.[16]

Presidential discretion does not end with the appointment process. All the manifold programs of the government have differential impacts on the various geographic areas of the nation, and so it is possible to reward and punish congressional friends and foes quite vigorously. Small Business Administration and Economic Development Administration loans to certain areas may get more and more difficult to obtain, as applications fail to "qualify." Pilot programs and demonstration projects may be funneled here rather than there. Defense contracts and public works may be accelerated in some areas, retarded in others.[17] Administrative decisions to open offices or consolidate operations of various Federal agencies may be made. All these activities are indispensable to the running of any large administrative apparatus, and it may be a matter of indifference administratively whether an installation is opened in Dallas or Houston, whether a regional head-quarters is in Portland or Seattle. However, these administrative decisions have great political impact, because they affect the prosperity of the areas where they are put into effect, and so they are often of acute concern to local political leaders. As a result, they can become weapons in the hands of a politically astute President.

The sheer high status of the Presidency is of course a formidable weapon. Only the crustiest and most independent congressmen and senators fail to warm to considerate personal treatment by a President of the United States. A private breakfast, a walk in the White House rose garden, an intimate conference—all duly and widely reported in the press—give a politician a sense of importance that not only may flatter his ego but also may remind him of his responsibilities as a national legislator, as a trustee of the common weal. He may then moderate his opposition or stiffen his resolve to support the President. After a session with Ronald Reagan, a freshman Democratic Representative from Texas said: "It's kind of like you were going on a hunting trip or playing golf with someone who's trying to do business with you."[18]

Of course this tactic does not always work. Here is an example from the Johnson Presidency:

> When numerous congressmen were unhappy about the closing of the VA hospitals, we had one of our frequent White House receptions for a group of congressmen and their wives. These receptions often featured briefings by cabinet members on current issues. At this particular one, the President personally responded to questions that had been raised about the VA hospital closings.
>
> He delivered a long and emotional oration in defense of the closings. "Our disabled boys deserve the best medical treatment we can give them," he declared. "Why, we're closing down one VA Hospital in a little Texas town that has become nothing more than a firetrap. The veterans are all being taken to a modern new hospital in Memphis, just as they deserve."
>
> His remarks stressed that his own state of Texas was losing a hospital in the

interests of better medical care for the veterans. He went on to say that the local people in the little Texas town had been upset about losing jobs because of the closing, but that was being resolved because the poverty program was making the former hospital into a Women's Job Corps center. The President concluded proudly that the local people were delighted and thought they'd get more revenue from the Job Corps than they had from the VA hospital. He was starting to sit down when a voice boomed out of the back of the room—the loud, rather husky voice of Congressman Harold Cooley of North Carolina.

"You gonna burn the women?" Cooley asked.

"What?" the President asked.

"You said it was a firetrap," Cooley said. "You gonna burn the women?"

Johnson's brilliant presentation was demolished by one question, and he stood speechless for a full minute, searching for a response.[19]

President Eisenhower once tried the personal touch with the indefatigable and colorful Representative Otto Passman, chief opponent of foreign aid.

In 1957, as the foreign aid bill was getting its final touches, President Eisenhower and his advisors decided to try an advance truce talk with Otto. They gave him the full treatment, and he recalls it with a nice touch of sadness . . . .

"It was kind of embarrassing, you understand," he told me in his musical southern voice. "I refer to it as the Passman trial. They sent for me in a long black Cadillac, I guess the first time I had ever been in one. I felt real important, which is not my usual way of feeling. When I got to the President's study at the White House, all the big shots were there. Admiral Radford and Secretary Dulles and the leaders of Congress. We had tea and little cakes, and they sat me right across from the President. They went around the room, asking for comments, one minute each. When they got to me, I said I would need more than one minute, maybe six or seven minutes, to tell what was wrong with their program. . . ."

Passman's lecture was complete with footnotes and fine print, figures down to the last thin dime, unobligated balances in the various foreign aid accounts, carry-over funds, reobligated, deobligated obligations, supplies in the pipeline, uncommitted balances, and so on—in that mysterious verbal shorthand that only a man who lives and breathes foreign aid could comprehend . . . After . . . everyone left, the President turned to his staff and said,

"Remind me never to invite that fellow down here again."[20]

These examples are not typical. Congressmen and senators generally find it hard to say no directly to the President of the United States, especially when he asks them nicely—but they may simply fail to do what he wants.

Another way of exploiting the prestige of the Presidency is the gambit of "going to the people." This process is usually described in a misleading way. What a President does when he goes to the people is try to focus the attention of the mass media and relevant interest groups on an issue. It is not normally possible in the course of one or a few fireside chats to provoke a ground swell of opinion change that promises to rearrange the composition of Congress unless congressmen knuckle under.[21] The ties that congressmen and senators have back home are typically multiple, strong, and of long standing. It is hard for a President to change all this while explaining the intricacies of a particular issue over television. He can, however, communicate his concern about the issue. He can increase its general visibility, stir up interest group activity, and, to a certain extent, set the terms in which it will be debated.

Congressional weapons have already been covered to a substantial degree. They include the power to delay and to fail to act, the power to cut appropriations and thus to curtail programs, the power to require the executive agencies to comply with stringent regulations, either by writing technical and specific laws or by legally requiring frequent reports and repeated authorizations.

Senatorial courtesy is a significant constraint on the presidential appointment power. Throughout the legislative labyrinth, different congressmen and senators are strategically placed to delay, modify, or defeat legislation and appropriations. There is also the power of impeachment, which has now twice been used against a President. In 1868 President Andrew Johnson was almost deposed in an impeachment and trial. In 1974 impeachment proceedings were started against President Nixon, but Mr. Nixon resigned before they could run their course.

As congressional leaders gingerly approached the question of impeachment of President Nixon in the spring and summer of 1974, they had to ask themselves whether this ultimate constitutional sanction had lain so long in disuse that it could no longer be employed. When the House Judiciary Committee, after months-long deliberations and a fascinating televised debate, voted three articles of impeachment, this question was decisively resolved. The contents of these three articles, especially when contrasted with two proposed articles of impeachment rejected by the committee, gave a clue to the conditions under which this sanction was likely to be employed.[22] Neither policy disagreements with congressional majorities nor petty crimes tending to contribute to a President's personal enrichment were accepted as grounds for impeachment: only serious transgressions against the political process itself were deemed sufficiently grave to count as "high crimes and misdemeanors" in the sense intended by the framers of the Constitution.[23] Thus the House Judiciary Committee placed at the very center of its concern the preservation of the system of norms and regulations by which national leaders are accountable to each other, and revived from its moribund condition a powerful method for ensuring that these norms are not lightly ignored.

One other weapon in the congressional arsenal deserves brief consideration: the power to investigate. This is a significant congressional activity, although one that has perhaps suffered from a surfeit of publicity. Investigations may move in many directions. Perhaps the most famous of these in modern times have been the Kefauver and McClellan investigations of crime and racketeering, various House Committee on Un-American Activities investigations of communism in the United States, the Army-McCarthy hearings of 1954, and the Ervin Committee hearings of 1973 on Watergate-related offenses. Of these, only the last two involved any sort of congressional scrutiny of the executive branch. One was also an inquiry into the practices of a senator and a subcommittee of the Senate that was under his leadership; the other began as an investigation of a President's campaign finance committee and from there worked its way into the White House.

Under ordinary circumstances—that is, barring the contemplation of impeachment—the President and his Executive Office are immune from congressional investigation; the precedents for this immunity stretch back to George Washington. However, Congress may inquire minutely into the workings of the rest of the executive branch, may probe for conflict of interest, may seek to reconstruct the premises on which decisions were made, may ferret out interoffice disagreements and expose all to the glare of publicity. Sometimes the public ventilation of policy disagreement is the purpose of congressional investigations, as was true of hearings after the dismissal of General MacArthur during the Korean war and of hearings by the Senate Foreign Relations Committee during the Vietnam war in which the Secretary of State and other members of the executive branch were subjected to sharp interrogation. Insofar as the President needs the various departments and agencies of the executive branch to execute his policies, this power of Congress to investigate constrains him.[24] In addition, the power of Congress to investigate may force the President to adopt extraordinary measures within the executive branch to investigate wrongdoing. Both President Truman and President Nixon set up special prosecutors within the Justice Department under severe pressure from Congress, and granted these prosecutors unusual independence. Both Truman and Nixon fired special prosecutors they had appointed, but only President Truman (who was not personally the target of the investigation) got away with it politically. In the case of the Nixon administration, the special prosecutor was held by the Supreme Court to enjoy such an unusual position that he could successfully become a party to a suit against his nominal superior, the President of the United States.[25] Because of the Nixon experience, a law providing for a special prosecutor was enacted requiring the Attorney General to appoint "independent counsel" to investigate allegations of improper conduct by high government or campaign officials.[26]

Finally, there is the congressional power of post-audit. The General Accounting Office, an agency of Congress, continuously audits expenditures of Federal funds after they are made to ascertain that they have been spent in accordance with law. This office may disallow expenditures and require restitution.[27]

THE LEGITIMACY OF CONFLICT

Let us now examine the legitimacy of conflict between Congress and the President. Curiously, the fact of conflict itself has a bad name with writers on political questions. In behalf of the President and his policies, Congress is charged with willful parochialism, with neglect of national needs, with a variety of immoral, illegal, and undignified activities—all of which are indicative, it is often held, of an overriding need for general reform of the legislative branch. In the words of a few book titles, Congress is "on trial,"[28] a sink of "corruption and compromise,"[29] responsible for the "deadlock of democracy,"[30] a "sapless branch"[31] of government. It is "in crisis"[32] and has a "house out of order."[33] "Congress," says still another title, "needs help."[34]

In behalf of Congress, it is urged that the country is, as is Congress, "essentially moderate." The President is trying to impose a tyranny of the majority. He wishes to go "too far, too fast." He cares not for the Constitution, for public order, for the American way. His actions verge on usurpation. Nobody, however, suggests in this connection that the Presidency be weakened as an institution; rather, it is urged that incumbents pull up their socks and act less like Presidents.[35]

In the light of our constitutional history, however, conflict between the two branches should come as no surprise. Indeed, the system was designed so that different branches would be captured by different interests and so that they would have to come to terms with one another peaceably in order to operate the system at all. This theory is explicitly stated in *The Federalist* (1788), which is the authoritative commentary on the Constitution by three Founding Fathers:

> To what expedient, then, shall we finally resort, for maintaining in practice the necessary partition of power among the several departments, as laid down in the Constitution . . . ? [B]y so contriving the interior structure of the government as that its several constituent parts may, by their mutual relations, be the means of keeping each other in their proper places . . . In order to lay a due foundation for that separate and distinct exercise of the different powers of government, which to a certain extent is admitted on all hands to be essential to the preservation of liberty, it is evident that each department should have a will of its own . . . [T]he great security against a gradual concentration of the several powers in the same department, consists in giving to those who administer each department the necessary constitutional means and personal motives to resist encroachments of the others.... Ambition must be made to counteract ambition.[36]

Indeed, if the constitution can be said to grant legitimacy to anything, surely it legitimizes conflict between Congress and the President.

It is often argued, however, that majoritarian principles are violated by one or another of the two great branches. A presidential veto may render ineffectual congressional majorities in both houses, or an administration bill may be stalled somewhere in the toils of the legislative process by a small minority. Aside from any general skepticism one may harbor that majority rule is always a good thing, there is often in any particular case a problem in identifying a relevant majority whose decisions are to be regarded as legitimate.

Different doctrines suggest different solutions. There is, for example, the doctrine of *party responsibility*. According to this doctrine, the will of the majority of the majority party within Congress, if it is the same as the President's party, should prevail. On the other hand, a doctrine of *congressional responsibility* would hold that the will of the majority within Congress as a whole should prevail.

There have been times within recent memory when these two majorities have been at loggerheads.[37] The majority within Congress as a whole from 1936 into the 1970s was more often than not composed of a coalition of Republicans and Southern Democrats. Northern and Western Democrats, who made up a clear majority of the majority party, frequently could not get a majority on the floor. Clem Miller, writing in the early 1960s, put the matter bluntly:

> What the correspondents need to do is to sit down with a stubby pencil and do some simple addition and subtraction. What we will find is that the combination of southern Democrats and northern Republicans can always squeak out a majority when they want to, and they want to on a great number of significant issues.... Actually, the Democratic party as nonsoutherners define it is a minority in the House.[38]

One way to resolve this dilemma when it occurs would be to regard the relevant majority as existing in the electorate. Those for whom the majority of people vote, nationwide, should prevail. The President is elected on a nationwide basis and congressmen and senators individually are not, but congressmen and senators act in concert; collectively, they are elected on a national basis. At this point, therefore, the argument must become intricate. The legitimacy of the presidential majority may be impugned because the electoral college in effect nullifies the votes accruing to presidential candidates in those states lost by narrow margins. Even when this does not actually deprive the winner of the popular vote of public office, as it did in 1888, it can lead to the election of a President who receives less than a majority of all the popular votes. This in fact has happened at least thirteen times, most recently in 1968, when Richard Nixon received 43.4

percent of the votes and Hubert Humphrey received 42.7 percent, the rest going to other candidates (mainly George Wallace).

The legitimacy of the congressional majority can be questioned on at least two grounds. Malapportionment in the states, it can be argued, forbids the expression of true majority sentiment in electing congressmen and senators.[39] And after they are elected, various characteristics of decision-making processes in the respective houses make the expression of the will of the majority of even these truncated representatives difficult and on some occasions impossible.

All these charges, it should be said, are perfectly true. It appears that nobody enters into the arena of national policy-making with an absolutely clean and unsullied right to have his will prevail because he was elected by majority sentiment. Furthermore, who knows why candidates are elected to public office? Most people vote the way they do out of party habit, not because they endorse any particular set of campaign promises or projected policies. Typically, small minorities care about selected policies. However, it is perfectly possible for a candidate to be elected by a majority that disagrees with *all* his policy preferences. It is also perfectly possible for a particular electorate to elect a President, a senator, and a congressman, none of whom agrees with either of the others to a significant extent about any public policies.[40] Therefore an attempt to justify particular policies advocated by congressmen or Presidents based solely on their supposed link to the electorate seems dubious.

What about reforms? Would it be possible to change a few features of the political system so that Congress and the President could at least claim legitimacy for their actions, if not on the grounds that they accurately expressed the will of a majority, then on the grounds that they represented more closely the majority choice of their respective electorates? On the presidential side, doing this would entail at least scrapping the electoral college and substituting direct popular election. In some quarters, the move would be popular. It would probably have the effect of loosening the hold that the modern long-term liberal presidential coalition has had on the office. Of course, the incentives to interest groups in the large, two-party states to give up their present access to the Presidency are not very great even though they are no longer at such a severe disadvantage in the other parts of the system.[41]

But the reapportionment decisions were aimed at equalizing the influence of voters in the elections of all legislatures, state and Federal, save only the U.S. Senate. Meanwhile, because of the third-party candidacies of George Wallace and John Anderson in fifty states in the 1968 and 1980 elections, Americans began to confront the possibility that in some future election no candidate would receive a majority in the electoral college, thus throwing the election into the House of Representatives; there, according to constitutional requirement, each state, no matter how populous, is entitled to only one vote.[42] On election night in 1968 (but not particularly since) commentators horrified themselves with this specter and may well have produced a ground swell of interest in direct elections. Direct elections, however, may not solve all the difficulties complained of in the present system. The unit rule of the electoral college, by providing winner-take-all procedures within each state,[43] actually discourages splinter parties. Only those parties that are securely anchored in at least one section of the country have even the smallest hope of scoring in the electoral college. Under the present system, splinter parties may draw marginal support away from one party or another in closely contested states, but in general that is all they can do. Under direct-election rules, however, any number can run and draw votes away from front-runners. This means that winners would likely have lower total votes, and so this system seems unlikely to do away with minority Presidents, if that is the contemplated end in view.

A second set of reforms looks toward changing Congress's internal decision-making procedures. In general, reform proposals seeking to bring congressional policy-making more closely into line with presidential preferences assume that Congress and the Presidency will be in the hands of the same party and suggest procedures to bring measures to the floor easily and to weaken the grip of the committees on them. These proposals identify Congress primarily as a great forum for debate.[44]

However it is reasonable to think of Congress as doing its most important work as a deliberative body in committee. By investing heavily in staff in recent years, and by giving greater power to its numerous decentralized subcommittees, Congress seems to be moving in this direction. Many very popular congressional reforms thus present the following difficulty. Insofar as congressmen weaken their committees, they weaken the one device they have to scrutinize the merits of legislative proposals. Committees encourage specialization and technical sophistication, even expertise. They are convenient agencies through which bridges can be built to the executive branch, making possible a flow of information so that Congress can act intelligently.

Typically, suggestions for congressional reform have their beginnings in modest dissatisfactions over the President's inability to persuade Congress to enact parts of his program. But like the comedian who begins by tugging at a stray thread and ends up unraveling his entire wardrobe, congressional reformers soon find themselves dismantling the entire political system in their mind's eye and suggesting instead a system modeled on the British government, where the legislature takes orders from the Cabinet, and the Cabinet from the Prime Minister.[45] This vision of tidiness is, however, not well suited to a nation in which conflict is a legitimate feature of the day-to-day processes of governing, in which sectional traditions are strong, and in which a substantial variety and number of interest groups have learned to expect that one or another part of the government will always be accessible to them.

Actually, most specific proposals for reform would, if enacted, fall far short of provoking a constitutional crisis. Moreover, in the wake of periodic landslides in elections, such as those that sent overwhelming Democratic majorities to Congress in 1958, 1964 and 1974, reforms have been enacted tending to make the committees and their chairmen more responsive to majorities within the Democratic caucus and to the elected party leadership in the House. Among these reforms have been the separate election of committee chairmen by secret ballot in caucus at the opening of each Congress, the removal of the power to make committee assignments from the Democratic members of the Ways and Means Committee to the somewhat more accessible caucus steering committee, and the enactment of a rule placing appointment of the Democrats on the Rules Committee in the hands of the Democratic party leader in the House. The special majority in the Senate required to defeat a filibuster has been changed from two-thirds of senators present and voting to three-fifths of the entire Senate. The House has installed electronic voting, opened committee meetings to spectators, permitted television coverage of its proceedings, and limited the number of committee and subcommittee chairmanships that can be held by a single member. Although not in strict obedience to a grand design, change has come to Congress without a constitutional upheaval.

SOURCES OF COOPERATION

The extent of conflict between Congress and the President is, in any event, easily overestimated. There are an impressive number of forces in the political system that encourage cooperation between the branches and that keep the conflict that does exist at a tolerable level. Certainly high on any list of such forces would be the effects of party membership.

Because American political parties are not highly organized, have no clear standards for membership, and are not highly ideological, it is easy to underestimate their claims on the loyalties of the faithful. But these claims are important, and especially so to politicians who hold office bearing the party label. Students of roll-call voting have repeatedly found that the best single predictor of the vote of a member of Congress is his party membership.[46] Also, because major portions of the congressional agenda are set by the President, it is clear that the party designation he shares with members of Congress is of enormous aid in promoting cooperation between the branches.

Party loyalty is, indeed, a very conscious part of congressional behavior.

When congressmen speak, as they often do, of making a record to run on, they are referring as much to the winning of the Presidency or of Congress as a whole for their party as to the winning of their own seats. The party label and the party record are meaningful entities to them, and much of the sharpest kind of partisan conflict on Capitol Hill revolves not around the specific merits of legislation so much as around the question of credit. Members of the party in opposition to the President must ask themselves whether they can afford to support programs that may help to perpetuate the administration in office. Conversely, members of the President's party ask whether they can afford not to support him. Thus party lines cut across the gulf between Congress and the Presidency.

To be sure, party loyalty is not so pervasive as to preclude opposition to parts of the President's program from within segments of the President's own party in Congress. Sectional, local, and factional preferences, strongly held within the constituencies of congressmen, including those of the President's own party, place a constraint on the cooperation congressmen can give to a President. Sometimes the very political survival of the congressman, who is, after all, subject to renomination and reelection on the local level, demands that he break on one or more issues with a President of his own party. On the other hand, winning coalitions in Congress can often be forged from bipartisan components. This tends to mute the effects of partisanship; it forces bipartisan participation in the formulation of legislation, enabling members of both parties to claim credit for programs that are popular with the presidential coalition but controversial within Congress. Cross-party alliances thus damp down conflict in general within the political system. Political leaders never know when they will need a few extra votes from the other side of the aisle—and they can rarely be sure precisely who among the opposition will defect on a large number of unspecified future issues. Thus it pays to fight fairly, to play only as roughly as they absolutely have to. This general rule applies to Presidents when dealing with opposition congressmen as well as to congressmen when dealing with opposition Presidents.

One congressman who understood this rule of the game particularly well was Joseph Martin, long-time Republican leader of the House. In his memoirs he spoke of his relations with Franklin Roosevelt.

> When he became President, I liked Roosevelt personally and admired—ruefully at times—his dynamic political skill . . . Like myself, he was a practical politician. That is what politicians should be. During his years in office, we met often . . . As members of the same trade, we understood one another well . . . One day I told him I needed a new road in the southern part of my district. He called in Louis McHenry Howe. "Louis," he said, "call MacDonald" —Thomas H. MacDonald, head of the Bureau of Public Roads—"and tell him I am sending down a black Republican, and I want to give him a road." And I got it . . . [47]

As a President serving with a Congress controlled in part by the opposition party, Ronald Reagan has employed the device of the bipartisan commission to damp down partisanship in selected areas of public policy where presidential leadership by other means was thought to be impractical. Thus commissions on the Social Security system, the MX missile, and Central American policy were formed for the purpose of winnowing alternatives and presenting them to Congress as a substitute for initiative by the President.[48]

Another rule of the game tending to confine conflict between Congress and the President is a kind of unwritten moratorium on partisanship that takes place at the start of a President's term of office. During this "honeymoon" period, while the President is organizing his administration, it is customary for most presidential nominees for the various top-level jobs in his administration to be confirmed with only the most perfunctory scrutiny. Even in cases when some senators have sincere reservations or when their political interests in their home states could be better served by other nominees, the custom is to withhold objection and to allow the President to surround himself with associates of his own choosing.

There is also a rather sizable number of occasions requiring joint presidential-congressional action in which neither partisanship nor sectional differences play a part. These occur most often in the realm of foreign affairs. When the President acts in international crises—as in Mr. Truman's decision to send troops to Korea, or Mr. Eisenhower's decision not to send troops to Indochina, or Mr. Kennedy's decision to blockade Cuba, or Mr. Johnson's decision to retaliate after the Gulf of Tonkin incident, or Mr. Ford's similar decision on the Mayaguez incident—he customarily consults with congressional leaders of both parties, and he can usually count on their strong support, at least for the duration of the crisis. Lack of consultation can be correspondingly costly, as Mr. Nixon may have discovered in the spring of 1970 when he sent American troops into Cambodia. There are also instances, seldom crises, when the President is hemmed in by Congress in foreign affairs, for example, in our long-term policies toward the People's Republic of China, in our relations with Germany and Britain before World War II, or in our capacity to fight limited wars after a few inconclusive years of heavy investment, as in the case of Vietnam.[49]

Finally, there are occasional periods of severe domestic difficulty in which presidential proposals find ready acceptance in Congress. One such period was the famous first 100 days of Franklin Roosevelt's first term of office, when the presidential honeymoon coincided with the depths of a depression. As we have seen, an impressive volume of legislation was enacted during this period, some of it remarkably innovative, but it would be wrong to suggest, as it sometimes is, that the 100 days were merely a demonstration of presidential mastery over Congress. Rather, both Congress and the President responded in much the same way to the urgency of external events.

Once the crisis had abated, a more familiar pattern of congressional response to presidential initiatives was gradually reestablished.[50]

Congress and the Presidency are like two gears, each whirling at its own rate of speed.[51] It is not surprising that, on coming together, they often clash. Remarkably, however, this is not always the case. Devices that harmonize their differences are present within the system: the effects of party loyalty and party leadership within Congress, presidential practices of consultation, the careful restriction of partisan opposition by both congressional parties, and the readily evoked overriding patriotism of all participants within the system in periods—which nowadays, regrettably, come with some frequency—universally defined as crises.

With all the snags and thickets that complicate relations between Congress and the Presidency, it is worth noting that cooperation between the two branches does take place. This remarkable fact can be explained only in part by referring to incentives built into the machinery of the system. In addition, the underlying political culture discourages ideological extremism and fanatical intransigence and places a premium on the political skills of negotiation, maneuver, and accommodation. These permit Congress and the President to get along in spite of their differences, to unite in times of national emergency, and yet to return another day to disagree.

TO EXPLORE
FURTHER

Good general analyses of the basic principles of American national government are scarce. I recommend E. Pendleton Herring's *The Politics of Democracy* (New York: Holt, 1940); Robert A. Dahl's *A Preface to Democratic Theory* (Chicago: University of Chicago Press, 1956); Dahl's less schematic, more historical, *Democracy in the United States*, 4th ed. (Boston: Houghton Mifflin, 1981); and a superb basic textbook in American government by Raymond E. Wolfinger, Martin Shapiro, and Fred I. Greenstein, *Dynamics of American Politics*, 2nd ed. (Englewood Cliffs, N.J.: Prentice-Hall, 1980).

For treatment of some of the cultural and social factors underlying American governmental institutions, Alexis de Tocqueville, *Democracy in America*, 2 vols. (New York: Vintage Books, Random House, 1956), is still, after a century and a half, indispensable. David Potter, *People of Plenty* (Chicago: Phoenix Books, University of Chicago Press, 1958) and Daniel Boorstin's stimulating trilogy *The Americans* (New York: Random House, 1958, 1965, 1973) explore themes important for an understanding of American politics. David B. Truman in *The Governmental Process* (New York: Knopf, 1953), written with a theory of interest groups firmly in mind, tells a great deal about "rules of the game." Charles E. Lindblom's book in this series, *The Policy-Making Process* (Englewood Cliffs, N.J.: Prentice-Hall, 1980), applies a useful and persuasive theory of decision-making to American government.

The most ambitious analytical work on the contemporary Presidency is Richard Neustadt's *Presidential Power*, 3rd ed. (New York: Wiley, 1980). It draws on a rich backlog of case material and on Neustadt's own experience as an aide to President Truman, but, curiously, it has stimulated only a little in the way of critical dialogue. See, for examples, William T. Bluhm, *Theories of the Political System* (Englewood Cliffs, N.J.: Prentice-Hall, 1965), pp. 246-59; Peter Sperlich, "Bargaining and Overload: An Essay on Presidential Power," in Aaron Wildavsky (ed.), *The Presidency* (Boston: Little, Brown, 1969), pp. 168-92; John Hart, "Presidential Power Revisited," *Political Studies* 25 (March 1977), pp. 48-61; Thomas E. Cronin, "Presidential Power Revised and Reappraised," *Western Political Quarterly* 32 (December 1979), pp. 381-95; James MacGregor Burns, *Leadership* (New York: Harper and Row, 1978), pp. 385-97; and the symposium in *Presidential Studies Quarterly* 11 (Summer 1981), pp. 341-63, with contributions from Bert A. Rockman, David G. Wegge, Norman C. Thomas, Harry A. Bailey, Jr., and Neustadt. Other treatments of the Presidency are Erwin C. Hargrove's *The Power of the Modern Presidency* (New York: Knopf, 1974); Clinton Rossiter's *The American Presidency* (New York: Harvest Books, Harcourt, Brace & World, 1960); Sidney Hyman's *The American President* (New York: Harper & Row, 1954); and Richard Pious's *The American Presidency* (New York: Basic Books, 1979). In *The Twilight of the Presidency* (New York: New American Library, 1970), George Reedy argues that the trappings of the office have increasingly removed occupants of the White House from reality. Students may also find useful Arthur Schlesinger, Jr.'s sober second thoughts on *The Imperial Presidency* (Boston: Houghton Mifflin, 1973), which he once so much admired. Neustadt, in addition, has contributed several impressive articles to the study of the Presidency, among them: "Presidency and Legislation: The Growth of Central Clearance," *American Political Science Review*, vol. 48 (September 1954), pp. 641-71; and "Presidency and Legislation: Planning the President's Program," *American Political Science Review*, vol. 49 (December 1955), pp. 980-1021. Four articles by Elmer E. Cornwell are also useful and relevant: "Wilson, Creel and the Presidency," *Public Opinion Quarterly*, vol. 23 (Summer 1959), pp. 189-202; "Coolidge and Presidential Leadership," *Public Opinion Quarterly*, vol. 21 (Summer 1957), pp. 265-78; "Presidential News: The Expanding Public Image," *Journalism Quarterly*, vol. 36 (Summer 1959), pp. 275-83; and "The Presidential Press Conference: A Study in Institutionalization," *Midwest Journal of Political Science*, vol. 4 (November 1960), pp. 370-89. See also Elmer E. Cornwell, *Presidential Leadership of Public Opinion* (Bloomington, Ind.: Indiana University Press, 1965) and, on a similar theme, Colin Seymour-Ure, *The American President: Power and Communication* (New York: St. Martin, 1982); and Michael B. Grossman and Martha Kumar, *Portraying the President: The White House and the News Media* (Baltimore: Johns Hopkins University Press, 1981). John H. Kessel has made an unusually rigorous effort at studying the Presidency comparatively, reported in two articles: "The Structure of the Carter White House," *American Journal of Political Science* 27 (August 1983), pp. 431-63, and "The Structures of the Reagan White House," *op. cit.* 28 (May 1984), pp. 231-58. The most penetrating recent book-length analysis of presidential power in the political system is James Sterling Young's forthcoming *The Puzzle of the Presidency.*

Revealing information about presidential decision-making often turns up in case studies. For example, see Herman Somers's *Presidential Agency* (Cambridge, Mass.: Harvard University Press, 1950), which discusses the operations of the Office of War Mobilization and Reconversion; Bernard C. Cohen's *The Political Process and Foreign Policy* (Princeton, N.J.: Princeton University Press, 1957), on the domestic politics of the Japanese peace treaty; Joseph Jones's *The Fifteen Weeks* (New York: Viking, 1955), on the establishment of the Marshall Plan; Aaron Wildavsky's *Dixon Yates: A Study in Power Politics* (New Haven, Conn.: Yale University Press, 1962); and Samuel P. Huntington's *The Common Defense* (New York: Columbia University Press, 1961). Dean Acheson, *Present at the Creation* (New York: Norton, 1969), is a valuable account of policy-making in the Truman Presidency and contains a superb capsule description of Mr. Truman as President. Robert J. Donovan's two books on the Truman Presidency, *Conflict and Crisis* (covering 1945-48) and *Tumultuous Years* (covering 1949-53), both published by W. W. Norton of New York in 1977 and 1982, respectively, are authoritative. Fred I. Greenstein's *The Hidden-Hand Presidency* (New York: Basic Books, Inc., 1982) is an important milestone in the scholarly rehabilitation of Dwight Eisenhower's Presidency, a trend that will undoubtedly go too far.

Basic sources on the Kennedy Presidency are Theodore Sorensen's *Kennedy* (New York: Harper & Row, 1965), and Arthur Schlesinger, Jr.'s *A Thousand Days* (Boston: Houghton Mifflin, 1965). Both are unremittingly adoring accounts. Less cloying are Hugh Sidey's *John F. Kennedy: President* (New York: Atheneum, 1963); and Herbert Parmet's *Jack: The Struggles of John F. Kennedy* (New York: Dial, 1980); and *JFK: The Presidency of John F. Kennedy* (New York: Dial, 1983). On foreign policy aspects of the Kennedy Presidency, see Roger Hilsman, *To Move a Nation* (Garden City, NY: Doubleday, 1967), and Graham Allison, *Essence of Decision* (Boston: Little, Brown, 1971). Perhaps the most sycophantic account of Kennedy is Benjamin C. Bradlee, *Conversations with Kennedy* (New York: Norton, 1975). For antidotes to Kennedy-worship, readers might consult Henry Fairlie, *The Kennedy Promise* (New York: Dell, 1974); Garry Wills, *The Kennedy Imprisonment* (Boston: Little, Brown, 1982); Peter Collier and David Horowitz, *The Kennedys* (New York: Summit, 1984); Joan Blair and Clay Blair, Jr., *The Search for JFK* (New York: Berkley, 1976); and David Halberstam's *The Best and the Brightest* (New York: Random House, 1969), which now and again slips over into carping. Useful explications of Kennedy era policy from the perspective of Kennedy appointees are contained in McGeorge Bundy, *The Strength of Government* (Cambridge, Mass.: Harvard University Press, 1968), and William Kaufmann, *The McNamara Strategy* (New York: Harper & Row, 1969). Perhaps the most balanced and informative account of public administration during the Kennedy administration is Victor Navasky's interesting book on the Justice

Department, *Kennedy Justice* (New York: Atheneum, 1971). For a good overview of Kennedy era economics see Seymour E. Harris, *Economics of the Kennedy Years* (New York: Harper & Row, 1964), and Walter Heller, *New Dimensions of Political Economy* (Cambridge, Mass.: Harvard University Press, 1966).

The best book on the early part of the Johnson Presidency is undoubtedly Rowland Evans and Robert Novak's *Lyndon B. Johnson: The Exercise of Power* (New York: New American Library, 1966). Eric Goldman's *The Tragedy of Lyndon Johnson* (New York: Knopf, 1968) has some useful passages; and Philip Geyelin's *Lyndon B. Johnson and World* (New York: Praeger, 1966) is excellent on foreign affairs. George Reedy, long a Johnson staff member, reflects on his experience and on his boss in *Lyndon B. Johnson: A Memoir* (New York: Andrews and McMeel, 1982). Important case studies about the impact of Vietnam on the Johnson Presidency are Townsend Hoopes, *The Limits of Intervention* (New York: McKay, 1969); Herbert Y. Schandler, *The Unmaking of a President* (Princeton, N.J.: Princeton University Press, 1977); and Larry Berman, *Planning a Tragedy* (New York: Norton, 1982). All observers of the Johnson Presidency are awaiting with uncommon interest the publication of the last two volumes of Robert Caro's trilogy *The Years of Lyndon Johnson*. The first volume, *The Path to Power* (New York: Knopf, 1982) brings Johnson up to 1942 and is enormously interesting.

On the Nixon Presidency, no serious student should overlook the *Submission of Recorded Presidential Conversations to the Committee on the Judiciary of the House of Representatives by Richard M. Nixon* (Washington, D.C.: Government Printing Office, 1974), or the various materials published by the House Judiciary Committee, including *Impeachment Inquiry, Hearings before the Committee on the Judiciary, House of Representatives Pursuant to Res. 803, Books I-III* (Washington, D.C.: Government Printing Office, 1974). An early appraisal of the Nixon Presidency is contained in Rowland Evans and Robert Novak, *Nixon in the White House: The Frustration of Power* (New York: Random House, 1971). A vigorous formulation of the fashionable pre-Watergate anti-Nixon position is Garry Wills, *Nixon Agonistes* (New York: New American Library, 1971), and an informative piece of pre-Watergate pro-Nixon puffery is Allen Drury, *Courage and Hesitation: Notes and Photographs of the Nixon Administration* (Garden City, N.Y.: Doubleday, 1971). Mr. Nixon's ablest defense so far has been made by his former speechwriter, William Safire, in *Before the Fall* (Garden City, N.Y.: Doubleday, 1975), which bears the same relationship to the Nixon Presidency as the Sorensen and Schlesinger books do to Kennedy's. The best overview of the Washington community during the last days of the Nixon administration is Elizabeth Drew's *Washington Journal* (New York: Random House, 1975). See also Richard Cohen and Jules Witcover, *A Heartbeat Away* (New York: Viking Press, 1974), and Carl Bernstein and Robert Woodward, *All the President's Men* (New York: Simon and Schuster, 1974), for accounts of aspects of the unraveling of the Nixon

Presidency. An extensive discussion of Nixon administration foreign policy is in Marvin Kalb and Bernard Kalb's uncritical *Kissinger* (Boston: Little, Brown, 1974). Equally unsparing in admiration of its main subject are two autobiographical volumes by Henry Kissinger, *White House Years* (Boston: Little, Brown, 1979) and *Years of Upheaval* (Boston: Little Brown, 1982).

The Gerald Ford administration is our unsung modern Presidency, and this is a great pity. In particular we lack any sort of evaluation of the stewardship of Ford's Cabinet appointees, many of whom were unusually able, including John Dunlop at Labor, Edward Levi at Justice, and William Coleman at Transportation. Aside from Ford's memoirs, *A Time to Heal* (New York: Harper & Row, 1979) and those of his wife, Betty, *The Times of My Life* (New York: Harper & Row, 1978), we have so far heard only from Ford's rather cranky long-time chief of staff Robert Hartmann, *Palace Politics* (New York: McGraw-Hill, 1980), who was somewhat shunted aside in the White House, from press secretary Ron Nessen in *It Sure Looks Different from the Inside* (Chicago: Playboy Press, 1978) and from a handful of journalistic observers, most notably the acerbic Richard Reeves in *A Ford, Not a Lincoln* (New York: Harcourt Brace Jovanovich, 1975); the workmanlike A. James Reichley in *Conservatives in an Age of Change* (Washington, D.C.: Brookings, 1981); and, in a repackaging of his careful and fair-minded *New Republic* essays, John Osborne, *White House Watch: The Ford Years* (Washington, D.C.: New Republic Books, 1977).

The Carter Presidency has generated several useful accounts. Perhaps least useful as history because of his selective memory is Jimmy Carter's own *Keeping Faith* (New York: Bantam Books, 1982), as Robert Kaiser demonstrates in a long review, "Wasn't Carter the President Who Said He'd Never Lie to Us?" *Washington Post Outlook* (November 7, 1982). However, what *Keeping Faith* may lack as a historical record it gains as a self-portrait of great documentary interest. Likewise some of the other Carter-era memoirs: Rosalyn Carter's *First Lady from Plains* (Boston: Houghton Mifflin, 1984); and National Security Advisor Zbigniew Brzezinski's *Power and Principle* (New York: Farrar, Straus, Giroux, 1983); especially when read in conjunction with Secretary of State Cyrus Vance's *Hard Choices* (New York: Simon and Schuster, 1983). See also press secretary Jody Powell's *The Other Side of the Story* (New York: William Morrow, 1984) and chief of staff Hamilton Jordan's *Crisis* (New York: Putnam, 1982).

The most voluminous consideration of the Carter Presidency so far is Betty Glad's *In Search of the Great White House* (New York: W.W. Norton & Company, 1980). For most purposes, however, the best book-length analysis of the Carter Presidency is Haynes Johnson's *In the Absence of Power* (New York: The Viking Press, 1980). High marks for prescience go to Jack Knott and Aaron Wildavsky for their "Jimmy Carter's Theory of Governing," *Wilson Quarterly* 1 (Winter 1977), pp. 49-67, who describe with great accuracy how Carter would address his presidential responsibilities based on a close reading of his campaign speeches and of Carter's own campaign autobiography, *Why Not the Best?* (New York: Bantam, 1975).

On the Reagan Presidency there are, so far, at least three indispensable books: Laurence I. Barrett's careful and thorough reconstruction of Reagan's first three years, *Gambling with History* (Garden City, N.Y.: Doubleday, 1983); Lou Cannon's biography, *Reagan* (New York: G.P. Putnam's Sons, 1982) by the journalist who knows the President best; and William Greider's fascinating and revealing series of interviews with David Stockman, President Reagan's budget director, in *The Education of David Stockman and Other Americans* (New York: Dutton, 1982). Two high-level refugees from the Reagan administration, both for various reasons dissatisfied with how they fared there, have already weighed in with informative memoirs: Paul Craig Roberts, *The Supply Side Revolution* (Cambridge, Mass.: Harvard University Press, 1984), and former Secretary of State Alexander Haig, *Caveat* (New York: Macmillan, 1984).

For more general material on the Presidency, see also the following: "The American Presidency in the Last Half-Century," *Current History*, vol. 39 (October 1960); "The Office of the American Presidency," *Annals*, vol. 30 (September 1956); "The Presidential Office," *Law and Contemporary Problems*, vol. 21 (Autumn 1956); and "The Presidency in Transition," *Journal of Politics*, vol. 21 (February 1949). Edward Corwin's classic, *The President: Office and Powers* (New York: New York University Press, 1957), is the foremost source on the legal and constitutional aspects of the presidential office. In the tradition of Corwin, see Louis Fisher, *President and Congress* (New York: Free Press, 1972). There are now a number of good readers on the Presidency that reprint many of the articles mentioned here. I will mention two. Aaron Wildavsky, *The Presidency* (Boston: Little, Brown, 1969); and my own *The Modern Presidency* (Washington, D.C.: University Press of America, 1973).

Two sources that provide much raw material for speculation on problems of presidential power are Robert Donovan's *Eisenhower: The Inside Story* (New York: Harper & Row, 1956), an account of Cabinet-level decision-making drawn from stenographic records of meetings of the Eisenhower Cabinet; and John Hersey's "Mr. President," *New Yorker*, 5 parts (April 7-May 5, 1951), a diary of a few days spent with President Truman. Hersey in 1975 spent a comparable period of time with President Ford and has reprinted both accounts in *Aspects of the Presidency* (New Haven, Conn.: Ticknor and Fields, 1980). Hersey was far less impressed with Ford than he was with Truman, and his hostility to Ford on ideological grounds comes through.

On staffing the Executive Office, see Edward Hobbes, *Behind the President* (Washington, D.C.: Public Affairs Press, 1954), and Lauren Henry, *Presidential Transitions* (Washington, D.C.: Brookings, 1960). Richard F. Fenno, Jr., *The President's Cabinet* (New York: Vintage Books, Random House, 1959), is a useful synthesis. For analytical articles on the Executive Office, see Don K. Price, "Staffing the Presidency," *American Political Science Review*, vol. 40 (December 1946), pp. 1154-68; Price, "The Office of the Chief Executive," *Public Administration Review*, vol. 14 (Autumn 1954), pp. 283-85; Warren Cikins, "The Council of Economic Advisors: Political Economy at the Crossroads," *Public Policy*, vol. 4 (1953), pp. 94-115; Corinne Silverman's ICP case, *The President's Economic Advisors* (University, Ala.: University of Alabama Press, 1959); Bertram Gross and John Lewis, "The President's Executive Staff During the Truman Administration," *American Political Science Review*, vol. 48 (March 1954), pp. 114-30; and George A. Graham, "The Presidency and the Executive Office of the President," *Journal of Politics*, vol. 22 (November 1950), pp. 599-621. More recent material includes books cited in the text by Walter Heller, Charles Schultze, and Paul Y. Hammond. Herbert Stein's *The Revolution in Fiscal Policy* (Chicago: University of Chicago Press, 1969) gives a historical overview of economic decisions made at the presidential level from Hoover through Kennedy, and his *Presidential Economics* (New York: Simon and Schuster, 1984) brings the story up to date. On the whole, I believe the most informative book-length work on presidential staff is still Patrick Anderson's *President's Men* (Garden City, NY: Doubleday, 1968).See also Roger Porter, *Presidential Decision-Making: The Economic Policy Board* (New York: Cambridge University Press, 1980).

Material on presidential nominating politics and on the presidential coalition is summarized in Nelson W. Polsby and Aaron Wildavsky, *Presidential Elections*, 6th ed. (New York: Scribner's, 1984). My book *Consequences of Party Reform* (New York: Oxford, 1983) describes how changes in presidential selection have rippled out into the political system and affected the conduct of the Presidency, interest groups, and the mass media.

The best scholarly work on the U.S. Senate in the contemporary era has been done by Ralph K. Huitt, primarily in a series of articles, which have been collected and reprinted in Huitt and Robert L. Peabody, *Congress: Two Decades of Analysis* (New York: Harper & Row, 1969). See also Donald R. Matthews's *U.S. Senators and Their World* (Chapel Hill, N.C.: University of North Carolina Press, 1960). It and William S. White's more informally written *Citadel* (New York: Harper & Row, 1957) are still of major importance in guiding contemporary thinking on the Senate, although each has deficiencies. Bertram Gross's *The Legislative Struggle* (New York: McGraw-Hill, 1953) is oriented toward legislative strategy and toward reform. H. Bradford Westerfield's *Foreign Policy and Party Politics* (New Haven, Conn.: Yale University Press, 1955) is an acute study of senatorial behavior in a particular issue area.

Two of the better senatorial biographies happen to be about mavericks: Richard Rovere, *Senator Joe McCarthy* (New York: Harcourt, Brace & World, 1959); and Robert A. Smith, *The Tiger in the Senate* (Garden City, N.Y.: Doubleday, 1962), about Wayne Morse. On McCarthy, Michael Straight's remarkable *Trial by Television* (Boston: Beacon Press, 1954) is perhaps the most revealing study yet published. More recent books on McCarthy are not especially good on the Senate, with the exception of Richard M. Fried, *Men Against McCarthy* (New York: Columbia University Press, 1976).

Also recommended are James T. Patterson's fine *Mr. Republican: A Biography of Robert A. Taft* (Boston: Houghton Mifflin, 1972); Senator Paul Douglas's memoirs, *In the Fullness of Time* (New York: Harcourt Brace Jovanovich, 1972); Neil MacNeil's *Dirksen* (New York: World Publishing Co., 1970); Bernard Asbell's excellent study of Edmund Muskie, *The Senate Nobody Knows* (Garden City, N.Y.: Doubleday, 1978); Hubert Humphrey's ebullient and informative autobiography *Education of a Public Man* (Garden City, N.Y.: Doubleday, 1976); and a full-scale biography of Humphrey, Carl Solberg, *Hubert Humphrey: A Biography* (New York: Norton, 1984).

On the House, see *Member of the House* (New York: Scribner, 1962) by the late Clem Miller, the newsletters of a gifted young congressman. This book does not merely explain the House as an institution, it evokes it. Robert L. Peabody and I (eds.), in *New Perspectives on the House of Representatives*, 3rd ed. (Chicago: Rand McNally, 1969), have gathered together a dozen essays and a short bibliography on aspects of contemporary House politics. Neil MacNeil, in *Forge of Democracy* (New York: McKay, 1963), does for the House what William White did for the Senate, with less flair for generalization but greater attention to historical anecdotage. George Galloway's *History of the House of Representatives* (New York: Crowell, 1961) is predominantly procedural in its concerns, as are his *Congress at the Crossroads* (New York: Crowell, 1946), an authoritative commentary on the Legislative Reorganization Act of that year, and *The Legislative Process in Congress* (New York: Crowell, 1962). Another valuable set of congressional memoirs is Jerry Voorhis's *Confessions of a Congressman* (Garden City, NY: Doubleday, 1948). Holbert N. Carroll's *The House of Representatives and Foreign Affairs* (Pittsburgh: University of Pittsburgh Press, 1958) is more inclusive than its title indicates. Charles O. Jones has written an exceptionally thoughtful and interesting text in *The United States Congress: People, Places, and Policy* (Homewood, Ill.: Dorsey, 1982). John Bibby and Roger Davidson's *On Capitol Hill* (New York: Holt, 1972) contains a good set of original case studies. Lewis A. Froman, Jr.'s useful *The Congressional Process* (Boston: Little, Brown, 1967) lays out strategic implications of congressional rules and procedures, as does Walter Oleszek's *Congressional Procedures and the Policy Process*, 2nd ed. (Washington, D.C.: Congressional Quarterly Press, 1984). A collection of general materials on Congress, including six previously unpublished letters by Clem Miller, is Nelson W. Polsby (ed.), *Congressional Behavior* (New York: Random House, 1971). Roll-call analysis is an important element in David Truman's *The Congressional Party* (New York: Wiley, 1959); Duncan MacRae's *Dimensions of Congressional Voting* (Berkeley, Calif.: University of California Press, 1958); Julius Turner's *Party and Constituency: Pressures on Congress* (Baltimore: Johns Hopkins Studies in Historical and Political Science, Series

LXIX, No. 1, 1951); and David Mayhew's *Party Loyalty among Congressmen* (Cambridge, Mass.: Harvard University Press, 1966). Outstanding work on congressional committees includes Richard Fenno's *Congressmen in Committees* (Boston: Little, Brown, 1973), and John Manley's *The Politics of Finance* (Boston: Little, Brown, 1970). See also David Price's *Who Makes the Laws?* (Morristown, N.J.: General Learning Co., 1972); David Vogeler's *The Politics of Congress* (Boston: Allyn and Bacon, 1974); Gary Orfield's, *Congressional Power: Congress and Social Change* (New York: Harcourt Brace Jovanovich, 1975); and David R. Mayhew's, *Congress: The Electoral Connection* (New Haven, Conn.: Yale University Press, 1974).

Perhaps the most original and noteworthy contemporary generalizations about congressional politics are contained in the work of Lewis A. Dexter. Some of this is reprinted in Peabody and Polsby (eds.), *New Perspectives on the House*, but more still can be found in the latter parts of Raymond Bauer, Ithiel de Sola Pool, and Lewis A. Dexter, *American Business and Public Policy* (New York: Atherton, 1963). This book, a study of interest group communication in reciprocal-trade legislation, is of great general interest. See also Dexter's *The Sociology and Politics of Congress* (Chicago: Rand McNally, 1969).

Most treatments of the process by which a bill becomes a law are case studies; an example is Stephen K. Bailey's well-written *Congress Makes a Law* (New York: Columbia University Press, 1950). Less detailed, and also less partisan, is H. Douglas Price's colorful "Race, Religion and the Rules Committee: The Kennedy Aid-to-Education Bills," in A. Westin (ed.), *The Uses of Power* (New York: Harcourt, Brace & World, 1962), pp. 1-71. Other good case studies are T. R. Reid, *Congressional Odyssey* (San Francisco: W.H. Freeman, 1980); Eric Redman, *The Dance of Legislation* (New York: Simon and Schuster, 1973); and Robert L. Peabody et al., *To Enact a Law* (New York: Praeger, 1972). General discussions of congressional routines can be found in Gross, *The Legislative Struggle*, Froman, *The Congressional Process*, Oleszek, *Congressional Procedures and the Policy Process*, and Edward F. Willett's lucid exposition of the procedural points, *How Our Laws Are Made* (Washington, D.C.: Government Printing Office, 1981).

Two classic works on the budgetary process are Richard F. Fenno, Jr.'s detailed and thoughtful *The Power of the Purse* (Boston: Little, Brown, 1966), on the congressional side of the appropriations process as it was before the extensive reforms of the 1970s; and Aaron B. Wildavsky's *The Politics of the Budgetary Process*, 4th ed. (Boston: Little, Brown, 1984), which deals more extensively with the executive side. For a sense of the history of budgetary problems, the reader should also consult *Organizing for National Security, Hearings before the Subcommittee on National Policy Machinery of the Senate Committee on Government Operations*, "The Budget and the Policy Process," part 8 (Washington, D.C.: Government Printing Office, 1961); and the task force reports and reports to Congress of the Commission on the Organization of the Executive Branch of the Government (second Hoover Commission, 1955). The relevant reports are titled "Budget and Accounting" (Washington, D.C.: Government Printing Office, 1955). More recently the work of Allen Schick, especially his *Congress and Money* (Washington, D.C.: Urban Institute, 1980), is indispensable. Schick is also the co-author, with Robert Keith, of the best up-to-date technical primer on the budgetary process, *Manual on the Federal Budget Process* (Washington, D.C.: Library of Congress, Congressional Research Service, 1982). *Federal Budget Report,* a bi-weekly newsletter edited by Stanley E. Collender and published by Touche Ross and Company in Washington, D.C., is an excellent source of ongoing information about budgetary politics. Collender has also written *The Guide to the Federal Budget* (Washington, D.C.: Urban Institute Press, 1985).

Much of the discussion by academic political scientists of conflict and cooperation follows Woodrow Wilson's *Congressional Government* (New York: Meridian, 1956). Works already cited by Gross, Carroll, Bailey, and Galloway express ideas congenial to Wilson's perspective. So also, with modifications that attempt to take explicit account of the American historical experience, does James M. Burns in *Deadlock of Democracy* (Englewood Cliffs, N.J.: Prentice-Hall, 1963). Defense of Congress is offered by William White and Neil MacNeil in works already cited.

The Congressional Record contains moderately reliable verbatim records of debates in Congress and much extraneous material—some of it quite entertaining. However, it cannot profitably be read by the serious beginner without concurrent use of the daily newspapers as a guide. *The Congressional Directory* and *The U.S. Government Organizational Manual* provide basic facts. All three are available by mail from the Government Printing Office in Washington, D.C. One private source, *Congressional Quarterly Weekly Reports* and annual *Almanac,* is outstanding in the accuracy, sophistication, and breadth of its coverage, especially of Congress. *National Journal,* also a weekly, provides thorough and well-documented articles on all aspects of Washington politics, with special emphasis on the executive branch. Three other reference works deserve mention as well: Michael Barone and Grant Ujifusa's *Almanac of American Politics 1984* (Washington, D.C.: National Journal, 1983) and Alan Ehrenhalt's *Politics in America* (Washington, D.C.: Congressional Quarterly, 1983) give encyclopedic and lively treatments of each and every Congressional district and the politics of incumbent members of Congress and senators; in *Vital Statistics on Congress, 1982* (Washington, D.C.: American Enterprise Institute, 1982), Norman Ornstein, Thomas E. Mann, Michael Malbin, and John Bibby give a statistical overview of Congress that is useful and enlightening.

NOTES

CHAPTER 1   On the American Political System

1. Woodrow Wilson, *Congressional Government* (New York: Meridian Books, 1956; 1st ed., 1884), pp. 23, 24, 30.

2. For the 1816 figures see *Historical Statistics of the United States; Colonial Times to 1957* (Washington, D.C.: Government Printing Office, 1960). Recent figures on executive branch employees are from the *Statistical Abstract of the United States 1982-83* (Washington, D.C.: Government Printing Office, 1982), p. 264, and show 2,855,000 civilian employees in the executive branch, and 2,083,000 uniformed personnel for 1981.

3. *U.S. Government Organization Manual 1982-83* (Washington, D.C.: Government Printing Office, 1982), pp. 62-66. In addition, there are specialized courts, including the Tax Court of the United States, territorial courts, the United States Court of Claims, the United States Customs Court, and the United States Court of Customs and Patent Appeals.

4. Although this decision was controversial at the time, some scholars now feel that the Court was acting under a mandate clearly implied by the Constitution. See Charles L. Black, Jr., *Perspectives in Constitutional Law* (Englewood Cliffs, N.J.: Prentice Hall, 1963), pp. 2-3.

5. See Robert A. Dentler and Marvin B. Scott, *Schools on Trial* (Cambridge,Mass.: Abt Books, 1981), esp. pp. 20-73.

6. See James Hamilton, *The Power to Probe* (New York: Random House, 1976).

7. See, in this case, Arthur Maass, *Muddy Waters* (Cambridge, Mass.: Harvard University Press, 1951).

8. *New York Times,* May 13, 1984.

9. Article I, Section 8, says, in part, "The Congress shall have power ... to raise and support armies, but no appropriation of money to that use shall be for a longer term than two years."

10. Article II, Section 3.

11. Twentieth Amendment, Section 2.

12. The Twenty-second Amendment reads, in part:

> No person shall be elected to the office of the President more than twice, and no person who has held the office of President, or acted as President, for more than two years of a term to which some other person was elected President shall be elected to the office of the President more than once.

Thus ten years is the absolute maximum time under the Constitution that any single person may serve as president.

13. See "Ergophobia," *The Economist* (August 13, 1983), p. 29. These examples are meant only to stack the deck against those who assert that the American political system is particularly bad by world standards. A more complex and interesting formulation of the problem would be to study the United States in the context of societies with similarly mixed populations and compare our solutions to problems of governing with theirs. See "The Wages of Envy," *The Economist* (August 28, 1983), p. 35, for a discussion of relations between Tamils and Singalese in Sri Lanka, a sad story that has many analogues elsewhere.

14. Two votes in the Senate for each state is an arrangement that was written into the Constitution (Article I, Section 3) by the famous "Connecticut Compromise" at the Constitutional Convention. It is almost certainly beyond the reach of change even by an ordinary constitutional amendment, because Article V of the Constitution provides that "no state, without its consent, shall be deprived of its equal suffrage in the Senate." See Max Farrand (ed.), *The Records of the Federal Convention of 1787*, rev. ed. (New Haven, Conn.: Yale University Press, 1937), volume I, pp. 343, 355, 363, 461, 470, 476.

15. The main decisions were *Baker* v. *Carr*, 369 *U.S.* 186 (1962), which took jurisdiction in state apportionment cases; *Wesberry* v. *Sanders*, 376 *U.S.* 1 (1964), which required substantial equality of populations within United States House districts; and *Reynolds* v. *Sims*, 377 *U.S.* 533 (1964), which forced the apportionment of both houses of bicameral state legislatures on the same population basis. For a thorough discussion of these and other cases, see Robert G. Dixon, *Democratic Representation* (New York: Oxford University Press, 1968). In *Wells* v. *Rockefeller*, 389 *U.S.* 421 (1969), the Court defined more exactly— and more narrowly—what "substantial equality" meant. See Nelson W. Polsby (ed.), *Reapportionment in the 1970's* (Berkeley: University of California Press, 1971). The line of cases continues to grow. For more recent commentary see Bernard Grofman, Arend Lijphart, Robert McKay, and Howard Scarrow, *Representation and Redistricting Issues* (Lexington, Mass.: Lexington Books, 1982).

16. Indeed, in *Karcher* v. *Daggett* 462 U.S. 725, [103 S.Ct. 2653] (1983) the Court demanded that congressional districts be more exactly equal in population than the U.S. census is capable of warranting.

17. Dixon, *Democratic Representation*, p. 455, shows on the basis of 1960 population figures that states having two members of Congress are most likely to lose out under the present formula for allocating congressional seats among the states.

18. Connoisseurs of the art form find much to admire in the redistricting that occurs after each decennial census. For instance, California Republicans brought a suit charging gerrymandering of congressional districts after the 1980 census gave several new seats to California. In a document supporting the suit, the political scientist Bernard Grofman described "glaring examples ... which wander without any rhyme or reason over the California landscape save to pick up (or submerge) pockets of partisan voting strength."

> For example [he says], ... District 6, which was a marginal Democratic-held seat in 1980, reaches out across the bay to add to the Democratic strength in the northern tip of San Francisco additional Democratic strength in Solano County (the Vallejo area) to dilute Republican strength in Marin County and to give rise to a narrow (52%) Democratic victory in 1982. This district, while slightly less contorted than its predecessor ("the water-connected gerrymander that Phil Burton concocted for his brother John"), is still readily contiguous only by sailboat.... District 12 ... makes a northward zap at the tip of the district to pick up a solid pocket of Republican strength. Thus, this pocket of Republican strength gets added to District 12, an already solidly Republican packed District.
>
> ... District 27 ... makes a sudden dart eastward in the middle section of the district to add solid Democratic votes to hold the district's Democratic edge. (Contiguous marginal and Republican areas inland are carefully skirted—left either to be submerged by the overwhelmingly Democratic strength in District 28, which was won in 1982 by Democratic incumbent Dixon with 79% of the vote, or to be packed into the lopsidedly Republican (and haphazardly shaped) District 42.

... District 44 goes through some remarkable contortions to pick up pockets of Democratic strength to guarantee a Democratic victory in this newly created district, and carefully skirts the Republican voters who have been packed into District 41 (won by Republican incumbent Lowery with 69% of the vote).

After the 1980 census the New Jersey legislature produced congressional districts variously labeled "the fishhook" (the 7th) and "the swan" (the 5th). Of the 3rd district, *Congressional Quarterly* reported, "when the Legislature created this district, some members complained that at high tide, it would cease to exist. Crafted to help [incumbent James J.] Howard, the new 3rd hugs the coastline in search of Democratic votes, avoiding inland Republican areas of Monmouth County." Larry Light, "New Jersey Map Imaginative Gerrymander," *Congressional Quarterly* (May 22, 1982), p. 1192.

Bizarre shapes are not always necessary to produce a highly political outcome. The Republican-dominated Arizona legislature divided the district of the most popular incumbent Democratic member of Congress into nice, squarish shapes, nevertheless forcing him to choose between running in a district that had more Democratic votes in it but more strangers, and a district that contained his home but that was loaded up with Republicans. See Larry Light, "New Arizona Districts: A Quandary for Udall," *Congressional Quarterly* (January 30, 1982), pp. 161-63.

19. Debate on changes of Senate rules, however, can be terminated only by a two-thirds vote of those present and voting.

CHAPTER 2   The Presidency

1. See Nelson W. Polsby and Aaron Wildavsky, *Presidential Elections*, 6th ed. (New York: Charles Scribner's Sons, 1984) for an extended discussion of political strategies in presidential elections.

2. Only the state of Maine counts votes differently. Its rules provide:

A presidential elector is elected from each congressional district and two at large ....

The presidential electors at large shall cast their ballots for candidates for President and Vice President of the political party which received the largest number of votes in the State. The presidential electors of each congressional district shall cast their ballots for the candidates for President and Vice President of the political party which received the largest number of votes in each congressional district.

In every election since at least 1936, all Maine electoral votes have been cast for the same candidate.

A handy summary of relevant state regulations is contained in Thomas Durbin and Michael Seitzinger, *Nomination and Election of the President and Vice President of the United States* (Washington, D.C.: U.S. Government Printing Office, 1980). The entry for Maine is on p. 356.

3. Ronald Reagan, who was a genuinely conservative Republican candidate in 1980, and a successful one, spent most of his campaign playing down his conservatism and benignly watching the Jimmy Carter candidacy self-destruct. See Albert R. Hunt, "The Campaign and the Issues," in Austin Ranney (ed.), *The American Elections of 1980* (Washington, D.C.: American Enterprise Institute, 1981), pp. 142-76. In 1984, running as the incumbent, he invoked Franklin Roosevelt and John Kennedy more frequently than Republican presidents.

4. Here is an example of Richard Nixon's 1968 thinking on the subject: "They tell me, 'You didn't hit him hard enough. Why don't you give them hell like Truman?' I explain that I not only have to appeal to partisan Republicans but also have to get Democrats to cross over. But [they] don't understand that. Occasionally I say a good word for Johnson or Humphrey. *It's a device, of course, to show I'm fair-minded,* but [they] don't see that. That's why [they] liked Barry so. He didn't give a damn about Democrats. But to win, you have to" (italics in original). Jules Witcover, *The Resurrection of Richard Nixon* (New York: Putnam, 1970), p. 135.

In the 1980 general election Ronald Reagan sought to expand his constituency by appealing to traditionally Democratic labor voters. Albert Hunt says:

> [Reagan] ... reversed several earlier positions to enhance his appeal to union members. Now he was promising that he wouldn't seek to extend antitrust laws to unions or repeal the Occupational Safety and Health Act (OSHA) or the Davis-Bacon Act ..., or eliminate the minimum wage or seek a national right to work law.

"The Campaign and the Issues," p. 158.

5. Letter to Lady Delamere, March 7, 1911.

6. See Elmer E. Cornwell, Jr., "Presidential News: The Expanding Public Image," *Journalism Quarterly*, vol. 36 (Summer 1959), pp. 275-83, for an ingenious demonstration of the increase, in this century, of news media attention to the President as compared with Congress. Other indications of the emotional centrality of the President in American life are contained in Leila Sussman, *Dear F.D.R.: A Study of Political Letterwriting* (Totowa, N.J.: Bedminster, 1963), and in studies of public opinion when Presidents die in office. A good summary of this literature is contained in Harold Orlansky, "Reactions to the Death of President Roosevelt," *Journal of Social Psychology*, vol. 26 (November 1947), pp. 235-66. See also Bradley S. Greenberg and Edwin B. Parker (eds.), *The Kennedy Assassination and the American Public* (Stanford, Calif.: Stanford University Press, 1965); Martha Wolfenstein and Gilbert Kliman (eds.), *Children and the Death of a President* (Garden City, N.Y.: Doubleday, 1964); and Fred I. Greenstein, "The Psychological Functions of the Presidency for Citizens," in Elmer E. Cornwell (ed.), *The American Presidency: Vital Center* (Chicago: Scott, Foresman, 1966), pp. 30-36. An up-to-date summary of presidential public relations is Michael B. Grossman and Martha Kumar, *Portraying the President: The White House and the News Media* (Baltimore: Johns Hopkins University Press, 1981).

7. *The Memoirs of Herbert Hoover*, vol. 2, *The Cabinet and the Presidency 1920-1933* (New York: Macmillan, 1952), p. vi. Recent sympathetic accounts of President Hoover's life include David Burner, *Herbert Hoover: A Public Life* (New York: Knopf, 1979); George H. Nash, *The Life of Herbert Hoover*, vol. 1, *The Engineer 1874-1914* (New York: W.W. Norton, 1983); and Gary Dean Best, *Herbert Hoover: The Postpresidential Years, 1933-1964* (Stanford, Calif.: Hoover Institution Press, 1983).

8. See *Memoirs.*, pp. 216ff, and esp. 217; and Victor L. Albjerg, "Hoover: The Presidency in Transition," *Current History* (October 1960), pp. 213-19. In 1949 Mr. Hoover was rated next to the bottom of the "average" category as a President by fifty-five social scientists. See Arthur M. Schlesinger, Sr., *Paths to the Present* (New York: Macmillan, 1949), pp. 93-111. In 1962 a ranking by a similar group of historians rated Mr. Hoover nineteenth out of thirty-one, fifth from the bottom of the "average" category, ten notches below Truman, who was rated "near great." Arthur M. Schlesinger, "Our Presidents: A Rating by 75 Historians," *New York Times Magazine* (July 29, 1962), pp. 12ff.

Later surveys more or less confirm this judgment. In 1970 a sociologist, Gary Maranell, reporting the result of a survey of 571 American historians, scored Mr. Hoover eighteenth in "general prestige assigned to the President at the present time." "The Evaluation of Presidents: An Extension of the Schlesinger Polls," *The Journal of American History* 57 (June 1970), pp. 104-13. Forty-nine historians and political scholars polled by the *Chicago Tribune* in 1982 rated Mr. Hoover twenty-first out of thirty-eight. Steve Neal, "Our Best and Worst Presidents," *Chicago Tribune Magazine* (January 10, 1982), pp. 8ff. At around the same time, historians Robert K. Murray and Tim H. Blessing asked nearly 2,000 historians nineteen pages' worth of questions. Their 846 respondents scored Hoover twenty-first ("average," bracketed by Van Buren and Hayes). "The Presidential Performance Study: A Progress Report," *The Journal of American History* 70 (December 1983), pp. 535-55. See also a secondary analysis of various polls by Arthur B. Murphy, "Evaluating Presidents of the United States," *Presidential Studies Quarterly* 14 (Winter 1984), pp. 117-26.

A perceptive discussion of Hoover's presidential style is James D. Barber, "Classifying and Predicting Presidential Style: Two 'Weak' Presidents," *Journal of Social Issues*, vol. 24 (July 1968), pp. 51-80.

9. Richard E. Neustadt, *Presidential Power* (New York: Wiley, 1960), p. 214.

10. *Ibid.*, p. 162.

11. In this connection, see E. P. Hayes, *Activities of the President's Emergency Committee for Employment* (Concord, N.H.: private printing, 1936), pp. 2-3, 6-10, 15, 38, 96, and *passim*. For a more sympathetic discussion of President Hoover's economic policies, see Herbert Stein, *The Revolution in Fiscal Policy* (Chicago: University of Chicago Press, 1969).

12. William E. Leuchtenburg, *In the Shadow of FDR* (Ithaca, N.Y.: Cornell University Press, 1983), p. ix. As Leuchtenburg remarks: "From 1945 to the present historians have unfailingly ranked [Roosevelt] with Washington and Lincoln, and the men who succeeded him found one question inescapable: How did they measure up to FDR?" p. xi. The 1949 and 1962 Schlesinger surveys, *op cit.*, placed Roosevelt third in rank behind Lincoln and Washington, as a "great" President, a judgment in which Clinton Rossiter concurs, *The American Presidency*, rev. ed. (New York: Harcourt, Brace & World, Harvest Books, 1960), p. 152. So do the more recent surveys: Maranell (1970) has Roosevelt third, and Neal (1982) and Murray and Blessing (1983) rate him second (below Lincoln, above Washington).

13. The foregoing quotations are from Pendleton Herring, "First Session of the Seventy-third Congress, March 9, 1933 to June 16, 1933," *American Political Science Review*, vol. 28 (February 1934), pp. 65, 67, and 75. See also his description of congressional handling of the banking crisis, *ibid.*, pp. 70ff., and, in general, Herring, *Presidential Leadership* (New York: Farrar and Rinehart, 1940), as well as his periodic reviews of congressional activity for the *American Political Science Review*: "1st Session of the 72nd Congress," vol. 26 (October 1932), pp. 846-74; "2nd Session of the 72nd Congress," vol. 27 (June 1933), pp. 404-22; "1st Session of the 73rd Congress," vol. 28 (February 1934), pp. 65-83; "2nd Session of the 73rd Congress," vol. 28 (October 1934), pp. 852-66; and "1st Session of the 74th Congress," vol. 29 (December 1935), pp. 985-1005.

14. James T. Patterson, *Congressional Conservatism and the New Deal* (Lexington: University of Kentucky Press, 1967), pp. 4-5. See also William E. Leuchtenburg, *Franklin D. Roosevelt and the New Deal* (New York: Harper & Row, 1963), pp. 41-62, and Joseph Alsop, *FDR: A Centenary Remembrance* (New York: Washington Square Press, 1982).

15. I am using this term in a sense slightly different from the usage of its coiner, Thomas C. Cochran, who in "The 'Presidential Synthesis' in American History," *American Historical Review*, vol. 53 (July 1948), pp. 748-59, argued for a greater infusion of social science theory and methods into historical inquiry and for an understanding of the lives of ordinary people in the past and not just those of political elites.

See also Martin Shapiro's discussion of what he calls the "New Deal myth" about the Supreme Court. "The Supreme Court from Warren to Burger" in Anthony King (ed.), *The New American Political System* (Washington, D.C.: American Enterprise Institute, 1978), especially pp. 188ff.

16. See Patterson, *Congressional Conservatism*.

17. See Jasper B. Shannon, "Presidential Politics in the South: 1938," *Journal of Politics*, vol. 1, nos. 2 and 3 (May and August 1939), pp. 146-70, 278-300; and Alsop, *op. cit.*, pp. 106-7.

18. Arthur Schlesinger, Jr., says that this characteristic of Roosevelt's Presidency was widely criticized at the time; this is one general point in the discussion of the Presidency at which many analysts have reversed themselves, perhaps mostly because of the influence of Schlesinger and Richard Neustadt. See Schlesinger, *The Coming of the New Deal* (Boston: Houghton Mifflin, 1958), pp. 521ff.

19. *Ibid.*, p. 528. See also an admiring memoir by Roosevelt's Secretary of Labor, Frances Perkins, *The Roosevelt I Knew* (New York: Viking, 1946); and by his speechwriter Samuel I. Rosenman, *Working with Roosevelt* (New York: Harper, 1952).

20. Francis Biddle, *In Brief Authority* (Garden City, N.Y.: Doubleday, 1962), p. 182.

21. Fillmore H. Sanford, reporting on a public opinion poll conducted in 1949 in Philadelphia, gives evidence of Roosevelt's overwhelming popular appeal four years after his death. Respondents gave Mr. Roosevelt his highest marks for gregariousness. A second theme of approval is related to Mr. Roosevelt's image as helper of materially deprived groups, such as "the poor" and "labor." "Public Orientations to Roosevelt," *Public Opinion Quarterly*, 15 (Summer 1951), pp. 189-216.

22. "Truman's Global Leadership," *Current History*, 39 (October 1960), p. 226.

23. See, in particular, Harry S Truman, *Memoirs, Year of Decisions* (Garden City, N.Y.: Doubleday, 1955), pp. 58-59, 95-99, 226-27; *Years of Trial and Hope* (1956), pp. 31-38 and *passim.* On the history of the Bureau of the Budget, see Larry Berman, *The Office of Management and Budget and the Presidency 1921-1979* (Princeton, N.J.: Princeton University Press, 1979). On the creation of the Council of Economic Advisers see Nelson W. Polsby, *Political Innovation in America: The Politics of Policy Initiation* (New Haven, Conn.: Yale University Press, 1984), pp. 100-112. For a discussion of the Council's early work, see Bertram M. Gross and John P. Lewis, "The President's Economic Staff During the Truman Administration," *American Political Science Review* 48 (March 1954), pp. 114-30.

24. Truman, *Years of Trial and Hope.*, pp. 35-36.

25. Neustadt, *Presidential Power*, p. 175.

26. Truman, *Years of Trial and Hope*, p. 194.

27. *Ibid.*, p. 193.

28. Truman, *Year of Decisions*, pp. 329-30.

29. See Robert J. Donovan, *Tumultuous Years: The Presidency of Harry S Truman, 1949-1953* (New York: Norton, 1982), pp. 114-18, 372-81.

30. See "Harry Truman, Foreign Policy Master-builder," *The Economist* (April 28, 1984), pp. 41-43.

31. See Polsby, *Political Innovation*, pp. 78-91; and Joseph M. Jones, *The Fifteen Weeks: February 21 to June 5, 1947* (New York: Viking, 1955).

32. See Elmer Davis, "Harry S Truman and the Verdict of History," *Reporter* (February 3, 1953), pp. 17-22; and Herbert Elliston, "The Stature of Harry Truman," *Atlantic Monthly* (February 1956), pp. 69-71. An excellent discussion of foreign affairs in the Truman administration and an affectionate portrait of President Truman is contained in Dean Acheson, *Present at the Creation* (New York: Norton, 1969). In the wake of Watergate, there developed a certain nostalgia for Mr. Truman's forthrightness, and this was no doubt fed by such uncritical works as Merle Miller, *Plain Speaking* (New York: Berkley-Putnam, 1974) and Margaret Truman's remembrance of her father, *Harry S Truman* (New York: Morrow, 1973). The centennial of Truman's birth in 1984 brought forth another round of tributes from his near-contemporaries. See, for example, William E. Leuchtenburg, "Give 'Em Harry," *The New Republic* (May 21, 1984), pp. 19-23, who concludes "Odds are that the history books, now and in the future, will say that Harry S Truman, born a century ago, ranks close to the top." This is the verdict of the various surveys of historians. Truman was not rated in the Schlesinger poll of 1948, but in 1962 he scored ninth, "near great," tied with Polk. The Maranell survey (1970) rated him seventh (below Wilson, above Jackson) for "general prestige" and he was eighth in the *Chicago Tribune* poll of 1982 and in the Murray-Blessing survey (1983).

33. The 1962 Schlesinger *New York Times Magazine* poll of seventy-five historians rated Eisenhower next to the bottom of the "average" category—three steps below Hoover and bracketed by Chester A. Arthur and Andrew Johnson. Out of a large number of sympathetic, well-informed, but nevertheless unfavorable assessments, see, for example, Dean Albertson, in Albertson (ed.), *Eisenhower as President* (New York: Hill and Wang, 1963), introduction; Neustadt, *Presidential Power*; Rossiter, *The American Presidency*; Emmett J. Hughes, *The Ordeal of Power* (New York: Atheneum Publishers, 1962; Dell, 1964)(by a speechwriter in the Eisenhower White House); Richard Rovere, *Affairs of State: The Eisenhower Years* (New York: Farrar, Straus & Cudahy, 1956). For favorable verdicts, see Merlo J. Pusey, *Eisenhower the President* (New York: Macmillan, 1956); Arthur Larson, *Eisenhower: The President Nobody Knew* (New York: Scribner, 1968); Herbert S. Parmet, *Eisenhower and the American Crusades* (New York: Macmillan, 1972); and, by the President's admiring younger brother, himself a distinguished public servant, Milton S. Eisenhower, *The President Is Calling* (Garden City, N.Y.: Doubleday, 1974), esp. Chapters 14-19.

34. The Maranell poll of 1970 shows Eisenhower in nineteenth place—between Hoover and Andrew Johnson—for "general prestige." By 1982, however, Eisenhower had begun to move up on the charts. The *Chicago Tribune* poll in that year ranked Ike ninth. See Neal. He was number eleven in the 1983 Murray-Blessing survey. A leading recent work in the political science literature that takes a favorable view of Eisenhower is Fred I. Greenstein's *The Hidden-Hand Presidency* (New York: Basic Books, 1982). As Herbert Parmet points out, Greenstein's

well-publicized work is not alone, "loading on additional details to what we have been reading about Ike since the early '70s. An introductory footnote lists seven books that have reappraised the Eisenhower Presidency.... [A]lmost all were the products of research that yielded essentially the same view of Eisenhower..." "Why We Liked Ike," *The New Leader* 65 (December 13, 1982), p. 16.

35. Neustadt, *Presidential Power*, p. 9 (italics in the original).

36. Martin Merson, *Private Diary of a Public Servant* (New York: Macmillan, 1955), p. 73. See also Norman Dorsen and John G. Simon, "A Fight on the Wrong Front," *Columbia University Forum* (Fall 1964), pp. 21-28.

37. Dwight D. Eisenhower, *Mandate for Change* (Garden City, N.Y.: Doubleday, 1963), pp. 319-21. Larson (*Eisenhower*, pp. 12-14) was an Eisenhower advisor and one of those who agrees.

38. See Greenstein, *The Hidden-Hand Presidency*, pp. 182-201.

39. Sherman Adams, *Firsthand Report* (New York: Popular Library, 1962), p. 92. In *Alliance Politics* (New York: Columbia University Press, 1970), Richard Neustadt suggests that there was less loss of presidential control over foreign policy than Adams implies. See pp. 103-6. Greenstein and his student, Richard Immerman, maintain that Adams exaggerated Eisenhower's detachment from policy-making. See Greenstein, pp. 87-91; and Richard H. Immerman, "Eisenhower and Dulles: Who Made the Decisions?" *Political Psychology* 1 (Autumn 1979), pp. 21-38.

40. Adams, *Firsthand Report*, p. 83.

41. *Ibid.*, p. 78.

42. Aaron B. Wildavsky, *Dixon-Yates, a Study in Power Politics* (New Haven, Conn.: Yale University Press, 1962), pp. 307-8. Greenstein claims that Eisenhower's studied incompetence in press conferences was calculated to draw fire away from him. He quotes Eisenhower's press secretary, James Hagerty:

> "President Eisenhower would say, Do it this way. I would say, If I go to the press conference and say what you want me to say, I would get hell. With that he would smile, get up and walk around the desk, pat me on the back and say, 'My boy, better you than me.'"

Another technique of Eisenhower's was double-talk. "Intentional evasiveness," Greenstein writes,

> ". . . was a standard Eisenhower press conference tactic. Sometimes, as in a March 16, 1955, press conference, he mixed vagueness with ambiguity studiously designed to have different effects on different audiences. The issue was whether, under what circumstances, and with what kinds of weapons the United States would defend Quemoy and Matsu. In his previous news conference, Eisenhower had warned that in the event of a "general war" in Asia the United States was prepared to use tactical nuclear weapons. Just before the following week's conference, the State Department conveyed through Hagerty the urgent request that the President not discuss this delicate matter further. Eisenhower reports that he replied, "Don't worry, Jim, if that question comes up, I'll just confuse them."

Fred I. Greenstein, *The Hidden-Hand Presidency*, pp. 91-92, 68-69.

43. See Neustadt, *Presidential Power*, pp. 64-80, 108-23; Hughes, *The Ordeal of Power*, pp. 205-9; Adams, *Firsthand Report*, pp. 354-75; and Charles J. V. Murphy, "The Budget and Eisenhower," *Fortune* (July 1957), pp. 96ff.

44. This is a condensation of President Truman's analysis of the actual power of the Presidency, the power to "persuade," quoted by Neustadt, *Presidential Power*, p. 10.

45. See esp. *ibid.*, p. 118.

46. See Robert Donovan, *Eisenhower: The Inside Story* (New York: Harper, 1956), for an authorized account of Cabinet meetings during Eisenhower's first term.

47. On Eisenhower's popularity, see Greenstein, *The Hidden-Hand Presidency*, pp. 4-6, 92-93; and Herbert Hyman and Paul Sheatsley, "The Political Appeal of General Eisenhower," *Public Opinion Quarterly* 17 (Winter 1953), pp. 443-60.

48. See, for example, Joseph Loftus, "Cabinet Holding Informal Talks," *New York Times* (July 25, 1961); and Richard F. Fenno, Jr., "The Cabinet: Index to the Kennedy Way," *New York Times Magazine* (April 22, 1962), pp. 13, 62-64.

49. Perhaps the most interesting contemporary account of Kennedy's White House is Joseph Kraft, "Kennedy's Working Staff," *Harpers* (December 1962), pp. 29-36.

50. See Nelson W. Polsby and Aaron Wildavsky, *Presidential Elections* 3rd ed. (New York: Charles Scribner's Sons, 1971), pp. 23-26; and Ithiel De Sola Pool, Robert P. Abelson, and Samuel L. Popkin, *Candidates, Issues and Strategies* (Cambridge: Massachusetts Institute of Technology, 1964), pp. 117-18. The best data on the attitudes of voters in the 1960 election are from the University of Michigan Survey Research Center. See Angus Campbell, Philip Converse, Warren E. Miller, and Donald E. Stokes, *Elections and the Political Order* (New York: Wiley, 1966), pp. 67-69, 78-124. On p. 92 the authors calculate that Kennedy's Catholicism was probably responsible for a net loss of 2.2 percent of the two-party vote nationwide.

51. The Democrats lost twenty-one seats in the 1960 election. Normally, at congressional elections held in the middle of a President's four-year term the President's party loses substantial ground in the House. Up until 1962 the twentieth-century average was forty-five seats. In the 1962 elections, however, the Democrats lost only three seats. Many observers interpreted this, incorrectly, as a sign of President Kennedy's 1962 popularity rather than as an indication of his unpopularity in 1960.

52. Tom Wicker, for example, complains of the lack of a Kennedy "hundred days." See *JFK and LBJ: The Influence of Personality upon Politics* (New York: Morrow, 1968), esp. p. 147. The idea that presidents must have a first hundred days of extraordinary accomplishment is, of course, a legacy of the Roosevelt era.

53. See Lawrence O'Brien, *No Final Victories* (Garden City, N.Y.: Doubleday, 1974), pp. 104-36. On Kennedy and Congress in general see Randall B. Ripley, *Kennedy and Congress* (Morristown, N.J.: General Learning Press, 1972); and John Hart, "Staffing the Presidency: Kennedy and the Office of Congressional Relations," *Presidential Studies Quarterly* 13 (Winter, 1983), pp. 101-10.

54. For a fine blow-by-blow account of the packing of the House Rules Committee in early 1961, see Neil MacNeil, *The Forge of Democracy: The House of Representatives* (New York: McKay, 1963), pp. 412-47.

55. See Richard W. Bolling, *Defeating the Leadership's Nominee in the House Democratic Caucus*, Inter-University Case Program No. 91 (Indianapolis: Bobbs-Merrill, 1965).

56. One of the most astute observers of Congress in those years was Sam Rayburn's assistant, D. B. Hardeman, whose reminiscences were recently published. Hardeman says:

> I've always thought that a major part of the Kennedy program would have passed had he lived; that at that time he was assassinated, the newspaper people ... forgot that there's a cycle in Congress, certainly in modern times: ... no activity in the first year of Congress until after Easter; then the easier legislation is put through one house or the other in the summer of that first year; then the tougher pieces of legislation have longer hearings and more involved operations so they seem to be held up. In the fall of the first year you go into sort of an inactive slump; and then, along in the spring of the second year of a Congress, you come to grips with these hard issues and you get them out of the way, one way or the other, in an election year. I think that is what would have happened in the case of the Kennedy program had he lived.

D.B.: Reminiscences of D. B. Hardeman, compiled by Larry Hufford (Austin: AAR/Tantalus, Inc., 1984), p. 114.

57. For informed discussion of the legislative effectiveness of both men, see Joseph Cooper and Gary Bombardier, "Presidential Leadership and Party Success," *Journal of Politics*, vol. 30 (November 1968), pp. 1012-27; Dan Cordtz, "Lyndon's Legislation," *Wall Street Journal* (August 11, 1965); and Hardeman, pp. 114-15.

58. See, for example, Roger Hilsman, *To Move a Nation* (Garden City, NY.: Doubleday, 1967), p. 56. "The minute I got back to my desk, the phone rang from the White House. 'By now,' a voice said, 'you will have been told that you are to be the new Assistant Secretary of State for Far Eastern Affairs,' I said that I had. 'You will also have been told to refrain from intruding

into military and strategic matters.' I admitted this, too. 'Well,' said the voice, 'the President wants you to understand that it was precisely because you have stood up to the Defense Department that you were chosen, and that he expects you to continue.' "

Examples from another domain can be found in Arthur Schlesinger, Jr., *A Thousand Days* (Boston: Houghton Mifflin, 1965), p. 138, on the appointment, which Kennedy initially opposed, of Kermit Gordon to the Council of Economic Advisors. "Finally [Council Chairman-designate Walter] Heller called on Kennedy ... hoping to get the matter settled. While he waited, he discussed the problem with [Kennedy's appointments secretary] Ken O'Donnell. O'Donnell asked whether Gordon was really the best man for the job. Heller said emphatically that he was. O'Donnell then said that he should stick to his guns and tell the President-elect that he had to have Gordon. Heller did so when he saw Kennedy a few minutes later. Kennedy said, 'Oh, all right,' picked up the phone and called Gordon in Williamstown." At another point (p. 656), Schlesinger says: "It was one of the Council's jobs to venture out ahead of policy. The President would say to Heller, 'I can't say that yet, but you can.' "

59. William Manchester reports that a tiny plaque on Kennedy's desk read: "Oh God, Thy sea is so great and my boat is so small." *Death of a President* (New York: Harper & Row, 1967), p. 8. The rather bombastic rhetoric of Kennedy's much-admired oratory on large occasions thus did a gross injustice to the essentials of his style as a presidential leader, if we can judge from offstage eyewitness reports such as Hilsman, *To Move a Nation*. See, for example, on p. 53, a quotation, in indirect discourse, of Kennedy discussing problems he was having with the State Department: "Everyone had his own style and people above as well as below, always had to do some adapting." On another occasion, Kennedy said, "There is always inequity in life. Some men are killed in a war, and some men are wounded, and some men never leave the country.... It's very hard in military or in personal life to assure complete equality. Life is unfair." Theodore C. Sorensen, *Kennedy* (New York: Harper & Row, 1965), p. 42. Sorensen comments (pp. 370, 371): "He assumed that we would all have to live indefinitely with national and international tensions and imperfect humans and solutions.... He entertained no delusions about himself or others, neither affecting nor accepting any pretensions of grandeur."

60. Though never employed full time in Kennedy's White House, as he had been in Truman's, Neustadt was a frequent visitor and consultant from his post as a professor of government at Columbia University. See Neustadt's, "Kennedy in the Presidency: A Premature Appraisal," *Political Science Quarterly*, vol. 79 (September 1964), pp. 321-34, subsequently incorporated into the 3rd edition (1980) of *Presidential Power*, pp. 147-61.

61. For accounts of the Bay of Pigs, see Schlesinger, *A Thousand Days*, pp. 233-47; Sorensen, *Kennedy*, pp. 291-309; Hilsman, *To Move a Nation*, pp. 26-39; Haynes Johnson, *The Bay of Pigs: The Leaders' Story of Brigade 2506* (New York: Norton, 1964); and Peter Wyden, *Bay of Pigs: The Untold Story* (New York: Simon and Schuster, 1979).

62. Neustadt, *Presidential Power, passim.*

63. David Halberstam, "The Very Expensive Education of McGeorge Bundy," *Harpers* (July 1969), p. 36. On the missile crisis, see Schlesinger, *A Thousand Days*, pp. 794-841; Sorensen, *Kennedy*, pp. 607-718; Hilsman, *To Move a Nation*, pp. 159-229; Elie Abel, *The Missile Crisis* (Philadelphia: Lippincott, 1966); and Robert F. Kennedy, *Thirteen Days: A Memoir of the Cuban Missile Crisis* (New York: W.W. Norton, 1969).

64. See Paul Y. Hammond, *The Cold War Years: American Foreign Policy Since 1945* (New York: Harcourt, Brace & World, 1969), for a good overview. Samuel P. Huntington, *The Common Defense* (New York: Columbia University Press, 1963); Jack Raymond, *Power at the Pentagon* (New York: Harper & Row, 1964); and Paul Y. Hammond, *Organizing for Defense* (Princeton, N.J.: Princeton University Press, 1961) are useful accounts of the pre-McNamara Pentagon.

65. See Frances Fitzgerald, *Fire in the Lake* (Boston: Little, Brown, 1972); Noam Chomsky, *American Power and the New Mandarins* (New York: Pantheon, 1969); and David Halberstam, *The Best and the Brightest* (New York: Random House, 1969). Wallace Thies provides a summary and critique of critics of the war policy in *When Governments Collide* (Berkeley: University of California Press, 1980), pp. 213-22.

66. A favorable assessment is William Kaufman, *The McNamara Strategy* (New York: Harper & Row, 1964). Less favorable is Richard Harwood and Laurence Stern, "McNamara: Debate Puts His Record on Trial," *Washington Post* (June 15, 1969). See also an informative follow-up on the Harwood-Stern article, by Joseph Califano, "Correcting the Record on McNamara," a letter to the editor of the *Washington Post* (July 1, 1969); and Paul Y. Hammond, "A Functional

Analysis of Defense Department Decision-making in the McNamara Administration," *American Political Science Review*, vol. 62 (March 1968), pp. 57-69.

67. See Walter Heller, *New Dimensions of Political Economy* (Cambridge, Mass.: Harvard University Press, 1966), for an account of this episode by its main architect. An enthusiastic description is contained in Norman MacRae, "The Neurotic Trillionaire," *The Economist* (May 10, 1969), pp. 26-35. Another, more measured account, placing the tax cut in historical perspective, is contained in Herbert Stein, *Revolution in Fiscal Policy*, pp. 372-453. See also Stein, *Presidential Economics* (New York: Simon and Schuster, 1984), pp. 89-122.

68. See William J. Barber, "The Kennedy Years: Purposeful Pedagogy" in Craufurd D. Goodwin (ed.), *Exhortation and Controls: The Search for a Wage-Price Policy 1945-1971* (Washington, D.C.: Brookings, 1975), pp. 135-91.

69. See Victor Navasky, *Kennedy Justice* (New York: Atheneum, 1971) for a discussion of the management of the Justice Department under Robert Kennedy.

70. An account that emphasizes Kennedy "style" is Benjamin C. Bradlee, *Conversations with Kennedy* (New York: Norton, 1975). Bradlee, who cultivated Kennedy as a social friend, was Washington bureau chief of *Newsweek* during the Kennedy Presidency and later became executive editor of the *Washington Post*.

71. For unfavorable assessments of the Kennedy administration, see Henry Fairlie, *The Kennedy Promise: The Politics of Expectations* (Garden City, N.Y.: Doubleday, 1973); Garry Wills, *The Kennedy Imprisonment: A Meditation on Power* (Boston: Little, Brown, 1982); and Bruce Miroff, *Pragmatic Illusions* (New York: David McKay Co., 1976). There were significant costs to the Kennedy style of governing. Consider this reflection by Harris Wofford, himself a loyal member of the Kennedy administration, in his memoir, *Of Kennedys and Kings* (New York: Farrar, Straus, Giroux, 1980), pp. 360-61:

> When I was told that [Undersecretary of State Chester] Bowles was not brought into the councils on the Bay of Pigs because he would be boring, I began to comprehend the kind of closure at the center of what from a distance seemed such an open New Frontier. The President was open to any view, any analysis, any person, no matter how iconoclastic, with one limitation: Kennedy did not want to be bored.

> Man-eating sharks, brutal analysis, and covert action were not boring. Lectures about morality, legality, and principles were. The secret use of power (to overthrow Castro or Diem) was not boring. The public support of Nehru or Nyerere was. Foreign aid and even perhaps the Peace Corps were boring. The CIA was not. Chester Bowles was often boring. [Deputy CIA Director] Richard Bissell never was.

> The witty, rough, sardonic language that Kennedy liked was stimulating, but the degree to which this style dominated the White House and became the common denominator of those to whom the President listened was self-defeating. Ted Sorensen, perhaps the most earnest and least cynical of the President's close colleagues, saw Kennedy as having won an inner struggle between the lure of luxury and statesmanship. In the White House that struggle seemed to me to be continuing, in new forms: it was a luxury to insist on not being bored.

72. Richard Donahue, who worked for President Kennedy on Capitol Hill, made this comment in a speech on April 4, 1963. It was reported the next day in the *Washington Post* by Julius Duscha, "Executive Legislative Rifts Described." See also Robert Spivack, "Seeking a Scapegoat," *New York Herald Tribune* (November 14, 1963).

73. "What They Say about J.F.K.: Congressmen Tell What's on Their Minds," *U.S. News and World Report* (July 30, 1962), p. 32.

74. Meg Greenfield, "Why Are You Calling Me, Son?" *The Reporter* (August 16, 1962), pp. 29-31.

75. Bobby Baker, *Wheeling and Dealing* (New York: Norton, 1978), p. 142.

76. Greenfield, "Why Are Your Calling Me, Son?" *op. cit.*

77. The term "Camelot" was a coinage that was applied retrospectively to the Kennedy administration by the President's widow in a sentimental interview with Theodore H. White, "For President Kennedy: An Epilogue," *Life* (December 6, 1963), pp. 158-59.

78. For an indication of this phenomenon, see Manchester, *Death of a President*, and Lawrence

F. O'Brien, *No Final Victories* (Garden City, New York: Doubleday, 1974), p. 164. O'Brien says (p. 180): "My decision to stay [in the Johnson White House] came at about the time that ... others of the Kennedy team were leaving the government, and there was some bitterness at my staying ... I knew that some of them hated my guts for staying with Lyndon Johnson." For a description of the effects of hostility between Kennedy and Johnson camps on the Johnson White House, see Eric Goldman, *The Tragedy of Lyndon Johnson* (New York: Knopf, 1969), pp. 17-20. On page 34, Professor Goldman describes the response of President Johnson's principal assistant to a story in the *Washington Post* about Goldman's appointment as a special consultant: "Jenkins' mild voice rose as he told me, 'You are not the Johnson Arthur Schlesinger. Nobody is going to be the Johnson anything of Kennedy. *This is a different administration*' " (italics in the original).

79. A preliminary assessment of President Johnson's administrative style is contained in Tom Wicker, "Johnson's Men: 'Valuable Hunks of Humanity,' " *New York Times Magazine* (May 3, 1964), pp. 11ff. A hostile, but fascinating study giving background biographical information about Johnson is Robert Caro's *The Years of Lyndon Johnson: The Pathway to Power* (New York: Knopf, 1982). This book, the first of three projected volumes, carries Johnson's biography up to 1944.

80. Stewart Alsop, *The Center* (New York: Harper & Row, 1968), p. 36.

81. See, for example, Goldman, *Tragedy of Lyndon Johnson, passim.,* and esp. p. 525.

82. Philip Geyelin, *Lyndon Johnson and the World* (New York: Praeger, 1966), pp. 13, 15. Compare Frances Perkins's similar comment about the presumably far more cosmopolitan Franklin Roosevelt, *The Roosevelt I Knew*, p. 97: "Roosevelt could 'get' a problem infinitely better when he had a vicarious experience through a vivid description of a typical case. Proceeding 'from the book,' no matter how logical, never seemed solid to him. His vivid imagination and sympathy helped him to 'see' from a word picture. Later, when the problems of unemployment became even more pressing, he heard many theoretical economic discussions, but he never felt certain about the theory until he saw a sweater mill located in a small village outside Pough-keepsie which had employed no more than one hundred and fifty people. Roosevelt talked with the employer, who was in despair. He talked to the workers, who were frightened and confused. In this way he got the economic and human problem all at once. He had a basis of judging whether a program would be practical by thinking of how it would apply to the sweater mill."

83. Among others, Wicker, *JFK and LBJ*, makes this argument.

84. David Wise, "The Twilight of a President," *New York Times Magazine* (November 3, 1968), p. 131.

85. The *New Yorker's* astute Washington commentator Richard H. Rovere wrote at the time: "It is the war in Vietnam and only the war in Vietnam that has brought him low...." "Letter from Washington," *New Yorker* (September 23, 1967), p. 159.

86. See Hedrick Smith *et al.,* "The Vietnam Policy Reversal of 1968," *New York Times* (March 6, 7, 1969); Richard Harwood and Laurence Stern, "The War and a Political Downfall: How Johnson Decided," *Washington Post* (February 9, 1969); Townsend Hoopes, *The Limits of Inter-vention* (New York: McKay, 1969); Clark Clifford, "Vietnam Reappraisal: The Personal History of One Man's View and How It Evolved," *Foreign Affairs*, vol. 47 (July 1969), pp. 601-22; and Herbert Y. Schandler, *The Unmaking of a President: Lyndon Johnson and Vietnam* (Princeton, N.J.: Princeton University Press, 1977).

President Johnson's version of the events recounted here was somewhat different from the view that emerges from the above five sources. He emphasized that he relied on advice from Secretary of State Rusk rather than, as the sources above argue, from the Defense Department. See Max Frankel, "Johnson Says Tet Victory Led to His '68 Peace Move," *New York Times* (February 8, 1970); and Lyndon B. Johnson, *The Vantage Point* (New York: Holt, Rinehart and Winston, 1971), pp. 365-424.

87. Don Oberdorfer, *Tet* (Garden City, N.Y.: Doubleday, 1971); Peter Braestrup, *Big Story* (Boulder, Col.: Westview, 1977), argues that the American reaction to Tet was based on an impression of the military situation that was falsely created by the news media.

88. See, for example, Joseph R. Slevin, "Hodges Shook up by Sudden Notice of LBJ's Acceptance of Resignation," *Washington Post* (January 7, 1965); and Rowland Evans and Robert

Novak, *Lyndon B. Johnson: The Exercise of Power* (New York: New American Library, 1966), pp. 343-44, on the departure from the USIA of the mortally ill Edward R. Murrow.

89. Anderson says:

A number of regular, periodic reports were required from the departments. In August 1967 the list included:

1. Advance newsmakers (every Thursday). Items of significant news value.

2. Informational activities (every other Monday). Specifics on speeches, press conferences, etc.

3. Legislature report (every Friday).

4. Personal report to the president (every two weeks). Brief letters— two pages—on current and anticipated activities.

5. Achievement report (every two months). Factual review of major accomplishments.

6. 90-day travel and speaking schedule (first of each month).

7. Cabinet policy report (monthly). Optional.

James E. Anderson, "Executive Management of the Bureaucracy and the Johnson Presidency: A Preliminary Exploration," delivered at the Annual Meeting of the American Political Science Association, September 1984.

90. William E. Leuchtenberg, "The Genesis of the Great Society," *Reporter* (April 21, 1966), pp. 35-39.

91. Evans and Novak, *Lyndon B. Johnson*, pp. 116-17.

92. See, for example, Tom Wicker, "Lyndon Johnson Is 10 Feet Tall," *New York Times Magazine* (May 23, 1965), pp. 23ff.

93. Goldman, *Tragedy of Lyndon Johnson*, pp. 102-3. See also George Reedy, *Lyndon B. Johnson: A Memoir* (New York: Andrews and McMeel, 1982). Reedy was a long-time member of Johnson's staff and for a while was White House press secretary. He writes of Johnson (pp. x, 157):

He was notorious for abusing his staff, for driving people to the verge of exhaustion— and sometimes over the verge; for paying the lowest salaries for the longest hours of work on Capitol Hill; for publicly humiliating his most loyal aides; for keeping his office in a constant state of turmoil by playing games with reigning male and female favorites.

There was no sense in which he could be described as a pleasant man. His manners were atrocious—not just slovenly but frequently *calculated* to give offense. Relaxation was something he did not understand and would not accord to others. He was a bully who would exercise merciless sarcasm on people who could not fight back but could only take it. Most important, he had no sense of loyalty.... To Johnson, loyalty was a one-way street: all take on his part and all give on the part of everyone else—his family, his friends, his supporters....

As a human being, he was a miserable person—a bully, sadist, lout, and egotist. He ... enjoyed tormenting those who had done the most for him. He seemed to take a special delight in humiliating those who had cast in their lot with him. It may well be that this was the result of a form of self-loathing in which he concluded that there had to be something wrong with anyone who would associate with him.

See also Caro, *The Path to Power, passim*; and the final reflections on Johnson of his former protégé Bobby Baker: "... when it got down to the licklog, friendship with Lyndon Johnson was a one-way street." *Wheeling and Dealing* (New York: Norton, 1978), p. 268.

94. Richard Harris, *A Sacred Trust* (New York: New American Library, 1966), pp. 215-16. Copyright (c) 1966 by Richard Harris. Originally published in *The New Yorker*.

95. A literature sprang up about Mr. Johnson, as it does with most Presidents, that can only be described as scurrilous. It is uncommon, however, for material of this kind to have a vogue in presumably intellectual circles, as did the anti-Johnson *Macbird*, a sophomoric parody. See Barbara Garson, *Macbird* (New York: Grove Press, 1967). Much more disturbing was the flow of responsible reporting and commentary giving prominence to unattractive features of Mr. Johnson's personality that seemed to be finding their way into the making and justification of

public policy and into the everyday lives of his associates. See, for example, John Osborne, "Concern About L.B.J.," *New Republic* (July 24, 1965), pp. 12-14; "Report on Washington," *Atlantic Monthly* (July 1966), p. 13; Henry Gemmill, "Capitol Malaise," *Wall Street Journal* (November 8, 1967); Warren Rogers, "The Truth About LBJ's Credibility Gap," *Look* (May 2, 1967); James Deakin, "The Dark Side of L.B.J." *Esquire* (August 1967), pp. 45ff.; Goldman, *Tragedy of Lyndon Johnson*; Wicker, *JFK and LBJ*; and Evans and Novak, *Lyndon B. Johnson*, all *passim*.

96. A valiant attempt to deal with some of these complaints can be found in Howard K. Smith, "Prologue," in James MacGregor Burns (ed.), *To Heal and to Build: The Programs of President Lyndon B. Johnson* (New York: McGraw-Hill, 1968), pp. 1-15.

97. Details on several such incidents may be found in Evans and Novak, *op cit.*, pp. 201-504. Apparently, "undue publicity" was given a specific definition in the Johnson administration: "Johnson became annoyed when he felt that Bundy was getting too much personal publicity.... Bundy several years later would tell a group of *Time* editors, 'The worst thing you could do with Lyndon Johnson was to go public with something, which with Lyndon Johnson meant anyone but himself.'" David Halberstam, "The Very Expensive Education of McGeorge Bundy," *Harpers* (July 1969), p. 36.

98. Evans and Novak, *Lyndon B. Johnson*, p. 504.

99. *Ibid.*, p. 505.

100. James Reston, "The Doubts and Regrets of the Johnson Dissenters," *New York Times* (March 9, 1969). This period in Washington politics inspired a novel by Douglass Cater, a respected member of the Johnson White House staff: *Dana: The Irrelevant Man* (New York: McGraw-Hill, 1970). See also George Reedy, *Johnson*; and the insightful comments of James C. Thomson, Jr., "Getting Out and Speaking Out," *Foreign Policy* 13 (Winter 1973-74), pp. 49-69. Thomson suggests that the problem is present to a degree in all administrations and that the costs of abrupt or principled departure are great for people who want to continue to pursue mixed careers, moving in and out of official position. He recalls, for example, that when Undersecretary of State Chester Bowles, in November 1961, rather than accepting a lesser post in the Kennedy administration, "prefer[red] to get out and speak out, President Kennedy's White House staff intermediary warned him 'We will destroy you.'" (p. 65).

101. John Pierson, "The Job Is Demanding, but the Little Extras Ease a President's Lot," *Wall Street Journal* (April 4, 1969).

102. In "Congress and Closed Politics in National Security Affairs," *Orbis*, vol. 10 (Fall 1966), pp. 737-53, H. Bradford Westerfield makes a parallel argument, though he does not attribute the increase of "closed politics" in national security affairs to explicit choices by President Johnson.

103. Recent contributions to the literature on both Presidents admirably illustrate the problems involved. See Bradlee, *Conversations with Kennedy*; William Manchester, *One Brief Shining Moment* (Boston: Little Brown, 1983); Jack Valenti, *A Very Human President* (New York: W.W. Norton, 1976); and Merle Miller, *Lyndon* (New York: Putnam, 1980) for examples of puffery. On the hostile side, see Wills, *The Kennedy Imprisonment*, and Caro, *The Path to Power*. Responsible writers have commented on the unusual difficulties that they have encountered in ascertaining basic facts about John Kennedy and the Kennedy family. See Joan and Clay Blair, Jr., *The Search for J.F.K.* (New York: Berkley Publishing Corp., 1976), pp. 13-15; and Peter Collier and David Horowitz, *The Kennedys* (New York: Summit Books, 1984), pp. 455-58.

104. Criminal charges, indictments, and convictions rippled out widely from the Watergate incident, related events, and efforts to prevent knowledge of these events from spreading. Eventually President Nixon's two top White House assistants, two former attorneys general, the White House counsel, several lesser White House assistants, the President's personal lawyer, and the former Secretary of Commerce were punished, and the President himself was named by a grand jury as a "co-conspirator" in various criminal acts. He was not indicted apparently because the Special Prosecutor instructed the grand jury that impeachment, not indictment, was the proper mechanism for bringing him to account. See Leon Jaworski, *Crossroads* (Elgin, Ill.: David C. Cook Publishing Co., 1981), pp. 181-83, 190; and "The Watergate Case: Where Are They Now?" *Congressional Quarterly* (July 28, 1984), pp. 1829-33.

105. A recitation of some of these complaints, among others, can be found in writings of

Nixon's tireless ex-speechwriter, William Safire. See, for example, "Nixon Never Did," *New York Times* (June 5, 1975), p. 37. On some of Johnson's activities, see Bill Gulley, as told to Mary Ellen Reese, *Breaking Cover* (New York: Simon and Schuster, 1980), pp. 44-112. Gulley was a marine officer in charge of various White House amenities (e.g., Camp David, White House helicopters) during several administrations as Director of the Military Office in the White House. His book gives an amazing account of Lyndon Johnson's exploitation of public funds for his own benefit. For example, he describes Johnson's preparations for retirement as follows (pp. 89-90):

> It was after Johnson's announcement, when he started preparing for his retirement, that we really got into abusing military assets—wholesale, you might say. He started moving people and equipment around so that by the time he got to Texas he was going to be very comfortable. It was all kept very quiet, and only a few people knew anything about it....
>
> We began by sending the big stuff down to Texas. Two planes were assigned from Andrews to Bergstrom—a Convair that seated thirty-two, which Johnson wanted specially configured, and a T-39, a small jet, which we also modified to suit him. And we sent down the air crews to go with the planes.
>
> We put two boats on Lake LBJ, ostensibly so Secret Service could follow him on the water, and we put a naval officer down there with them, full time. He operated whichever boat Johnson was using, and he stayed at the ranch, at government expense, until LBJ died.
>
> We transferred his favorite stewards, who acted as valets, and his favorite chili-cooker. We made arrangements so he could use certain military services: he wanted the barber from Bergstrom to continue to come to the ranch and cut his hair; he wanted to use the commissary and the PX; and we stationed a heart specialist at Brooke Army Hospital nearby.
>
> GSA fixed up several offices for him in Austin; then we put a helicopter at Bergstrom to take him between Austin and the ranch and provided a crew for that. Tom Mills, the Navy chief who gave the President and Mrs. Johnson rubdowns, was promoted to lieutenant and transferred down there, where he doubled as a ranch hand. In 1976, three years after LBJ *died*, Tom was still on the ranch, and on the Navy payroll. He's a lieutenant commander now.
>
> At the same time all this was going on, we were sending big transport planes, C-141s, out of Andrews with truckloads of stuff for Texas.

Copyright © 1980 by Bill Gulley and Mary Ellen Reese. Reprinted by permission of Simon and Schuster, Inc. I have no way of knowing whether this, or the rest of Gulley's account is true. Not a word of it has, to my knowledge, been publicly denied or disputed by anyone in a position to know the facts.

106. I have already quoted (footnote 100 and the accompanying text) James Reston's rather mysterious allusion to President Johnson's "fascination with the intimidating power of the FBI and the Internal Revenue Service."

An example of this fascination has surfaced in Jon Bradshaw, "Richard Goodwin: the Good, the Bad and the Ugly," *New York* (August 18, 1975), p. 37: "'When he heard I wanted to resign,' said Goodwin, 'he jocularly threatened to put the FBI and the IRS on me, saying there would be no place in the world where I could hide that he could not rout me out. He even threatened to draft me.'" Presidential speechwriter Goodwin left the Johnson White House evidently without coming to harm, but it is conceivable that Johnson used the same speech on others who did not share his robust sense of humor.

I have made no special study of this subject but, at the risk of contributing unduly to the political cynicism of readers, can point to the following evidence that abuses of power such as came to light in the Watergate investigations were in some measure precedented.

On February 27, 1975, Attorney General Edward Levi testified before a congressional committee that FBI director J. Edgar Hoover kept secret files dating back to 1920, and kept them meticulously up to date. From time to time Mr. Hoover would share tidbits from these files with Presidents and attorneys general (cf. corroborative testimony by Biddle, *In Brief Authority*, pp. 258-61). The *New York Times* report of Levi's testimony says: "Mr. Levi cited instances in which incumbent Presidents had ordered the bureau to report on the activities of members of Congress. Justice Department officials later said that Presidents Kennedy, Johnson and Nixon had indulged in this practice." "[I]n 1964 ... a former White House aide, Bill Moyers, asked the bureau to gather data on campaign aides to Senator Barry Goldwater ... Mr. Moyers made the request on behalf of President Johnson a few weeks before the election...." Nicholas M. Horrock, "Levi Details Wide Scope of Hoover's Secret Files," *New York Times* (February 28, 1975), p. 1.

This story also mentions President Johnson's asking the FBI to inquire if Treasury Department officials investigating his former protégé, Bobby Baker, had any connections with Robert Kennedy, and Mr. Johnson's receiving information of an FBI investigation of the telephone toll records of members of the staff of Republican vice-presidential candidate Spiro T. Agnew in 1968. Evidently, Mr. Johnson caused the hotel room of Martin Luther King, Jr., to be wiretapped and bugged at the Democratic National Convention of 1964. See Ronald Kessler, "FBI Tapped King at 1964 Convention," *Washington Post* (January 26, 1975), p. 1; and David Garrow, *The FBI and Martin Luther King, Jr.* (New York: Penguin Books, 1981), pp. 118, 168-69, who indicates that the Rev. King's telephone was tapped by the FBI in the Kennedy administration as well, with the knowledge of both John and Robert Kennedy (pp. 67, 100, 157).

Here is Bradlee, *Conversations with Kennedy* (pp. 111-12), quoting President Kennedy on June 14, 1972: "[Jim Patton, President of Republic Steel] asked me 'Why is it that all the telephone calls of all the steel executives in all the country are being tapped?' and I told him that I thought he was being wholly unfair to the Attorney General and that I was sure it wasn't true. And he asked me 'Why is it that all the income tax returns of all the steel executives in all the country are being scrutinized?' and I told him that, too, was wholly unfair, that the Attorney General wouldn't do any such thing ... And, of course, Patton was right." See also Alan Dershowitz, "Unchecked Wiretapping," *New Republic* (May 31, 1975), pp. 13-17. Evidently, President Kennedy made extensive secret recordings of White House telephone calls and meetings during the last 16 months of his 34-month Presidency. Their contents have not been disclosed, but no one has responsibly alleged that they might contain evidence of knowledge of impeachment offenses. Edward A. Gargan, "Kennedy Secretly Taped Sessions in White House," *New York Times* (February 4, 1982).

107. For their account, see Carl Bernstein and Bob Woodward, *All the President's Men* (New York: Simon and Schuster, 1974). Perhaps the most useful compendium of material on Watergate is Congressional Quarterly's volume *Watergate: Chronology of a Crisis* (Washington, D.C., 1975).

108. For an expansion of this view, see my essay "Alienation and Accountability in the Nixon Administration," in Nelson W. Polsby, *Political Promises* (New York: Oxford University Press, 1974), pp. 6-14.

109. For an account of Nixon's views on this question, see William Safire, *Before the Fall* (Garden City, N.Y.: Doubleday, 1975), pp. 307-15.

110. A meticulously detailed and interesting account of Washington during Watergate which documents many of these points is Elizabeth Drew, *Washington Journal* (New York: Random House, 1975).

111. The most thorough account of the early Nixon Presidency is Rowland Evans and Robert Novak, *Nixon in the White House: The Frustration of Power* (New York: Random House, 1971).

112. See the comments of one close observer, Herbert Stein, on Shultz in the Nixon Cabinet, *Presidential Economics*, pp. 145ff.

113. A brief description of Mr. Nixon's administrative strategy by a member of the Nixon administration is contained in Richard Nathan's *The Plot That Failed: Nixon and the Administrative Presidency* (New York: Wiley, 1975).

114. The tip of the iceberg was revealed in a story in the normally prosaic, civil service routine-oriented *Federal Times*, Inderjit Badhwan, "Government-wide Patronage Deals" (September 25, 1974). See also "Documents Relating to Political Influence in Personnel Actions at the De-

partment of Housing and Urban Development," published by the Subcommittee on Manpower and Civil Service of the House of Representatives Committee on Post Office and Civil Service, December 12, 1974 (Washington, D.C.: U.S. Government Printing Office, 1974), and Dom Bonafede, "Nixon Personnel Staff Works to Restructure Federal Policies," *National Journal* (November 12, 1971), pp. 2440-48. On July 19, 1973, the *Washington Post* published a list of 94 persons formerly employed in Mr. Nixon's 1972 campaign effort or on the White House staff who had been deployed out into Cabinet departments or regulatory agencies. This was characterized as a "partial list."

115. Statement of Dwight Ink, before the Subcommittee on Civil Service, House Committee on Post Office and Civil Service (Washington, D.C., February 28, 1984).

116. See Lou Cannon, "OEO Chief Savors Shutdown," *Washington Post* (February 4, 1973); Jules Witcover, "OEO Dismantlers Proceed with Speed, Zeal: Fear Rumors Plague Staff," and Austin Scott, "Plans to Neutralize Hill Revealed," *Washington Post* (February 17, 1973).

117. See Richard L. Garwin, "Presidential Science Advising," in Wallace T. Goldin (ed.), *Science Advice to the President* (New York: Pergamon Press, 1980), p. 127; James S. Coleman, "The Life, Death, and Potential Future of PSAC," in *ibid.*, pp. 135-37; David Z. Robinson, "Politics in the Science Advising Process," in *ibid.*, p. 162; and David Z. Beckler, "The Precarious Life of Science in the White House," *Daedalus* 103 (Summer 1974), pp. 127-28.

118. See Raymond J. Waldmann, "The Domestic Council: Innovation in Presidential Government," *Public Administration Review* 36 (May/June 1976), pp. 260-68.

119. See Larry Berman, *The Office of Management and Budget and the Presidency, 1921-1979* (Princeton, N.J.: Princeton University Press, 1979), pp. 116-26.

120. It is difficult to get a wholly reliable count of Executive Office of the President employees because of the propensity of Presidents to "borrow" staff from other executive agencies so as to make their own establishment look smaller than it is. Representative Morris Udall looked into the matter in 1972 and produced Table 17: "A Report on the Growth of the Executive Office of the President, 1955-1973," Committee on Post Office and Civil Service, U.S. House of Representatives (Washington, D.C.: 1972), p. 5. See also Lou Cannon, "White House Staff: Nixon's Is Record in Size," *Washington Post* (January 7, 1973); John Pierson, "Nixon's Bills: Costs of Presidency Are Put at $70 Million, but No One Is Certain," *Wall Street Journal* (March 10, 1970); and two articles by John Herbers for the *New York Times*, "Nixon's Presidency: Expansion of Power" (March 4, 1973) and "Nixon's Presidency: Centralized Control" (March 6, 1973). Since 1978, under the terms of the White House Personnel Authorization Employment Act, the number of detailees on the White House staff from other parts of the executive branch has to be reported annually. John Hart, in "The President and His Staff" (1984), an unpublished paper, gives a useful compilation of these reports, which shows the number of White House employees as of September 30, 1983, as 313. At other times of the year it seems likely that this number is somewhat higher.

121. The press release proclaiming the reorganization is dated January 5, 1973, to coincide with the beginning of Mr. Nixon's second term. Useful background material is contained in *Papers Relating to the President's Departmental Reorganization Program: A Reference Compilation* (Washington, D.C.: Government Printing Office, 1972). The reorganization plan never took effect.

122. Drew, *Washington Journal*, pp. 27-28. See also Philip Kurland, *Watergate and the Constitution* (Chicago: University of Chicago Press, 1978). Kurland, a distinguished and rather conservative constitutional lawyer, writes (p. 219):

... [T]he tools for the execution of the "plebiscitary Presidency" were not Nixon creations. Nixon revealed not a capacity for innovation but only a capacity for imitation. What he did do was to utilize devices created by predecessors, who used them sparingly, while he used them persistently; who used them in isolation, while he used them in combination; who used them unsuccessfully, while he used them successfully, until they failed him in the end.

He was an innovator, however, in a way that showed less imitation of his presidential predecessors than of governors of less democratic nations. He created a presidential, political police force; he rejected the basic concept of Anglo-American political freedom, the rule of law. And he effected both these changes in American political tradition—

TABLE 17 Executive Office of the President—Total Permanent Positions*

	1955	1965	1970	1971	1972	1973
The White House Office	262	255	250	533	540	510
Executive Residence	72	77	75	75	75	75
The Domestic Council[a]				52	70	66
National Security Council	28	50	75	70	75	79
Special projects						
Special assistance to the President[a]				39	39	39
Council of Economic Advisers	33	44	56	57	57	57
Council on Environmental Quality[a]			30	54	57	65
National Aeronautics and Space Council		27	26	21	16	16
National Commission on Productivity[a]					20	20
Office of Consumer Affairs[a]				35	50	52
Office of Emergency Preparedness		250	227	235	223	223
Office of Intergovernmental Relations[a]			9	9	9	9
Office of Management and Budget[a]	435[b]	480[b]	555	657	684	660
Office of Science and Technology		34	54	50	50	50
Office of Telecommunications Policy[a,c]		40	63	48	65	65
Special Action Office Drug[a]					172	174
Special Representative for Trade Negotiations		28	23	30	34	46
President's Advisory Commission of Governmental Reorganization	6					
Office of Defense Mobilization	294					
President's Commission on Equal Opportunity Housing		10				
President's Commission on Equal Opportunity		18				
National Council on Marine Resources			20			
President's Advisory Council on Executive Reorganization			30			
Total, from budget documents	1130	1303	1493	1965	2236	2206
Add, details from other agencies	273	273	273			
Total	1403	1576	1766	1965	2236	2206

[a] New offices added since January 1969.
[b] Known as Bureau of Budget.
[c] Prior to 1970 was part of OEP.
*The Post Office and Civil Service Committee has never updated the Udall report. The *National Journal White House Phone List,* rev. ed. (Washington, D.C., November 4, 1981) provides a rough count of total permanent positions for that year: there are 2,073 names on the list.

Source: Udall, "Growth of the Executive Office," p. 5.

deeply embedded in the Constitution—through the device of the White House Office.

Legislation that resulted in part from congressional responses to the Nixon Presidency included the War Powers Act and the Impoundment Control provisions of the Congressional Budget Act. These and other measures adopted a device known as the "legislative veto," an attempt on the part of Congress to limit presidential power by requiring the express approval of one or another house of Congress to administrative regulations or executive actions. Between 1950 and 1976 over 200 different bills containing legislative vetoes were enacted, 160 of them between 1970 and 1976. Joseph Cooper and Patricia Hurley, "The Legislative Veto: A Policy Analysis," *Congress and the Presidency* 10 (Spring 1983), pp. 1-24. In 1983, in *INS* v. *Chadha* 103 S. Ct. 2764 (1983), the Supreme Court ruled that legislative veto provisions were unconstitutional, and required that instead Congress express its wishes by legislating in the usual way, by passing bills in identical form through both Houses and obtaining the President's signature. The Court held that the House, in vetoing an attorney general's decision to suspend the deportation of Jagdish Rai Chadha, "took action that had the purpose and effect of altering the legal rights, duties and relations of persons, including the attorney general, Executive Branch officials, and Chadha, all outside the legislative branch" (103 S. Ct. at 2784).

123. A tape of a White House meeting between President Nixon and his legal counsel John Dean, on September 15, 1972, appears to sanction the collection of an "enemies list." The President is quoted as saying: "I want the most comprehensive notes on all those who tried to do us in.... They are asking for it and they are going to get it. We have not used the Bureau and we have not used the Justice Department but things are going to change now." Mr. Dean replied: "What an exciting prospect." Dean had written a memorandum to White House domestic policy czar John D. Ehrlichman dated August 16, 1971, inquiring "how we can use the available federal machinery to screw our political enemies" and listing twenty "priority" candidates for this treatment.

124. The White House asked the IRS to audit Democrats. Ehrlichman testified to the Ervin Committee that "I wanted them to turn up something and send [O'Brien] to jail before the election, and unfortunately it didn't materialize." Quoted in Elizabeth Drew, *Washington Journal: The Events of 1973-1974* (New York: Macmillan, 1975), p. 321.

Jimmy Breslin recounts a description by then House Majority Leader Thomas P. O'Neill of what was going on: "There would be a guy who always was a big giver and nobody was hearing from him. I'd go over the lists for our dinner and I'd say, 'Hey, where is so and so? He always was a helluva good friend of ours. Why haven't we heard from him?' So I'd call the guy and he'd call me back and he'd say, 'Geez, Tip, I don't know what to tell you. Nine IRS guys hit me last week and I'd like to stay out of things for a while.' I began getting that from a lot of people.... That's what it was like. All our old friends, our best friends, were afraid to come around. Well, you didn't have to draw a map for me to let me know what was going on. It was a shakedown. A plain old-fashioned goddammed shakedown. I can read pressure. I could see what they were doing. And then out comes this great big newspaper ad. Democrats for Nixon. And the ad had all the names of our people on it. The day the ad came out, they were calling me up saying, 'Tip, I had to sign the ad. They sandbagged me. It's either sign the ad or go into the soup.'" *How the Good Guys Finally Won* (New York: Viking, 1975) pp. 15, 16. See also Arlen J. Large, "Playing Hardball with Tax Returns," *Wall Street Journal* (May 30, 1974); Deborah Shapley, "White House Foes: Wiesner Target of Proposal to Cut MIT Funds," *Science* (July 20, 1973), pp. 244-46.

125. An excellent summary of White House attempts to change the shape of television news is Thomas Whiteside, "Annals of Television: Shaking the Tree," *New Yorker* (March 17, 1975), pp. 41-91. The quote is at p. 61. See also William Porter, *Assault on the Media: The Nixon Years* (Ann Arbor: University of Michigan Press, 1976).

126. Clem Miller, *Member of the House* (New York: Scribner, 1972), p. 93. Miller has a superb little essay on pp. 119-22 on the norms of personal restraint that govern members of Congress in their relations with one another.

127. For this story see Bernstein and Woodward, *All the President's Men*, p. 105. Other difficulties between newspapers and the Nixon administration are discussed in Sanford J. Ungar, *The Papers and the Papers* (New York: Dutton, 1972); Lewis W. Wolfson, *The Press Covers Government* (Washington, D.C.: American University, Department of Communication, 1973); and John Pierson, "A Report from Our Man on the 'Enemy' List," *Wall Street Journal* (July 2, 1973).

128. Whiteside, "Annals of Television." See also Daniel Schorr, *Clearing the Air* (Boston: Houghton Mifflin, 1977), pp. 71-86.

129. The Nixon campaign of 1972 is authoritatively estimated to have raised $61,400,000, more than twice as much as any other presidential campaign in history, before or since. See Herbert Alexander, *Financing Politics*, 3rd ed. (Washington, D.C.: Congressional Quarterly Press, 1984), p. 7.

William Safire, *Before the Fall*, (p. 549) says: "By the summer of 1972 the decision had been made to spend the campaign kitty on re-electing the President, and not to share much of it with Republican candidates in local campaigns."

130. William Safire's account is in Safire, *op cit.*, pp. 654-55. Caspar Weinberger, Nixon's Secretary of Health, Education and Welfare, has referred to the first Cabinet meeting after the 1972 election at which wholesale resignations were demanded as "the most shocking thing I've ever been through." He is quoted in John Hersey, *The President* (New York: Knopf, 1975), p. 26. See also Norman C. Miller, "Bitter Bureaucrats: Unhappiness Mounts as Nixon Keeps on Housecleaning," *Wall Street Journal* (March 22, 1973).

131. See Donovan, *Tumultuous Years*, pp. 340-71.

132. See Theodore H. White, *Breach of Faith* (New York: Atheneum, 1975), pp. 250-75.

133. Good early accounts of these aspects of Mr. Nixon's work habits are contained in Robert B. Semple, Jr., "Nixon's Style as Boss Combines Desires for Order and Solitude," *New York Times* (January 12, 1970); John Pierson, "The Nixon Style: President Seeks Order in His Decision-making but Events Intrude," *Wall Street Journal* (July 7, 1969); Don Oberdorfer, "The Presidency: Still Very Private After First Year," *Washington Post* (January 18, 1970); and Richard F. Janssen, "Turmoil at the Top: An Inaccessible Nixon Stirs Anger and Despair within Administration," *Wall Street Journal* (May 8, 1970). See also Saul Pett, "Nixon on Nixon: Tough Decisions Require Calm," *Washington Post* (January 14, 1973); Haynes Johnson, "A Revealing, but Most Private, President," *Washington Post* (January 20, 1973).

134. Perhaps the best picture of this is contained in Safire, *Before the Fall, passim*. See also Lou Cannon, "The Siege Psychology and How It Grew," *Washington Post* (July 29, 1973).

135. See Earl Mazo and Stephen Hess, *Nixon: A Political Portrait* (New York: Popular Library, 1968), for a friendly account of Nixon's early campaigns. Far less friendly is William Costello, *The Facts About Nixon* (New York: Viking, 1960).

136. Safire, pp. 152-55, makes the point that Nixon's "standard as a modern President ... was John F. Kennedy." Bill Gulley worked as a White House liaison with former Presidents in the Ford administration. His description of his first meeting with the recently resigned Nixon testifies to Nixon's acute consciousness of precedents created by benefits granted to his predecessors:

> When [Nixon] spoke he was curt and direct, and he was mainly concerned with getting his "entitlement." "Look," he said, "I'm entitled to anything that any other former President is entitled to. Goddamn, you know what I did for Johnson, and you know I did things for Ike and Truman, and, goddamn it, I expect to be treated the same way. When I travel I expect military aircraft; I expect the same support I provided. I expect communications and medical personnel, everything they had. And, goddamn it, you tell Ford I expect it."

Gulley, *Breaking Cover*, pp. 115-16.

137. Safire, pp. 688-93, and esp. p. 692. This is also consistent with the themes of most of Mr. Nixon's major publications since his resignation. See *The Real War* (New York: Warner Communications, 1980); and *Real Peace* (Boston: Little, Brown, 1983).

138. A thorough account is Marvin Kalb and Bernard Kalb, *Kissinger* (New York: Dell, 1975). See also Henry Kissinger, *White House Years* (Boston: Little, Brown, 1979), and Kissinger, *Years of Upheaval* (Boston: Little, Brown, 1982).

139. See Safire, *Before the Fall*, pp. 388 ff.

140. A good account of Mr. Ford's career up to the Nixon pardon is Jerald F. terHorst's *Gerald Ford and the Future of the Presidency* (New York: The Third Press, 1974). Mr. terHorst was a Grand Rapids journalist who moved to Washington and became a respected member of the

Washington press corps. He was President Ford's first presidential press secretary and resigned when Ford pardoned President Nixon.

141. Richard Reeves, *A Ford, Not a Lincoln* (New York: Harcourt Brace Jovanovich, 1975), pp. 39f. It is worth noting that the Congress was controlled by Democratic majorities in both House and Senate and that therefore the Democratic Speaker of the House, Carl Albert, was first in line for the succession to the Presidency as long as there was no Vice-President. Nevertheless, there was wide agreement that Nixon's nominee should be a Republican, and Ford had no difficulty on partisan grounds in being confirmed.

142. This phrase occurred in Ford's first address as President to a joint meeting of Congress, on August 12, 1974. See also Fred L. Zimmerman, "In Washington Now, Some Hear 'Sound of Peacefulness,'" *Wall Street Journal* (August 19, 1974); and the memoir by Ford's long-time chief assistant and speechwriter, Robert T. Hartmann, *Palace Politics* (New York: McGraw-Hill, 1980), pp. 192-350, *passim*. There is strong evidence that Ford's attitude toward Congress was no mere pose. The writer John Hersey obtained unusual access to the Ford White House and published a diary of his observation of Mr. Ford's working routines during the week of March 10-15, 1975. In particular, Hersey was amazed at Ford's personal fondness for members of Congress with whom he was frequently locked in legislative combat. He describes a legislative strategy meeting in the oval office:

> The President stirs with pleasure—it almost seems as if he has suddenly walked through a door into his real self. Familiar names: the old horse-trading routines. Even his hands seem independently to enjoy themselves now as they settle into the little enactments of bargaining they know so well—counting, weighing, arresting; a finger encircles a thumb (We have that man), knuckles rap the desk (Try again), the whole hand flaps (He's hopeless), reminiscences about motions to recommit like memories of great football games. The names like candies in his mouth: Frank, Gale, Hugh, John, Al, Herman, Gaylord, Barber, Mike....

John Hersey, *The President* (New York: Knopf, 1975), p. 60. See also pp. 73-75.

Ford's feelings were cordially reciprocated by members of Congress. A. James Reichley, *Conservatives in an Age of Change* (Washington, D.C.: Brookings Institution, 1981), quotes Abner Mikva, a militantly liberal Illinois Democrat (p. 333):

> President Ford and the Ford administration had a very supportive relationship with Congress. He did not want the right things—in fact he did not want very much at all. But there was a warm feeling in Congress toward Ford.

Richardson Preyer, the distinguished Democratic moderate from North Carolina said (Reichley, p. 333): "Ford ... was trusted, even among those who strongly disagreed with him."

143. Hartmann, pp. 199-200.

144. Richard Reeves reports the following incident:

> It was immediately clear that Ford was personally reluctant to move quickly to change the Nixon White House, and it was decided at the transition team meeting the first day that [former Governor William] Scranton should brief the President on the functions and operations of the White House staff. Haig volunteered to help and told Scranton he would schedule a meeting with the President at 9:30 the next morning, August 10. In fact, the August 10 schedule produced later by Haig's staff showed a meeting between Ford and Haig at 8:30 *A.M.*
>
> When Scranton arrived at 9:30, he was met by Terry O'Donnell, who had been Nixon's appointments secretary; he was told that Ford and Haig were in conference, and his orders from Haig were not to disturb them. When the chief of staff came out of the Oval Office, he told Scranton the briefing was over, he had already handled it.

Reeves, *A Ford, Not a Lincoln*, p. 74. See also Hartmann, *Palace Politics*, pp. 203-4. Haig was not the only troublesome Nixon holdover. Reeves says (pp. 75-76):

> On August 14 [press secretary Jerald] terHorst announced that the [Watergate-related White House] tapes "have been ruled to be the personal property of former President Nixon." The ruling, he said, had been made by the White House legal staff with the

agreement of the Justice Department and Special Watergate Prosecutor Leon Jaworski. "The decision was made independent of President Ford," terHorst added. "He concurs in the decision."

[Holdover Nixon White House deputy counsel Fred] Buzhardt had informed terHorst of the ruling earlier in the day. The press secretary, concerned that there were still no Ford people on the legal staff, asked whether the Justice Department and special prosecutor were involved with the ruling. "They're aboard," was the answer, according to terHorst.

But within minutes of terHorst's announcement, when the news was broadcast, both Attorney General William Saxbe and Jaworski said they were never part of an agreement; Buzhardt had merely informed them of his own ruling. TerHorst, who had first told Ford of the agreement, went back to the President, embarrassed and angry—they had been taken.

The next day Ford overruled the decision.

145. *A Discussion with Gerald R. Ford: The American Presidency* (Washington, D.C.: American Enterprise Institute, 1977), p. 4.

146. Rockefeller's confirmation hearings provided a seemingly irresistible opportunity for the House and Senate to inquire into the finances of one of America's richest families. See *Nomination of Nelson A. Rockefeller to be Vice President of the United States*, Hearings before the Committee on the Judiciary, House of Representatives, Ninety-third Congress, 2d Session, November 21, 22, 25, 26, 27, December 2, 3, 4, 5, 1974 (Washington, D.C.: Government Printing Office, 1974).

147. See John Osborne, *White House Watch: The Ford Years* (Washington, D.C.: New Republic Books, 1977), pp. xxiv-xxxiii.

148. For the story of the Levi confirmation, see "Ford to Nominate Levi, Coleman," *Washington Post* (January 15, 1975). Levi was a considerable success as attorney general. See "Levi Looks Back at Justice," *Time* (December 20, 1976), p. 72; and Anthony Lewis, "A Test on Wiretaps," *New York Times* (April 20, 1977).

149. See "A Pardon for Nixon and Watergate Is Back," *Congressional Quarterly Weekly Report* 32 (September 14, 1974), pp. 2454-63. The Gallup poll figures show that before the pardon, in early September 1974, 66% of all respondents approved of the way Ford was handling his job. After the pardon, on September 8, the *New York Times* commissioned a poll (reported in *C.Q.* of September 14, 1974, p. 2463) in which 32% said Ford was doing a "good" job, and 62% disapproved of the pardon. The next regular Gallup poll showed 50% giving overall approval of Ford's Presidency, a drop of 16 points in less than a month.

150. See "Nixon Fund Request," *Congressional Quarterly Weekly Report* (September 21, 1974), p. 2571.

151. Grover Cleveland was the all-time champion caster of presidential vetoes (8.6 per month in his first term, 3.54 per month in his second) followed by Franklin Roosevelt (4.41 vetoes per month), Harry Truman (2.60), and Dwight Eisenhower (1.89). Ford, who like most of the others served with a Congress controlled by the opposing party, comes in at 1.83 vetoes a month. Next is Ulysses S. Grant with 0.97. See Louis Fisher, *The Politics of Shared Power* (Washington, D.C.: Congressional Quarterly Press, 1981), p. 26. See also A. James Reichley, *Conservatives in an Age of Change*, who claims that "no fewer than thirty-nine of Ford's vetoes were against bills that would have significantly and directly affected the federal budget. Most of the others dealt with foreign policy, energy, or general economic policy. During his brief tenure Ford undoubtedly vetoed more bills raising important substantive issues than any previous president" (p. 325).

152. See Norman J. Ornstein and David W. Rohde, "Shifting Forces, Changing Rules, and Political Outcomes: The Impact of Congressional Change on Four House Committees," in Robert L. Peabody and Nelson W. Polsby (eds.), *New Perspectives on the House of Representatives* 3rd ed. (Chicago: Rand McNally, 1977), pp. 186-269.

153. See Allen Schick, *Congress and Money: Budgeting, Spending, and Taxing* (Washington, D.C.: Urban Institute, 1980).

154. Osborne, p. xiii.

155. Osborne, p. xv.

156. Gerald R. Ford, *A Time to Heal* (New York: Harper & Row, 1979), pp. 352-53.

157. For fragments of evidence see Albert R. Karr, "The 'Wild Man' of Transportation," *Wall Street Journal* (October 27, 1975); and "Levi Looks Back at Justice," *Time* (December 20, 1976).

158. Ford was a varsity football player at the University of Michigan and for a time earned his keep at Yale Law School by coaching. His only presidential rival as an athlete would be the compulsive outdoorsman Theodore Roosevelt. See Edmund Morris, *The Rise of Theodore Roosevelt* (New York: Coward, McCann & Geoghegan, 1979), pp. 99-118, 200-225, 270-89.

159. As Ford himself ruefully admitted. See Ford, *A Time to Heal*, pp. 343-45.

160. See Reichley, *Conservatives in an Age of Change*, pp. 395-96.

161. Ford, *A Time to Heal*, pp. 327-28.

162. Mr. Ford has written:

> According to [Robert] Teeter's polls, the public viewed me as a "nice guy" who wasn't quite up to the Oval Office's demands.... [They] also disclosed that all my traveling in 1975 had hurt my standing with the voters. Therefore I should remain in the capital and be as "Presidential" as possible.

Ford, *A Time to Heal*, p. 348.

163. Robert Axelrod, "1976 Update," *American Political Science Review* 72 (June 1978), p. 622-24.

164. As Jody Powell, his press secretary, pointed out, "...President Carter readily admits to a weakness for hyperbole and the superlative." Jody Powell, *The Other Side of the Story* (New York: Morrow, 1984), p. 48.

165. Carter set a pattern in dealing with his vice president that was unique and exemplary. Vice President Mondale had an office in the west wing of the White House, near the Oval Office. His staff was integrated into Carter's White House staff. He received carte blanche to go to all meetings held for the President's benefit, all CIA briefings and meetings on national security including National Security Council, and Cabinet meetings. Mondale's biographer says:

> To make sure that Mondale missed nothing else of significance, Carter directed his staff to supply the vice president with detailed, advanced copies of his presidential schedule. Mondale was to feel free to join any meeting involving Carter. Nothing was to be off-limits—not even the most sensitive negotiations with foreign leaders or strategy sessions involving the most crucial national security question—the attempt to reach agreement with the Soviet Union on a Strategic Arms Limitation Treaty. Of at least equal significance was Mondale's location at a major sluice gate in the enormous paperflow generated by Carter. Mondale was in what the White House bureaucratically called the "loop": every piece of paper Carter saw, he would see. It meant he could study sensitive foreign-intelligence reports before they reached Carter and then later read the presidential directives and notations they inspired. The process bolstered Mondale's clout enormously.

Finlay Lewis, *Mondale* (New York: Harper & Row, 1980), pp. 237-38.

166. See Charles O. Jones, "Keeping Faith and Losing Congress: The Carter Experience in Washington," *Presidential Studies Quarterly* 14 (Summer 1984), pp. 437-45; Haynes Johnson, *In the Absence of Power* (New York: Viking, 1980); and Polsby, *Consequences of Party Reform*, pp. 105-14.

167. They also claimed that something called "the Washington establishment" was hostile to them. Carter's top assistant, Hamilton Jordan, wrote:

> Because Jimmy Carter was not a product of Congress and was not well known to the Washington establishment, there was an inordinate curiosity about him.... It was bad enough that they didn't know him and had no stake in his candidacy, but to make matters worse, Carter had defeated their various darlings in the battles around the country. There was a subtle but strong feeling when we arrived in Washington that "Well, OK, you Georgians—you won the big prize through gimmicks, good fortune, and by running against Washington. But now we are going to show you who's boss in this town!"

> ... For almost four years, the Washington establishment had been like a pack of jackals lurking near a wounded animal, smelling its blood, but hiding in the bushes and peering out only from time to time. Now that their prey was dead, they descended on the carcass with a vengeance.

Hamilton Jordan, *Crisis*, pp. 156, 358.

168. See Norman J. Ornstein and David W. Rohde, "Shifting Forces, Changing Rules, and Political Outcomes: The Impact of Congressional Change on Four House Committees," in Peabody and Polsby (eds.), *New Perspectives on the House of Representatives*, pp. 186-269.

169. See Norman J. Ornstein, Robert L. Peabody, and David W. Rohde, "The Contemporary Senate: Into the 1980s," in Lawrence C. Dodd and Bruce I. Oppenheimer (eds.), *Congress Reconsidered* (Washington, D.C: Congressional Quarterly Press, 1981), pp. 13-30.

170. "As characterized by one member, the House has become a 'fast breeder reactor' for amendments. Between 1963 and 1970 the total number of appropriations amendments, for example, was 441 but within the 1971-77 period, the number increased to 715." Joseph Cooper and Melissa P. Collie, "Structural Adaptation in the House: Multiple Reference and Interunit Committees in Organizational Perspective," a paper delivered at the 1981 annual meeting of the American Political Science Association, September 3-6, 1981, p. 34. See also Barbara Sinclair, "The Speaker's Task Force in the Post-Reform House of Representatives," *American Political Science Review*, vol. 75 (June 1981), pp. 397-410 (esp. p. 399).

171. Ben W. Heineman, Jr., and Curtis A. Hessler, *Memorandum for the President* (New York: Random House, 1981), p. xix.

172. Tom Wicker, "Whatever Became of Jimmy Carter?" *Esquire* (July 1984), pp. 78-84.

173. Ibid.

174. See Eric L. Davis, "Legislative Liaison in the Carter Administration," *Political Science Quarterly*, 94 (Summer 1979), pp. 287-301.

175. Charles O. Jones has assembled much pertinent evidence on this point from the testimony of members of President Carter's White House staff. See Jones, "Carter and Congress: From the Outside In," delivered at the Annual Meeting of the American Political Science Association, Washington, D.C., September 1984. Haynes Johnson recounts:

> One day in December 1976, in Plains, Tip O'Neill told Carter: "Mr. President, I want you to understand something. Some of the brightest men in America are in this Congress of the United States. Don't make the mistake of underestimating them. They've been there for years, and on any specific piece of legislation they know why every comma, every semicolon, every period is there. We want to work together, but I have a feeling you are underestimating the feeling of Congress and you could have some trouble." Carter instantly replied: "I'll handle them just as I handled the Georgia legislature. Whenever I had problems with the Georgia legislature I took the problems to the people of Georgia."

In the Absence of Power (New York: Viking, 1980), p. 22. See also David S. Broder, "A 'Most Puzzling Maneuver,'" *Washington Post* (March 16, 1977); John Herbers, "The Carter-Congress Rift May Just Have Started," *New York Times* (March 27, 1977); Albert R. Hunt, "Jimmy Carter vs. Congress?" *Wall Street Journal* (March 25, 1977); and Tom Wicker, "Whatever Became of Jimmy Carter?"

176. This theory was given a fine exposition by Jack Knott and Aaron Wildavsky in "Jimmy Carter's Theory of Governing," *The Wilson Quarterly* 1 (Winter 1977), pp. 49-67. Their construction of the theory is based on Carter's campaign speeches.

177. For more on Jimmy Carter's background, see his campaign autobiography, *Why Not the Best* (New York: Bantam Books, 1975). On Woodrow Wilson there is an enormous literature. A particularly interesting psychological study is Alexander L. George and Juliette L. George, *Woodrow Wilson and Colonel House* (New York: John Day, 1956).

178. Jimmy Carter, *Keeping Faith* (New York: Bantam Books, 1982), pp. 69-71. Carter originally promised to reduce the number of separate agencies of the Federal government from an estimated 1,900 to 200. Jack Knott and Aaron Wildavsky, "Jimmy Carter's Theory of Gov-

erning," p. 510. This proved impossible to accomplish. It is also hard to say where he got the number 1,900 from.

179. See Thomas H. Hammond and Jack H. Knott (eds.), *A Zero-Based Look at Zero-Base Budgeting* (New Brunswick, N.J.: Transaction Books, 1980), pp. 98-102. "ZBB has so metamorphosed into incremental budgeting that the only thing left is its smile floating in the air" (p. 102).

It proved to be easy to give an account of zero-based budgeting that reduced it to absurdity. Here is an example, a fictional dialogue between "the chairman of the House Appropriations Committee and a Cabinet Secretary":

CHAIRMAN: Good morning, Mr. Secretary. We are happy to have you here. And what are you Secretary of, may I ask?
SECRETARY: I'm the Secretary of Defense.
CHAIRMAN: Very interesting. And what does your department do?
SECRETARY: We defend the country, sir.
CHAIRMAN: And how do you do that?
SECRETARY: By maintaining a strong military force.
CHAIRMAN: I see. Have you done any cost-benefit analysis of the value of defending the country?
SECRETARY: Well———
CHAIRMAN: Have you considered whether it would be possible to defend the country more cheaply without your department?

Herbert Stein, "How About Zero-Based Revenue?" *Wall Street Journal* (January 3, 1977).

180. "About 95 percent of top bureaucrats reaching retirement age—those between 55 and 59 with 30 years of federal experience—are deciding to leave, compared with about 18 percent in 1978, the General Accounting Office (GAO) reports" (p. 1296). William J. Lanouette, "SES: From Civil Service Showpiece to Incipient Failure in Two Years," *National Journal* (July 18, 1981), pp. 1296-99.
Of the Reagan administration sequel Hugh Heclo writes:

. . . [W]ithin the executive branch all the new management tools for performance appraisals and financial incentives have been accompanied by more distant rather than closer working relations between political appointees and career executives, particularly in the first term of the Reagan administration. At the end of 1983, two-thirds of the alumni of the Federal Executive Institute reported the "political/career interface" as having a negative effect on management effectiveness (in April 1981 the percentage had been 40%). In another survey of public executive attitudes, a majority of respondents felt that their agencies' performance appraisal system had little effect on performance, had not improved communication between superiors and subordinates, and was not worth the cost of administration. After five years operation, 40% of those who originally joined the new Senior Executive Service in 1979 had left government.

"Washington and Whitehall Revisited: An Essay in Constitutional Lore," a paper presented at the British/American Festival in Durham, North Carolina (June 12/13, 1984), p. 21.

181. Much of the material in the following paragraphs is drawn from Nelson W. Polsby, *Consequences of Party Reform* (New York: Oxford University Press, 1983), pp. 102-5. See also Richard F. Fenno, Jr., *The President's Cabinet* (Cambridge, Mass.: Harvard University Press, 1959).

182. Jimmy Carter, *Keeping Faith*, p. 84.

183. *Ibid.*, p. 86.

184. *Ibid.*, p. 93.

185. Haynes Johnson, *In the Absence of Power* (New York: Viking, 1980), pp. 188-89. Copyright © 1980 by Haynes Johnson. Reprinted by permission of Viking Penguin, Inc.

186. See Congressional Quarterly, *Energy Policy* (Washington, D.C.: Congressional Quarterly Inc., 1979), pp. 33-37, 43.

187. See *Consequences of Party Reform*, pp. 108ff.

188. For a summary of public opinion ratings on President Carter, see Polsby, *Consequences of Party Reform,* p. 229 (notes 64-67).

189. See Nelson W. Polsby, "The Democratic Nomination," in Austin Ranney (ed.), *The American Elections of 1980* (Washington, D.C.: American Enterprise Institute, 1981), pp. 37-60.

190. The most detailed description of these events is Elizabeth Drew, "Phase: In Search of a Definition," *The New Yorker* (August 27, 1979), pp. 45-73. See also *Consequences of Party Reform,* pp. 116ff.

191. Carter identifies them as Secretary of Treasury Michael Blumenthal and Secretary of HEW Joseph Califano. See *Keeping Faith,* pp. 116-17.

192. See *Keeping Faith,* pp. 115-16; Drew, "Phase: In Search of a Definition," pp. 59-64.

193. These reactions are summarized in Polsby, *Consequences of Party Reform,* pp. 119-23.

194. Elizabeth Drew, "Our Far-Flung Correspondents: Settling In," *The New Yorker* (February 28, 1977), pp. 82-88.

195. The demonstration of this argument is central to *Consequences of Party Reform, op cit.*

196. President Carter's description is contained in *Keeping Faith,* pp. 317-407.

197. See Polsby, *Consequences of Party Reform,* p. 128.

198. Jordan, *Crisis,* pp. 352-54.

199. Hamilton Jordan said:

> I remember Carter's other defeat, at the hands of Lester Maddox in 1966, and how [Carter] had packed up his family and driven off into the night without thanking his campaign workers.

Jordan, *Crisis,* p. 351.

Carter's early 1980 concession among other things led to complaints about the effects of election day information on turnout. See Raymond Wolfinger and Peter Linquiti, "Tuning In and Turning Out," *Public Opinion,* vol. 4 (February/March 1981), pp. 56-60. On Carter's role, see John Fogarty, "Carter Saw No Harm in Conceding Early," *San Francisco Chronicle,* November 7, 1980; John Balzar, "Demos Hurt by Early TV Vote Report," *ibid.,* March 11, 1981; Kenneth Reich, "State Democrats Bitter on Carter's Early Concession," *Los Angeles Times,* November 5, 1980; William Endicott, "Anti-Carter Vote Seen in State Races," *ibid.,* November 6, 1980; and Roger Smith, "Early Concession Costly: State Party Leaders Sure Carter 'Paralyzed' Effort," *ibid.,* November 7, 1980.

200. See Nelson W. Polsby, "Party Realignment in the 1980 Election," *The Yale Review* 72 (Autumn 1982), pp. 41-54.

201. The administrative tactic of not filling vacancies in the executive branch proved not only effective, but enduring. The Council of Economic Advisors, sometimes a source of uncomfortable economic analysis, was simply ignored and given no chairman—indeed not even an acting chairman—for months after Martin Feldstein left the chairmanship in July 1984; the National Science Foundation had no deputy director and no assistant directors—all presidential appointments—for much of Reagan's first term. See Jonathan Fuerbringer, "Whither the Council of Economic Advisors?" *New York Times* (August 30, 1984); John Walsh, "IBM's Bloch Named to Lead NSF," *Science* 224 (June 22, 1984), p. 1318.

202. On President Reagan and Congress, see Dick Kirschten, "The Pennsylvania Ave. Connection—Making Peace on Capitol Hill," *National Journal,* vol. 13 (March 7, 1981), pp. 384-87; Richard E. Cohen, "The 'Revolution' on Capitol Hill: Is It Just a Temporary Coup?" *ibid.,* vol. 13 (August 19, 1981), pp. 1537-41; and Stephen J. Wayne, "Congressional Liaison in the Reagan White House: A Preliminary Assessment of the First Year," in Norman J. Ornstein (ed.), *President and Congress: Assessing Reagan's First Year* (Washington, D.C.: American Enterprise Institute, 1982), pp. 44-65.

203. The key votes were: Gramm-Latta I on May 7, 1981, Gramm-Latta II on June 26, 1981, and final passage of the tax bill on July 31, 1981.

204. In a publication of the Council on Foreign Relations, *Time* magazine's Soviet specialist Strobe Talbott writes:

> Not only did [President Reagan] allow Soviet-American relations to deteriorate seriously

(in doing that he had plenty of help from the Soviets themselves), but he also conveyed the impression, certainly during his first two years in office, that the relationship *ought* to be bad: the Soviets were such murderous, deceitful scoundrels that competition and confrontation were the only appropriate forms for the relationship; the Soviets did not deserve détente, by that or by any other name.

The Russians and Reagan (New York: Vintage Books, 1984), p. 70.

205. See I. M. Destler, "The Evolution of Reagan Foreign Policy," in Fred I. Greenstein (ed.), *The Reagan Presidency: An Early Assessment* (Baltimore: The Johns Hopkins University Press, 1983), pp. 117-58.

206. Lou Cannon wrote:

... Most of the time, President Reagan was intuitively keen but intellectually lazy. His ignorance was his armor, shielding him from harsh realities which might have discouraged some of his boldest initiatives while gradually weighing down his presidency. He did not know how the federal budget worked or understand the threat to the environment from toxic wastes and acid rain or realize that the Soviets, for all their menace to human freedom, had in fact fulfilled a number of their treaties. He did not understand that a conservative agenda for America could be as costly as a liberal one. He did not recognize that the "racetrack" method of MX-basing he thought he was rejecting had been discarded long ago by President Carter, not recently by Caspar Weinberger. He did not know enough. And he did not know how much he didn't know.

Because of Reagan's knowledge gaps, his presidential news conferences became adventures into the uncharted regions of his mind. His advisers prepared the President as carefully as they could and crossed their fingers in hopes that the questioning would coincide with the preparation. Often, however, their well-intentioned concern that Reagan might display his ignorance contributed to the President's problems rather than solving them. Much of the time in Sacramento, Reagan held weekly press conferences, and the brief interval between them enabled his advisers to anticipate most of the questions. In Washington, Reagan met with the press so infrequently that it was difficult for even the most skillful briefers to anticipate what ground the questions might cover. Unlike Richard Nixon, Reagan was not stiff and fearful with reporters. And unlike Carter, he displayed a cheerful sense of humor which he was willing to employ at his own expense. Reagan liked many of the reporters and they liked him, even though he often could not recall their names. But he found the presidential press conference, with its discomforting demands on both conceptual understanding and detail, a perpetual struggle. Being hard of hearing did not help. Reagan could not catch many of the questions, particularly from the back of the crowded briefing room. This combination of poor hearing and limited knowledge transcended Reagan's communicative skills, dimming the luster of the Great Communicator's triumphant solo performances on national television. Reagan had so much trouble understanding the questions that the White House communications office finally installed a small loudspeaker on the left of the podium just below camera range. From then on he could at least understand the questions, even if he was not always able to answer them.

Reagan (New York: G.P. Putnam's Sons, 1982), pp. 372-73. Reprinted by permission of the Putnam Publishing Group from *Reagan* by Lou Cannon. Copyright © Lou Cannon 1982. See also Laurence I. Barrett, *Gambling with History*, esp. pp. 23ff, 31, 54ff, 223, 255; and John J. Fialka, "A Question of Depth: Reagan Intellect Surprises Some," *Wall Street Journal* (August 6, 1984), p. 38.

207. "The Presidential Shield," *Washington Post National Weekly Edition* (October 22, 1984), p. 4.

208. See Cannon, *Reagan*, pp. 371-401.

209. On internal battles in the Reagan White House, see Steven R. Weisman, "Now, Talk of New Strains Among the Top Aides," *New York Times* (March 31, 1983); Lou Cannon and David Hoffman, "Reagan Tugged by Rival Strategists," *Washington Post* (April 17, 1983); "A House Divided Against Itself...," *Conservative Digest* (May 1983), pp. 10-33; and Barrett, esp. pp. 218-51.

210. See John H. Kessel, "The Structures of the Reagan White House," *American Journal of Political Science* 28 (May 1984), pp. 231-58; Francis X. Clines, "James Baker: Calling Reagan's Re-election Moves," *The New York Times Magazine* (May 20, 1984), pp. 52-68; Jack W. Germond and Jules Witcover, "The Rise of Jim Baker," *The Washingtonian* 18 (October 1982), pp. 144-47, 184-88; and Barrett, *Gambling with History*, pp. 372-87.

211. Robert Ajemian says flatly:

> It was ... [Presidential Assistant Michael J.] Deaver who had pushed for William Clark as National Security Advisor and then, realizing he had made a mistake, turned on him, once more with Nancy Reagan's approval. Today Clark will not speak to Deaver and acknowledges his greeting only when Reagan is present.

"Making Reagan Be Reagan," *Time* (August 27, 1984), p. 21. See also "The White House: Cloak and Dagger Stuff," *The Economist* (September 1, 1984), pp. 21-23; Cannon, *Reagan, passim.*; and Barrett, *Gambling with History*, pp. 326-35.

212. See Cannon, *Reagan, passim.*; and Barrett, *Gambling with History*, pp. 94-106.

213. The standard descriptive term was that Mr. Reagan was "detached." For example, see Ajemian, "Making Reagan Be Reagan," pp. 20-21:

> In a presidency like this one, where the Chief Executive is so detached, so indifferent to detail, so psychologically unable to deal with personal conflict ....

> By all accounts the President is by nature a passive man who needs to be set in motion by others.

An article in the *New York Times* summarized a few examples of Presidential detachment:

> First came the difficulties the President had in reading a 16-word sentence that opened the Olympic Games ... then came an episode at his ranch when Mr. Reagan seemed unable to think of an answer to a reporter's question about the apparent collapse of the possibility of talks with the Soviet Union on curbing outer space weapons. While the President smiled, his wife, Nancy, was overheard prompting him: "Doing everything we can." Mr. Reagan repeated the phrase ....

> Michael K. Deaver, the deputy White House chief of staff, ... [said] that it was true that Mr. Reagan sometimes had "difficulty staying awake" at Cabinet meetings because the meetings were "sometimes boring."

> White House officials say that although they have never seen Mr. Reagan actually fall asleep at meetings, he sometimes dips his head and then shakes it in an effort not to nod off.

Steven R. Weisman, "Western White House: How Reagan Spent His Vacation, Really Spent It," *New York Times* (August 15, 1984).

Perhaps the most stunning example of Presidential detachment of all came at the start of Mr. Reagan's second term when his White House chief of staff, James Baker, and his Secretary of Treasury, Donald Regan, worked out an arrangement to swap jobs without consulting the President, and informed him of the new arrangement a day before it was announced publicly. "President Designates Regan White House Chief of Staff, Switching Him with Baker," *New York Times* (January 9, 1985).

214. See John L. Palmer and Isabel V. Sawhill (eds.), *The Reagan Experiment* (Washington, D.C.: The Urban Institute Press, 1982), for an early assessment. For a later one, the same editors produced *The Reagan Record* (New York: Ballinger, 1984). Other global evaluations of the Reagan Presidency as of the fall of 1984 include *Newsweek* (August 27, 1984) and a series in the *New York Times*: Hedrick Smith, "Reagan's Effort to Change Course of Government," *New York Times* (October 23, 1984); Peter T. Kilbourn, "Reagan Economic Record Called Good but Mixed," *ibid.* (October 24, 1984); David E. Rosenbaum, "In Four Years, Reagan Changed Basis of the Debate on Domestic Programs," *ibid.* (October 25, 1984); Leslie H. Gelb, "Reagan Foreign Policy: Shifting Aim," *ibid.* (October 26, 1984). On Sunday, October 28, 1984, the *Times'* lead editorial reviewed the Reagan Presidency in detail while endorsing President Reagan's opponent, Walter Mondale.

215. William Howard Taft, *Our Chief Magistrate and His Powers* (New York: Columbia University Press, 1916), pp. 138ff.

216. From Arthur B. Tourtellot, *Presidents on the Presidency* (Garden City, NY: Doubleday, 1964), pp. 55-56.

217. Leonard D. White, *The Federalists: A Study in Administrative History* (New York: Macmillan, 1948), p. 89. For a running account of the contrast between these two theories of presidential power in American administrative history, see also White's *The Jeffersonians* (New York: Macmillan, 1951), esp. pp. 29ff., and *The Jacksonians* (New York: Macmillan, 1954), esp. pp. 56ff.

218. Schlesinger, "Our Presidents," p. 12. See also Thomas A. Bailey, *Presidential Greatness: The Image of the Man from George Washington to the Present* (New York: Appleton-Century-Crofts, 1966).

219. A recent example of this empirical regularity from British experience was the effect of the Falkland Island war of 1983 in dramatically boosting the popularity of Prime Minister Margaret Thatcher. See Robert Worcester and Simon Jenkins, "Britain Rallies 'Round the Prime Minister," *Public Opinion* (June/July 1982), pp. 53-55.

220. Sudden crisis involving external threat and vigorous presidential activity seem best designed to provoke this response, at least in the short run. John E. Mueller's "Presidential Popularity from Truman to Johnson," *American Political Science Review*, vol. 64 (March 1970), pp. 18-34, emphasizes that these benefits are visible only in the short run; however, he documents the presence of the phenomenon. Mueller argues that the war in Vietnam did not follow the same pattern, but his finding on this point may be contaminated by other, stronger factors contributing to President Johnson's unpopularity. For further discussion of this point, see Kenneth N. Waltz, "Electoral Punishment and Foreign Policy Crises," in James N. Rosenau (ed.), *Domestic Sources of Foreign Policy* (New York: Free Press, 1967), pp. 263-93.

The Korean war hurt President Truman with public opinion in the long run. See Angus Campbell et al., *The American Voter* (New York: Wiley, 1960), pp. 48-50. But perhaps the main reason the Korean war was unpopular was that Truman decided to limit the war and called for a *partial* rather than an all-out mobilization. See Samuel P. Huntington, *The Soldier and the State* (New York: Random House Vintage Books, 1964), pp. 387-91. For a general discussion of Vietnam and public opinion, see Richard A. Brody, "How the Vietnam War May Affect the Election," *Trans-action*, vol. 5 (October 1968), pp. 16, 23; and Sidney Verba et al., "Public Opinion and the War in Vietnam," *American Political Science Review*, vol. 61 (June 1967), pp. 317-33. A thorough update of this literature emphasizing the effects on mass opinion of news reports of elite attitudes is contained in Richard Brody, "International Crises: A Rallying Point for the President?" *Public Opinion* 6 (December/January 1984), pp. 41-43.

221. For an excellent and full account see Richard Cohen and Jules Witcover, *A Heartbeat Away* (New York: Viking, 1974).

222. See Hamilton Jordan, *Crisis: The Last Year of the Carter Presidency* (New York: Putnam, 1982), pp. 235-38, 291-93; and Betty Glad, *Jimmy Carter: In Search of the Great White House* (New York: W. W. Norton, 1980), pp. 415, 422.

223. See "The Reagan 45," *The New Republic* (April 16, 1984), pp. 5-7.

224. *Ibid.*, p. 7.

225. This list is from Clinton Rossiter's *The American Presidency*, rev. ed. (New York: Harcourt, Brace & World, 1960), chap. 1.

226. Richard Neustadt, "The Presidency at Midcentury," *Law and Contemporary Problems*, vol. 21 (Autumn 1956), p. 610.

227. Joseph Alsop, *FDR: 1882-1945, A Centenary Remembrance* (New York: Washington Square Press, 1982), pp. 92-93.

228. See Herman M. Somers, *Presidential Agency* (Cambridge, Mass.: Harvard University Press, 1950).

229. See Hart, "Staffing the Presidency: Kennedy and the Office of Congressional Relations."

230. Being verbose souls, as well as highly visible, most press secretaries in recent years have published memoirs of their experiences in the White House. See e.g., Pierre Salinger, *With Kennedy* (Garden City, N.Y.: Doubleday, 1966); Ron Nessen, *It Sure Looks Different from the Inside*

(Chicago: Playboy Press, 1978); Herbert Klein, *Making It Perfectly Clear* (Garden City, N.Y.: Doubleday, 1980); and Jody Powell, *The Other Side of the Story* (New York: Morrow, 1984).

231. Robert Pierpoint, *At the White House* (New York: Putnam, 1981), p. 126.

232. Herbert Klein, *Making It Perfectly Clear*, p. 185.

233. *National Journal* (April 25, 1981), p. 681.

234. National Journal, *The White House Phone Directory*, 1983 ed.

235. A sympathetic observer of the Nixon administration gives an especially vivid example of this process in a transcript of a Ziegler press conference on October 27, 1970—well before Watergate and its aftermath totally soured relations between President Nixon and the press:

QUESTION: Ron, as the President takes off on this last campaign push before the election, does he still feel that the Republican party has the chance to gain control of the Senate?

ZIEGLER: I don't think that the President really ever said that, Stu. So I would reject the statement that you attribute to the President before answering your question.

QUESTION: I didn't attribute any statement to the President.

ZIEGLER: But to answer your question, the President said that the races across the country are very close.... The President has referred to, as you know, the majority of one, not necessarily relating to party division but a change of a seat or two which could be of value to the administration as we proceed in the next two years. Most of the major issues have been determined on two to three votes, four to five votes. So it is felt that a change of one or two seats could be very helpful.

QUESTION: Does that indicate, Ron, that the President no longer feels that it is likely that the Republicans will gain control of the Senate?

ZIEGLER: I'm not going to predict what the outcome of the election might be. It is too close, I think, to do that. I can only state what the President's objective is and what it has been. That is to assist where he can in areas where there is an opportunity for a Republican victory or where he has been particularly close to an individual who is running for office and someone who is waging a good effort. How it will come out, I don't know. But I would say that we are optimistic.

QUESTION: Do you then define success as a gain of one seat in the Senate?

QUESTION: What are you optimistic about?

ZIEGLER: I am optimistic about the way things will turn out.

QUESTION: Are you optimistic about gaining a seat or two, or four or five, or control of the Senate or what?

ZIEGLER: I am not going to predict. It is difficult to say.

QUESTION: Would you consider the gaining of one or a majority of one a significant achievement?

ZIEGLER: I would say that it would be a success if there were one or two changes in certain seats and within those changes the person elected would be of such persuasion that he would generally support the President's objectives. On the House side, closing the gap between 30 to 35, which is the traditional loss, would be a worthwhile achievement, too.

QUESTION: You said in certain seats.

QUESTION: What seats are you talking about when you say in certain seats? There are quite a number of Democrats that are up in the Senate at this time and not too many Republicans. Do you mean every one of those Democratic seats?

ZIEGLER: I am not going to go through state by state and give you an assessment of each race. I am giving you our general concept, but I will not be drawn into what seats or what kind of seats. I am giving you a general concept. That is all I am prepared to do....

QUESTION: ... If I understood you correctly, you said it would be a success if there were one or two changes in certain seats in the Senate. Since Republicans now have 43 Senate seats, are you saying that a gain of one or two, bringing it up to 44 or 45 seats, would be a success?

ZIEGLER: No, you missed the point of what the President has been saying. I am not going to predict how the Senate will come out in terms of what will happen in the division of seats gained by the Republicans or seats held by the Democrats. What I am saying is that a change, a net change, within the Senate, all Senate seats, a change of one or two of those who are in office now, could be of some assistance to the President if those changes fall within those seats not on party lines, but on ideological lines, where they generally would be of the persuasion that would be of support to the President. The major issues in the past two years have been determined by two to three votes or maybe slightly more. Many times the four to five votes would have been influenced by the decision of the one or two as the major issues were being discussed. But what I am giving you here is not particularly new or fresh. The President stated that at every speech he has made.

QUESTION: They don't need to be Democrats or Republicans? They could be Conservatives or something like that, as long as you get one or two?
ZIEGLER: They don't necessarily have to be Conservatives.
QUESTION: Then the defeat of a Liberal in New York would be successful?
ZIEGLER: I am not going to extend my remarks.
QUESTION: Could you give us an example of one or two? Are you referring to the Supreme Court nominations? Which are the two or three votes you just talked about?
ZIEGLER: If you have been in Washington for any time, you are well versed on the issues.
QUESTION: As I recall, most of the legislative issues were passed by an overwhelming majority.
ZIEGLER: There were many major issues in the last Congress, if you have been reading the papers you would be aware, that were very close in their votes.
QUESTION: We know what we think. We want to know what you think.
ZIEGLER: I am not giving you any more on what I think at this time.
QUESTION: Do you mean the Supreme Court nominees and the ABM vote?
ZIEGLER: Any other questions?

James Keogh, *President Nixon and the Press* (New York: Funk & Wagnalls, 1972), pp. 40-43.

236. See Polsby, *Political Innovation,* pp. 106-7.

237. "Science: The Doors to the White House Reopen," *Congressional Quarterly* 32 (October 12, 1974), pp. 2834-40. The best ongoing coverage of the political activities of the scientific community is contained in the news section of *Science* magazine. See, for example, Philip M. Boffey, "The Hornig Years: Did LBJ Neglect His Science Advisor?" *Science* (January 31, 1969), pp. 453-58; John Walsh, "Science Politics: An Invitation from the White House," *Science* (October 26, 1973), pp. 365-68; Barbara J. Culliton, "Office of Management and Budget: Skeptical View of Scientific Advice," Science (February 1, 1974), pp. 392-96. An early view of the growth of scientific advice to the President is Daniel Lang, "A Scientist's Advice," *New Yorker* (January 19, January 26, 1963) which is a profile of Kennedy's science advisor Jerome Wiesner. See also the memoirs of Eisenhower's two advisors, George G. Kistiakowsky, *A Scientist at the White House* (Cambridge, Mass.: Harvard University Press, 1976); and James R. Killian, Jr., *Sputnik, Scientists, and Eisenhower* (Cambridge, Mass.: The MIT Press, 1977). Killian was the first Presidential Science Advisor, and he describes the formation of PSAC in 1958 after the Soviet Union launched Sputnik.

238. My source for this often-quoted passage is Laura Fermi's charming memoir, *Atoms in the Family* (Chicago: University of Chicago, 1954), pp. 165-66.

239. Killian, *Sputnik, Scientists, and Eisenhower,* p. 16.

240. "Other EOP Offices: Supporting the President," *National Journal* (April 25, 1981), p. 696.

241. See Roger B. Porter, *Presidential Decision-Making: The Economic Policy Board* (New York: Cambridge University Press, 1980), p. 237; and John Ehrlichman, *Witness to Power* (New York: Pocket Books, 1982), pp. 63, 72-73.

242. These are, in order of the seniority of their posts (date of the department's establishment given in parentheses), the Secretaries of State (1789), Treasury (1789), and Defense (1947) (as successor to the Secretary of War in Washington's Cabinet); the Attorney General (1870); the Secretaries of Interior (1849), Agriculture (1862), Commerce (1913), Labor (1913), Health and Human Services (as successor to Health, Education, and Welfare, 1953), Housing and Urban Development (1965), Transportation (1966), Energy (1977), and Education (1979). Others may

be invited to Cabinet meetings at the discretion of the President. The Postmaster General, originally fifth in line, now heads a public corporation and no longer occupies a Cabinet position.

243. See Donovan, *Eisenhower*. The best general treatment of Presidents and their Cabinets is Richard F. Fenno, Jr., *The President's Cabinet* (New York: Random House Vintage Books, 1959). On Cabinet and subcabinet appointment processes, see Dean E. Mann and Jameson Doig, *The Assistant Secretaries* (Washington, D.C.: The Brookings Institution, 1965).

244. In the first Reagan administration there were seven such "cabinet councils": Economic Affairs, chaired by the Treasury Secretary; Natural Resources and Environment, chaired by the Interior Secretary; Commerce and Trade, chaired by the Commerce Secretary; Human Resources, chaired by the Secretary of Health and Human Services; Food and Agriculture, chaired by the Secretary of Agriculture; Legal Policy, chaired by the Attorney General; and Management and Administration, chaired by Presidential Counselor Edwin Meese.

See Barrett, *Gambling with History*, p. 72.

245. On the NSC under Eisenhower, see Paul Y. Hammond, *Organizing for Defense* (Princeton, N.J.: Princeton University Press, 1961), esp. pp. 353-63; and Dillon Anderson, "The President and National Security," *Atlantic Monthly* (January 1956), pp. 42-46. On the NSC under Kennedy, see, for example, the account of the Cuban missile crisis given by the *New York Times*, "Cuban Crisis: A Step by Step Review" (November 3, 1962); and Abel, *The Missile Crisis*. Kennedy's NSC, under McGeorge Bundy, was changed from a long-range planning group staffed by careerists into a much more activist organization oriented to the short-range needs of the President and staffed by a mixture of foreign policy professionals from within and outside the government.

See also, in general, the following documents of the U.S. Senate Subcommittee on National Policy Machinery: "Organizational History of the National Security Council," Committee Print, 86th Cong., 2d Sess. (1960); "Organizing for National Security: The National Security Council," *Hearings, May 10 and 24, 1960*, Part IV (1960); I. M. Destler, "National Security Advice to U.S. Presidents," *World Politics* 29 (January 1977), pp. 143-76; and I. M. Destler, Leslie H. Gelb, and Anthony Lake, *Our Own Worst Enemy* (New York: Simon and Schuster, 1984), esp. pp. 165-237.

246. Henry A. Kissinger, "The National Security Council," *Report of the Senate Subcommittee on National Security and International Operations, Committee on Government Operations*, 91st Cong., 2nd Sess. (March 3, 1970), pp. 1-2.

247. *Ibid.*, p. 5. More recently, see Anna Kasten Nelson, "National Security I: Inventing a Process (1945-1960)," pp. 229-62 and I. M. Destler, "National Security II: The Rise of the Assistant (1961-1981)," pp. 263-96, both in Hugh Heclo and Lester Salamon (eds.), *The Illusion of Presidential Government* (Boulder, Col.: Westview Press, 1981). See also Lawrence J. Korb and Keith D. Hahn (eds.), *National Security Policy Organization in Perspective* (Washington, D.C.: American Enterprise Institute, 1981).

248. See Leslie Gelb, "Why Not the State Department?" *The Washington Quarterly*, Special Supplement (Autumn 1980), pp. 25-40.

249. A good measure of the relative prominence of NSC advisors is the amount of notice they get in the newspapers. I. M. Destler has collected figures showing:

Number of Entries for Assistants in *The New York Times* Index

BUNDY	ROSTOW	KISSINGER	SCOWCROFT	BRZEZINSKI
38 (1961)	31 (1966)	150 (1969)	16 (1976)	147 (1977)
15 (1962)	18 (1967)	145 (1970)		145 (1978)[a]
21 (1963)	56 (1968)	292 (1971)		112 (1979)
29 (1964)		592 (1972)		130 (1980)[b]
91 (1965)				

[a]*The New York Times* was on strike from August 10 through November 5, 1978, and published only an abbreviated, "for the record" edition during this period.
[b]Based on semimonthly indexes.

I. M. Destler, "National Security II: The Rise of the Assistant," in Heclo and Salamon, *The Illusion of Presidential Government*, p. 275. See also I. M. Destler, "A Job that Doesn't Work," *Foreign Policy* 38 (Spring 1980), p. 84; and Kissinger, *White House Years*, pp. 26-32.

250. Peter Szanton, "Two Jobs, Not One," *Foreign Policy* 38 (Spring 1980), pp. 89-90. Reprinted with permission from *Foreign Policy* 38 (Spring 1980). Copyright 1980 by Carnegie Endowment for International Peace.

251. It is not the only such agency: the National Security Agency, the Defense Intelligence Agency, and the State Department, among others, gather foreign intelligence.

252. See Somers, *Presidential Agency*.

253. See "New Name Is Given U.S. Planning Office," *New York Times* (December 14, 1968).

CHAPTER 3 The Senate

1. For a more thorough discussion of the Congress in comparative perspective, see my article "Legislatures" in Fred I. Greenstein and Nelson W. Polsby (eds.), *Handbook of Political Science*, vol. 5 (Reading, Mass.: Addison-Wesley, 1975), pp. 257-319.

2. David Kozak reports the views of sixteen senators who were formerly House members on House-Senate differences in "House-Senate Differences: A Test Among Interview Data," presented to the Annual Meeting of the American Political Science Association, 1984. See also Norman J. Ornstein, "The House and the Senate in a New Congress," in Thomas E. Mann and Norman J. Ornstein (eds.), *The New Congress* (Washington, D.C.: American Enterprise Institute, 1981), pp. 363-83.

3. There is hard evidence on the differences between the publicity accorded members of the Senate as compared with the House. See, for example, Stephen Hess, *The Washington Reporters* (Washington, D.C.: Brookings, 1981), p. 101; Michael J. Robinson and Kevin R. Appel, "Network News Coverage of Congress," *Political Science Quarterly* 94 (Fall 1979), pp. 410-11, and especially, Joe S. Foote and David J. Weber, "Network Evening News Visibility of Congressmen and Senators," a paper presented to the Radio-television Journalism Division, Association for Education in Journalism and Mass Communication Annual Convention, Gainesville, Florida, August 1984. Foote and Weber found that senators on average were mentioned more than six times as often as House members, and that while House news coverage was almost entirely restricted to the official leadership, 90 percent of all senators received at least some publicity.

4. Actually, by 1911, twenty-nine of the forty-six states were holding direct elections for the U.S. Senate, to which their legislature gave *pro forma* assent. See George E. Mowry, *The Era of Theodore Roosevelt and the Birth of Modern America* (New York: Harper & Row Torchbooks, 1958), pp. 80, 264.

5. Senators are, however, on average somewhat more vulnerable to defeat than members of the House once the election takes place:

Members Reelected as Percentage of Those Seeking Reelection

YEAR	SENATE	HOUSE
1970	77.4%	94.5%
1972	74.1	93.6
1974	85.2	87.7
1976	64.0	95.8
1978	60.0	93.7
1980	55.2	90.7

Source: Norman J. Ornstein, Thomas E. Mann, Michael J. Malbin, and John F. Bibby, *Vital Statistics on Congress, 1982* (Washington, D.C.: American Enterprise Institute, 1982), pp. 46-48.

6. I have elaborated on the argument that follows in several places: "Goodbye to the Inner Club," *Washington Monthly*, vol. 1 (August 1969), pp. 30-34; "Policy Analysis and Congress," *Public Policy*, vol. 18 (September 1969), pp. 61-74; "Strengthening Congress in National Policy-Making," *Yale Review*, vol. 59 (June 1970), pp. 481-97, the first and last of which are reprinted in Nelson W. Polsby (ed.), *Congressional Behavior* (New York: Random House, 1971). See also Nelson W. Polsby, *Political Innovation in America: The Politics of Policy Initiation* (New Haven, Conn.: Yale University Press, 1984).

7. For a more traditional formulation of the commandment to specialize and its meaning, see Donald Matthews, *U.S. Senators and Their World* (Chapel Hill, N.C.: University of North Carolina Press, 1960), pp. 95-97.

8. Many of these specialties, to be sure, turn out to be dictated at least in part by committee assignments. See William Chapman, "'Mr. Clean Air': At Last Being a Republican Pays Off for Vermont's Stafford," *Washington Post* (December 22, 1981); Ward Sinclair, "Sen. Magnuson Is 'Mr. Health' for NIH," *Washington Post* (February 19, 1980); and Michael R. Gordon, "Sam Nunn for the Defense—Georgia Boy Makes Good as the Gentle Pentagon Prodder," *National Journal* (March 31, 1984), pp. 611-14.

9. See E. E. Schattschneider, *The Semi-Sovereign People* (New York: Holt, 1960), pp. 78-96.

10. In 1979 House proceedings began to be televised on cable television. They swiftly developed a small but devoted audience, and, predictably, members—especially a small and determined group of Republicans—began to devote substantial time and energy to playing to this audience. See Diane Granat, "The House's TV War: The Gloves Come Off," *Congressional Quarterly* (May 19, 1984), pp. 1166-67.

11. I argue in *Consequences of Party Reform* (New York: Oxford University Press, 1983), pp. 11-13, that the Kefauver hearings on organized crime, televised throughout the east and midwest in March 1951, is a key event. At that point, national publicity began to impinge significantly on senatorial careers—and hence on senatorial preoccupations.

12. From 1960 to 1984 ten different individuals have been nominated for President by the two major parties. Two of them (Carter and Reagan) were governors; the rest were Washington-based: senators or vice presidents. From 1920 to 1956 thirteen individuals were nominated. Five held Washington-based jobs at the time (I arbitrarily include Dwight Eisenhower); eight did not. Three of these were governors of New York (Smith, Roosevelt, Dewey).

13. See Louis Harris, "Why the Odds Are Against a Governor's Becoming President," *Public Opinion Quarterly*, vol. 23 (Fall 1959), pp. 361-70. J. Stephen Turett argues that the problems governors have had in recent years have not, however, increased the rate at which they have left office. See Turett's "The Vulnerability of American Governors, 1900-1969," *Midwest Journal of Political Science*, vol. 15 (February 1971).

14. See Robert Evans and Robert Novak, *Lyndon B. Johnson: The Exercise of Power* (New York: New American Library, 1966), esp. pp. 88-118.

15. Joseph S. Clark, *Congress: The Sapless Branch* (New York: Harper & Row, 1964), p. 5.

16. See Martin Schram, "Minority Boss: Sen. Robert C. Byrd, Skilled Only, Maybe, in Making the Trains Run," *Washington Post* (May 31, 1981); and Martin Tolchin, "Byrd Persuasive as Senate Chief," *New York Times* (March 27, 1977).

17. With some exaggeration, Baker described the majority leadership in his time as "a janitor's job. Robert Byrd and I open the Senate every morning." Dennis Farney, "Baker Is Ready for 'Civilian' Life," *Wall Street Journal* (August 8, 1984). See also David Shribman, "Despite Serious Setbacks, Dole Has Displayed Strength Under Pressures of Senate GOP Post," *Wall Street Journal* (May 8, 1985).

18. Alan Ehrenhalt, "Harrison Williams and the New Senate," *Congressional Quarterly* (March 20, 1982), p. 655. As Ehrenhalt points out, this has implications for the way senators handle all sorts of business. In the instant case, the problem was ethics. Ehrenhalt says:

> The old Senate had its own elaborate standards for personal behavior, but they were essentially private ones. Today's standards are public and ... [senators] feel enormous pressure to deal ... in a way that satisfies public opinion.

19. Charles O. Jones gives the following vignette:

> On the Senate side, I walked in on the tail end of a staff meeting in Senator Heinz's office. Since the room was very crowded, the first question I asked Geoffrey Garin, the legislative assistant, after the meeting was: "What is the size of the staff?" The answer was 33 people in the Washington office and 22 in Pennsylvania (11 in Pittsburgh, 9 in Philadelphia, and 2 in Harrisburg). I remember thinking at the time that this was probably at least as much patronage as was available to some cabinet officers.

Charles O. Jones, *The United States Congress* (Homewood, Ill.: The Dorsey Press, 1982), p. 40.

20. Norman Ornstein, Thomas Mann, Michael Malbin, and John Bibby, *Vital Statistics on Congress, 1982* (Washington, D.C.: American Enterprise Institute, 1982), pp. 110, 113.

21. Spencer Rich, "An Invisible Network of Hill Power," *Washington Post* (March 20, 1977).

22. See Eric Redman, *The Dance of Legislation* (New York: Simon and Schuster, 1973). For other instances, see David E. Price, *Who Makes the Laws?* (Cambridge, Mass.: Schenkman Publishing Co., 1972).

23. Senators meeting this description are now legion: Edward Kennedy, Richard Lugar, Robert Dole and Gary Hart are a few current examples that come immediately to mind. Their success in senatorial politics can be contrasted with the relative isolation and ineffectiveness of similarly inclined senators in an earlier era. See, for example, Alan Drury's discussion of Senators Carl Hatch and Joseph Ball in *A Senate Journal 1943-1945* (New York: McGraw-Hill, 1963).

24. As Humphrey said:

> I would become a national leader, if I could, with a national base, with a national constituency. The Senate would be my forum for expounding a point of view, for attracting and persuading people beyond my senatorial audience. There would be time enough to "work" the Senate after I gathered some additional, external power.

Hubert H. Humphrey, *The Education of a Public Man* (Garden City, N.Y.: Doubleday & Co., Inc., 1976), p. 147.

25. Notable among these students, as we shall see, was Ralph Huitt of the University of Wisconsin.

26. Ralph K. Huitt, "The Outsider in the Senate: An Alternate Role," *American Political Science Review*, vol. 55 (September 1961), pp. 566-67. This description summarizes work by William S. White, *Citadel* (New York: Harper & Row, 1956), and Donald Mathews, *U.S. Senators and Their World* (Chapel Hill, N.C.: University of North Carolina Press, 1960). The inner-club hypothesis had many proponents and was routinely invoked as a way of describing the placement of individual senators in the status structure of the Senate. See, for example, Joseph Kraft, "King of the U.S. Senate," *Saturday Evening Post* (January 5, 1963), pp. 26-27; Senator Joseph Clark, "The Senate Establishment," *Congressional Record*, daily ed. (February 18-28, 1963), pp. 2413-26, 2524-31, 2703-7, 2763, 2764, 2766, 2771, 2773; Allan Nevins, *Herbert H. Lehman and His Era* (New York: Scribner, 1963), esp. pp. 369-70.

27. Donald Matthews, "The Folkways of the U.S. Senate," originally in *American Political Science Review*, vol. 53 (December 1959), pp. 1064-89, and reprinted extensively. It also appears in Matthews, *U.S. Senators and Their World*, pp. 92-117.

28. As Ross K. Baker tells it,

> For several years after arriving in the Senate in 1912 as a freshman from the new state of Arizona, Carl Hayden maintained the respectful silence then expected of new members. One day, however, in a burst of youthful exuberance, he resolved to make a speech. It wasn't a very controversial speech but he felt that he had been a Senator long enough to comment on a minor matter affecting his state. As Mr. Hayden returned to his seat, an aged colleague approached him and hissed: "You just *had* to talk, didn't you?"

Ross K. Baker, "Upstart Senate Frosh," *New York Times* (November 13, 1979).

29. Dean Acheson, *Sketches from Life of Men I Have Known* (New York: Popular Library, 1962), p. 111.

30. White, *Citadel*, p. 87.

31. *Ibid.*, pp. 84, 92.

32. *Ibid.*, pp. 85.

33. *Ibid.*, pp. 75-76. See also Humphrey, *Education of a Public Man*, pp. 129-131. In an article published while he was Whip, Humphrey said, among other things, "the legislative branch has not been performing its functions with the order and effectiveness the nation deserves ... the rules and traditions of Capitol Hill are not sacred..." and he offered seven concrete proposals for reform. "To Move Congress Out of Its Ruts," *New York Times Magazine* (April 7, 1963), pp. 89ff.

34. Ralph Huitt, "Democratic Party Leadership in the Senate," *American Political Science Review*, vol. 55 (June 1961), p. 338. Both parties make committee assignments through their steering committees, subject to the general rule that a senator is entitled to keep whatever assignments he already has. Thus these committees handle transfers as vacancies occur and place freshman members. Republicans generally proceed strictly according to seniority for all vacancies. Democrats under the Johnson rule gave themselves more leeway. This change led to charges that committee placements were subject to manipulation by Johnson designed to affect policy outcomes. See Clark, "The Senate Establishment."

35. White, *Citadel*, p. 92.

36. *Ibid.*, p. 91.

37. *Ibid.*, p. 83; Nevins, *Herbert H. Lehman*, pp. 369-70.

38. See, for example, Senator Paul Douglas of Illinois on his colleague Herbert Lehman:

> Generous in deed and hospitality, with purse and heart open to every unfortunate, Herbert was the very embodiment of friendly and hopeful compassion.

Paul H. Douglas, *In the Fullness of Time* (New York: Harcourt Brace Jovanovich, Inc., 1971), pp. 198, 242.

39. White, *Citadel*, p. 10.

40. To my knowledge the only exhaustive list of inner-club members ever compiled was Clayton Fritchey's "Who Belongs to the Senate's Inner Club?" *Harper's* (May 1967). Fritchey listed fifty-three members and provisional members, more than a majority. Eight others, being freshmen, were ineligible.

41. The national visibility of Humphrey and Johnson, recently vice president and President respectively, makes citations to descriptions of their personalities unnecessary. As to the others, a reader might consult appropriate entries in a reference work such as *Current Biography*. In addition, for Mansfield, see John G. Stewart, "Two Strategies of Leadership: Johnson and Mansfield" in Nelson W. Polsby (ed.), *Congressional Behavior* (New York: Random House, 1971), pp. 61-92; and Douglass Cater, "The Contentious Lords of the Senate," *Reporter* (August 16, 1962), p. 28. For Alben Barkley, see White, *Citadel*, pp. 105-6. For Robert A. Taft, see James T. Patterson, *Mr. Republican: A Biography of Robert A. Taft* (Boston: Houghton Mifflin, 1972). For Everett Dirksen, see Neil MacNeil, *Dirksen* (New York: World, 1970), William Barry Furlong, "The Senate's Wizard of Ooze: Dirksen of Illinois," *Harper's* (December 1959), pp. 44-49; Murray Kempton, "Dirksen Delivers the Souls," *New Republic* (May 2, 1964), and Meg Greenfield, "Everett Dirksen's Newest Role," *Reporter* (January 16, 1964). For Kenneth Wherry, see White, *Citadel*, p. 106, and Acheson, *Sketches from Life of Men I Have Known*, pp. 112-14. For William Knowland, see Rowland Evans and Robert Novak, "Inside Report: Knowland's Return," *Washington Post* (June 28, 1963), p. A19. For Eugene Millikin, see Beverly Smith, "The Senate's Big Brain," *Saturday Evening Post* (July 4, 1953), p. 76. For Styles Bridges, see "The Congress," *Time* (December 8, 1961), p. 25. For Arthur Vandenberg, see Dean Acheson, *Sketches from Life of Men I Have Known*, pp. 109-11; and Richard H. Rovere, *The American Establishment* (New York: Harcourt, Brace & World, 1946), pp. 189-91. For Ernest McFarland, see David B. Truman, *The Congressional Party* (New York: Wiley, 1959), pp. 113, 303-4. For Thomas Kuchel, see *Congressional Quarterly* (May 4, 1962), p. 740. For Russell Long, see T. R. Reid, *Congressional Odyssey* (San Francisco: W.H. Freeman and Co., 1980), esp. pp. 115-19, 130-31. For Hugh Scott, see "Hugh Scott: Pussycat on a Hot Tin Roof," *Washington Post* (February 24, 1975). For Robert Byrd, see Robert Sherrill, "The Embodiment of Poor White Power," *New York Times Magazine* (February 28, 1971), p. 90.

42. In the entire history of the Senate, 14 women have served as Senator, only 5 of them for more than a year. They are:

Rebecca Latimer Felton	D-Georgia	Nov. 21-22, 1922[a]
Hattie Caraway	D-Arkansas	Dec. 8, 1931-Jan. 3, 1945
Rose Long	D-Louisiana	Feb. 10, 1936-Jan. 3, 1937
Dixie Bibb Graves	D-Alabama	Aug. 20, 1937-Jan. 10, 1938
Gladys Pyle	R-South Dakota	Nov. 8, 1938-Jan. 3, 1939[b]
Margaret Chase Smith	R-Maine	Jan. 3, 1949-Jan. 3, 1973
Eva Bowring	R-Nebraska	Apr. 26-Nov. 8, 1954
Hazel Abel	R-Nebraska	Nov. 8-Dec. 31, 1954
Maurine Neuberger	D-Oregon	Jan. 3, 1961-Jan. 3, 1967
Elaine Edwards	D-Louisiana	Aug. 7, 1972-Jan. 3, 1973
Maryon Allen	D-Alabama	June 8, 1978-Jan. 3, 1979
Muriel Humphrey	D-Minnesota	Jan. 26, 1978-Jan. 3, 1979
Nancy Landon Kassebaum	R-Kansas	Jan. 3, 1979-
Paula Hawkins	R-Florida	Jan. 3, 1981-

[a] Filled vacancy caused by Senator Thomas Watson's death; the next day she gave up the seat to Senator Walter George, the elected candidate for the vacancy.
[b] Not sworn in.
Sources: Esther Stineman, *American Political Women* (Littleton, Col.: Libraries Unlimited, Inc., 1980), pp. 191-97; and National Women's Political Caucus, *National Directory of Women Elected Officials 1982* (Washington, D.C., 1982), p. 15.

43. *Congressional Record*, daily ed. (February 19, 1963), p. 2399.

44. Alan Ehrenhalt, "In the Senate of the '80s, Team Spirit Has Given Way to the Rule of Individuals," *Congressional Quarterly* (September 4, 1982), p. 2182.

45. This technique is still in use. See Charles Mohr, "Senator Disrupts Arms Hearing by Citing Rule on Committee Hours," *New York Times* (October 17, 1979).

46. Ralph Huitt, "The Outsider in the Senate: An Alternate Role," *American Political Science Review*, vol. 55 (June 1961), pp. 569-70.

47. Mary McGrory, "Morse Tackles an 'Untidy World' "*Washington Evening Star* (November 17, 1963).

48. Excerpts from "Israel's Best Friend in Congress" (October 29, 1973), p. 54, reprinted by permission from TIME, The Weekly Newsmagazine; Copyright 1973 Time, Inc. All rights reserved.

49. Kenneth Crawford, "The Senate's Ways," *Newsweek* (January 14, 1963), p. 27.

50. Gerald R. Rosen, "What Maggie Wants, Maggie Gets," *Dun's Review*, April 1972, p. 38. Reprinted with the permission of *Dun's Review*, April 1972, Copyright, 1972, Dun & Bradstreet Publications Corporation.

51. Spencer Rich, "Allen A Master of New-Style Filibuster," *Washington Post* (July 1, 1974), p. A2.

52. Bobby Baker, *Wheeling and Dealing* (New York: Norton, 1978), pp. 100-101.

53. Spencer Rich, "Senate Democrats in Flux," *Washington Post* (August 13, 1972), p. A1.

54. These numbers change every two years with the entry of a newly elected freshman class. The point, however, remains the same: that in recent times there has been a lot of turnover in the Senate and its political center of gravity has shifted away from veteran members and toward newcomers.

55. Martin Tolchin, "Howard Baker: Trying to Tame an Unruly Senate," *New York Times Magazine* (March 28, 1982), p. 74.

56. Huitt, "Democratic Party Leadership in the Senate," pp. 337-38.

57. See, for example, "Mansfield's Ideas on Leadership," *Washington Sunday Star* (November 17, 1963).

58. Arlen J. Large, "Capitol Traffic Jam," *Wall Street Journal* (February 18, 1969).

59. Alan Ehrenhalt, "Senate Leader's Job: Curbing Individualism," *Congressional Quarterly* (April 7, 1984), p. 819.

60. Rosen, "What Maggie Wants, Maggie Gets," p. 38.

61. Matthews, *U.S. Senators and Their World*, p. 153.

62. George Goodwin, "The Seniority System in Congress," *American Political Science Review*, vol. 53 (June 1959), p. 433.

63. This impression is confirmed by Steven S. Smith and Christopher J. Deering, *Committees in Congress* (Washington, D.C.: Congressional Quarterly Press, 1984), pp. 111-19, who report a greater diversity of goals among Senators than House members and acknowledge that Senate committees tend to have broad mandates.

64. On Jackson's role in establishing a rationale for a strong State Department in the Kennedy administration, see Roger Hilsman, *To Move a Nation* (Garden City, NY: Doubleday, 1967), pp. 22, 555-56. A famous successor to Tom Hennings' chairmanship of the Subcommittee on Constitutional Rights of the Senate Judiciary Committee was Sam Ervin of North Carolina.

65. This term was originally used to refer to unbranded range cattle presumably belonging to the Maverick family of San Antonio, Texas.

66. White, *Citadel*, p. 126. For accounts of Senator McCarthy's deviant behavior, see Richard A. Rovere, *Senator Joe McCarthy* (New York: Harcourt, Brace & World, 1959); and esp. Michael Straight, *Trial by Television* (Boston: Beacon Press, 1954).

67. Ward Sinclair, of the *Washington Post*, gives an illustration:

> In an institution where trust is the glue that binds, Sen. James A. McClure (R-Idaho) has a problem: some of his senatorial colleagues don't trust him.
>
> McClure's problem became visible on the Senate floor last week when it took him hours to get agreement to begin debate on a revision of federal irrigation law that will benefit big farmers in the West.
>
> At least five "holds" had been placed on the irrigation bill by senators who objected to its being called up for consideration. Part of it was because of substance, part retaliation, part distrust.
>
> Such a personal reaction is unusual in the Senate. Although members routinely disagree on issues, they do so in faith that their points of view and their legislative proposals will get fair hearings.
>
> McClure's difficulties, according to various senators and staff aides, stem from his leadership on the Energy and Natural Resources Committee, of which he became chairman when Republicans took control of the Senate last year.
>
> "He plays games with the committee and tries to be Mr. Nice Guy," said one senator who declined to let his name be used. "But he's a little too slick. You can be the toughest kind of fighter in this place, but you better be honest."...
>
> "If you say you've got a 'technical' amendment, it had better be a technical amendment," [said another senator]. "And you better not lie to a fellow senator.... This thing is not the subject of a lot of conversation around here, but a look or a glance tells you what's on members' minds."...
>
> McClure's series of contretemps over committee business led one member to say, "There are four or five senators that all of us on both sides of the aisle are concerned about, and McClure is one of them."

Ward Sinclair, "Idaho's McClure, Head of Energy Panel, Is a Capitol Hot Potato," *Washington Post* (July 6, 1982).

68. Raymond Bauer, Ithiel de Sola Pool, and Lewis Anthony Dexter, *American Business and Public Policy* (New York: Atherton, 1963), pp. 66-68.

69. See Huitt, "The Outsider in the Senate," esp. pp. 574-75.

70. Ralph K. Huitt, "The Morse Committee Assignment Controversy: A Study in Senate Norms," *American Political Science Review*, vol. 51 (June 1957), p. 317.

71. *Ibid.*, p. 329. Huitt concludes from his study of party bolting in the Senate that this form of extreme deviance is rarely punished, and when it is punished, the consequences are rarely lasting. See also A. Robert Smith, *The Tiger in the Senate* (Garden City, N.Y.: Doubleday, 1962), esp. pp. 179-201; and Clarence E. Berdahl, "Party Membership in Congress," *American Political Science Review* (April, June, August 1949), pp. 309-21, 492-508, 721-34.

72. See Hugh A. Bone, "Introduction to Senate Policy Committees," *American Political Science Review*, vol. 50 (June 1956), pp. 339-59; and "Some Notes on Congressional Campaign Committees," *Western Political Quarterly*, vol. 9 (March 1956), pp. 116-37.

73. From 1953 to 1955 Johnson was Minority Leader; from 1955 to 1960, Majority Leader.

74. See, for example, Truman, *The Congressional Party*, pp. 293-94.

75. Evans and Novak, *Lyndon B. Johnson*, pp. 104-5.

76. Bobby Baker, who was Secretary of the Senate when Johnson was Majority Leader, describes this ongoing process during those years:

> I was always on the lookout to gain information that might one day secure a key vote. Certain Senate junkets were highly prized and the competition to be named to them was brisk and fierce. If I happened to hear a certain senator's wife say that she loved South America or had a special thing for Africa, I filed the information away and at the proper time worked to get her husband named to official trips going that way—and made certain, of course, that not only the senator but also his lady knew who'd taken care of the matter; since senators' wives were permitted on most such junkets, I often made valuable new allies. If for sentimental or historical reasons a senator had an urge to be assigned to a certain desk—as new Senator Ted Kennedy wanted to occupy his brother Jack's old spot—I did everything possible to help. One did not merely go looking for votes when they were needed on a given bill, but constantly did the mule work—some of it dull and bothersome—that might store up residues of goodwill for the future.

Wheeling and Dealing, p. 69.

77. A useful comparison of Johnson and Mansfield is John G. Stewart, "Two Strategies of Leadership," in Polsby (ed.), *Congressional Behavior*, pp. 61-92. See also Spencer Rich, "Quiet Revolt Under Way in Senate," *Washington Post* (January 26, 1975), p. A1.

CHAPTER 4   The House of Representatives

1. John Beckler, "Men in Dotage Hamstringing House," *Washington Post* (April 3, 1964); "House Freshman Raps 'Old Men,'" *Washington Star* (April 3, 1964).

2. See Mary Russell, "Hill's Reform Democrats Make Gains," *Washington Post* (December 3, 1974). The quotation is from Philip Burton of California, newly elected chairman of the House Democratic Caucus. The metaphor had something of a vogue at the opening of the Ninety-fourth Congress (at least in the *Washington Post*). "As Representative John Moss (D-Calif.) said: 'The winds of change have swept down to the committee level.'" Mary Russell, "House Units Feel Impact of Freshman," *Washington Post* (January 22, 1975).

3. Richard L. Lyons, "House Freshman Sees No Big Effort to 'Knock Off' Chairmen," *Washington Post* (January 27, 1975).

4. Not many women have, in the past, served in Congress. In the Ninety-eighth Congress (1983), a historical high point, there were twenty-one female members of the House of Representatives and two female Senators.

5. Carolyn Hagner Shaw, "Protocol, Address of Officials and Social Forms," *The Social List of Washington and Social Precedence in Washington* (Washington, D.C.: Shaw, 1963), pp. 10-14. Senators are outranked by the President, former Presidents and their widows, the vice president,

Speaker of the House, members and retired members of the Supreme Court, foreign ambassadors and ministers, the Cabinet, and a few other officers of the executive branch. Representatives are outranked by all of these and by the governors of states, acting heads of executive departments in the absence of the Cabinet member, and former vice presidents.

6. As Charles O. Jones notes, "senators have nearly twice as many committee and subcommittee assignments as House members—10.68 in 1979 as compared to 5.89 in the House." *The United States Congress* (Homewood, Ill.: The Dorsey Press, 1982), p. 277. Many Senate subcommittees exist mainly as a way of augmenting the staff available to their chairmen, and seldom meet. Richard D. Lyons, "28 Senate Subcommittees Held No Meetings in 1975," *New York Times* (April 4, 1976). Before the reforms of 1977, which shrank the number of subcommittees somewhat, each senator served on an average of 18 committees and subcommittees. Minority leader Everett Dirksen said:

> I would not dare say to the people of Illinois that I knew all about the things that go on, when I serve on 5 subcommittees of the Committee on Appropriations, on 7 subcommittees of the Committee on the Judiciary, and on 3 subcommittees of the Committee on Government Operations. To do so I would really need roller skates, to get from one subcommittee to another, without even then knowing entirely everything about every subject matter which is considered by the various committees.

Quoted in Walter J. Oleszek, *Overview of the Senate Committee System*, prepared for the Commission on the Operation of the Senate (Washington, D.C., April 23, 1976), p. 16.

7. There are 154 regular committees and subcommittees in the House. Committee chairmen may chair only one subcommittee, and ranking subcommittee members, who control minority staff, likewise overlap ranking members on the full committee only slightly. This gives nearly 300 strategically located positions on some subcommittee or other. Republican, minority, leadership positions (Minority Leader, Whips, Conference officers) number 27, and on the Democratic side, with its enormous group of at-large and zone assistant whips, there are 77 posts regarded as "leadership" positions. In addition, there are eleven select committees and subcommittees.

Although these positions vary greatly in the scope of their influence, and some individuals have more than one, it is clearly the case that responsibilities and power in the House have spread to more and more members in recent years.

8. *Congressional Government* (New York: Meridian Books, Inc., 1956; 1st ed., 1884), pp. 85-86.

9. See Barbara W. Tuchman, "Czar of the House," *American Heritage*, vol. 45 (December 1962), pp. 33-35, 92-102; George Galloway, *History of the House of Representatives* (New York: Crowell, 1961), pp. 52-53; Samuel W. McCall, *The Life of Thomas Brackett Reed* (Boston: Houghton Mifflin, 1914), pp. 162-72; and Lewis Deschler (ed.), *Constitution, Jefferson's Manual, and Rules of the House of Representatives* (Washington, D.C.: Government Printing Office, 1961), sections 52 and 863.

10. See George Norris, *Fighting Liberal* (New York: Collier Books, 1961), pp. 121-32; Blair Bolles, *Tyrant from Illinois* (New York: Norton, 1951), pp. 200-24.

11. Remarks of Clarence Cannon, *The Leadership of Speaker Sam Rayburn: Collected Tributes of His Congressional Colleagues*, 87th Cong., 1st Sess., House Document 247 (Washington, D.C.: Government Printing Office, 1961), pp. 15, 16.

12. Remarks of Carl Vinson, *ibid.*, p. 13.

13. These reforms, the product of rules changes urged by the House Democratic caucus, apply so long as Democrats control the House. Whether they would survive intact under a Republican House majority remains to be seen.

14. See, for example, Stephen K. Bailey, *Congress Makes a Law* (New York: Columbia, 1950), pp. 151-53.

15. See Norman J. Ornstein, "Causes and Consequences of Congressional Change: Subcommittee Reforms in the House of Representatives, 1970-73," in Ornstein (ed.), *Congress in Change* (New York: Praeger, 1975), pp. 88-114.

16. See Nelson W. Polsby, Miriam Gallaher, and Barry Spencer Rundquist, "The Growth of the Seniority System in the U.S. House of Representatives," *American Political Science Review*,

vol. 63 (September 1969), pp. 787-807. Subcommittee chairmen are also nearly always selected on the basis of committee seniority or, less frequently, subcommittee seniority. See Jack A. Goldstone, "Subcommittee Chairmanships in The House of Representatives," a communication to the *American Political Science Review* 69 (September 1975), pp. 970-71.

17. See Ornstein, "Causes and Consequences of Congressional Change."

18. See Charles M. Tidmarch with the assistance of Paul D. Ginsberg, "Politics, Power, and Leadership in Congressional Subcommittees," delivered at the Annual Meeting of the American Political Science Association, September 1984; Nicholas Cohodas, "From Activist to Obstructionist: Peter Rodino Turns Judiciary into a Legislative Graveyard," *Congressional Quarterly* (May 12, 1984), pp. 1097-1102; Jacqueline Calmes, "Banking Chairman: Secretive but Successful," *Congressional Quarterly* (September 8, 1984), pp. 2198-2202; Dennis Farney, "Again, Peter Rodino Turns up at Center of Political Dispute," *Wall Street Journal* (June 25, 1984).

19. In 1974 Malcolm Jewell and Chu Chi-Hung showed that assignments to these three committees were the most demanded by Members of the House: "Membership Movement and Committee Attractiveness in the U.S. House of Representatives, 1963-1971," *American Journal of Political Science* 18 (May 1974), pp. 433-41. Despite organizational changes in the House weakening the power of all three committees, especially Rules, these three committees still led the rest by the criterion of attractiveness to members in 1981. Bruce A. Ray, "Committee Attractiveness in the U.S. House, 1963-1981," *American Journal of Political Science* 26 (August 1982), pp. 609-13.

20. See John F. Manley, "The House Committee on Ways and Means: Conflict Management in a Congressional Committee," *American Political Science Review*, vol. 59 (December 1965), pp. 927-39.

21. See George Galloway, *The Legislative Process in Congress* (New York: Crowell, 1953), pp. 612ff.

22. See Neil MacNeil, *Forge of Democracy* (New York: McKay, 1963), p. 159.

23. Ornstein, "Causes and Consequences of Congressional Change," p. 110.

24. The "task forces" of the Budget Committee function in ways similar to subcommittees.

25. See, for example, the discussion of the Rules Committee under Chairman Howard W. Smith, in MacNeil, *Forge of Democracy*. See also H. Douglas Price, "Race, Religion, and the Rules Committee," in A. Westin (ed.), *The Uses of Power* (New York: Harcourt, Brace & World, 1962); and Clem Miller, in John Baker, *Member of the House* (New York: Scribner, 1962), *passim.*

26. See Richard F. Fenno, Jr., "The House of Representatives and Federal Aid to Education," in R. L. Peabody and N. W. Polsby (eds.), *New Perspectives on the House of Representatives* (Chicago: Rand McNally, 1963). An excellent case study showing Barden at his most effective is John E. Moore, "Controlling Delinquency: Executive, Congressional and Juvenile, 1961-64," in Frederic N. Cleaveland and associates, *Congress and Urban Problems* (Washington, D.C.: Brookings, 1969), pp. 110-72.

27. See Nicholas Masters, "Committee Assignments in the House of Representatives," *American Political Science Review*, vol. 55 (July 1961), pp. 345-57; and Kenneth A. Shepsle, *The Giant Jigsaw Puzzle* (Chicago: The University of Chicago Press, 1978).

28. John F. Bibby (ed.), *Congress off the Record* (Washington, D.C.: American Enterprise Institute, 1983), p. 8.

29. *Ibid.*, p. 6.

30. Mr. O'Brien's obituaries were most informative. For example, the *Washington Post*, April 15, 1964, told this anecdote: "Rep. O'Brien was a great friend of the late Speaker Sam Rayburn and regularly called on Rayburn a few days in advance of crucial House votes. On one such occasion, according to a Rayburn aide, Rep. O'Brien ambled into Rayburn's office and asked, 'How do you want them fellows to vote, Mr. Speaker?' Rayburn told him. 'They'll be there,' Mr. O'Brien replied."

31. It is no cliché to say that they don't make them like that any more. By 1984 the number of Democratic members from Illinois had shrunk to only 12, eight of them from Chicago. Most were still responsive to suggestions from Dan Rostenkowski of Illinois, the son of a Chicago alderman who was chairman of the House Ways and Means Committee.

32. See Masters, "Committee Assignments in the House of Representatives," *Cannon's Precedents 8.* section 2179, 2195; and Floyd M. Riddick, *The U.S. Congress: Organization and Procedure* (Manassas, Va.: National Capitol Publishers, 1949), pp. 164-68.

33. See David Truman, *The Congressional Party* (New York: Wiley, 1959); Julius Turner, *Party and Constituency* (Baltimore: Johns Hopkins, 1951); and David R. Mayhew, *Party Loyalty among Congressmen: The Difference between Democrats and Republicans, 1947-1962* (Cambridge, Mass.: Harvard University Press, 1966).

34. Nelson W. Polsby, "Two Strategies of Influence in the House of Representatives: Choosing a Majority Leader, 1962," in Peabody and Polsby (eds.), *New Perspectives on the House of Representatives* (Chicago: Rand McNally, 1963), p. 342. The quote is from an interview with Representative Tom Steed of Oklahoma.

35. The Speaker, through his power of recognition on the floor, by tradition has exclusive control over the conditions under which legislation may be brought to the floor and passed by unanimous consent, or under suspension of the rules (by two-thirds vote). Each party also has a committee of three "objectors" who object to the passage of particular bills by unanimous consent if certain conditions are not met, for example, if they authorize more than one million dollars of expenditure, if they fail to receive clearance from the executive, or if they are controversial between the parties. See Rep. Wayne Aspinall, "The Consent Calendar," *Congressional Record*, vol. 109 (February 4, 1963), part 2, pp. 1630-31.

36. See Polsby, Gallaher, and Rundquist, "Growth of the Seniority System;" and MacNeil, *Forge of Democracy*, p. 96.

37. The 1984 Congressional Staff Directory lists 47 such groups, among them the Congressional Rural Caucus, the Congressional Wood Energy Caucus, the Pro-Life Caucus, and the Sophomore Republican Class of the 97th Congress Caucus. This, if anything, understates the number that are now operating. See Susan Webb Hammond, "Congressional Caucuses and Party Leaders," paper delivered at the Annual Meeting of the American Political Science Association, Washington, D.C., September 1984.

38. Mark F. Ferber, *The Democratic Study Group: A Study of Intra-Party Organization in the House of Representatives*, unpublished Ph.D. dissertation (Los Angeles: University of California at Los Angeles, 1964); Kenneth Kofmehl, "Institutionalization of a Voting Bloc," *Western Political Quarterly*, vol. 17 (June 1964), pp. 256-72; and Richard W. Bolling, *Defeating the Leadership's Nominee in the House of Democratic Caucus*, ICP #91 (Indianapolis: Bobbs-Merrill, 1970).

39. Charles O. Jones, "Minority Party and Policy-Making in the House of Representatives," *American Political Science Review*, vol. 62 (June 1968), pp. 481-93; and Robert L. Peabody, *The Ford-Halleck Minority Leadership Contest, 1965*, Eagleton Institute Cases in Practical Politics, no. 40 (New York, 1966).

40. See John F. Manley, "The Conservative Coalition in Congress," *American Behavioral Scientist* 17 (November-December 1973), pp. 223-47.

41. See Bolling's *House Out of Order* (New York: Dutton, 1965) for an analysis laying stress upon the Speaker and the Democratic caucus as the likeliest instruments for countering the conservative coalition.

42. See John R. Johannes, *To Serve the People* (Lincoln: University of Nebraska Press, 1984).

43. Some scholars argue, in addition, that recent improvements in the capacity of members of Congress to advertise themselves through energetic and efficient casework has enormously strengthened their chances of reelection. See Morris P. Fiorina, *Congress: Keystone of the Washington Establishment* (New Haven, Conn.: Yale University Press, 1977).

44. Jerry Voorhis, *Confessions of a Congressman* (Garden City, N.Y.: Doubleday, 1948), p. 233.

45. See Lewis A. Dexter, "The Representative and His District" and "What Do Congressmen Hear?" both printed in revised and expanded forms from earlier publications in Nelson W. Polsby, Robert A. Dentler, and Paul A. Smith, *Politics and Social Life* (Boston: Houghton Mifflin, 1963), pp. 485-512. See also John W. Kingdon, *Congressmen's Voting Decisions* (New York: Harper & Row, 1981).

46. See, for example, David Rogers, "Coming of Age in the House: Lungren and Frank Gain Credibility," *Wall Street Journal* (October 4, 1984).

47. One method of communication is, in a small way, eroding the anonymity of House members. In recent years proceedings on the House floor have been televised, and broadcast not only in the Capitol building and House offices, but also to a small but devoted audience of subscribers to the CSPAN cable network. An enterprising group of young Republicans have seized on this opportunity by regularly occupying the hours that the House sets aside for the routine statements of members with an orchestrated series of partisan statements. These members are becoming known to the CSPAN audience.

CHAPTER 5   National Policy-Making I : The Legislative Labyrinth

1. Defeat at the committee stage is the predominant means by which measures are winnowed out in both Houses. Once a bill reaches the floor, the odds overwhelmingly favor enactment. Stanley Bach points out with respect to floor action, that "During the 95th and 96th Congresses, the House passed 3013 measures and defeated 72; in the Senate, 2626 measures were passed and only 8 were defeated." "Parliamentary Strategy and the Amendment Process: Rules and Case Studies of Congressional Action," *Polity* 15 (Summer 1983), p. 573.

2. The most important exceptions are taxing and spending bills, which must begin in the House. Measures for spending money will be considered at length in the next chapter.

3. Article II, Section 2.

4. Walter J. Oleszek, *Congressional Procedures and the Policy Process*, 2nd ed. (Washington, D.C.: Congressional Quarterly, Inc., 1984), pp. 77-78. The Speaker now has the power to refer bills concurrently to different committees, to split the contents of bills between committees, and to refer bills to different committees seriatim.

5. For an extremely complex example, involving maneuvers between rival agencies of the executive branch as well as presidential ambitions and party rivalry, see E. W. Kenworthy, "Ocean-Dumping Bill by Muskie Appears to Outmaneuver Nixon," *New York Times* (November 18, 1970).

6. Tabulations demonstrating this point for the Senate in the field of foreign affairs are contained in James A. Robinson, *Congress and Foreign Policy-Making* (Homewood, Ill.: Dorsey, 1962), pp. 99-100.

7. Interview by the author, March 25, 1963.

8. See Richard E. Neustadt, "Presidency and Legislation: the Growth of Central Clearance," *American Political Science Review*, vol. 48 (September 1954), pp. 641-71; Robert S. Gilmour, "Central Legislative Clearance: A Revised Perspective," *Public Administration Review* 31 (March-April 1971), pp. 150-58; and Joel Havemann, "White House Report: OMB's Legislative Role in Growing More Powerful and More Political," *National Journal Reports* 5 (October 27, 1973), pp. 1589-98.

9. Lewis A. Dexter, "What Do Congressmen Hear?" in Nelson W. Polsby, Robert A. Dentler, and Paul A. Smith (eds.), *Politics and Social Life* (Boston: Houghton Mifflin, 1963), p. 492.

10. Richard Harris, "Annals of Legislation: The Turning Point," *New Yorker* (December 14, 1968), p. 84.

11. When this is not the case and senior committee members oppose the bill, the chances are that the House will report no bill in the first place or that the chairman will pursue some strategy other than the one suggested here to hasten hearings.

12. See Walter Goodman, *The Committee* (Boston: Little Brown, 1963).

13. Under rules reformed in 1973, executive sessions, that is, sessions of committees held behind closed doors with observers excluded, are increasingly rare, even for committee mark-ups.

14. Clem Miller, in J. W. Baker (ed.), *Member of the House* (New York: Scribner, 1962), pp. 13, 14, 15.

15. An alternative method of bringing bills to the floor similar to unanimous consent is by

suspension of the rules, which is accomplished by a two-thirds vote and always with the cooperation of the Speaker. It is clearly unsuited for the passage of most controversial legislation.

16. Since the passage of the Budget and Impoundment Act of 1974, appropriations bills conform to the guidelines of the Budget resolution before they can be brought to the floor.

17. Congressman Richard Bolling, "The Keeper of the Rules: Congressman Smith and the New Frontier," CBS Reports, January 19, 1961.

18. In 1967 liberal Democratic committee members finally overran Judge Smith's successor as chairman (William Colmer of Mississippi) and forced through a few token changes in committee procedure. Among the changes was the establishment of a regular meeting time, which under House rules all committees were and are supposed to have anyway.

19. Tom Wicker, "Again that Roadblock in Congress," *New York Times Magazine* (August 7, 1960). The committee did, in fact, have the power to call itself to order, but the process is laborious and would have been extremely insulting to Judge Smith. See Lewis Deschler, *Constitution, Jefferson's Manual and Rules of the House of Representatives* (Washington, D.C.: Government Printing office, 1961), Section 734.

20. *Congressional Record*, daily ed. (July 25, 1963), p. 12621.

21. Richard Bolling, "The House Committee on Rules," speech delivered at the Midwest Conference of Political Scientists, Columbia, Missouri, May 11, 1961, p. 6.

22. The House, unlike the Senate, does not provide a desk for each member in the chamber in which they meet; it has only banks of seats. These tables are the only working surfaces available to members.

23. H. Douglas Price, "The Congress: Race, Religion and the Rules Committee," in A. F. Westin (ed.), *The Uses of Power* (New York: Harcourt, Brace & World, 1962), p. 60. The recording of votes in the committee of the whole makes it far more difficult to skulk, as in the good old days.

24. See Bertram Gross, *The Legislative Struggle* (New York: Holt, 1952), p. 267.

25. James M. Landis, "The Legislative History of the Securities Act of 1933," *George Washington Law Review*, vol. 28 (October 1959), pp. 29-49. Quoted passage, pp. 43-45. Reprinted by permission of *George Washington Law Review*.

26. From 1913 to 1968 there were 1,270 vetoes, including 524 pocket vetoes. Only 37 vetoes were overridden. From 1969 to 1983 there were 154 vetoes, including 55 pocket vetoes, and 21 were overridden.

CHAPTER 6   National Policy-Making II : The Budgetary Process

1. Richard E. Neustadt, *Presidential Power* (New York: Wiley, 1960), p. 33.

2. Statement of Hon. David E. Bell, "Organizing the National Security. The Budget and the Policy Process," *Hearings Before the Subcommittee on National Policy Machinery*, part 8 (Washington, 1961), pp. 1134-35.

3. Statement of Hon. Wilfred J. McNeil, *ibid.*, pp. 1060-61. For a similar statement by President Nixon's first budget director, see Robert P. Mayo, "Meeting Public Needs: An Appraisal," *National Tax Journal* 25 (September 1972), pp. 335-42.

4. The inexorable growth of the American economy and population made it clear that 1966 was going to be the last year in which the administrative budget would be under $100 billion. For President Johnson, this figure was politically a magic number; in 1964 he had opened a sizable credibility gap with the press by broadly hinting that the budget would go over $100 billion, so that the eventual figure, which he knew would be less, would be publicized as a great exercise in governmental self-denial and frugality.

When the administrative budget finally cracked President Johnson's magic ceiling, the time seemed ripe to consolidate it with trust-fund expenditures, a move that had long been recommended by experts in this recondite field. The budget documents were written so as to permit accurate comparisons with previous years. Thus the retrospective addition of trust-fund expenditures recorded that the $100 billion mark had been passed long since. See Rowland Evans and Robert Novak, *Lyndon B. Johnson: The Exercise of Power* (New York: New American Library, 1966), pp. 368-76; and James Deakin, *Lyndon Johnson's Credibility Gap* (Washington, D.C.: Public Affairs Press, 1968), p. 50: "To reporters keeping vigil in Austin late in December 1966, the word was passed by one of those ubiquitous 'high administration sources' that the new federal budget would be $135 billion to $140 billion.... Reporters recalled the great budget hoax of 1964, when the President protested mournfully that it would be practically impossible to keep spending under $100 billion, then sandbagged them with a $97.7 billion total."

5. Art. I, Sec. 9, paragraph 7.

6. One of the most confusing features of congressional procedure is the fact that the appropriations process parallels the regular legislative process. When a bill becomes a law, it may *authorize* the expenditure of money for stipulated purposes, but this does not mean that that amount of money will actually be *appropriated* to this end. How much money is appropriated depends on the process I am about to describe. Normally, to initiate a program, it is necessary to go through the legislative process to provide authorization and then the budgetary process to provide money.

The annual budget document may also provide for money which is supposed to be spent over more than one year, as, for example, in the case of a complicated long-range building program. Thus the language of the appropriations process makes distinctions between "budget authority" (the legal right to spend) and "outlays" (actual expenditures).

7. This means that at any point in time somewhere in the Federal government officials have to be concerned with at least three different annual budgets: the budget they are currently spending, the budget that is next in the pipeline, and the budget that is being planned for at this forecasting stage. See Jacques Gansler, "Reforming the Defense Budget Process," *The Public Interest* 75 (Spring 1984), pp. 62-75.

8. No doubt the role of inflation in determining the income of the government will change with the indexing of income tax rates.

9. Some Presidents have tried, with uneven success, to influence the economy by taking nonfinancial measures. These have gone by various names: e.g., jawboning, voluntary wage-price guidelines, private-sector initiatives, a publicity campaign to "Whip Inflation Now."

10. The Reagan administration attempted to slow down this so-called "bracket creep" by sponsoring a provision in the Economic Recovery Tax Act of 1981 that indexes tax liabilities for inflation. See Paul Craig Roberts, *The Supply-Side Revolution* (Cambridge, Mass.: Harvard University Press, 1984), p. 164.

11. Table 15 shows the extent to which Federal budgets predict actual Federal expenditures. Inaccurate predictions of receipts appear to account for the major source of error in dollar terms. This is understandable; it makes sense for political leaders to see to it that estimates of income are given optimistically in budget forecasting, because doing this permits them to ask for a larger budget without incurring a predicted deficit— and all the political (or at least propaganda) disadvantages that go with it.

12. Presidents vary in the extent to which they involve themselves in budgetary decision-making. Harry Truman was famous for his attentiveness to the budget. Richard Nixon, on the other hand, delegated virtually all budgetary decision-making to his OMB director and interposed an almost impregnable wall of budget officials between himself and governmental agencies, including his own appointees, the Cabinet officers who headed these agencies. Gerald Ford, an old House Appropriations Committee hand, went thoroughly into budgeting details himself. Ronald Reagan delegated extensively to his OMB director, David Stockman, on details and restricted his participation to setting overall policy. See Laurence I. Barrett, *Gambling with History* (Garden City, N.Y.: Doubleday, 1983), p. 142.

13. In the jargon of budget makers, the supply of last year's goods and services at this year's prices is known as a "current services budget," the starting point for budget making.

14. These results are not very different from those reported by Robert J. Art on the defense budget between 1950 and 1984. "On average Congress gave to the President about 97 or 103% of what it initially asked for, although it was more likely to give him less than more.... The President's request for the fiscal year was routinely cut, but Congress appropriated more for that fiscal year than for the previous one." Robert J. Art, "Congress and the Defense

Budget," unpublished, July 1984. Art shows considerable jumps in the defense budget from year to year associated with war mobilization (e.g., in the 1950's for Korea and the 1960's for Vietnam), but for most years the defense appropriation looks a lot like the appropriation for the year before: 10 percent or less change in twenty-one years, more than 10 percent change in thirteen years.

15. William Greider, *The Education of David Stockman and Other Americans* (New York: Dutton, 1982), p. 57.

16. Allen Schick, "The Problem of Presidential Budgeting," in Hugh Heclo and Lester Salamon (eds.), *The Illusion of Presidential Government* (Boulder, Col.: Westview, 1981), p. 86.

17. Bureau of the Budget is the former name of the Office of Management and Budget. The name was changed by the Nixon administration in 1970. The Nixon administration also gave the OMB a greater political role. As the *Wall Street Journal* reported: "The assistant directors for the budget have been removed from the Civil Service and their jobs made more political.... [They] have phones plugged into the White House switchboard and they now act as 'desk men' for the departments and agencies; when a Cabinet officer has a problem, he's expected to call them first." John Pierson, "Who's in Charge? Coming Cabinet Moves Point Up the Big Decline of Secretaries' Role," *Wall Street Journal* (November 20, 1970).

18. Statement of Hon. Maurice Stans, in *Hearings*, p. 1096.

19. Bell, *ibid.*, pp. 1142-43.

20. See two symposia on the PPBS appearing in the *Public Administration Review* in December 1966 and March/April 1969; David Novick, *Program Budgeting* (Cambridge, Mass.: Harvard University Press, 1965); and Charles L. Schultze, *The Politics and Economics of Public Spending* (Washington, D.C.: Brookings, 1968).

21. See Allen Schick's informative "A Death in the Bureaucracy: The Demise of Federal PPB." *Public Administration Review* 33 (March/April 1973), pp. 146, 156.

22. See Aaron Wildavsky, *The Politics of the Budgetary Process*, 4th ed. (Boston: Little Brown, 1984), pp. 202-21; Peter Pyhrr, *Zero-Base Budgeting* (New York: Wiley, 1973); and Thomas Hammond and Jack Knott (eds.), *A Zero-Based Look at Zero-Base Budgeting* (New Brunswick, N.J.: Transaction Books, 1980).

23. See Edward H. Hobbs, *Behind the President* (Washington, D.C.: Public Affairs Press, 1954), chap. 2; and Louis Brownlow, *A Passion for Anonymity* (Chicago: University of Chicago Press, 1958), Part III.

24. The severe disruptions that followed the attempt of one President, Mr. Eisenhower, to ignore his part of this bargain are discussed by Neustadt, *op. cit.*, pp. 64-80.

25. These quotations were drawn from appropriations subcommittee hearings by Aaron B. Wildavsky and summarized in an unpublished essay. This essay, enlarged and refined, became Wildavsky's *The Politics of the Budgetary Process*. It is now in its fourth (1984) edition.

26. "Agriculture-Environmental and Consumer Protection Appropriations for 1974," *Hearings Before the Subcommittee on Agriculture-Environmental and Consumer Protection*, Committee on Appropriations, House of Representatives, Ninety-Third Congress, First Session (Washington, D.C.: Government Printing Office, 1973), pp. 184-85.

27. Barry Blechman, Edward Gramlich, and Robert Hartman, *Setting National Priorities: The 1976 Budget* (Washington, D.C.: Brookings, 1975), p. 196. Entitlement programs, such as Social Security and Unemployment Insurance, spend money without going through the annual appropriations process. People entitled by law to benefits receive checks that are drawn on the Social Security and Unemployment Insurance trust funds.

28. These committees have only limited functions, namely, to hold hearings on and report two concurrent resolutions annually. The resolutions give overall figures on revenues and expenditures of the government for the next fiscal year. By law, as we shall presently see, a device known as "reconciliation" may be attached to the later resolution. This requires committees of Congress to report changes in the programs under their supervision sufficient to reconcile expenditures under these programs with the overall expenditure total given in the resolution.

　　The House committee has twenty-five members: five chosen from the Appropriations Committee, five from the Ways and Means Committee, and the rest from other committees of the House. Unlike all other House committees, membership on the Budget Committee is rotated, with no member except the chairman (whose term is also limited) and a member representing the leadership for each party permitted to serve for more than six years out of every ten. The Senate committee consists of sixteen senators, all permanent members, who beginning in 1977 have been permitted only one other major committee assignment.

My discussion of the reconciliation process owes a great deal to the field interviews and other research of John Gilmour.

29. The first chairman, Al Ullman of Oregon, served briefly before resigning to take over the chairmanship of the Ways and Means Committee. See, in general, Lance T. LeLoup, "Process versus Policy: The U.S. House Budget Committee," *Legislative Studies Quarterly* 4 (May 1979), pp. 227-54.

30. The Congressional Budget Office rapidly grew into a sizable and respected professional organization, with 218 employees in 1981. No doubt one possible model for its product much in the minds of those who wrote the 1974 legislation was the series of books, called *Setting National Priorities*, giving detailed analyses of selected aspects of the budgets of 1971 through 1974 and published by the Brookings Institution. This series continued annually until 1984 when the title became *Economic Choices*. See, for example, Joseph Pechman (ed.), *Setting National Priorities: The 1984 Budget* (Washington, D.C.: Brookings, 1983). One co-author of these books, Alice M. Rivlin, became the first director of the Congressional Budget Office. Under her leadership, the CBO developed a high professional reputation for careful and useful forecasting. By 1984 Aaron Wildavsky, ordinarily no fan of economic forecasting, said: "The CBO is now considered the best source of budget numbers in Washington." Wildavsky, *The Politics of the Budgetary Process*, p. 238. See also Schick, *Congress and Money: Budgeting, Spending, and Taxing* (Washington, D.C.: Urban Institute, 1980), pp. 131-65; and Joel Havemann, *Congress and the Budget* (Bloomington: Indiana University Press, 1978), pp. 100-122.

31. The reader who wishes to track the formation of the House and Senate Budget Committees and the Congressional Budget Office will find many useful articles on these subjects in weekly editions of *National Journal* and *Congressional Quarterly* from 1974 onward. See, for example, *C.Q.* for September 7, 1974, p. 2415, or *N.J.* for April 5, 1975, p. 495. Also see Joel Havemann, *Congress and the Budget*, pp. 3-37.

32. This was the Omnibus Budget Reconciliation Act of 1981, Public Law 97-35, which takes up 576 pages in the statute books. At the time, in the summer of 1981, the President was still benefiting from a post-election honeymoon, which had been extended by the rush of sympathy occasioned by the unsuccessful attempt on his life that had hospitalized him at the end of March. It was then widely believed that his election had signaled a fundamental rightward realignment of the electorate, and that therefore these budget reductions could be considered a popular mandate, as the President urged on television preceding the vote in the House of Representatives:

> The President's televised address, in April, was masterly and effective: The nation responded with a deluge of mail and telephone calls, and the House of Representatives accepted Reagan's version of budget reconciliation.

Greider, *The Education of David Stockman and Other Americans*, p. 42.

33. As Allen Schick points out, reconciliation was a great presidential success in 1981, but it has not been used comprehensively since. Perhaps it can never be used in this fashion again. See Schick, *Reconciliation and the Budgetary Process* (Washington, D.C.: American Enterprise Institute, 1982).

34. Art. I, Sec. 7. The classic work on the contemporary budget process from the congressional side is Richard F. Fenno, Jr., *The Power of the Purse* (Boston: Little, Brown, 1966). For a more current view see Schick, *Congress and Money*, pp. 415-82.

35. Norman Ornstein and David Rohde, "Shifting Forces, Changing Rules and Political Outcomes: The Impact of Congressional Change on Four House Committees," in Robert Peabody and Nelson W. Polsby, *New Perspectives on the House of Representatives* (Chicago: Rand McNally, 1977), pp. 186-269.

36. Schick, *Congress and Money*, pp. 431-32. Although this pattern was relatively new for appropriations subcommittees in the 1980s, it was not at all uncommon to see members of

Congress sort themselves out into the subcommittees of substantive committees according to their constituency or intellectual interests, as Charles O. Jones demonstrated in 1961 for the Agriculture Committee in his classic article "Representation in Congress: The Case of the House Agriculture Committee," *American Political Science Review* 55 (June 1961), pp. 358-67.

37. Congressional Budget Office, *Baseline Budget Projection for Fiscal Years 1985-1989* (Washington, D.C.: U.S. Government Printing Office, 1984), pp. 22-25.

38. Programs that provide cash transfer payments from the Federal government to individuals are typically "entitlements," i.e., payments to which people are entitled by law. Examples of entitlement programs are Old Age, Survivors and Disability Insurance (OASDI), which is more familiarly known as Social Security. Social Security expenditures were $170.7 billion in fiscal year 1983, financed through an OASDI trust fund which in turn derives its revenues from a payroll tax on employers and employees. Medicare expenditures were $52.5 billion in FY1983, and it is financed in the same manner as OASDI. Another entitlement is officially known as Aid to Families with Dependent Children (AFDC), popularly known as "Welfare," and in FY1983 it cost a total of $8.4 billion, which was paid out of general revenues. See Committee on Ways and Means, U.S. House of Representatives, *Background Material and Data on Major Programs Within the Jurisdiction of the Committee on Ways and Means* (Washington, D.C.: U.S. Government Printing Office, 1983); and *Budget of the United States Government, Fiscal Year 1985* (Washington, D.C.: U.S. Government Printing Office, 1984).

39. Arthur W. Macmahon, "Congressional Oversight of Administration: The Power of the Purse," *Political Science Quarterly*, vol. 58 (July, September, 1943), reprinted in R. L. Peabody and N. W. Polsby (eds.), *New Perspectives on the House of Representatives* (Chicago: Rand McNally, 1963), p. 351.

40. Richard F. Fenno, Jr., "The House Appropriations Committee as a Political System," *American Political Science Review*, vol. 50 (June 1962), pp. 310-24.

41. Schick, *Congress and Money*, p. 420.

42. Schick, *Congress and Money*, pp. 420-23.

43. *Hearings Before the House Committee on Appropriations, Subcommittee on the Treasury, Postal Service and General Government Appropriations*, 97th Congress, 2nd Session, Part 4 (Washington, D.C.: U.S. Government Printing Office, 1982), p. 214.

44. *Hearings Before the Agriculture Subcommittee of the House Appropriations Committee*, 93rd Congress, 1st Session, Part 1 (Washington, D.C.: U.S. Government Printing Office, 1973), p. 204.

45. A famous description of how decision-makers can make decisions in the absence of detailed knowledge is Warner Schilling, "The H-Bomb Decision: How to Decide Without Actually Choosing," *Political Science Quarterly* 74 (March 1961), pp. 24-46.

46. This colorful phrase has been around quite a while. George Washington used it to refer to the Senate as contrasted with the House.

47. Fenno, "The House Appropriations Committee as a Political System," p. 316.

48. *Ibid.*, p. 312.

49. *Ibid.*, p. 316.

50. Rowland Evans and Robert Novak, "Inside Report: King Clarence," *Washington Post* (June 5, 1963).

51. Author's interview, July 16, 1963. The congressman exaggerated somewhat. Subcommittee reports average perhaps one-half inch in thickness.

52. When the Appropriations Committee goes to the Rules Committee, it does so to obtain special orders protecting itself against points of order on the floor calling attention to violations of the Budget Act (since no appropriations bill is supposed to be taken up before the House passes a Budget resolution, as it sometimes is unable to do) or to legislative provisions in an appropriations bill.

53. Fenno, *The Power of the Purse*, pp. 449-53.

54. See Norman J. Ornstein, Thomas E. Mann, Michael J. Malbin, and John F. Bibby (eds.), *Vital Statistics on Congress, 1982* (Washington, D.C.: American Enterprise Institute, 1982), Table 7-8, p. 154.

55. Schick, *Congress and Money*, p. 438.

56. See Joseph Cooper and Melissa Collie, "Structural Adaptation in the House: Multiple Reference and Interunit Committees in Organizational Perspective," a paper delivered at the 1981 meeting of the American Political Science Association, September 3-6, 1981, p. 34.

57. Schick, *Congress and Money*, pp. 427-33.

58. *Ibid.*, pp. 433-36.

59. *Ibid.*, p. 436.

60. Ralph K. Huitt, "Congressional Organization and Operations in the Field of Money and Credit," *Fiscal and Debt Management Policies* (Englewood Cliffs, N.J.: Prentice-Hall, 1963), pp. 433-34, summarizes evidence on this point. See also Robert Ash Wallace, *Congressional Control of Federal Spending* (Detroit: Wayne State University, 1960), pp. 27-28, and Fenno, *The Power of the Purse*, p. 450. During the Reagan administration, the Republican Senate was somewhat less openhanded than the Democratic House.

61. In addition, subcommittee vacancies in the Senate have always been filled according to seniority, a process that tends over time to allocate senators according to their programmatic interests. This has recently become the practice in the House as a part of the reduction in the powers of chairmen. Schick says that as a result, Appropriation subcommittees contain increasingly more program advocates and fewer members who care about loyalty to subcommittee norms.

> The switch to self-selection spelled a serious decline in group identifications and the rise of individualistic, disintegrative values on House Appropriations.

Schick, *Congress and Money*, p. 432

62. The only live option other than passing an appropriations bill is to send it back to the conference committee. If it is defeated on the floor of either chamber, then the Federal agencies affected have to go out of business, and this event is likely to have severe repercussions, including the inconvenience of a substantial number of constituents.

63. Impoundments must be reported to Congress; the Comptroller General, a Congressional employee who heads the General Accounting Office, will report them to Congress if the administration does not.

CHAPTER 7   Conflict and Cooperation

1. *Congressional Quarterly*, authoritative supplier of these numbers, is properly diffident in reporting them, and it points out that major and minor matters, close votes and lopsided wins, administration initiatives and congressional initiatives are all lumped together, that only roll-call votes are counted without regard for measures that may have been abandoned or compromised or put through on a voice vote. See "Voting Record of '81 Shows the Romance and Fidelity of Reagan Honeymoon on Hill," *Congressional Quarterly Almanac 1981* (Washington, D.C.: Congressional Quarterly, 1982), p. 18-C.

2. One such Senator was Lyndon Johnson, who got his start in politics as a New Deal Democrat but by the time he was elected to the Senate in 1948, had changed his tune, as Senate aide Bobby Baker recalls:

> "Now," he drawled, "I know your job is to assist the Senate Democratic leadership. I know you count noses and maybe you lobby a little bit to help the Democratic program. Fine. But I gotta tell you, Mr. Baker, that my state is much more conservative than the national Democratic party. I got elected by just eighty-seven votes and I ran against a caveman." He toyed with a pencil, drumming it on the desk, and said, "I cannot always vote with President Truman if I'm going to *stay* a senator. I am a Texan and I've got a Southern constituency so I'm going to be more conservative than you would like me to be or than President Truman would like me to be. President Truman's about as popular as measles in Texas, and you'll waste your time trying to talk to me when I know it would cut my own throat to help him."
>
> I asked the senator-elect what issues likely would give him the most trouble.

"Well," he said, "I'm committed to the continuation of the Taft-Hartley Act. Labor's not much stronger in Texas than a popcorn fart, and so I can't vote to repeal it. I'm for the natural gas bill and for the tidelands bill. Frankly, Mr. Baker, I'm for nearly anything the big oil boys want because they hold the whip hand and I represent 'em. Yeah, I represent farmers and working men and when I can help President Truman help 'em, I'll do it. But you tell the president for me, and you tell your leaders in the Senate for me, that the New Deal spirit's gone from Texas and I'm limited in what I can do. Hell, half the people from Texas are against me! If I go to voting for the Fair Employment Practices Commission and so on, they've got a good start toward forming a lynch mob. I need time to mend my own fences, and then I'll worry about President Truman's."

Bobby Baker, *Wheeling and Dealing* (New York: Norton, 1978), pp. 40-41.

3. See Nelson W. Polsby, "Coalition and Faction in American Politics: An Institutional View," in S. M. Lipset (ed.), *Party Coalitions in the 1980's* (San Francisco: Institute for Contemporary Studies, 1981), pp. 153-78.

4. See John F. Manley, "The Conservative Coalition in Congress," *American Behavioral Scientist,* vol. 17 (November-December 1973), pp. 223-47.

5. See Raymond Wolfinger and Robert B. Arsenau, "Partisan Change in the South, 1952-1976," in Louis Maisel and Joseph Cooper (eds.), Sage Electoral Studies Yearbook, vol. 4: *Political Parties: Development and Decay* (Beverly Hills, Calif.: Sage Publications, 1978), pp. 179-210.

6. Calculations based on *Congressional Quarterly* statistics.

7. E. E. Schattschneider, "United States: The Functional Approach to Party Government," in Sigmund Neumann (ed.), *Modern Political Parties* (Chicago: University of Chicago Press, 1956), pp. 194-215 (esp. pp. 210ff.); and E. E. Schattschneider, *The Semisovereign People* (New York: Holt, 1960), pp. 78-96.

8. See Raymond E. Wolfinger and Joan Heifetz, "Safe Seats, Seniority, and Power in Congress," *American Political Science Review,* vol. 59 (June 1965), pp. 337-49.

9. For a discussion of these changes, see Nelson W. Polsby, *Consequences of Party Reform* (New York: Oxford University Press, 1983).

10. Dean Acheson, *Sketches from Life of Men I Have Known* (New York: Harper & Row, 1961), pp. 144-45.

11. Paul Duke, "The Foreign Aid Fiasco," *Reporter* (January 16, 1964), p. 22.

12. John Pierson, "Nixon Talent Hunt: Off to a Good Finish," *Wall Street Journal* (May 9, 1969). Other newspaper accounts of the early tribulations of the Nixon administration in the same vein include Marjorie Hunter, "Dirksen Holds Up Rights Appointment," *New York Times* (May 2, 1969), and Warren Unna, "Postal Rate Increase Is Jeopardized by Congressional Anger at Blount," *Washington Post* (May 17, 1969).

13. T. R. Reid, "The Capitol," *Washington Post* (June 25, 1977). See also "House Democrats Say Carter's Patronage Policy Saps Party Discipline," *New York Times* (June 15, 1977).

14. Two and a half years into the Carter administration, Jordan said:

I am not well known and I recognize that.... Most of the Congressmen that are criticizing my elevation to chief of staff don't know me. That's not their fault; that's my fault. I have not made the effort to know them.

"Jordan's 'Beautiful' But Who's Jerdun?" *New York Times* (July 28, 1979).

In his memoirs, Carter's press secretary Jody Powell confesses:

I must say in all honesty that one of my great regrets is that I did not make a greater effort to get the President together socially with small groups of journalists—not the White House correspondents, who are fearful of becoming too close to a President and probably with good reason, but editors, columnists, and some of the senior network people.

Jody Powell, *The Other Side of the Story* (New York: Morrow, 1984), p. 208.

15. The scale on which President Nixon exercised this impoundment capacity led to lawsuits compelling expenditures and to congressional action to curb the practice. See Louis Fisher,

"Presidential Spending Discretion and Congressional Controls," *Law and Contemporary Problems* 37 (Winter 1972), pp. 137-72; and Warren J. Archer, "Executive Impounding of Funds: The Judicial Response," *University of Chicago Law Review* 40 (Winter 1972), pp. 328-56. An implication of the Supreme Court ruling in the *Chadha* case (1983) evidently is that the legislative veto cannot be used to thwart presidential impoundments of funds. A thorough review of the rather murky legal situation into which the *Chadha* case plunged the government is Louis Fisher, "One Year After INS v. Chadha: Congressional and Judicial Developments" (Washington, D.C.: Congressional Research Service, The Library of Congress, June 23, 1984). On impoundment, see p. 9. Impoundment seems likely to be one area where we can expect more skirmishing between the branches.

16. In the case of appointments to the federal judiciary, elaborate arrangements are not uncommon. For example, senators from New York in the 1980's worked out a formula giving three-fourths of the federal judicial appointments to the senator from the President's party and the remaining fourth to the senator from the opposing party. There was no necessity for the President to go along, but there were great political risks if he failed to do so. See David Margolick, "Nomination for Federal Court Stalled," *New York Times* (June 24, 1984).

Bobby Baker gives another example, from the Kennedy administration, when Vice President Johnson attempted to ride roughshod over his nemesis, the senior Democratic senator from Texas, Ralph Yarborough:

> Sixteen of the Johnson men required confirmation in 1961. Nothing happened. Not a nomination was acted on. Senator Yarborough had exercised his right, and an old Senate tradition, in going to the proper chairmen and labeling each of LBJ's nominees as "personally obnoxious" to him. This is a device by which senators traditionally have stopped confirmation of home-state nominees of whom they disapprove. It is *always* honored; no president or vice-president or any other outsider can persuade the Senate not to honor that rule.
>
> It became necessary for the administration to approach Senator Yarborough hat in hand. "Give me half the appointments in Texas," Ralph Yarborough said. "Have Lyndon withdraw eight of his nominees and I'll clear the other eight. And it's got to be fifty-fifty from this day forward." It was.

Wheeling and Dealing (New York: Norton, 1978), pp. 146-47.

17. A number of examples of this process received considerable publicity during President Carter's drive for renomination in 1980. Joseph Kraft reported:

> Governor Bob Graham of Florida, who is due to place the President's name in nomination, was given, from funds usually reserved for natural disasters, money to take care of a wave of Cuban refugees who came to Florida last winter. Lynn Cutler, a commissioner in Black Hawk County, who helped vitally in the Iowa caucuses, was given grants that enabled a meat-packing plant in Waterloo to stay open.

Joseph Kraft, "The Carter Machine," *Washington Post* (August 12, 1980).
The state of Maine received $75.2 million in federal grants during January, compared with only $15 million in November and $23 million in December. Federal grants to New Hampshire doubled from December to January in preparation for its February delegate selections. (Timothy B. Clark, "As Long As Carter's Up He'll Get You a Grant," *New York Times* [April 21, 1980]; and Clark, "Carter Plays Santa Claus for His Reelection Campaign," *National Journal* [April 5, 1980], pp. 548-53.) Stories abounded about HUD and Transportation grants won and lost by communities on the basis of whether prominent public officials endorsed the President or not. Los Angeles, where Mayor Tom Bradley backed the President, did well; Chicago, where the fickle Mayor Jane Byrne jumped to Senator Kennedy, was reported to be in trouble. East St. Louis, Illinois, where Mayor Carl Officer endorsed Carter, got a $7.8 million federal courthouse; Carbondale, Illinois, where Congressman Paul Simon endorsed Kennedy, unexpectedly lost a HUD grant. (Timothy D. Schellhardt, "Carter, Who Railed against Pork-Barrel Politics in 1976, Now Exploits Them for Illinois Primary," *Wall Street Journal* [March 6, 1980].)
    None of this was coincidental, as journalists discovered when they inquired of Federal officials. Hedrick Smith reported in the *New York Times*:

> The Carter administration is boldly working the politics of incumbency this fall by directing federal aid to its political allies and timing aid announcements for maximum political impact on states involved in the early stages of the 1980 campaign.
>
> The Florida caucuses last weekend produced a gush of federal aid into Florida, but they were only the first stream of what White House officials candidly acknowledge is a much broader Niagara of federal aid being steered toward Iowa, New Hampshire, Illinois, New York, Massachusetts, North Carolina, and Minnesota.

Hedrick Smith, "White House Using Grants to Woo States in Campaign," *New York Times* (October 17, 1979).

18. Laurence I. Barrett, *Gambling with History* (Garden City, N.Y.: Doubleday, 1983), p. 150.

19. Lawrence O'Brien, *No Final Victories* (Garden City, N.Y.: Doubleday, 1974), pp. 172-73. Copyright 1974 by Lawrence F. O'Brien. Reprinted by permission of Doubleday & Company, Inc.

20. Rowland Evans, Jr., "Louisiana's Passman: The Scourge of Foreign Aid," *Harper's* (January 1962), pp. 78-83. Copyright 1961 © by Harper's Magazine Foundation. All rights reserved. Reprinted from the January 1962 issue by special permission.

21. President Carter found this out in connection with his energy policy. *Congressional Quarterly* comments:

> In his speech to the nation April 18, 1977, explaining the need for his energy program, President Carter observed:
>
> "I am sure each of you will find something you don't like about the specifics of our proposal.... We can be sure that all the special interest groups in the country will attack the part of this plan that affects them directly."
>
> Six months later, Carter again tried to sell the public his energy program via television Nov. 8, and he noted: "I said six months ago that no one would be completely satisfied with this national energy plan. Unfortunately, that prediction has turned out to be right."
>
> Gallup Polls throughout the year demonstrated one of the biggest obstacles Carter faced: About half the nation refused to take the energy crisis very seriously.
>
> In mid-December, Gallup reported that 40 per cent of the nation's people believed that the U.S. energy situation was "very serious"; another 42 per cent viewed it as "fairly serious." Fifteen per cent, Gallup said, saw the problem as "not at all" serious.
>
> Those figures had remained virtually unchanged since early April, before the President's plan was presented, Gallup said. "...[A]pproximately half of the public can be said to be relatively unconcerned about our energy problems," Gallup wrote in late June. Despite all the political fury in Washington, despite repeated presidential addresses and unceasing media attention, the American public's views on energy changed barely at all in 1977.
>
> The absence of a strong body of public opinion behind Carter's program made it difficult to repel sophisticated lobbying campaigns against the plan waged by committed special interests. As Energy Secretary Schlesinger summed up Oct. 16 on CBS television's "Face the Nation:"
>
> "...[T]he basic problem is that there is no constituency for an energy program. There are many constituencies opposed. But the basic constituency for the program is the future...."

Congressional Quarterly, *Energy Policy* (Washington, D.C., 1979), p. 35.

22. The first article of impeachment accused Nixon of numerous acts "in a course of conduct or plan designed to delay, impede and obstruct the investigation" of the break-in of the Watergate offices of the Democratic National Committee, "to cover up, conceal and protect those responsible; and to conceal the existence and scope of other unlawful covert activities." The second article charged that Nixon "repeatedly engaged in conduct violating the constitutional rights of citizens, impairing the due and proper administration of justice and the conduct of lawful inquiries"—including misuse of the FBI, the Central Intelligence Agency,

and the Internal Revenue Service. The third article charged him with obstructing the impeachment investigation of the House Judiciary Committee itself by "wilfully disobeying" subpoenas requiring him to produce material in his possession believed necessary for their inquiry.

Rejected articles of impeachment accused President Nixon of unjustly enriching himself. by tax evasion, and unlawfully spending federal money on private property belonging to him, and of unlawfully concealing from Congress bombing operations in Cambodia.

See Report of the Committee on the Judiciary, House of Representatives, *Impeachment of Richard M. Nixon*, August 20, 1974.

23. An authoritative examination of the historic meaning of "high crimes and misdemeanors" is contained in Raoul Berger, *Impeachment: The Constitutional Problems* (Cambridge, Mass.: Harvard University, 1973), pp. 53-102.

24. On investigations in general, see Telford Taylor, *Grand Inquest* (New York: Simon and Schuster, 1955); and James Hamilton, *The Power to Probe* (New York: Random House, 1976).

25. See *U.S.* v. *Nixon* 418 *U.S.* 683 (1974).

26. Ethics in Government Act (1978) (Public Law 95-521); Extension and Revision (1983) (Public Law 97-409).

27. See Gerald G. Shulsinger, *The General Accounting Office: Two Glimpses* (University, Ala.: University of Alabama Press, 1956), ICP case 35; and Frederick C. Mosher, *The GAO* (Boulder, Col.: Westview Press, 1979).

28. James M. Burns, *Congress on Trial* (New York: Harper & Row, 1949).

29. H. H. Wilson, *Congress: Corruption and Compromise* (New York: Holt, 1951).

30. James M. Burns, *The Deadlock of Democracy* (Englewood Cliffs, N.J.: Prentice-Hall, 1963).

31. Joseph S. Clark, *Congress: The Sapless Branch* (New York: Harper & Row, 1964).

32. Roger H. Davidson, David M. Kovenock, and Michael K. O'Leary, *Congress in Crisis* (Belmont, Calif.: Wadsworth, 1966).

33. Richard Bolling, *House Out of Order* (New York: Dutton, 1965).

34. Philip Donham and Robert J. Fahey, *Congress Needs Help* (New York: Random House, 1966). The genre is apparently inexhaustible. See also Harold Laski, *The American Presidency* (New York: Harper & Row, 1949); Drew Pearson and Jack Anderson, *The Case Against Congress* (New York: Simon and Schuster, 1968); Warren Weaver, Jr., *Both Your Houses* (New York: Praeger, 1972); Mark J. Green, with others, *Who Runs Congress?* 3d ed. (New York: Viking, 1979); Daniel Rapoport, *Inside the House* (Chicago: Follett Publishing Co., 1975); and Philip Brenner, *The Limits and Possibilities of Congress* (New York: St. Martin's Press, 1983).

35. This point of view was once more common than it is nowadays. See Ernest S. Griffith, *Congress: Its Contemporary Role* (New York: New York University Press, 1961); James Burnham, *Congress and the American Tradition* (Chicago: Regnery, 1949); and Arthur Maass, *Congress and the Common Good* (New York: Basic Books, 1983).

36. *The Federalist*, 51. The authorship of this number has been disputed between Alexander Hamilton and James Madison. Madison is now regarded as the most likely author. See Jacob Cooke's "Introduction" to *The Federalist* (Middletown, Conn.: Wesleyan University, 1961), and an ingenious attempt to resolve the issue by Frederick Mosteller and David L. Wallace, "Inference in an Authorship Problem," *Journal of the American Statistical Association*, vol. 58 (June 1963), pp. 275-309.

37. An exploration of this problem, along with several other issues, is contained in Willmoore Kendall, "The Two Majorities," *Midwest Journal of Political Science*, vol. 4 (November 1960), pp. 317-45.

38. Clem Miller, *Member of the House*, ed. John W. Baker (New York: Scribner, 1962), p. 123.

39. Even so, in 1980, Democratic House candidates received 50.4 percent of the vote. Ronald Reagan received 50.8 percent of the vote for president. Norman Ornstein, Thomas Mann, Michael Malbin, and John Bibby, *Vital Statistics on Congress, 1982* (Washington, D.C.: American Enterprise Institute, 1982), pp. 38-39; and Austin Ranney (ed.), *The American Elections of 1980*, Appendix A, pp. 352-53.

40. In 1980 almost a third of the congressional districts (143 of them or 32.8 percent) split their vote between President and House candidates. See Ornstein, Mann, Malbin, and Bibby,

Vital Statistics on Congress, 1982, p. 53. The literature on these points is immense. See, in particular, Angus Campbell, Philip Converse, Warren Miller, and Donald Stokes, *The American Voter* (New York: Wiley, 1960); and V. O. Key, Jr., *Public Opinion and American Democracy* (New York: Knopf, 1961). In a later book Key attempts to introduce a modification into this picture of the electorate, mainly by analyzing the small minority of voters who switch from one election to the next. See V. O. Key, Jr., *The Responsible Electorate* (Cambridge, Mass.: Belknap, Harvard University, 1966).

41. This and other proposed reforms of the presidential party and electoral system are examined in Nelson W. Polsby and Aaron B. Wildavsky, *Presidential Elections* (New York: Charles Scribner's Sons, 1984), pp. 208-66. See also Lawrence Longley and James D. Dana, Jr., "New Empirical Estimates of the Biases of the Electoral College for the 1980's," *Western Political Quarterly* 37 (March 1984), pp. 157-75.

42. See Neal R. Peirce and Lawrence D. Longley, *The People's President* (New Haven, Conn.: Yale University Press, 1981) for the parade of horrors.

43. There is a minor exception: the state of Maine. See chapter 2, footnote 2.

44. Examples of this style of argument may be found in Woodrow Wilson, *Congressional Government* (New York: Meridian, 1956; originally published 1885); in Holbert N. Carroll, *The House of Representatives and Foreign Affairs* (Pittsburgh: University of Pittsburgh Press, 1958); and in many of the writings of George Galloway. See, for example, Galloway's *The Legislative Process in Congress* (New York: Crowell, 1953).

45. For a recent version of this style of argument see Lloyd N. Cutler and C. Douglas Dillon, "Can We Improve Our Constitutional System?" *Wall Street Journal* (February 15, 1983); and Cutler, "To Form a Government," *Foreign Affairs* 59 (Fall 1980), pp. 126-43.

46. See Julius Turner, *Party and Constituency: Pressures on Congress* (Baltimore: Johns Hopkins, 1951); David B. Truman, *The Congressional Party* (New York: Wiley, 1959); Lewis A. Froman, Jr., *Congressmen and Their Constituencies* (Chicago: Rand McNally, 1963), pp. 88-89; Avery Leiserson, *Parties and Politics* (New York: Knopf, 1958), p. 379.

47. Joe Martin (as told to Robert J. Donovan), *My First Fifty Years in Politics* (New York: McGraw-Hill, 1960), pp 68-71.

48. On President Reagan's use of commissions in general:

> Partisan bickering over Social Security reform led Reagan to appoint a "National Commission on Social Security." The recommendations of the commission were quickly endorsed by both Reagan and [House Speaker] O'Neill, and were then promptly passed into law. (*Congressional Quarterly* [January 22, 1983], pp. 155-60.)

> After Congress turned down one scheme for basing the MX missile, called "dense pack," early in 1983 Reagan appointed a commission to find a militarily and politically acceptable basing mode for the new missile. (*Congressional Quarterly* [April 16, 1983], pp. 727-28.)

> To develop support for policies in Latin America, Reagan appointed a commission headed by Henry Kissinger. It recommended a comprehensive package of policies for the Caribbean region. (*Congressional Quarterly* [February 25, 1984], pp. 443-47.)

See also Thomas R. Wolanin, *Presidential Advisory Commissions* (Madison: University of Wisconsin Press, 1975).

49. The War Powers Act, passed on November 7, 1973 over Nixon's veto, requires the President to report to Congress within 48 hours on any commitment of troops to "hostilities." Essentially it allows the President to involve U.S. troops but requires that they be removed within 60 days unless Congress approves a resolution specifically authorizing their continuation, or else declares war. *Congressional Quarterly Almanac 1973* (Washington, D.C.: Congressional Quarterly, 1974), pp. 905-17.

Because the legislation involves what looks like a legislative veto, its constitutional standing is now in question. The Reagan administration used this opening to bargain with Congress over the time during which he would be permitted to commit troops in connection with the invasion of Grenada in 1984. For further comments on the legislative veto, see Chapter II, footnote 122.

50. See E. Pendleton Herring, *Presidential Leadership* (New York: Farrar and Rinehart, 1940), pp. 31-32, 42-45, 52-59, and *passim.*

51. Herring, who uses a similar image, remarks that "In looking at the operations of Congress and the executive, we may see with Ezekiel, De little wheel run by faith/ And de big wheel run by de grace ob God/ 'Tis a wheel in a wheel/ Way in de middle of de air." *Ibid.*, p. x.

INDEX